Library of
Davidson College

THE LONG WAIT

**Recent Titles in
Contributions in Military Studies**

Jailed for Peace: The History of American Draft Law Violators, 1658-1985
Stephen M. Kohn

Against All Enemies: Interpretations of American Military History from Colonial Times to the Present
Kenneth J. Hagan and William R. Roberts

Citizen Sailors in a Changing Society: Policy Issues for Manning the United States Naval Reserve
Louis A. Zurcher, Milton L. Boykin, and Hardy L. Merritt, editors

Strategic Nuclear War: What the Superpowers Target and Why
William C. Martel and Paul L. Savage

Soviet Military Psychiatry: The Theory and Practice of Coping with Battle Stress
Richard A. Gabriel

A Portrait of the Israeli Soldier
Reuven Gal

The Other Price of Hitler's War: German Military and Civilian Losses Resulting from World War II
Martin K. Sorge

The New Battlefield: The United States and Unconventional Conflicts
Sam C. Sarkesian

The Other Desert War: British Special Forces in North Africa, 1940-1943
John W. Gordon

Military Psychiatry: A Comparative Perspective
Richard A. Gabriel, editor

Wars without Splendor: The U.S. Military and Low-Level Conflict
Ernest Evans

The Ambiguous Relationship: Theodore Roosevelt and Alfred Thayer Mahan
Richard W. Turk

TIMOTHY J. BOTTI

THE LONG WAIT

The Forging of the Anglo-American
Nuclear Alliance, 1945–1958

Contributions in Military Studies, Number 64

GREENWOOD PRESS

New York • Westport, Connecticut • London

Library of Congress Cataloging-in-Publication Data

Botti, Timothy J., 1956-
 The long wait.

 (Contributions in military studies, ISSN 0883-6884 ;
no. 64)
 Bibliography: p.
 Includes index.
 1. Nuclear weapons—United States. 2. Nuclear
weapons—Great Britain. 3. United States—Military
relations—Great Britain. 4. Great Britain—Military
relations—United States. I. Title. II. Series.
U264.B68 1987   355'.0271'0973   87-7530
ISBN 0-313-25902-X (lib. bdg. : alk. paper)

British Library Cataloguing in Publication Data is available.

Copyright © 1987 by Timothy J. Botti

All rights reserved. No portion of this book may be
reproduced, by any process or technique, without the
express written consent of the publisher.

Library of Congress Catalog Card Number: 87-7530
ISBN: 0-313-25902-X
ISSN: 0883-6884

First published in 1987

Greenwood Press, Inc.
88 Post Road West, Westport, Connecticut 06881

Printed in the United States of America

The paper used in this book complies with the
Permanent Paper Standard issued by the National
Information Standards Organization (Z39.48-1984).

10 9 8 7 6 5 4 3 2 1

For my parents,
Claire and Robert E. Botti

CONTENTS

Abbreviations	ix
1. Introduction	1
2. The Illusion of Cooperation	7
3. Protecting the Atomic Monopoly	17
4. Movement toward Limited Cooperation	25
5. The British Want More	37
6. The United States Agrees to Cooperate—Almost	47
7. Out of the Question	65
8. Running in Place	71
9. Who Shall Be Consulted on the Use of Atomic Bombs?	79
10. Full Consideration?	89
11. The Struggle for Control of Atomic Energy Policy	97
12. Activity—but No Action	105
13. Getting Organized	111
14. Fundamental Decisions	121
15. Amending the McMahon Act	133
16. Striving to Achieve a Minor Victory	143
17. Cooperation on Hold	151
18. Deceiving the JCAE	157
19. First Catalyst for Nuclear Partnership	167
20. Eisenhower Takes Command	175
21. Political Complications	185
22. Second Catalyst for Nuclear Partnership	199

23.	Clearing the Final Hurdle	213
24.	Partnership at Last	229
25.	Conclusion	243
	Bibliography	251
	Index	257

ABBREVIATIONS

AEC	Atomic Energy Commission
CDT	Combined Development Trust
CPC	Combined Policy Committee
DOD	Department of Defense
EDC	European Defense Community
IAEA	International Atomic Energy Authority
ICBM	Intercontinental Ballistic Missile
IRBM	Intermediate Range Ballistic Missile
JCAE	Joint Committee on Atomic Energy (U.S. Congress)
JCS	Joint Chiefs of Staff
JSSC	Joint Strategic Survey Committee
MDAP	Mutual Defense Assistance Program
MLC	Military Liaison Committee
NATO	North Atlantic Treaty Organization
NSC	National Security Council
OEEC	Organization of European Economic Cooperation
PPS	Policy Planning Staff (U.S. State Department)
RAF	Royal Air Force
SAC	Strategic Air Command
SACEUR	Supreme Allied Commander Europe
SPAL	South Pacific Air Lines
USAF	United States Air Force
USN	United States Navy

THE LONG WAIT

1
INTRODUCTION

Out of the fiery crucible of World War II emerged the most powerful nation in the history of the world. Unlike the other major combatants, the United States in August 1945 possessed a vibrant economy, strong industries, and an unscathed homeland. American losses from December 1941 to the surrender of Japan totaled less than 500,000, a relatively low number in comparison to British fatalities and a small fraction of Soviet deaths. Twelve million well-equipped and well-trained military personnel were in uniform. And then there was the atomic bomb. Although the only two operational weapons had been used against Hiroshima and Nagasaki, the United States alone possessed the knowledge and industrial expertise to manufacture more. As long as the monopoly lasted, American leaders were certain of ultimate victory in any worldwide conflict.

Yet American leaders realized that in the long run the United States needed the cooperation of other nations to insure economic prosperity and to maintain a favorable strategic position vis-à-vis the Soviet Union. Unfortunately, Britain, the principal wartime ally, had been exhausted by its six-year struggle against Hitler's Germany. Before that country would be able to contribute materially to the accomplishment of American goals, British financial health had to be restored. In December 1945, therefore, the U.S. government granted Britain a large postwar loan. Under the Truman Doctrine of March 1947, the United States relieved Britain of the burden of strategic responsibility for the Eastern Mediterranean. The British were left free to concentrate on protecting the Middle East. Next, the United States moved to buttress all of Western Europe. Beginning in April 1948, the Marshall Plan provided billions of dollars to repair war-damaged economies and helped to restore the region's natural defenses against internal subversion and outside pressures. Already admirers of British efforts to develop Western European defense ties, the Americans actively encouraged and then joined the North Atlantic Treaty Organization (NATO) in 1949. Despite British difficulty with American assertions about the breadth of the international Communist threat, by the outbreak of the Korean War in June 1950, Anglo-American relations were approaching the intimacy of the wartime alliance.

The same degree of intimacy did not develop, however, in the critical field of atomic energy. Possessed of an atomic monopoly and hopeful of preserving it, the Truman administration did not permit the kind of functional collaboration with the British that had existed during the war. The root of the problem lay in certain wartime agreements and British inequality in those arrangements. Because the British had signed away all right to information necessary for the construction of large-scale plants and manufacture of atomic bombs, they found themselves in the postwar period without an intact atomic energy infrastructure. They were, in addition, partially ignorant of how to build one. Nor were the Americans willing to reestablish and expand cooperation concerning atomic energy. Because they had decided upon a policy of trying to secure an international control agreement, they avoided significant commitment to the British. Had they wanted a nuclear partnership, however, they probably could have had one on very favorable terms. Confronted by the reality of heavy expenditures for atomic energy development, the British would likely have agreed to submerge the British program into the American—but only if they could have obtained access to American atomic weapons information. They also would have asked for control of a small supply of atomic bombs and cooperation on the commercial development of atomic energy. But in 1945-46 American policymakers would not consider this.

The Congress, meanwhile, with the tacit approval of the administration, worked in 1946 on legislation designed to preserve the atomic monopoly and severely restrict the flow of secret information to foreign governments. Called the Atomic Energy or McMahon Act of 1946, the law worked well. Thereafter, the administration could attempt no improvement in nuclear relations with the British without congressional approval. The Joint Congressional Committee on Atomic Energy (JCAE), the watchdog committee set up by the McMahon Act, closely monitored administration negotiations and retained near veto power over proposed agreements. Using divisions among the policymakers to increase its influence, the committee became a major factor in preventing full partnership in the nuclear field.

Another factor limiting cooperation was British self-inflicted wounds. Untimely spy scandals and unwillingness to improve security standards destroyed opportunities for collaboration created by East-West tensions and especially by Soviet development of the atomic bomb. British insistence on stressing past cooperation rather than demonstrating British potential for future contributions, moreover, did not impress the practical-minded Americans. They did not believe the British had much to offer. Indeed, the

Introduction 3

British atomic energy program proceeded at a relatively leisurely pace and produced an atomic detonation only in October 1952. Owing mainly to cooperation in the control of critical raw materials and introduction of American strategic bombers into Britain in 1948, the British preserved a marginal nuclear connection but little more. The sorry state of nuclear relations became a troubling irritant and an anomaly in the harmonious feeling that generally characterized Anglo-American postwar relations.

The anomaly endured into the 1950s. Even after Winston Churchill returned to power in October 1951, the Americans evidenced little enthusiasm for cooperation. Much respected by the Americans and in a stronger political position than the outgoing Labour government, Churchill tried to restore American confidence in Britain's worth as a reliable nuclear partner. Efforts were undertaken to correct British security standards—a very sore point with the Americans because of the aforementioned spy scandals—insistent and reasoned requests were made for coordination of nuclear strategy between the British and American chiefs of staff, and dogged progress was made in the manufacture of Britain's atomic bomb. Lastly, the late 1954 decision to expand greatly the British stockpile of atomic weapons and to undertake the development of the hydrogen bomb significantly increased the value of British cooperation to the United States in the nuclear sphere.

But British actions alone, though important, were not sufficient to restore Anglo-American nuclear cooperation. The change of American administration in 1953, together with international developments and continuing concerns about Soviet aggression, finally put cracks in the solid wall of American resistance to collaboration. The second important step toward closer nuclear ties occurred when Dwight D. Eisenhower became President in January 1953. Far more sympathetic to British pleas for cooperation than his predecessor and acutely aware of the necessity of tightening defense ties with principal allies to face the growing Soviet challenge (symbolized by the Soviet hydrogen bomb test of August 1953), he favored nuclear collaboration from the start. Accordingly, he campaigned actively for a change in the McMahon Act to permit broader information exchanges and greater cooperation with the British. Cooperation was all the more imperative, he argued, because of his "New Look" defense strategy emphasizing maximum reliance on nuclear weapons. Successful in persuading Congress in 1954 to amend the law, he was then able, in June 1955, to conclude with the British a limited agreement for cooperation in both the military and commercial/industrial uses of atomic energy. Although far short of what the British had desired and ultimately unworkable due to Atomic Energy Commission (AEC) and JCAE objections to releasing information that might have revealed atomic weapon design and manufacturing data, the June 1955 pact set the stage for further efforts at cooperation.

In 1956, for example, administration officials secretly negotiated an agreement to transmit to the British nuclear submarine propulsion information. Members of the JCAE were not at first informed. When in June they learned of it, they rose in a storm of protest and forced the President to postpone implementation of the arrangement. They were adamant that the British not get American nuclear submarine propulsion information until they agreed to reveal all British nuclear secrets useful in the commercial application of nuclear power. This pattern of administration scheming and Joint Committee obstructionism might have continued indefinitely had not the Suez crisis occurred in fall 1956 and convinced Eisenhower that he must finally assume an active and vigorous role in Anglo-American nuclear affairs.

Relations had been so strained over Suez, Eisenhower realized, that only a dramatic gesture like offering Britain American nuclear-armed intermediate range ballistic missiles would suffice to conciliate British leaders. This offer he did decide to make early in 1957 along with implementation of the agreement on nulear submarine propulsion information and negotiations on other areas of military nuclear cooperation. It seemed as though Anglo-American nuclear relations were on a fast track to success. But negotiations again bogged down over details, minor and major, and were complicated by political pressure on the British government to declare in favor of a moratorium on nuclear testing. Opposition in the JCAE, moreover, while waning, was still troublesome. In the end, it took the Soviet Sputnik success of October 1957 to convince British and American officials that they must settle their differences and conclude a broad agreement in the nuclear field. Only in that way would they increase the collective strength vis-à-vis the Soviets and enhance the national security of both countries.

Sputnik also had the effect of swinging a decisive majority of the JCAE and Congress in favor of increased nuclear ties with Britain and other allies. While congressional leaders still wanted to be certain that the United States obtained substantial benefit from opening the vault of nuclear secrets, they understood that U.S. national security and the defense of Western Europe would be substantially enhanced by Anglo-American nuclear cooperation. Even so, they forbade transfer of American hydrogen bomb information and wrote into the 1958 amendments to the 1954 Atomic Energy Act restrictions against communication to allies other than Britain of information that would assist those nations to acquire a nuclear weapons capability. They did not want to take any action to escalate dramatically the nuclear arms race and the proliferation of nuclear weapons.

On July 3, 1958, the British and Americans concluded an agreement that established a stable, long-term nuclear alliance between the two countries. Although periodic disagreements developed in the future due to the dominant American role and genuine differences of opinion, the alliance endured. Inadequate nuclear ties would no longer be an anomaly in the overall Anglo-American relationship.

Introduction

Three agreements pertaining to Anglo-American wartime atomic relations are critical for an understanding of postwar relations—the Quebec Agreement of August 19, 1943, the Agreement and Declaration of Trust of June 13, 1944, and the Hyde Park Memorandum of September 19, 1944. The Quebec Agreement required the British to submerge their atomic program into the American program. Both countries pledged never to use the bomb or give information about it to anyone without consent of the other. Because the United States assumed the "heavy burden of production" of the bomb, the British left the distribution of "any postwar advantages of an industrial or commercial character" to the President. The Prime Minister would accept for Britain what the President considered "just and fair" and "in harmony with the economic welfare of the world." The agreement provided for full and effective collaboration, but only in the field of scientific research and development. In the field of design, construction, and operation of large-scale plants, data exchanges would take place as "necessary and desirable" to complete the project at the earliest moment. A Combined Policy Committee (CPC) with three American, one Canadian, and two British officials would make the ad hoc arrangements and other decisions necessary to carry out the agreement.[1]

Despite protests from scientific advisors Drs. James B. Conant and Vannevar Bush that the atomic partnership would lead to an unfortunate coupling of British and American postwar foreign policies and result in foreclosure of an atomic energy agreement with the Soviets, President Franklin D. Roosevelt assented to the pact. He believed that an Anglo-American atomic partnership was one key to peace in the postwar world and took a second step in that direction, without the knowledge of his advisors, in the Hyde Park Memorandum. He and Winston Churchill agreed that full collaboration in developing atomic energy for "military and commercial purposes should continue after the defeat of Japan unless and until terminated by joint agreement."[2]

These two agreements, and the Agreement and Declaration of Trust that created a Combined Development Trust (CDT) under the CPC for the control of uranium and thorium supplies in areas beyond the physical and legal jurisdiction of Britain and the United States,[3] were executive agreements made by Roosevelt under his authority as President. Although binding on the United States internationally and part of the supreme law of the land, they had less force than treaties approved by the Senate. They would have to be considered null and void should Congress pass contrary legislation. Knowledgeable about the American political system, the British understood this and sought stronger commitment after the war.[4]

As a practical matter, the Quebec Agreement placed the British in a position of inferiority in the nuclear relationship. Nowhere in the agreement did the United States promise to give Britain the "secret" of the atomic bomb—the technical information required to design, construct, and operate the large-scale plants necessary for the manufacture of fissionable material and to build the bomb itself. Nor did the United States promise to transfer industrial or commercially valuable information discovered during the development of the bomb. The President had sole discretion to decide what the British would receive. Churchill and his successors, it must be said, expected far-ranging cooperation after the war and recognition of Britain's right to share the benefits of the wartime project. Their disappointment and bitterness would be great when cooperation and recognition did not materialize for many years.

NOTES

1. U.S. Department of State, *United States Treaties and Other International Agreements*, 5:1114.

2. Aide-Memoire Initialed by Roosevelt and Churchill, Hyde Park, September 19, 1944, Roosevelt Papers, *Foreign Relations of the United States* (hereafter cited as *FRUS*), Conference at Quebec, 1944, 2: 492-93; Richard G. Hewlett and Oscar E. Anderson, Jr., *The New World: A History of the United States Atomic Energy Commission*, Vol. 1 (USAEC, 1972), pp. 326-28.

3. Agreement between the United States and United Kingdom for the Establishment of the Combined Development Trust, Hyde Park, June 13, 1944, lot file 55D540, box 2, *FRUS*, 1944, 2:1026-28.

4. *U.S. v. Belmont*, 301 U.S. 324 (1937), established that executive agreements were binding on the United States internationally and part of the supreme law of the land; James L. Gormly, "The Washington Declaration and the 'Poor Relation': Anglo-American Atomic Diplomacy, 1945-46," *Diplomatic History* 8 (Spring 1984): 127.

2
THE ILLUSION OF COOPERATION

> Our "secret" in respect to atomic bombs probably will not be a "secret" for more than five years; but it seems to me that during these five years we must keep it to ourselves through every possible precaution so that we can exercise maximum international pressure for effective and dependable international control.
>
> —Senator Arthur Vandenberg, April 18, 1946[1]

At a meeting of the Combined Policy Committee (CPC) in Washington on July 4, 1945, the British and Americans, in accordance with the Quebec Agreement of August 19, 1943, agreed jointly to use the atomic bomb against Japan. There was no debate. In fact, the British representatives were far more concerned with allocation of uranium supplies by the Combined Development Trust (CDT). Although while the war lasted all supplies had to be given to the United States for production of weapons for possible use against still-defiant Japan, the British worried that should the war end abruptly, they would be left without any stocks with which to start up an atomic energy program in the British Isles. Their only satisfaction was that according to the Agreement and Declaration of Trust of June 13, 1944, any excess uranium not required for American weapons manufacture would be held by the CDT for allocation by the CPC at a later date.[2]

Wartime collaboration between the United States and Britain in all fields, including development of the atomic bomb, had been very close, so that the British in the last days of the war looked forward to continuation of the Anglo-American alliance after Japan was subdued. Clement Attlee, leader of the British Labour party and new Prime Minister from August 1, 1945, admitted as much in a telegram to President Harry S. Truman on August 8. The recent detonation of an atomic device over Hiroshima, he said, mandated a "reevaluation of policies and readjustment of international relations." He wanted to join with Truman in a "joint declaration of our intentions to utilise the existence of this great power not for our own ends, but as trustees for humanity in the interests of all peoples in order to promote peace and justice in the world."[3]

Fine words; but postwar realities made many American policymakers nervous about giving up control of the atomic bomb, or even sharing the "secret" with other nations including Britain. Still others, like Secretary of War Henry Stimson, looked into the future and predicted an atomic arms race between the Soviet Union and the United States if the United States failed to invite the Soviets into an atomic partnership. The danger of such an arms race was even greater if the Soviets perceived that the British and Americans were combining against them. The issue of the atomic bomb, Stimson wrote to the President on September 11, was the key to future Soviet-American relations. He wanted a direct proposal put to the Soviets for an agreement between the Soviets, Americans, and British to control atomic energy and make use of it for industrial and humanitarian purposes. He proposed that the United States, as a gesture of good faith, stop manufacturing bombs, halt further weapons development, and impound all bombs already manufactured. But he did not put forward a plan for international control of atomic energy. Since only Britain, the United States, and the Soviet Union had demonstrated their potential power and responsibility in the war, the Soviets would scoff at giving smaller, less-important countries a role in controlling atomic energy. Under Secretary of State Dean Acheson and Under Secretary of War Robert P. Patterson (who succeeded Stimson on September 27, 1945) were in substantial agreement.[4]

Eager to make a statement about the atomic bomb and American atomic energy policy, Truman gave a speech on the subject before Congress on October 3, 1945, just two weeks after soliciting opinions from administration officials at a cabinet meeting. His address was an attempt to walk a fine line between some form of international control, a popular idea with the public, and safeguarding the secret of the bomb for the United States. He was proposing, he said, initial discussions with the wartime allies, Britain and Canada, prior to talks with other nations (that is, the Soviet Union) that would then take place "in an effort to effect agreement on the conditions under which cooperation might replace rivalry in the field of atomic energy." But he also stated his intention not to disclose information relating to the manufacturing process leading to the production of the atomic bomb itself. In other words, the United States would support international control as long as a system could be divided to prevent other nations from building the bomb.[5]

Truman's speech alarmed officials on both sides of the Atlantic. Within his own administration, Secretary of State James F. Byrnes and General Leslie R. Groves, head of the Manhattan Engineering District (the organization in control of the atomic bomb project), regretted that the President had mentioned international control of atomic energy before the postwar international situation had become clearer and peace treaties had been drawn up and signed. Secretary of the Navy James F. Forrestal made his feelings known more bluntly. He opposed the idea of turning over the atomic bomb to "a piece of paper"—an international control agreement with the Soviets—and feared allowing even the British a say in the future of the bomb. To avoid their meddling, he wanted to disband the CPC.[6]

The predominant American military sentiment, reflected by Forrestal, was that the United States should take steps to guarantee for as long as possible American atomic superiority. Estimating that the United States held a five-year technological lead in the nuclear field, the Joint Strategic Survey Committee (JSSC) advised that the U.S. government take steps to control all uranium sources, accelerate to the greatest extent possible atomic research and development, set in place severe security standards and otherwise follow a policy of achieving the highest degree of secrecy, and accumulate rapidly a sufficiently large stockpile of weapons to implement strategic war plans if necessary. The importance of maintaining close contact with Britain and Canada was not mentioned.[7]

Truman's speech also had the effect of stirring up the British Parliament and press to demand that Attlee make a statement on British atomic energy policy. Newspaper editors in particular scored what they considered too strong an emphasis by the American government on secrecy and not enough on trusting allies. Having already set up a research establishment in the United Kingdom and having proceeded with plans for an atomic pile for research and development purposes, Attlee proposed a conference with himself, Truman, and Canadian Prime Minister Mackenzie King to discuss a common plan for atomic energy development. The United States soon agreed and scheduled the conference to begin in Washington on November 10, 1945.[8]

American policymakers went to work belatedly drawing up the American position. But it was the War Department rather than the State Department that took the lead. After Byrnes showed little enthusiasm for Patterson's suggestion that the State Department, with War Department assistance, conduct a thorough examination of the international aspects of atomic energy in preparation for the conference, Patterson met with Vannevar Bush, director of the Office of Scientific Research and Development, to ask for his ideas. He then ordered Lieutenant R. Gordon Arneson, General Groves's atomic energy advisor, to undertake a study of the current state of Anglo-American atomic relations. Arneson was to review the Quebec Agreement, Agreement and Declaration of Trust (neither Patterson nor Bush knew about the Hyde Park Memorandum),[9] Stimson's September 11, 1945, proposal, and Patterson's memorandum of September 26, 1945, based on Bush's memorandum of September 25, 1945. He was to produce a tentative set of proposals for revision of past agreements with the British and Canadians. He was also ordered to draw up a negotiating approach to the Soviets concerning international control and a plan for the establishment of a United Nations Organization (UNO) for the control of atomic energy.[10]

Meanwhile, on November 5, 1945, Bush drew up his own recommendations. Since the war was now over, he wrote, the Quebec Agreement and its provisions were no longer operative. They had to be renegotiated and replaced, preferably by a permanent agreement ratified by the Senate that would be compatible with a future agreement on international control of atomic energy by the U.N. To do this, the Anglo-American treaty must deal not only with cooperation on control of raw materials—a continuation of the CPC and CDT arrangement—but must insure that clauses dealing with information exchanges or political relations were temporary in nature and subject to revision or cancellation once a UNO was established. Specifically, he wanted no exchange of information necessary for the manufacture of atomic bombs and cancellation of two potentially embarrassing (for both countries) clauses from the Quebec Agreement. These were the provision limiting British activity in commercial and industrial aspects of atomic energy and the provision giving Britain veto power over American use of the atomic bomb. With respect to negotiating with the Soviet Union and drawing up an international control agreement, he advised a step-by-step approach providing for the establishment of a UNO to disseminate all fundamental scientific information, including data on atomic fission. Free travel by scientists would then be guaranteed, followed by establishment of an internationally constituted inspection system, still without a right of control. Only then, after many years of preparation, would nations in possession of raw materials turn over their stocks for use in nuclear power plants. The United States would do the same with its raw materials and its stock of atomic bombs but would at no time provide information on the manufacture of atomic weapons to any other nation.[11]

The final American position, solidified without State Department participation, adopted much of Bush's plan with one interesting addition. In talks with the British, the Americans would still insist that the effective cooperation of the Soviets be proven in practice before the United States agreed to give authority over atomic energy to a UNO. But before canceling the Quebec Agreement clause limiting British activity in the commercial and industrial aspects of atomic energy, the United States would ask for control of all uranium and thorium in the British Commonwealth.[12]

The British had an entirely different conception of what an international control agreement should look like and what relations with the United States should be. Some ministers favored sharing with the Soviets not only fundamental scientific knowledge but the practical know-how of manufacturing the bomb as well—this even though Britain did not then have the information itself to give. Wisely, Attlee argued before the full cabinet that cooperation with the Soviet Union ought to be limited to scientific knowledge only. He carried the day. He also won out on Anglo-American relations. He came to the conference intending to maintain as close cooperation with the United States as possible and to begin production of a British atomic bomb with American help at an early date. The Quebec Agreement, he believed, had established a good framework in the CPC for policy coordination and information exchange, and the CDT too should remain intact to continue joint control of raw materials.[13]

Yet he also realized that Britain's bargaining position was not a strong one. The legal and moral argument he would try to employ to persuade the Americans to establish an effective nuclear partnership depended upon the promises given by Roosevelt to Churchill and encapsuled in the Hyde Park Memorandum of September 19, 1944. The problem, as analyzed in a British chiefs of staff study, was that nothing in the Hyde Park document indicated that it had been intended to supersede the far more detailed Quebec Agreement. Indeed, both agreements had been concluded by the President and Prime Minister without authorization of Congress or Parliament. They could thus be more easily repudiated as wartime agreements no longer in force in peacetime. Even more distressing, neither Truman nor Byrnes had shown a readiness to share American atomic secrets with Britain. Nevertheless, Attlee was confident that the Americans would prove reasonable. He approached the conference in a hopeful frame of mind.[14]

If the British came expecting fulfillment of Roosevelt's promises and united in their determination to achieve full partnership, the Americans entered the conference in a state of disarray. Truman, as the British later realized, did not understand the essence of the wartime agreements and was (like his advisors) ignorant of the Hyde Park Memorandum. The American position as interpreted by Patterson, Bush, and Groves, in addition, had only been cast in its final form on November 10, 1945. That same day Attlee and King arrived, and the next day the first meetings took place. It is remarkable that although Patterson, Bush, Groves, and their aides had done the detailed preparation for the conference, they were excluded from these early discussions. They only came into the talks in a meaningful way on November 14.

At the direction of President Truman, no verbatim accounts were kept of the first meetings held on November 11, 1945, on the presidential yacht *Sequoia* as it cruised the Potomac River. Present at the initial meeting were the three heads of government only. They were subsequently joined by Byrnes, Truman's chief of staff Admiral William D. Leahy, Sir John Anderson, chairman of the United Kingdom Advisory Committee on Atomic Energy, British Ambassador to the United States Lord Edward Halifax, Canadian Ambassador to the United States Lester B. Pearson, and the Canadian Prime Minister's secretary Leslie Rowan. The primary topic of conversation was international control. Although agreement in principle to

American proposals for free exchange of scientific information and eventual international control came quickly, the British opposed the kind of careful approach Bush had proposed. They especially disapproved the requirement for physical inspection of atomic energy installations. Their feeling was that the Soviets would never agree to on-site inspection and that therefore insistence on the point would doom the international control idea. In any event, consensus was only hammered out when Bush joined the discussions late on Tuesday, November 13, and insisted on the American point of view. Formal agreement came late the next night.[15]

Finding common ground for bilateral relations proved just as difficult. Discussions on this latter set of issues were hampered by a fundamental misunderstanding concerning what each side wanted. In a series of meetings on November 14 and 15, 1945, attended by Canadian representatives, Americans Patterson, Groves, and Arneson, and Britons Anderson, British military representative in Washington Field Marshal Sir Henry Wilson, and British Embassy Counsellor Roger Makins, the participants set forth their views and attempted to revise the Quebec Agreement in accordance with the wishes of their superiors.[16]

Speaking for the British was Anderson, a Conservative who had been in charge of the British atomic energy program in 1941 and had served as Lord President of the Council in Churchill's wartime government. The British government, he declared, wanted full interchange of personnel and full cooperation in the nuclear field. It also desired revision of the Quebec Agreement clause limiting British activity in the commercial and industrial aspect of atomic energy. But since the Quebec Agreement had placed that decision in the President's hands, the British would abide by whatever decision the Americans arrived at. In these talks, he did not specify that full cooperation meant giving Britain access to weapons information. Without agreeing or disagreeing with Anderson's proposal for full cooperation, Groves suggested that as a quid pro quo the British would have to bring all uranium and thorium in the British Commonwealth under control of the CDT to be allocated on the basis of demonstrated need. But he too failed to make himself completely understood. What he meant but did not say was that since the United States alone had an intact infrastructure for the manufacture of bombs, it alone should make use of the uranium and thorium.[17]

Ultimately, no substantial agreement could be reached. To break the impasse, Anderson and Groves decided to draw up a Memorandum of Intention to set forth basic guidelines for a new Anglo-American atomic agreement to be written later by the CPC. After considerable wrangling over wording, the document was signed on November 16, 1945. Keeping intact the CPC and CDT, Anderson and Groves ignored the question of industrial and commercial rights and softened the clauses on consent for use of the atomic bomb and disclosure of information to third parties to read "consultation." On the question of raw material allocation and information exchange, the memorandum was equally weak. Allocation would be on the basis of need, in the common interest, and for scientific research, military, and humanitarian purposes; but the CPC would decide later in "light of then existing conditions and on a fair and equitable basis" who needed what. Although the words "full and effective cooperation" had been incorporated into the document at Anderson's insistence, they applied only to the field of basic scientific research and did not, the Americans made sure, change the fundamental meaning of the agreement. Cooperation in development, design, construction, and operation of plants was recognized as desirable in principle but was limited, at Groves's insistence, to "*ad hoc* arrangements as may be approved from time to time by the CPC as mutually advantageous." The United States had the right, in effect, to refuse to help the British build an atomic bomb.[18]

At the end of the conference, the three heads of government issued a public statement expressing a desire for full and effective cooperation without realizing the confusion of interpretation in their own minds and the minds of their advisors. The Americans came away believing that they had escaped without commitment and had bought time to play out their plan for international control. They would not, they thought, have to give the British atomic energy information in the near future. The British, on the other hand, believed that they had come away with a promise to establish real cooperation and to draw up a new partnership. They did not comprehend just how wrong they were for many months.

In the House of Commons on November 22, 1945, Attlee spoke confidently of what had been accomplished at the Washington conference and the possibilities for effective international control. The United States, Canada, and Britain, he said, had had full and frank discussions and were working on plans for future cooperation in the field of atomic energy. In point of fact, the CPC did not establish a subcommittee to draft an agreement until December 4, and Attlee overestimated greatly the speed with which the Americans would move. The international control problem had to be resolved first. Even more ominous, the American Congress had begun to assert itself on a wide variety of issues including atomic energy. Senators Tom Connally (D., Texas), chairman of the Foreign Relations Committee, and Arthur Vandenberg (R., Michigan), ranking Republican on the committee, told the President at the public signing ceremony on November 15 that they should have been consulted before the conference. They suspected that the administration intended far too much cooperation with the British. With regard to international control of atomic energy, Connally, Vandenberg, Brien McMahon (D., Connecticut) and others on the newly created Special Senate Committee on Atomic Energy demanded that the administration develop an effective system of security through inspection and control before giving out classified information even to trusted allies. They knew almost nothing about Anglo-American wartime atomic cooperation and clearly intended the ban to prevent exchanges of information with the British. Late in 1945 they began work on legislation to restrict severely if not forbid entirely such exchanges.[19]

Congressional fears about Anglo-American nuclear cooperation were exaggerated. The administration had no intention of giving away American nuclear secrets to the British or to anyone else. Administration policy discussions leading up to the mid-November conference in Washington and the American position at the conference itself demonstrated just how determined administration policymakers were to prevent acquisition by other powers of the "secret" of the atomic bomb. But the British, by interpreting American words and smiles in the most favorable light, convinced themselves that the administration did intend to cooperate in the nuclear field and maintained this belief into the new year. A rude awakening awaited them.

NOTES

1. Arthur H. Vandenberg, Jr., *The Private Papers of Senator Vandenberg* (Boston: Houghton Mifflin, 1952), pp. 252-53.

2. Minutes of Meeting of CPC, Washington, July 4, 1945, SCI Files, *Foreign Relations of the United States* (hereafter cited as *FRUS*), 1945, 2:12-14.

3. Attlee to Truman, London, August 8, 1945, S/AE Files, *FRUS*, 1945, 2:36-37.

4. Memorandum by Stimson, Washington, September 11, 1945; Memorandum by Acheson, Washington, September 25, 1945; Memorandum by Patterson, Washington, September 26, 1945, S/AE Files, *FRUS*, 1945, 2:41-44, 48-55.

5. *Public Papers of the Presidents: Harry S. Truman, 1945* (Washington, D.C.: U.S. Government Printing Office, 1961), pp. 362-66.

6. Minutes of Meeting of Secretaries of State, War, and Navy, October 10, 1945, 740.00119 EW/10-1045, *FRUS*, 1945, 2:55-57.

7. JCS 1477/1, October 30, 1945, CCS 471.6 (8-15-45), sec. 1, Modern Military Branch, National Archives.

8. Attlee to Truman, London, October 16, 1945, Department of State Records, RG 59, Decimal Files 1945-1949, box 4617, file 811.2423, National Archives; James L. Gormly, "The Washington Declaration and the 'Poor Relation': Anglo-American Atomic Diplomacy, 1945-46," *Diplomatic History* 8 (Spring 1984): 130-31; *New York Times*, Oct. 28, 1945, p. 33; Oct. 31, 1945, p. 6.

9. *Public Papers of the Presidents, Truman, 1945*, p. 453.

10. Memorandum by Arneson, Washington, April 17, 1946, S/AE Files, *FRUS*, 1945, 2:63-69.

11. Memorandum by Bush, Washington, November 5, 1945, S/AE Files, *FRUS*, 1945, 2:69-73.

12. Memorandum by Arneson, Washington, April 17, 1946, S/AE Files, *FRUS*, 1945, 2:63-69.

13. Margaret Gowing, *Independence and Deterrence: Britain and Atomic Energy, 1945-1952*, vol. 1 (London: Macmillan, 1974), pp. 69-70, 72-73; Gormly, "Washington Declaration," pp. 126-27.

14. Ibid.

15. Gormly, "Washington Declaration," pp. 133-35; Gregg Herken, *The Winning Weapon: The Atomic Bomb in the Cold War, 1945-1950* (New York: Alfred A. Knopf, 1980), pp. 63-65; John W. Wheeler-Bennett, *John Anderson, Viscount Waverly* (London: Macmillan, 1962), pp. 334-35.

16. Leslie R. Groves, *Now It Can Be Told* (New York: Harper & Row, 1962), pp. 403-5. Delegated to help draw up the Memorandum of Intention, Groves informed Patterson that he had been excluded from the early meetings. He thought the State Department had wanted it that way. Patterson was startled, as was Byrnes when told, but Groves managed as best he could from past knowledge.

17. Memorandum by Arneson, Washington, April 17, 1946, S/AE Files, *FRUS*, 1945, 2:63-69; Francis Williams, *A Prime Minister Remembers* (London: William Heinemann, 1961), p. 102.

18. Memorandum by Arneson, Washington, April 17, 1946; Memorandum by Groves and Anderson, Washington, November 16, 1945, S/AE Files, *FRUS*, 1945, 2:63-69, 75-76.

19. 416 *H.C. Deb.* 5s., p. 607; Minutes of Meeting of CPC, Washington, December 4, 1945, SCI Files, *FRUS*, 1945, 2:86-89; John A. Munro and Alex I. Inglas, "The Atomic Conference of 1945 and the Pearson Memoirs," *International Journal* 29 (Winter 1973-74): 90-109; Vandenberg, *Private Papers of Senator Vandenberg*, pp. 225-27, 234-35; Dean Acheson, *Sketches from Life of Men I Have Known* (New York: Harper & Brothers, 1959), pp. 124-25; *New York Times*, Nov. 29, 1945, p. 4; Dec. 20, 1945, p. 8; Dec. 29, 1945, p. 1. The frustration of Vandenberg and other senators was all the more pronounced because of a feeling of having been shunted aside in the early part of World War II by President Roosevelt.

3
PROTECTING THE ATOMIC MONOPOLY

> I can see nothing in the Washington declaration [of November 15, 1945], or in the [U.N.] assembly resolution, which requires us to dissolve our partnership, either in the exchange of information or in the control of raw materials, until it can be merged in a wider partnership; I should be sorry to think that you did not agree with this view.
>
> —Attlee to Truman, June 7, 1946[1]

In January 1946 the British requested permission for a scientific team to attend the upcoming atomic bomb trials at Bikini Atoll in July. The U.S. government agreed. British experts, the Joint Chiefs of Staff (JCS) advised, had special knowledge that could help in planning and execution of the tests. From a military point of view, their participation was highly desirable. The British were encouraged. By permitting them many times the number of military and civilian observers allowed to any other member nation of the new U.N. Atomic Energy Commission, the United States was acknowledging the special relationship that existed between the United States and Britain.[2]

The British also hoped for a favorable American response to the report of the subcommittee of the CPC that had been established on December 4, 1945, to draw up a comprehensive proposal for a new atomic energy agreement. Yet when the CPC met in Washington on February 15, 1946, to consider the plan, the Americans hesitated. Since the proposed agreement, Byrnes told Halifax, would have to be registered with the Secretariat of the U.N. in accordance with U.N. article 102, the administration would have to consider the matter carefully. With public opinion so strongly supportive of international control of atomic energy, he explained, the United States might not want to let the world know that it was contemplating new bilateral nuclear arrangements with the British.[3]

In reality, what had happened was that General Groves, even while serving on the CPC subcommittee with Makins and Pearson, had opposed any proposal that would tighten Anglo-American nuclear relations. On February 13, 1946, therefore, he wrote a memorandum to Byrnes charging that the subcommittee plan called for a relationship tantamount to a military alliance. He complained that the United States would end up bearing almost the entire financial and developmental burden—just as during the war—while Britain would be free to develop atomic energy for commercial and industrial purposes. Under the plan, moreover, Britain could veto American use of the atomic bomb and, undeservedly in his opinion, enjoy the full benefits of the combined effort including benefits arising from the wartime program. The subcommittee plan was flawed in two other ways, he advised. It ran counter to the American proposal in the U.N. for international control (and thus would cause a stir if Congress and the public found out about it), and it permitted the British to build large-scale plutonium-producing plants in Britain (on February 15, 1946, the British informed the Americans that they did in fact intend to build such a plant in Britain). Plants located in North America, he insisted, made better strategic sense. Convinced that Groves's objections had substance, Byrnes informed Halifax of the American reservations.[4]

Groves was correct that a new Anglo-American nuclear agreement would have been inconsistent with international control of atomic energy. He was also correct that the subcommittee proposal, as written, would have left the British free to develop atomic energy for commercial and industrial purposes while still enjoying the full benefits of cooperation with the United States in the military field. But he was inaccurate in his other objections. Contrary to the assertions in his memorandum, the British would have contributed a fair share of the financial and developmental cost of the project, would have had only a right of consultation, not veto power, on the use of the bomb and disclosure of information to third parties, and would have had to commit all raw materials (considerable deposits of uranium and thorium from British Commonwealth sources) to the CDT for allocation by the CPC. Half the members of the CPC, in addition, were Americans. Since the Canadian representative usually backed the American point of view, the United States would probably have had little trouble guaranteeing adequate supplies for the American program.[5]

Regardless of the points in the subcommittee report, however, the British position at this time contained a good measure of flexibility and rationality. The British were fully aware of the potential cost of developing atomic energy and would have been quite willing to cooperate with the Americans in all fields of atomic energy, including commercial and industrial activities. Militarily, they were under no illusions. On January 1, 1946, the British chiefs of staff sent a report to Attlee advising that Britain needed atomic bombs as soon as possible to deter attack by a potential aggressor. But they also informed him that it would take five years before an independent British program could produce the necessary fissionable material to make bombs. Although the chiefs wanted two atomic piles for greater production of bombs and to keep a potential aggressor in the dark about how many bombs Britain could produce, the government decided that the country could initially afford only one. Even so, there was some debate as to where to put the plant. Sir James Chadwick, scientific advisor to the British members of the CPC, and Professor John Cockcroft, director of the British atomic research establishment, favored location at Chalk River in Canada. A prepared site with ample water, it would give political advantages vis-à-vis the United States. The political advantages were that the United States would be far more likely to agree to a nuclear partnership if atomic installations and stockpiles of raw materials were located in North America. Most British policymakers, it must be said, wanted location of at least one atomic pile in Britain. National pride was involved, but there was also the point that location in Canada would mean sharing the cost, and therefore the control, of the pile and the weapons material produced with the Canadians.[6]

Despite British readiness to attempt to satisfy American concerns, serious negotiations did not occur concerning the subcommittee plan. Instead, the Americans procrastinated and in the process ruffled British feelings. Even more alarming from the British point of view, Truman administration officials appeared willing to give in to atomic monopolists in Congress and agree to provisions in the atomic energy bill to restrict information exchanges and cooperation with foreign governments. They would do so in order to win over key congressmen to the idea of civilian, as opposed to military, control of atomic energy. Attlee told American Ambassador to Britain Averell W. Harriman that if the bill became law, Britain would build nuclear plants for military as well as commercial/industrial production of atomic energy. Although intended as a warning, this was another clear indication of flexibility in the British position. Should the United States agree to an Anglo-American nuclear partnership, Attlee was implying, the British might be willing to forego manufacture of atomic bombs in the British Isles.[7]

Having expected a quick decision in favor of the subcommittee proposal, the British became quite cross when it did not occur. On March 5, 1946, Acheson repeated to Halifax a statement of the official American position. It was politically impossible, he said, to agree to a secret exchange because U.N. article 102 required that all atomic energy accords be submitted to the U.N. Atomic Energy Commission for review. The United States, then, had to wait to see if progress could be made on international control. Facilely, the British members of the CPC drew up a clever response to be presented at the next CPC meeting. Conceding that article 102 did prevent a new agreement, they asserted that it did not legally bar fulfillment of old ones. They proposed, therefore, adoption of the subcommittee proposal based on cooperation under the wartime Quebec Agreement. Some revisions would have to be made in the old accord to insure effective collaboration—and these revisions were point for point the same as the subcommittee proposal —but this could be considered temporary and subject to permanent revision when the U.N. Atomic Energy Commission made its recommendations on international control.[8]

The British also intended to raise the question of raw material allocation at the next CPC meeting. They wanted control of a portion of CDT supplies received in the trust from V-J Day (August 14, 1945) through February 28, 1946, and half the supplies accumulated from March 1 through the end of 1946. The American members of the CPC had a different idea. They preferred allocation based on need and reiterated that position in preparation for an April 15 meeting of the CPC insisted upon by the British and set to take place at the State Department. At that meeting Halifax protested the American allocation formula and said that it would leave the British program with no supplies through February 28 even though Britain had paid 50 percent of the cost. General Groves responded bluntly. According to the Quebec Agreement, he said, allocations were made on the basis of need, not payment. Since the British had no plants in actual operation, they should get no supplies. Acceptance of the British proposal, he asserted, would force partial shutdown of American plants. After further debate, it was agreed that no decision could be taken, and the matter was delegated to a subcommittee composed of Acheson, Bush, Groves, Makins, and Chadwick for further study. Discussions then turned to the British plan for cooperation. Halifax, following Attlee's instructions to force the Americans' hand, made a detailed request for information on construction and operation of atomic energy plants. Although fearing a negative reply, he was nevertheless shocked by the firmness of the American response, backed by the Canadians. The United States, the Americans said, rejected out of hand the British proposal because it created difficulties with U.N. article 102, changed the basis of cooperation as set forth in the Quebec Agreement, and preempted atomic energy discussions in the U.N. about international control. Quite vigorously, the British countered that the November 15, 1945, declaration by Truman, Attlee, and King calling for "full and effective cooperation" was being ignored, but the Americans would not listen. The meeting ended in a complete impasse.[9]

While the British realized that the Americans were quite serious about international control, they also believed that their powerful ally wanted to continue to monopolize the benefits, military and otherwise, of atomic energy. Attlee was outraged. He sent Truman a telegram the next day and had Halifax question Byrnes as to the deeper reasons for the American refusal. The answer, first to Halifax and then to Attlee, defined the difference in interpretation of the Memorandum of Intention of November 16, 1945. But it did not set forth substantive reservations like those Groves had listed for Byrnes in mid-February 1946. The United States, Byrnes said, had only agreed to full and effective cooperation in basic research, not in development, design, construction, and operation of plants. The British would get no information of an industrial nuclear nature or data on how to build a bomb. Truman then explained in a letter to Attlee that sentiment in favor of international control was so strong that the American public would not support the construction of another atomic plant in the United States, let alone one constructed with American assistance in Britain.[10]

On the basis of the printed language of the Quebec Agreement and Memorandum of Intention, the American position was correct. The United States had no obligation to hand over its most sensitive nuclear information to the British. But there was also the question of the spirit of the Quebec Agreement, supported by the Hyde Park Memorandum (the American copy of which still could not be located). The British could make the case that they had submerged their program into the American with the understanding that information and assistance would be forthcoming after the war. Certainly this was Roosevelt's intention. The problem was that he was alone in this sentiment and that the Hyde Park Memorandum was very general in nature and an executive statement of future intention, not a treaty or even an accord comparable to the Quebec Agreement. Well aware of the American constitutional framework, the British, as has been shown, unquestionably realized that further agreement would be needed to give force to Roosevelt's commitment. No doubt the British did submerge their program expecting postwar American assistance, but it is clear that with the sole and admittedly important exception of Roosevelt, the Americans never intended to establish full and effective cooperation in all fields of atomic energy.

They did, however, intend to continue cooperation for the control of raw materials and met three times with the British in April 1946 to discuss allocation. Stung by the American refusal to consider a nuclear partnership, the British at first took a very tough line. Since they had paid for half the raw materials going into the CDT from V-J Day, they said, they wanted half for the same time period. Bargaining for the Americans, Groves staked out an equally stubborn position. He refused to consider any proposal that did not adopt as its basis the principle of need. He complained in two April 29, 1946, memoranda to Acheson and Bush that acceptance of a compromise proposed by Makins (giving the United States all stocks to March 31, 1946, and dividing the stocks equally from April 1 to December 31, 1946) would reduce production in American plants. British contribution to the overall program, he wrote, was very small, the supply of available raw material was not sufficient to justify building additional plants by a nation, Britain, "destined to be partner of ours in any major military operation," and the United States, shouldering the major burden of the joint effort, should take advantage of its present production capacity to build up a large strategic reserve of bombs in preparation for a possible future war with the Soviets.

He thought that the real reason the British wanted to begin building up a stockpile of raw materials was to take advantage of the commercial and industrial uses of atomic energy—an inefficient, uneconomical division of resources and efforts. But location of commercial plants or raw material stockpiles in Britain was in itself dangerous, he asserted, because such installations could be easily destroyed or neutralized in a war. The numbers, he insisted, told the tale. Proven high-grade uranium reserves in the Belgian Congo, the main source, were estimated at 7,700 tons. The British wanted half the 2,700 tons coming into the CDT from April 1 through December 31 and projected their needs at 5,400 tons for the next three years. Yet the United States needed 400 more tons in 1946 than the British were offering and 230 tons a month thereafter. The United States must flatly reject the compromise plan, he concluded.[11]

Acheson, Patterson, and Bush thought otherwise. They understood that the British were so angry about the American rejection of the proposed nuclear partnership that they would end cooperation on the control of raw materials and all Anglo-American nuclear contacts rather than accept less than Makins's compromise plan. After all, the British were paying half the cost, and the United States could not afford to lose British cooperation in securing uranium and thorium from British Commonwealth countries. They overruled Groves, therefore, and agreed to the formula giving each country 1,350 tons of Belgian Congo uranium for the period April 1 through December 31, 1946. Allocation for future years was left unresolved.[12]

Meanwhile Attlee, even as his government pushed through Parliament major pieces of legislation to nationalize key British industries (and in the process alarmed an already uneasy American Congress about the prospects of virulent socialism in Britain), sent a second message to Truman on June 7, 1946. He proudly put forward the British case. Britain, he asserted, had made very important contributions to the common war effort. British leaders and scientists had cooperated in the development of atomic energy, had been responsible for the invention of radar and jet propulsion, and had freely given the technology for these devices to the United States. They had sacrificed as well the independent British atomic energy program for the common good in the belief that the Americans would share information and give assistance later. Their two countries continued to cooperate in the control of raw materials critical for making atomic bombs. Why not do likewise in the exchange of nuclear information?[13]

Even had Truman been swayed by this appeal, it was too late for effective action. He himself had facilitated passage of the atomic energy bill by publicly throwing his support behind Senator McMahon's version. On July 26, 1946, the day after the United States concluded the Bikini Atoll trials to test the effects of atomic bombs underwater and on warships, the final Atomic Energy Act of 1946 providing for civilian control and severe restrictions on information exchanges with foreign governments passed the full Congress. The President signed it without objection. Anglo-American nuclear relations had disintegrated to a single link based on joint control of raw materials, and cooperation in that area was strained. Simultaneously with the passage of the McMahon Act, the British demanded that the Americans adopt the principle that whoever received raw materials from the CDT after V-J Day pay for it. Since the Americans had received all stocks through the end of March 1946, the British said, they should reimburse the British government for what it had already paid. The Americans quietly agreed.[14]

Margaret Gowing, in *Independence and Deterrence: Britain and Atomic Energy, 1945-1952*, states that she sees it as "extraordinary" that the McMahon Act passed without administration objection. But in fact the substance of that legislation accurately reflected the predominant sentiment in both administration and Congress in 1945 and 1946. Aside from Eisenhower, Acheson, and a few other State Department officials, most policymakers preferred to preserve the atomic monopoly and the strategic and other benefits exclusive control would bring. They saw no pressing need to cooperate with the British.[15]

Certainly the majority of Congress did not. Isolationists like Senator Bourke B. Hickenlooper (R., Iowa) fought hard for preservation of the atomic monopoly and received significant support from the Unilateralist wing of the Republican party. Unilateralists, although favorable to an active American foreign policy, disliked formal alliances with foreign powers. They pressed, rather, for economic self-sufficiency and strong air and naval forces with which to prevent foreign influence on American policy. They, like the anti-internationalists, frowned on revealing nuclear information. "If it were possible," Senator Vandenberg, leader of the Unilateralists, wrote in mid-November 1945, "to keep this secret in our possession indefinitely, this would be my first and emphatic choice because we know that America will not use this devastating weapon for aggressive purposes." After the Republicans gained substantial majorities in both houses of Congress in November 1946, opposition to nuclear cooperation with allies reached its zenith.[16]

Because of the strength of congressional opposition to nuclear cooperation and because the McMahon Act explicitly forbade revealing information on the manufacture or use of atomic weapons, the production of fissionable material, or the use of fissionable material for production of power, the administration soon discovered that it had little room to maneuver. Even inhibited was the President's ability to adjust to changing circumstances requiring closer defense ties with important allies. By letting the offending provisions pass into law uncontested, the administration had painted itself into a very uncomfortable diplomatic corner.[17]

NOTES

1. Attlee to Truman, June 7, 1946, S/AE Files, *Foreign Relations of the United States* (hereafter cited as *FRUS*), 1946, 1:1249-53.

2. Memorandum by Byrnes, Washington, January 5, 1946, 811.2423/1-546; Minutes of Meeting of Secretaries of State, War, and Navy, Washington, February 5, 1946, 811.2423/2-546, *FRUS*, 1946, 1:1203-4; JCS 1552/4, Washington, January 2, 1946, Department of State Records, RG 59, Decimal Files 1945-1949, box 4617, file 811.2423, National Archives.

3. Minutes of Meeting of CPC, Washington, February 15, 1946, S/AE Files, *FRUS*, 1946, 1:1213-15.

4. Memorandum by Groves, Washington, February 13, 1946; Statement by Halifax, Washington, February 15, 1946, S/AE Files, *FRUS*, 1946, 1:1204-7, 1215-16.

5. Draft Report to CPC by a Sub-Committee, Washington, February 15, 1946, S/AE Files, *FRUS*, 1946, 1:1207-13.

6. 416 *H.C. Deb.* 5s., pp. 1529-30; Margaret Gowing, *Independence and Deterrence: Britain and Atomic Energy, 1945-1952*, vol. 1 (London: Macmillan, 1974), pp. 169-70, 172-73.

7. Kenneth Harris, *Attlee* (London: Weidenfeld and Nicolson, 1982), pp. 284, 286.

8. David E. Lilienthal, *The Journals of David E. Lilienthal*, vol. 2, *The Atomic Energy Years, 1945-1950* (New York: Harper & Row, 1964), p. 26; Proposal by British Members CPC, Washington, undated, S/AE Files, *FRUS*, 1946, 1:1218-23.

9. Memorandum on Allocation by British Members CPC, Washington, undated; Memorandum by U.S. Members CPC, Washington, April 9, 1946; Minutes of Meeting CPC, Washington, April 15, 1946, S/AE Files, *FRUS*, 1946, 1:1225-31; John W. Wheeler-Bennett, *John Anderson, Viscount Waverly* (London: Macmillan, 1962), p. 337.

10. Attlee to Truman, London, April 16, 1946, S/AE Files; Memorandum of Conversation by Byrnes, Washington, April 18, 1946, 811.2423/4-1846; Truman to Attlee, Washington, April 20, 1946, 841.646/4-2046, *FRUS*, 1946, 1:1231-37.

11. Memorandum by Groves, Washington, April 29, 1946; Memorandum by Groves, Washington, April 29, 1946, S/AE Files, *FRUS*, 1946, 1:1238-41.

12. Memorandum for Files by Hancock, Washington, May 1, 1946; Memorandum by Acheson, Bush, and Groves, Washington, May 7, 1946, S/AE Files, *FRUS*, 1946, 1:1242-43, 1245-46.

13. Attlee to Truman, London, June 7, 1946, S/AE Files, *FRUS*, 1946, 1:1249-53.

14. Memorandum by Joint Secretaries of CPC, Washington, July 26, 1946; Minutes of Meeting CPC, July 31, 1946, S/AE Files, *FRUS*, 1946, 1:1254-57; Gregg Herken, *The Winning Weapon: The Atomic Bomb in the Cold War, 1945-1950* (New York: Alfred A. Knopf, 1980), p. 124.

15. Gowing, *Independence and Deterrence* 1: 105-10; Andrew J. Pierre, *Nuclear Politics: The British Experience with an Independent Strategic Force, 1938-1970* (London: Oxford University Press, 1972), pp. 118, 120.

16. Justus D. Doenecke, *Not to the Swift: The Old Isolationists in the Cold War Era* (London: Associated University Presses, 1979), pp. 59-60; David W. Reinhard, *The Republican Right since 1945* (Lexington: University Press of Kentucky, 1983), pp. 4, 20, 30-31; Arthur H. Vandenberg, Jr., *The Private Papers of Senator Vandenberg* (Boston: Houghton Mifflin, 1952), pp. 252-54.

17. Public Law 585, 79th Cong., 60 Stat. 755-775; Francis Duncan, "Atomic Energy and Anglo-American Relations, 1946-1954," *Orbis* 12 (Fall 1969): 1188-1207.

4
MOVEMENT TOWARD LIMITED COOPERATION

> In the likely event of failure of U.N. atomic energy discussions, the country must reconsider its diplomacy. For example, we shall have to consider the possibilities of combining with other nations in a U.N. without Russia; or a limited alliance with other countries which cooperated closely with us during the war; or a series of movements in the U.N. serving to isolate the Soviet Union and show up its intransigence and its aggressive intention on several points; e.g., subversion of civil liberties in satellite states and indirect aggression against member countries.
> —Robert A. Lovett, July 28, 1947[1]

At the end of the war, most formal military contacts between the British and Americans ended. Lower level discussions did take place, but not until Field Marshal Sir Bernard Law Montgomery visited the JCS in late 1946 did coordinated planning revive. After that, due to the increasing danger of conflict with the Soviets, military contacts were extensive and led to discussion of strategic questions. The British and Americans also shook hands economically and politically. In December 1945 a loan agreement for $3.75 billion was signed. A year later the two governments fused their zones of occupation in Germany. In March 1947 the United States in the Truman Doctrine agreed to take over responsibility from the British for assisting in the defense of Greece and Turkey in the Eastern Mediterranean. In June 1947 the idea for the Marshall Plan was hatched. Mutual interest and a common adversary convinced British and American leaders that they still needed each other.

If growing East-West tensions, the British reasoned, made necessary improved military, economic, and diplomatic ties, why should they not also require closer cooperation in the field of atomic energy? They had reason to hope that the Americans would come around to their way of thinking. George C. Marshall, former wartime Army chief of staff, became secretary of state in January 1947 and brought an attitude sympathetic toward the old wartime alliance. Robert A. Lovett, Marshall's under secretary of state (from July 1, 1947), also appeared inclined toward improved contacts with the British. A banker and former assistant secretary of war for aid, Lovett was also valuable for his friendship with Senator Vandenberg, key figure on the JCAE.[2]

But there were bureaucratic problems that boded ill for the chances of rapid improvement in Anglo-American nuclear relations. By creating the five-man AEC to manage all aspects of the nuclear program and by investing the JCAE with statutory authority to serve as a watchdog of that program, the McMahon Act had greatly complicated policy-making on atomic energy matters for the American government. The likelihood of intra-administration disagreement and exploitation of disagreement by congressmen was significantly increased. Nor were the lines of communication between important government agencies fully open in January 1947. A Military Liaison Committee (MLC) headed by Rear Admiral William S. Parsons had also been created by the McMahon Act for the purpose of coordinating policy between the War Department and the AEC. But already Chairman of the JCAE Hickenlooper was complaining that the AEC was not talking to and briefing properly the MLC. And there was great need for communication between the military and the AEC. Upon taking office, AEC Chairman David E. Lilienthal, former head of the Tennessee Valley Authority, discovered that the American nuclear program was in a deplorable condition. The United States had only one dozen atomic bombs in its arsenal, most not ready for immediate use, and the program was producing just two additional bombs a month. To make matters worse, neither the President nor the JCS had been informed that there were not enough bombs to carry out strategic war plans. Not until the end of 1948 did the stockpile reach an adequate level.[3]

Relations between the War and State departments, despite Marshall's presence in the latter agency, were also very bad. Contacts were limited to communications between the two secretaries and between Deputy Under Secretary of State H. Freeman Matthews and Major General James H. Burns. Friends from both departments had to meet secretly to avoid controversy. It was not until Marshall became secretary of defense in September 1950 and Lovett under secretary of defense that regular State-Defense Department (JCS) meetings took place.[4]

The American policy-making bureaucracy, then, was not functioning well with respect to atomic energy matters. But the British did not appear to understand. Instructed to investigate again the possibilities of concluding a new Anglo-American nuclear partnership, Makins met in late January 1947 with Lilienthal and the other AEC commissioners. He heard only bad news.

The McMahon Act, Lilenthal advised, officially ended wartime arrangements and all provisions for cooperation. In his opinion, a new agreement would have to be worked out for joint control of raw materials and submitted to Congress for its approval.[5]

Considering the hostility of the JCAE toward any cooperation on nuclear matters with foreign governments,[6] Makins must have been very much alarmed by Lilienthal's gloomy statement. But prompted by Halifax and Field Marshal (now Lord) Wilson, he tried again. This time he went to Acheson with a comprehensive proposal calling for an exchange of personnel to examine fully each other's information and activities. More specifically, even while acknowledging that the McMahon Act technically prevented such exchanges, the British wanted solutions to 12 to 14 critical problems they were having in their atomic energy program. The United States, Makins suggested, could justify such action by reinterpreting the McMahon Act to apply only to information acquired after passage of the act. Developments and discoveries in atomic energy that occurred before passage could legally be exchanged. Acheson replied that the administration could not so cavalierly circumvent the law. But for what in plain words was Makins asking? Just what did the "12 or 14 problems" refer to exactly? Makins told him. The British government, he said, wanted information on the whole field of preparing ingredients for the atomic bomb. Having already thrown cold water on reinterpretation of the McMahon Act, Acheson could only promise to consult other interested parties within the administration and return a formal reply.[7]

Although rejection of most of the British plan was all but a foregone conclusion, Marshall asked on February 11, 1947, one week before the Soviets blocked in the U.N. a U.S.-sponsored plan for international control of atomic energy, for a JCS study of the strategic implications of locating a large-scale nuclear plant in Britain. The JCS reply, based on a report by the Joint Strategic Survey Committee (JSSC), was that such a location would be "disadvantageous to the security interests of the United States" for four basic reasons. First, the JCS believed that commitment of resources to build a plant would result in an enormous drain on the British economy. Besides, commercial use of nuclear power was years away, and the JCS suspected that the British request was aimed at acquiring information only (without undertaking actual development) so that Britain could keep up with the United States and emerge later in a favorable position to exploit for maximum advantage the industrial uses of atomic energy.[8]

Second, location of a nuclear plant in the British Isles would mean positioning large stockpiles of raw materials in Britain. This would be a problem because diversion of raw materials into the British program would severely impair the ability of the more important American program to produce enough atomic bombs to meet minimum American military requirements. Third, giving secret information to the British increased dangerously the possibility of leaks to the Soviets. While the JSSC had nothing but praise for British military security, it criticized harshly the security records of "certain British scientists on atomic energy matters." Finally, the JSSC study pointed out that locating a nuclear installation and raw materials stockpile in Britain would put these critical facilities within easy bombing range of the European continent. The plant itself might even be destroyed or seized in a modern airborne assault. It would be far better, far sounder from a purely strategic viewpoint, to concentrate all nuclear activities in American plants (east of the Cascades and west of the Appalachians) and so facilitate conversion of usable raw materials into atomic bombs.[9]

This assessment was definitely too pessimistic for the conditions prevailing in 1947. Even though British air defenses were relatively poor, Soviet bombing capability was even weaker. Air power in Soviet military doctrine was seen as tactical, for the support of large advancing armies, and so the Soviets had neglected to build a strategic bomber force. They had no aircraft carriers, moreover, and only developed short- and medium-range bombers after 1948. They certainly did not have the ability to invade Britain and seize plants or stockpiles of raw materials. The real danger was that eventually the Soviets would manufacture atomic weapons and strategic bombers to carry them and have the capability to destroy any European target. Had the JCS and JSSC postulated that such Soviet development was possible in the near future and would then pose a serious risk to nuclear facilities in Britain, they would have been on firmer ground.

On the issues of diversion of raw materials from the American program and the danger of security breaches, however, the criticisms were more legitimate. The British program was in fact incapable of producing bombs and would be until 1952. Diversion of large amounts of uranium and thorium into the British Isles would, considering the relative scarcity of those two commodities in 1947, slow down American bomb production. In security matters too the JCS had cause for concern. Donald C. Maclean, British Embassy official and member of the CPC, and Klaus Fuchs, important British nuclear physicist, were both Soviet agents and would both take part in upcoming negotiations between the United States and Britain on nuclear cooperation.[10]

When on February 18, 1947, the Soviets blocked the American plan for international control in the U.N., a consensus began to build among American policymakers that the United States ought to move closer to the British on nuclear matters. One important advocate was General Dwight D. Eisenhower, chief of staff of the U.S. Army. From the first, Eisenhower had been critical of maximum security on nuclear matters insofar as it interfered with Anglo-American cooperation. He preferred to emphasize the transitory nature of the atomic monopoly and the long-term need for the United States to cooperate militarily and otherwise with allies and to coordinate strategic planning. When telling Wilson in early March, just before Truman's decision to extend aid to Greece and Turkey, that the JCS thought location of nuclear plants in the British Isles unwise, he chose not to mention the JCS's strategic reservations. Instead he emphasized that the Americans feared that the British government might be subject in the future to pressure from the Soviets threatening consequences Britain might not be willing to bear. Within the administration he also worked for Anglo-American nuclear reconciliation. He told Lilienthal that because of their wartime contributions, the British deserved better treatment. British socialism, he added, did not pose as grave a security risk as some suggested.[11]

But Eisenhower's view was still not widely accepted even after talks in Moscow on the German question between the United States, Soviet Union, Britain, and France broke down at the end of April 1947. What really propelled reconsideration of American policy was the raw material situation. The AEC estimated that the United States would need far more uranium than previously calculated and reported that the only way to meet minimum requirements was to secure more of the British share of the output going into the CDT from the Belgian Congo uranium mines. Concerned, the commissioners went to the JCAE. At a meeting on May 5, 1947, in which he described the nation's nuclear program in some detail, commissioner Carroll L. Wilson revealed information about the British the JCAE had not known. Senator Connally and others were stunned to hear that the British knew the fundamentals of how to make an atomic bomb. Reacting to their surprise, Lilienthal suggested that they immediately ask the State Department for a full briefing on the past history of Anglo-American atomic cooperation and learn the facts.[12]

On May 12, 1947, Under Secretary of State Acheson held this very important briefing session and sought to impress upon the minds of the members of the JCAE a favorable view of past Anglo-American atomic cooperation. The wartime relationship had been close, he said, with valuable contributions by British, Canadian, and other scientists in the Manhattan Project. Although the Quebec Agreement provided for full exchange of information only for the field of scientific research and development of atomic energy, the British and Americans had collaborated completely on the control and allocation of critical raw materials. They were continuing to collaborate in the CPC and CDT. President Roosevelt, furthermore, had promised full partnership in all aspects of atomic energy in the Hyde Park Memorandum of September 19, 1944, and the desirability of establishing a full partnership was recognized by President Truman after the November 1945 conference. Three obstacles to future cooperation still existed, however. The McMahon Act provisions severely restricting information exchanges, executive branch responsibility to Congress, and even the international control idea—still formally alive—all made relations with the British very difficult. These conditions had to change before a long-term solution to the raw material problem could be negotiated.[13]

The JCAE had much to ponder and so did the policymakers. The raw material problem was real and would grow worse later when decisions were made to accelerate the atomic energy program for more rapid bomb production. Just as alarming, if not more so, Soviet nuclear development was proceeding apace and might produce a bomb sooner than projected.

The replacement of Acheson by Lovett on July 1, 1947, expedited the reevaluation of nuclear policy. Both the State Department and AEC had been studying whether under the McMahon Act the administration could use information as a bargaining chip to insure adequate supplies of raw materials from the British. Now Lovett, concerned that the Soviets were stalling in the U.N. discussions on international control until they manufactured their first atomic bomb, approved a State Department Policy Planning Staff (PPS) proposal for a reorientation of American nuclear policy. The August 21, 1947, proposal was written by George F. Kennan, first head of the PPS. The United States, Kennan advised, should continue negotiating in the U.N. for an international control agreement but should also embark upon a public campaign to demonstrate to the world that Soviet intransigence was responsible for the U.N. impasse and that the United States was in the right. Simultaneously, the administration should open discussions with the British and Canadians about the meaning of the impasse and announce publicly the fact that these discussions were taking place. An absence of meaningful dialogue with the British and Canadians on nuclear matters was hurting overall relations and might have a detrimental effect on raw materials cooperation in the future. Already the State Department had had to advise the British to expect no progress on their request for information until after the next report of the U.N. Atomic Energy Commission to the U.N. Security Council in September.[14]

Opposition to Kennan's proposal for a dramatic improvement in Anglo-American cooperation centered around the two groups originally opposed to cooperation—hard-line atomic monopolists and international controllers, the former especially well represented on the JCAE. On August 29, 1947, Hickenlooper wrote Marshall protesting the arrangement with the British for control of raw materials. The British, he declared, were not close to being able to use their growing stockpile to make weapons. The presence of that stockpile in the British Isles, moreover, was providing a potential target to the Soviets in a possible future war. He was in favor of withholding economic aid unless they agreed to transfer all excess raw materials to North America. The United States, he said, was only trying to stabilize the world and "incidentally pull British chestnuts out of the fire." Economic coercion was a tactic also favored by Bernard Baruch, the American representative to the U.N. on atomic energy matters. But he had another reason for opposing cooperation with the British. He did not want to chance giving information only to have the British turn it over to other countries and thereby make more difficult effective international control.[15]

By October 1947, due to AEC complaints that the stocks of uranium available to the United States were grossly insufficient to keep American nuclear plants operating, almost everyone realized that the United States needed some agreement with the British to increase the American share of raw materials in the CDT. Kennan lobbied for his view within the administration in a PPS memorandum on October 24. In essence, he asserted, the United States could secure the materials needed by offering a combination of verbal concessions (such as recognizing that existing British industrial projects represented a "legitimate claim on raw materials") and a promise to seek from Congress in the next legislative session wider authority to exchange information when in the President's opinion such exchanges would " contribute to national security."[16]

Because Kennan's proposal also recognized the "desirability of the principle of assisting" the British to develop atomic energy for "peaceful uses" in the British Isles, members of the National Military Establishment (created by the National Security Act of 1947) and AEC objected. New Secretary of Defense Forrestal said at a meeting of the American members of the CPC on November 5, 1947, that although the military would support exchanging information with the British to achieve the goal of increasing the allocation of raw materials to the United States, he and his advisors could not sanction any plan that permitted location of a large nuclear plant in the British Isles. Edmund A. Gullion, special assistant to Under Secretary of State Lovett for atomic energy matters, tried to persuade him to reconsider. Since the British were adamant about building their plant, he said, with or without American help, and since they wanted it predominantly for industrial purposes, why not agree to assist in exchange for a reduction in the British share of raw materials and a transfer of most of their stockpile to the United States?[17]

To this suggestion Lilienthal and Vannevar Bush raised objections. The kind of assistance Gullion was proposing, Lilienthal charged, would require new legislation from Congress—unlikely considering the mood of the JCAE —and would result in some loss of security. He and Bush preferred limited data exchanges under the present law. The United States should agree to answer specific questions only, not to give information on the whole field of atomic energy. Seeing the lack of support for the broader approach, Marshall requested that the various agencies revise their recommendations for negotiations with the British and reconvene at a later date.[18]

Not only did the State Department have to adjust its proposals to satisfy the concerns of the National Military Establishment and AEC, it also had to worry about JCAE reaction. On November 16, 1947, Lovett and Forrestal met with Senators Vandenberg and Hickenlooper to forestall a move by the JCAE to threaten economic coercion to pressure the British into concessions on atomic energy. When the Senators warned that they would advise Congress to put conditions on long-term loans to the British or cut off aid completely should the British prove obstinate or unreasonable in negotiations, Lovett tried to reassure them. The State Department, he declared, could persuade the British to drop their right of consultation on the use of the atomic bomb and agree to ship the bulk of their raw material stockpiles to the United States or Canada without congressional action. Nothing as drastic as economic coercion was needed.[19]

The possibility of JCAE interference in negotiations with the British alarmed Lovett. He attempted, therefore, two days before the American members of the CPC were to meet with Vandenberg and Hickenlooper, to convince other administration officials that he needed more latitude to conduct negotiations. With a freer hand, he said, he might just clinch an agreement with the British before Congress became directly involved. Although Forrestal quickly concurred, Lilienthal, General Counsel for the AEC Herbert S. Marks, and Bush rebuffed him. They wanted the State Department to open discussions, find out what the British wanted and had to offer, and then consult with the JCAE. Despite Kennan's and Lovett's warnings about unhappy consequences if the British thought the Americans were stalling in negotiations, Lilienthal would give no "blank check." The most he would allow was to have the AEC and the military give the State Department a sense of how far to go in the negotiations and support State Department officials when they argued with the JCAE to keep the raw material and aid questions separate.[20]

The meeting on November 26, 1947, with Vandenberg and Hickenlooper, despite Lovett's fears, went smoothly, and by December 5 the State Department had a negotiating position acceptable to all. It did not offer as much freedom of action as Kennan's original proposal but was at least a workable plan. Keeping separate the questions of information exchange and raw material allocation, the United States would try to convince the British to bring all present raw material stocks beyond current operating needs to North America. It would then offer limited exchanges of information, but only in designated fields (not to include weapons information areas) and only if such exchanges promoted American national security. At the special insistence of the JCAE, the United States would demand that the Quebec Agreement and other past arrangements except for the CPC and CDT be officially terminated so that the United States no longer need consult on the use of the atomic bomb. The JCAE agreed to refrain from threatening economic pressure unless the negotiations stalled and the British refused to compromise. The committee members were given assurances they would be kept apprised of developments and of the terms of the agreement before anything was signed.[21]

Keeping the negotiations moving along at a rapid pace was extremely important, Lovett knew, because Vandenberg had decided to delay debate in Congress on the European Recovery Program (Marshall Plan) until December 17, 1947. The senator from Michigan wanted to see how negotiations with the British on nuclear cooperation were progressing before giving his critical support to passage of the bill. Lovett hastily informed the British and Canadians that the United States was ready to open talks, accordingly, and left them only a few days to prepare their positions. The British did not realize that the Americans wanted to talk primarily because of the raw material problem. Although they understood that the Americans were deeply interested in increasing their supplies of raw materials, they also believed that the Americans had decided to open negotiations because they, like the British, were alarmed at the worsening international situation and generally desired to pool information and technical experience. They also noted the presence of more Anglophiles in key positions in the Truman administration than had been the case in 1945-46. Confident, then, of significant progress on information exchanges, they intended to be accommodating on raw materials. They would insist only on retaining enough uranium and thorium to build up a stock of material. They would also raise the question of weapons information and the production of fissionable material but would not insist on agreement. The most important thing was that they secure a satisfactory information exchange agreement and concede no restriction on their right to build plants or accumulate uranium or atomic weapons in the British Isles.[22]

Opening negotiations in Washington on December 10, 1947, the members of the CPC quickly established a subcommittee to study likely areas of cooperation on information exchanges and set up a working group to consider a new raw materials agreement. They planned, if the talks were successful, to make a public announcement attesting to the fact that the British, Canadians, and Americans had succeeded in improving nuclear relations. Progress, as Lovett and the State Department had hoped, was rapid. On December 12 the subcommittee on information proposed exchanges in nine areas—declassified subjects, health and safety, research uses of radioisotopes and stable isotopes, fundamental nuclear and extranuclear properties of all elements, detection of distant nuclear explosions (important to detect future Soviet atomic detonations), fundamental properties of reactor materials, extraction chemistry, design of natural uranium reactors, and general research experience with low power reactors. The report was accepted at once. More difficult was the question of raw material allocation. The British scowled at American assertions that location of stockpiles and large-scale plants in Britain was unwise and doubted whether the raw material supply situation was as bad as the Americans suggested. New sources of uranium in South Africa, they maintained, would provide more ore than originally thought possible. Sufficient stocks would be available, therefore, to feed the voracious appetite of the American program while still permitting the British to maintain a healthy stockpile. Subsequently, the British agreed to give the United States the entire uranium production from the Belgian Congo for the next two years but no stocks presently in Britain. A subcommittee was set up to iron out differences.[23]

Although the overall negotiations had by December 17, 1947, gone very well, Kennan worried about the reaction of the JCAE to the hang-up over a new raw materials agreement. As approved by Vandenberg and Hickenlooper, the American proposal stipulated that most of the British stockpile be transferred to North America. Yet British Foreign Secretary Ernest Bevin and others in the British cabinet were blocking the transfer on "emotional grounds." Bevin in particular was sensitive to the argument that raw material stockpiles and large-scale plants might not be safe in the British Isles and was determined to resist American efforts to cut back the British program.[24]

Kennan's and the State Department's fears that the JCAE would overreact and rashly attempt to use economic coercion to force the British to make concessions if the nuclear negotiations did not pan out. Once a compromise was finally worked out and explained to the JCAE, the members agreed that it was the best the United States could get and gave their approval. On January 7, 1948, the new agreement, known as the Modus Vivendi, was signed. According to its provisions, the United States would receive all supplies from the Belgian Congo for the next two years and would receive portions of the British stockpile to reach a minimum figure of 2,547 tons of raw materials if the Belgian Congo amount was insufficient. On the question of information exchanges, the United States and Britain agreed to cooperate in the nine areas recommended by the first subcommittee, although Lilienthal made sure that the AEC had full discretionary authority over release of information to the British. Because the British retained contacts with Commonwealth scientists from New Zealand, Australia, and South Africa who had worked on the Manhattan Project, they were permitted to continue information exchanges with these countries in several areas. These were declassified subjects, health and safety, detection of distant nuclear explosions, survey methods for source material, cooperation on extraction of ores, design information on research reactors, and general research experience. But the Modus Vivendi officially ended all previous nuclear agreements except for those dealing with joint control of raw materials. The CPC and CDT would continue. The British right of consultation on the use of the atomic bomb, however, would not. As Vandenberg and Hickenlooper had insisted, the President's freedom of action for ordering the use of the bomb was now secured.[25]

For the British, the Modus Vivendi appeared to be a triumph. They had given up raw material supplies they would probably never use, achieved a moderate but meaningful first step toward complete exchange of nuclear information, and set the stage for further efforts to tighten cooperation. The Americans, in addition, had seemed to accept location of raw material stockpiles and plants in the British Isles. This had been a key point in persuading the cabinet to relent and permit the clause shipping some uranium from the British stockpile to the United States. Acceptance by the Americans of stockpiles and plants in Britain had a more important consequence. It meant that the Americans might be more inclined to acquiesce in, if not assist, the manufacture by Britain of atomic bombs and their deployment in the British Isles.[26]

On the American side, the agreement was also viewed in a favorable light. The British right of consultation on the use of the atomic bomb—although generally considered by the Americans to be without force since the end of the war—had officially been terminated. More positively, the uranium problem was solved (for two years only), better feeling between the two allies effected, and security for the most important nuclear secrets preserved. The United States had again made no promise to give Britain information for the building of large-scale plants and manufacture of atomic bombs. Also significant was the performance of the policy-making establishment. Despite the time and effort required to reach consensus (and despite stubborn congressional resistance), the American government had proven it could take necessary action to improve nuclear cooperation with its chief ally.

NOTES

1. Memorandum by Lovett, Washington, July 28, 1947, S/AE Files, *Foreign Relations of the United States* (hereafter cited as *FRUS*), 1947, 1:829-30.

2. Dean Acheson, *Present at the Creation* (New York: W. W. Norton, 1969), pp. 236-37.

3. Walter Millis, *The Forrestal Diaries* (New York: Viking Press, 1951), pp. 240-41; Gregg Herken, *The Winning Weapon: The Atomic Bomb in the Cold War, 1945-1950* (New York: Alfred A. Knopf, 1980), pp. 196-98, 241.

4. Dean Acheson, *Sketches from Life of Men I Have Known* (New York: Harper & Brothers, 1959), pp. 162-63.

5. Memorandum by Lilienthal, Washington, January 29, 1947, S/AE Files, *FRUS*, 1947, 1:784.

6. *Joint Atomic Energy Hearings*, 80th Cong., 1st sess., February 10, 1947, pp. 289-94.

7. Memorandum of Conversation by Acheson, Washington, February 1. 1947, S/AE Files, *FRUS*, 1947, 1:785-89.

8. JCS 1748/1, "Effect on U.S. Security of Atomic Energy Plants Located in the U.K." by JSSC, February 25, 1947, CCS 471.6 (8-15-45), sec. 4, Modern Military Branch, National Archives; Patterson and Forrestal to Marshall, Washington, undated, S/AE Files, *FRUS*, 1947, 1:798-99.

9. Ibid.

10. Robin Higham and Jacob W. Kipp, eds., *Soviet Aviation and Air Power: An Historical Review* (London: Brassey's, 1977), pp. 198-99; C. J. Bartlett, *The Long Retreat: A Short History of British Defence Policy, 1945-1970* (London: Macmillan, 1972), pp. 49-50; Douglas to Marshall, London, April 23, 1947, Department of State Records, RG 59, Decimal Files 1945-1949, box 5850, file 841.646, National Archives.

11. JCS 1477/2, December 6, 1945, CCS 471.6 (8-15-45), sec. 1, Modern Military Branch, National Archives; Margaret Gowing, *Independence and Deterrence: Britain and Atomic Energy, 1945-1952*, vol. 1 (London: Macmillan, 1974), pp. 118-19; David E. Lilienthal, *The Journals of David E. Lilienthal*, vol. 2, *The Atomic Energy Years, 1945-1950* (New York: Harper & Row, 1964), pp. 217-21.

12. Lilienthal, *Journals*, 2: 175-76; Richard G. Hewlett and Francis Duncan, *Atomic Shield: A History of the U.S. Atomic Energy Commission*, vol. 2 (Uni-

versity Park: Pennsylvania State University Press, 1969), p. 274; Memorandum by Lilienthal, Washington, April 23, 1947, USAEC files, *FRUS*, 1947, 1:804-6.

13. Statement by Acheson to Executive Session of JCAE, Washington, May 12, 1947, S/AE Files, *FRUS*, 1947, 1:806-11.

14. Memorandum of Conversation by Gullion, Washington, June 5, 1947, S/AE Files; Marshall to Embassy in U.K., Washington, June 17, 1947, 501.BC Atomic/6-1147; Memorandum by Lovett, Washington, July 28, 1947, S/AE Files; Memorandum by Gullion, Washington, August 21, 1947, S/AE Files; Report by PPS (PPS/7), Washington, August 21, 1947, PPS Files, *FRUS*, 1947, 1:817, 517-19, 829-30, 832-33, 603-14.

15. Hickenlooper to Marshall, Washington, August 29, 1947; Memorandum of Conversation by Gullion, Washington, September 10, 1947, S/AE Files, *FRUS*, 1947, 1:833-34, 645-46.

16. Hewlett and Duncan, *Atomic Shield*, pp. 275-76; Memorandum by Kennan and Gullion (PPS 11), Washington, October 24, 1947, S/AE Files, *FRUS*, 1947, 1:844-47; Millis, *Forrestal Diaries*, pp. 310-11.

17. Minutes of Meeting of U.S. Members CPC, Washington, November 5, 1947, S/AE Files, *FRUS*, 1947, 1:852-60.

18. Ibid.

19. Memorandum of Conversation by Forrestal, Washington, November 16, 1947, S/AE Files, *FRUS*, 1947, 1:864-66.

20. Minutes of Meeting of U.S. Members CPC, Washington, November 24, 1947, S/AE Files, *FRUS*, 1947, 1:866-70; Lilienthal, *Journals* 2: 259.

21. Minutes of Meeting of U.S. Members CPC with Chairman JCAE and Chairman Senate Foreign Relations Committee, Washington, November 26, 1947, S/AE Files; Lovett to Douglas, Washington, December 4, 1947, 841.6359/12-447; Lovett to Marshall in London and Washington, December 6, 1947, 841.6359/12-647, *FRUS*, 1947, 1:870-86.

22. Gowing, *Independence and Deterrence* 1: 243-45; Lovett to Douglas, Washington, December 4, 1947, 841.6359/12-447, *FRUS*, 1947, 1:879-81.

23. Douglas to Marshall, London, December 13, 1947, 841.6359/12-1347; Memorandum of CPC Meeting, Washington, December 15, 1947, S/AE Files; Record of Teletype Conference, Bohlen and Kennan, London and Washington, December 17, 1947, S/AE Files, *FRUS*, 1947, 1:896-903, 905-6.

24. Record of Teletype Conference, Bohlen and Kennan, London and Washington, December 17, 1947, S/AE Files, *FRUS*, 1947, 1:905-6.

25. Memorandum of Conversation by Gullion, Washington, January 7, 1948; Minutes of Meeting CPC, Washington, January 7, 1948; Statement by Lovett before JCAE, January 21, 1948, S/AE Files, *FRUS*, 1948, 1:677-91.

26. Gowing, *Independence and Deterrence* 1: 248-49.

5
THE BRITISH WANT MORE

> Senator Hickenlooper stated that it was his understanding that England's primary activity was to be along the lines of power production, and there was no indication of their entering into weapons production. He now finds that they are actively engaged in the production of plutonium, which could mean nothing to him but the production of weapons.
> —excerpt from August 12, 1948 meeting between Hickenlooper, Vandenberg, and Forrestal[1]

By December 1947 Ernest Bevin, the British foreign secretary, was completely disillusioned about the possibilities for postwar cooperation with the Soviet Union. In early 1948, as a consequence, he pushed for organization of the Western European nations into a defense alliance closely linked to the United States. After the Communist coup in Czechoslovakia in late February and March, Britain concluded the Brussels Treaty, a 50-year military alliance with France, Belgium, the Netherlands, and Luxemburg. Pleased by the tougher British stance, the American Congress approved the Marshall Plan for massive economic assistance to Western Europe and passed the Vandenberg Resolution in June, urging the United States to associate itself with Western European defense. The next month the Soviets imposed a land blockade on Berlin. The ensuing ten-month-long crisis unified the West and facilitated creation of NATO in April 1949.

Direct military cooperation between the United States, Britain, and Canada had by spring 1948 become a necessity due to the growing Soviet threat. In response, planning officers from the three countries met in Washington in May to approve HALFMOON, an outline emergency war plan. The planners foresaw a Soviet offensive against the European land mass, an attack on Middle East oil, and an attempt to neutralize the British Isles by air attack. The allied reply would be a strategic air offensive highlighted by attacks by bombers based in Britain. When the Berlin blockade began in July, the United States took steps to give itself the partial capability to carry out the plan. B-29 Superfortresses were sent to air bases in East Anglia in Britain. Although not modified to carry atomic bombs until 1949-50, and not actually equipped with them until mid-1951, B-29s were deployed in increasing numbers until Britain became the primary base for a possible strategic bombing campaign. By the end of 1948 there were three groups operating out of seven bases.[2]

To the British chiefs of staff, increasingly strained relations with the Soviets, dramatized by the February 25, 1948, Communist coup in Czechoslovakia, made urgent a more thorough examination of Britain's strategic vulnerability and measures to be taken to insure the defense of the British Isles. It quickly became clear that British defenses against air attack were very weak and that in the future Britain would have to rely on a policy of deterrence to ward off a possible atomic bomb assault by the Soviet Union. The problem was, however, that—aside from a winter 1947-48 U.S. Air Force Directorate of Intelligence study suggesting that 70 atomic bombs delivered on target would devastate the Soviet Union—no rational estimate had ever been made of the number of atomic bombs Britain, together with the United States, would need to deter the Soviets. The British chiefs tried. Predicting that the Soviets would within a few years develop the atomic bomb and begin stockpiling, they suggested that in 1957 the United States and Britain would need a total of 600 atomic bombs. Britain's share should be 200. And yet Britain in 1948 had the projected capacity with its two planned atomic piles to produce enough fissionable material for only 100 bombs by 1957. It could reach 200 by 1959 if it added a third pile and built a high-separation diffusion plant to produce highly enriched uranium 235, but this was not practical. British finances were already badly strained from trying to recover from the war, and the most the government could finance was three piles and a low-separation diffusion plant to be constructed in 1950.[3]

The March 17, 1948, Brussels Treaty with France, Belgium, the Netherlands, and Luxemburg, the British chiefs knew, improved Britain's defense posture in Europe. But the only way to accelerate the British nuclear program was to get help from the Americans. The British military already acknowledged that Britain could not fight another world war without the United States—especially a world war fought with atomic weapons.[4] But if the Americans could be persuaded that the time was right to cooperate in all areas of atomic energy development, Britain might still be able to construct its share of the deterrent force by the close of the 1950s. The British government, too, recognized the logic of trying to make progress in Anglo-American nuclear relations. The Modus Vivendi, British leaders thought, had created a much better atmosphere for cooperation. The Americans must now come to understand that the current international situation required coordination of effort in all fields.

In March 1948, therefore, they informed the Americans that they had, from January 1947, been conducting research and development on atomic weapons in a special section of the Ministry of Supply under the direction of Lord Charles Portal, former British chief of the air staff, 1940-45. The work was at the stage where total secrecy was too difficult to maintain and might impede progress on the project. The British government would soon go public with the news. Making no request for weapons-related information at this time, they nevertheless gave the Americans the clear impression that they would do so in the near future. This impression was reinforced when Admiral Sir Henry Moore, head of the British Naval Mission in Washington, had breakfast with Secretary of Defense Forrestal at the end of the month and discussed the British decision to manufacture atomic bombs.[5]

Some members of the AEC, particularly Lewis L. Strauss, a Wall Street financier and retired admiral, were alarmed by the news of the British atomic bomb development. Whether because of this news or out of genuine concern not to violate the McMahon Act, the AEC moved very slowly in fulfilling the information exchanges agreed to in the Modus Vivendi and failed to meet British expectations. The U.S. government would comply with the provisions of the agreement, but only after every precaution had been taken to insure that no information not authorized by the AEC and the military be exchanged and only if the information were being exchanged for information of equal value.[6]

On May 28, 1948, an AEC technical team composed of scientists Walter H. Zinn, George L. Weil, and Charles W. J. Wende arrived in Britain for a firsthand look at the British atomic energy program. On a visit to the main British research facilities at Harwell on May 30, they discovered that the British were apparently working more vigorously to produce plutonium for atomic bombs than they were in trying to develop atomic energy for electric power generation. The state of the British program was such, they reported shortly after their return to the United States in early June, that the British had made considerable progress and would eventually manufacture an atomic bomb. Commissioner Strauss was adamantly opposed to helping any country obtain the atomic bomb. He attempted at a meeting of the AEC on June 30 to persuade his colleagues to block exchanges of information in areas vital for further British progress—fundamental properties of reactor materials, technological developments in equipment and production processes, and weapons design. An equal exchange of information, he reminded the commissioners, had been the fundamental basis of the Modus Vivendi. Since the British had no information of equal value to trade, the United States could properly stop all contacts. Although inclined to go forward with the information exchanges (especially in the area of fundamental properties of reactor materials), Lilienthal agreed to seek the advice of the National Military Establishment and State Department at the next meetings of the American members of the CPC on July 6 and 7 before calling for a final vote of the AEC.[7]

At those meetings—at which Strauss, not a member of the CPC, was not present—Lovett, Donald C. Carpenter, deputy to the secretary of defense on atomic energy matters and head of the Military Liaison Committee (MLC), and William Webster, Carpenter's assistant, told Lilienthal that as long as the United States continued to receive adequate supplies of raw materials, they did not favor any action to oppose British development of an atomic bomb. When the British program finally succeeded, Lovett suggested, the United States could perhaps attempt to persuade the British government to store all British bombs in Canada for safekeeping, but that could be done later. It was decided to continue cooperation along the lines of the Modus Vivendi and even consider new areas of cooperation on information exchanges if the British made a formal request.[8]

Realizing suddenly that he was fighting alone against the nearly unanimous opinion of the other policymakers that cooperation on nuclear matters with the British was the proper policy to follow and ought to be safeguarded if not expanded in order to assure British cooperation on control and allocation of raw materials, Strauss arranged to meet with Forrestal on July 8, 1948, prior to a morning meeting of the AEC. He took a cautious line. He had no objections, he said, to British possession of atomic weapons, just as long as they did not manufacture them in the British Isles. That would be unwise. Forrestal shrugged off his complaint. By exchanging information with the British, he said, the United States was insuring its supplies of critical raw materials. Successful production of atomic bombs by the British, moreover, would boost their self-confidence and make Britain a more dependable ally. Strauss was still disturbed. Information exchanges and the British atomic bomb project, he maintained, were dangerous for American security. Secret information could be leaked through the British program to the Soviets and British weapons and nuclear installations would be subject to surprise invasion and capture in a war.[9]

Unable to rouse Forrestal from what he considered a complacent sense of security, Strauss attended the AEC meeting at 10:30 A.M. and listened to Lilienthal relate the discussions that had taken place at the July 6 and 7, 1948, meetings. Shaking his head in disbelief that the State Department and National Military Establishment could be so blind in this matter, he reminded the commissioners that at the time of the negotiations of the Modus Vivendi he had been insistent that the United States only agree to general areas of information exchanges so that the AEC would have the right to review specific British requests for information and weed out the dangerous ones. Now, in the two reports (AEC 43/11 and 43/13) before them, the commissioners were being asked to approve something very dangerous—an exchange of information on the fundamental properties of reactor materials. That exchange would go far beyond the general area agreed to on January 7, 1948. Since the specific data proposed for the exchange would greatly assist the British in producing atomic weapons, and since he doubted that the formal policy of the United States was to aid any country, even the United Kingdom, to develop atomic weapons, he opposed the exchange. Commissioner W. W. Waymack and Lilienthal countered that Strauss's objection went to the basic thrust of national policy, already decided, and that the proposed information exchanges as set forth in AEC 43/11 and 43/13 were "clearly within the scope of the January 7 agreement." But Strauss suggested that the secretaries of state and defense might not be aware of the extent of the British bomb project and that the President too should be made to understand what was at stake. Lilienthal was patient. He repeated that at the July 6 and 7 meetings, Lovett and he had fully explained the implications of the Zinn-Weil-Wende report and what it said about British nuclear activities. However, in order to satisfy Strauss that every proper precaution was being observed to see that American nuclear secrets were being protected, he proposed that the AEC, after consultation with the National Military Establishment, make a prompt report of the situation to the JCAE. The report would take the form of a general review of the progress of the technical cooperation program. The full commission voted to accept Lilienthal's suggestion. But they also approved, over Strauss's objections, the recommendation for information exchanges with the British set forth in AEC 43/11 and 43/13.[10]

If Lilienthal thought he had temporarily calmed Strauss's fears, he was mistaken. A few days later, Strauss came back to discuss the matter and was so worked up that "his hands were trembling most of the time" and he wanted to go directly to the President to brief him. Then he blurted out what he really thought of the British. They were too far to the left, he said, and might give away the secret of the atomic bomb to the Communists. Some of them—British Communists—sat in Parliament. Lilienthal quickly called Lovett to warn him of Strauss's mood, and Lovett complained that if Strauss kept on, British Intelligence would hear of his comments. He wanted Lilienthal to get Forrestal and Bush and straighten Strauss out.[11]

It is clear at this juncture that in the minds of State Department officials, military leaders, and a majority of the AEC, the importance of improving relations with the British either for the good of the overall relationship itself or for such matters as maintaining cooperation on joint control and allocation of raw materials and expansion of the American right to use British air bases outweighed potential damage done by leaks of information through the British program to the Soviet Union. It also outweighed the danger posed by location of nuclear installations, raw material stockpiles, and even atomic weapons in Britain, although it must be remembered that American policymakers did not believe the British were close to producing an atomic bomb or would be for some time. Under these circumstances, they favored giving the British most of what they wanted up to and including some information that might be of help in building an atomic bomb.

The extent to which AEC commissioners were willing to go was revealed in the Cyril Smith affair. The incident was played out as the Soviets, reacting to Western efforts to bring West Germany back into the economic, political, and military mainstream of Western Europe, began their blockade of all rail and road traffic from West Germany to Berlin on July 24, 1948. After the full AEC approved the exchange of information with the British on the fundamental properties of reactor materials on July 8, Commissioner James B. Fisk authorized Smith, an American scientist of British background and member of the General Advisory Committee to the AEC, to visit Harwell in Britain to brief the British. But Fisk interpreted "fundamental properties of reactor materials" as including basic metallurgy of plutonium—critical information for making an atomic bomb. Sending Smith off on his trip at the end of July, he gave no instructions to withhold that data. Meanwhile, Donald Carpenter heard unofficially from Admiral Moore that the British government would soon ask for atomic weapons information. After telling Lilienthal, Lovett, and Fisk of this development on August 3, Carpenter went to Senator Hickenlooper to convince him that granting the British request when it came would be a prudent step. Aghast, Hickenlooper arranged to meet with Strauss on August 11. On that very day, by coincidence, Strauss finally saw Fisk's authorization for Smith to discuss with the British basic metallurgy of plutonium and frantically tried to have Sumner T. Pike, acting AEC chairman in Lilienthal's absence from Washington, contact Smith and stop the exchange. Pike at first refused.[12]

The next day Hickenlooper and Vandenberg demanded a meeting with Forrestal, who called in Bush and Carpenter, and protested the proposed exchange as a violation of the law. Data on basic metallurgy of plutonium was weapons information, they said, and outside the boundaries of the Modus Vivendi. Despite Bush's insistence that the British plutonium atomic bomb program had been known to many in the American program before the signing of the Modus Vivendi and that no excitement at confirmation of this news was warranted, Hickenlooper was furious. He insisted the exchange be stopped. With Vandenberg, he demanded that the MLC exercise more control over the flow of information to the British. That flow, Forrestal reminded, could not be halted completely because securing raw materials was the primary American objective and stopping all exchanges would damage that goal. But he did instruct Carpenter to call Pike and convince him to direct Smith to withhold the controversial information. This was done.[13]

A few days later, on August 16, 1948, Carpenter tried to warn the British from making a request for atomic weapons information at that time. The JCAE was alert and aroused, he told Dr. F. N. Woodward, director of the British scientific mission in Washington. But if the British agreed to manufacture their weapons in Canada, the committee might be persuaded to relent. Woodward refused. The British military, he said, considered Canada just as vulnerable as Britain.[14]

The British obviously felt that they had waited long enough for the American policy-making bureaucracy to sort itself out and the administration to come to the conclusion that improved nuclear ties with Britain were desirable. They decided to ignore Carpenter's warning. On September 2, 1948, therefore, Moore handed Forrestal the official British request, written by British Defense Minister Albert V. Alexander. Describing the British program as "well-launched," Alexander asked for an exchange of information on atomic weapons and said that the United States should comply for the common interest. Both would be stronger if they worked together. Likely areas in which the British would need assistance were metallurgy and fabrication of plutonium, proximity fuses, and arming and safety devices in aircraft carrying atomic bombs. To discuss the British request, Carpenter and Woodward met again on September 16. Mistaking the provisions of the Modus Vivendi, Carpenter told Woodward that he thought the British had agreed to consult before undertaking the manufacture of atomic weapons. No, Woodward corrected, there was no provision for consultation, just notice in advance of building a bomb. The British had complied. When Carpenter tried again to persuade Woodward that manufacturing the British bomb in Canada would be wise, Woodward became angry. England was just as safe as Canada, he insisted, and this was something about which all British leaders agreed. Carpenter too showed annoyance. He reiterated his earlier statement that the British government should not have made a request for weapons information at this time and bluntly stated that American security could be damaged if the United States agreed to give the British weapons information and it was leaked to Moscow. This was too much for Woodward. He shot back that British security on nuclear matters might well be better than American. He indignantly invited the United States to send representatives to review British security and declared that with or without American assistance Britain would press on with its program to build a bomb. Carpenter asked what the British attitude would be if the United States gave Britain atomic bombs in exchange for discontinuing the British program. Woodward expressed no opinion. Higher authority would have to decide.[15]

Other British and American officials subsequently backed away from the confrontational postures assumed by Woodward and Carpenter in their acrimonious meeting. But even though John H. Henderson of the British Embassy staff assured Arneson, now special assistant to Lovett, that the British Isles could be defended against realistic threats (fifth-column action, for example), confided that even with American help the British program would not succeed in building a bomb in the near future, and spoke of Britain's critical dependence upon the United States for its defense and the defense of Western Europe. American opinion about British atomic weapons production remained steadfast. Lovett told British Ambassador Sir Oliver Franks that the JCS considered a British weapons program located in the British Isles far too vulnerable to Soviet attack. The United States would not give Britain information on the basic metallurgy of plutonium.[16]

Knowing that the British were extremely disappointed at this latest rebuke to their quest for expanded cooperation, Arneson and most of the AEC commissioners feared that they would retaliate by stalling negotiations for a new raw materials agreement for 1950-51. Since three-quarters of the American supply as late as 1951 came from the Belgian Congo, and since the United States needed British assistance to bargain with the South Africans for uranium ore becoming available in large quantities in 1952 and 1953, British retaliation in the raw materials area could have a devastating impact on American uranium supplies. On November 2, 1948, the day of Truman's surprise defeat of Thomas Dewey, Arneson told Lovett that although the State Department could do nothing to change the decision on the British request for weapons information, it could throw its weight on the side of improved cooperation in the nine fields and counterbalance the tightening of restrictions caused by JCAE pressure on the MLC. Lovett favored the idea but was forced to tell Franks that further negotiations would have to wait until 1949 when the atmosphere would presumably become more receptive. By then, failure of international control would be complete, the Democrats would take control of the Senate (ousting hardliner Hickenlooper from the chairmanship of the JCAE and replacing him with the more reasonable McMahon), and the battle over control of atomic energy currently being waged within the administration by the National Military Establishment and the AEC would have been resolved. Franks sensibly agreed that the British could wait.[17]

American wishes had won out again. But State Department officials had to wonder how long the British would go on deferring to administration desires without receiving greater compensation in the form of increased cooperation, especially American assistance for British efforts to build or obtain the atomic bomb. And it was clear that the United States' chief ally would obtain a bomb—with or without American assistance. British defense requirements and a desire for greater political influence in Europe and the world, although tempered by economic realities, made certain that the British would indeed carry through with their atomic bomb project. But what would their attitude be if they succeeded without American help? Would they—weapons in hand and pressured by European allies (most notably France) to share information—look with favor on American nonproliferation and maximum-security policies? Would they recall with satisfaction the conclusion to the Cyril Smith affair and the American rejection of their request for atomic weapons information? Would they still listen with sympathy and understanding to State Department explanations that opposition from the JCAE (and AEC commissioner Strauss), not stubbornness by the administration, blocked cooperation? Or would they reject all excuses and deny the United States any influence over British nuclear policy? Alarmed by this possibility and convinced of the positive benefits of cooperation, American policymakers amenable to closer Anglo-American nuclear ties set about formulating proposals for a sea change in American nuclear policy. They prepared to present these proposals when the second Truman administration took office.

NOTES

1. Memorandum of Meeting by Carpenter, Washington, August 12, 1948, *Foreign Relations of the United States* (hereafter cited as *FRUS*), 1948, 1: 734-37.

2. JCS 1844/4, May 6, 1948, and JCS 1844/6, May 13, 1948, CCS 381 USSR (3-2-46), sec. 13, in Kenneth W. Condit, *The History of the Joint Chiefs of Staff: The Joint Chiefs of Staff and National Policy*, vol. 2, *1947-1949* (Wilmington, Del.: Michael Glazier, 1979), pp. 288-93; Raymond Dawson and Richard Rosencrance, "Theory and Reality in the Anglo-American Alliance," *World Politics* 19 (October 1966): 27; Hewlett, *Atomic Shield*, pp. 538-39.

3. Margaret Gowing, *Independence and Deterrence: Britain and Atomic Energy, 1945-1952*, vol. 1 (London: Macmillan, 1974), pp. 215-23.

4. "Some British Strategic Problems," a lecture by Sir John Slessor at U.S. National War College, April 1948, in Sir John Slessor, *The Great Deterrent* (New York: Frederick A. Praeger, 1957), pp. 78-80.

5. Memorandum of Conversation by Gullion, Washington, March 19, 1948, S/AE Files, *FRUS*, 1948, 1:70-701; Walter Millis, *The Forrestal Diaries* (New York: Viking Press, 1951), p. 407.

6. Gowing, *Independence and Deterrence* 1:256; Memorandum Approved by State-Army-Navy-Air Force Coordinating Board, Washington, June 15, 1948, SANACC Files, lot 52M45, *FRUS*, 1948, 1:575-76.

7. Hewlett and Duncan, *Atomic Shield*, pp. 286-88.

8. Minutes of Meeting of U.S. Members CPC, Washington, July 6, 1948, S/AE Files, *FRUS*, 1948, 1:719-23.

9. Hewlett and Duncan, *Atomic Shield*, p. 288; CM 184, July 8, 1948, AEC (Department of Energy, Freedom of Information Act, photocopy).

10. CM 184, July 8, 1948, AEC (DOE, FOI, photocopy).

11. David E. Lilienthal, *The Journals of David E. Lilienthal*, vol. 2, *The Atomic Energy Years, 1945-1950* (New York: Harper & Row, 1964).

12. Hewlett and Duncan, *Atomic Shield*, pp. 289-92.

13. Memorandum of Meeting by Carpenter, Washington, August 12, 1948; Memorandum by Bush, Washington, August 12, 1948, S/AE Files, *FRUS*, 1948, 1:734-39; Millis, *Forrestal Diaries*, pp. 471-72.

14. Hewlett and Duncan, *Atomic Shield*, p. 293.

15. Moore to Forrestal, Washington, September 1, 1948; Memorandum of Conversation by Carpenter, Washington, September 16, 1948, S/AE Files, *FRUS*, 1948, 1:750-52, 755-58.

16. Memorandum for File by Arneson, Washington, September 22, 1948; Memo-

randum by Arneson, Washington, September 27, 1948; Memorandum of Conversation by Wendel, Washington, September 30, 1948, S/AE Files, *FRUS*, 1948, 1:766-75; Hewlett and Duncan, *Atomic Shield*, p. 294.

17. Hewlett and Duncan, *Atomic Shield*, pp. 173, 546; "Development, Growth, and State of the Atomic Energy Industry," *Joint Atomic Energy Hearings*, 84th Cong., 1st sess., February 3, 1955, pp. 111, 113-14, 118; Memorandum by Arneson, Washington, November 2, 1948; Memorandum of Conversation by Lovett, Washington, November 16, 1948, S/AE Files, *FRUS*, 1948, 1:781-86.

6

THE UNITED STATES AGREES TO COOPERATE—ALMOST

> I believe public sentiment is ready to support a strong Presidential drive for the kind of setup we ought to have at this time. Bearing in mind that our international proposals appear stymied, must we not try to establish some system (with Britain and Canada) which will integrate and make most effective the knowledge and skills available in each country, allocate production and other effort in the most efficient and effective way, and keep the major producing units in the United States?
> —David E. Lilienthal, August 19, 1949[1]

The year 1949 was crucial for Anglo-American nuclear relations. It was the year in which the American policymakers finally achieved substantial consensus and it was the year in which the Soviets manufactured and successfully detonated an atomic bomb. This latter event temporarily gave the administration the upper hand in dealing with JCAE opposition to information exchanges and improved cooperation.

Paralleling the situation in 1947, the early part of 1949 saw important personnel changes in key administration posts, tilting the balance in favor of improved ties to the British. Secretary of State Marshall and Under Secretary of State Lovett stepped down and were replaced in January by Dean Acheson, truly an Anglophile, and James E. Webb. In March an exhausted James Forrestal resigned and was succeeded by Louis A. Johnson. Not favorable to Britain by any means, Johnson nevertheless did not initially exert himself in nuclear matters. On the MLC William Webster replaced Donald Carpenter as chairman and did exert himself. He strongly advocated a reassessment by the administration of nuclear relations with the British and helped arrange an informal conference on January 24 and 25, 1949, at Princeton University to find a policy to replace the provisions of the Modus Vivendi, now generally considered unsatisfactory.

Chaired by Robert Oppenheimer, chairman of the General Advisory Committee to the AEC, and attended by Dr. James B. Conant, president of Harvard University, Webster, Lieutenant General Lauris Norstad, deputy chief of staff for operations of the United States Air Force (USAF), and Major General Kenneth Nichols, member of the MLC, all representing the military, Carroll Wilson and Joseph Volpe for the AEC, and Kennan, Arneson, and George H. Butler, deputy director of the PPS, for the State Department, the conference produced several recommendations. In terms of procedure, the participants said, the agencies within the administration should agree among themselves on an appropriate policy, should then approach the JCAE for approval of that policy, and should finally sound out the British and Canadians. They should ask the allies whether they would be willing to agree to three broad principles—consultation on location of nuclear production facilities with due respect for strategic considerations, coordination of programs for effective use of raw materials, and coordination of disclosure of information to other governments to prevent or delay development of atomic energy in other countries. Although it was expected that Congress would be a hard sell, the participants recommended that the President base the proposal for improved nuclear cooperation on the argument that the British would soon have an atomic bomb with or without American help and that collective security would be enhanced by cooperation. An Anglo-American–Canadian nuclear partnership would fit nicely with the Rio Pact (for Western Hemispheric defense), the Marshall Plan, and the North Atlantic Treaty Organization soon to be brought into existence on April 4, 1949, in Washington by signatures of the foreign ministers of the United States, Britain, France, and other Western European states.[2]

The British were soon going to have the atomic bomb anyway, the Princeton conference participants hypothesized, and the United States could not stop them. They wanted the bomb for reasons of national prestige, because of the supposed freedom of action it would give in foreign affairs, and because of continued uncertainty about the American commitment to Western European security and to assisting the British nuclear program. Although the fact of the British nuclear project was not negotiable, other issues might be. Strategically, the JCS still believed that location of plants and material in the British Isles was a mistake and that in the event of war those plants and stockpiles would be quickly destroyed or rendered useless. British production capacity for building bombs would then be lost. In exchange for American assistance to help them accelerate the pace of their nuclear project, however, the British might agree to relocate a significant part of their program in the North American continent, either Canada or the United States. Likewise, such relocation would prove beneficial from the standpoint of raw materials. Already the new uranium recovery process (REDOX) for recycling depleted materials had improved the raw material situation so that American estimates projected sufficient supplies of uranium for both the British and American programs through 1955. If the British now submerged most of their program into the far more efficient American one, significant additional quantities of raw materials could be saved. Then there was the argument pertaining to overall efficiency and economics. It was an uneconomical division of personnel, information, and resources, the Americans believed, to keep the British and American programs independent of each other. Especially in terms of new ideas, the United States would receive substantial benefit from a fusion of British and American techniques and personnel. The United States, as an alternative, might attempt to continue information exchanges and cooperation in non-weapons areas, but this would be very impractical. Because of the great mass of information already in British hands, any further information exchange was bound to be helpful for their progress toward building a bomb.[3]

Since American objectives, the participants went on to suggest, were to obstruct Soviet progress in developing the atomic bomb, better the American position vis-à-vis the Soviets, reduce the vulnerability of production capacity and stockpiles to destruction by Soviet attack, improve means of delivering atomic bombs against Soviet targets, and coordinate atomic energy policy with overall foreign policy, the United States should initiate a complete interchange of information—including weapons information—with Britain and Canada for the most effective use of raw materials, other resources, and effort. They should also establish effective coordination with respect to information disclosures to other governments. Full freedom of action for each country within its own program would (theoretically) be preserved, the CPC would continue, and dissemination of nuclear information to third parties, including Commonwealth countries, would be carefully controlled. To insure maximum strength and public support for the new partnership, Congress would be asked to confirm the new agreements. The nuclear pact would be related to, but not made part of, the North Atlantic Treaty Organization.[4]

The Princeton conference produced recommendations that, had they come two years or even one year earlier, would have met solid objection from members of the National Military Establishment on the grounds that full and effective cooperation with the British would create serious danger of leaks to the Soviets. Now, although military leaders still insisted that major nuclear installations not be located in the British Isles, they were prepared to acknowledge that overall cooperation with Britain, in the context of the strained international situation and East-West tensions, had to be secured. Improved nuclear cooperation, they further admitted, was a vital link in Anglo-American relations that needed to be strengthened. Lilienthal's thinking too had undergone a dramatic change from the time he first took office as head of the AEC. In January 1947 he had had three narrow objectives—to protect the security of American nuclear secrets, to guarantee adequate raw material supplies, and to adhere to the letter of the law as written in the provisions of the McMahon Act. Only slowly had he come to realize that the American program would benefit from improved cooperation with the British, both in terms of the control and allocation of raw materials and in the advances that would come with the fusion of the British and American programs. He had also broadened his thinking enough to see the importance of improved nuclear ties for overall Anglo-American relations. Convinced that the Princeton conference recommendations could be the basis for a new policy, he led the AEC in a vote on February 5, 1949, to adopt them as the basis for greater cooperation with the British and Canadians. Strauss was the sole dissenter.[5]

Backed now by Lilienthal and most of the AEC and with the Princeton recommendations in hand, Acheson approached the President and tried to overcome his reluctance to share atomic weapons information with the British. It was for the purpose of keeping nuclear work out of unsafe Britain, Truman replied, that President Roosevelt had entered into the wartime partnership. He was just continuing the policy. But Acheson persuaded him that a reassessment was in order. On February 10, 1949, the President appointed a Special Committee to the National Security Council (NSC) with Acheson (secretary of state) as chairman and with Forrestal (secretary of defense), Lilienthal (chairman of the AEC), Sumner T. Pike of the AEC, and Admiral Sidney W. Souers, executive secretary of the NSC, as members. Acheson and the others tapped Kennan and Arneson from the State Department, Webster and Nichols from the National Military Establishment, and Wilson and Volpe from the AEC to form a working group to do the staff work. Dwight Eisenhower, then president of Columbia University, was invited to participate.[6]

Borrowing many of the recommendations of the Princeton conference, the Special Committee issued its report on March 2, 1949. The McMahon Act was no obstacle to improved Anglo-American nuclear cooperation, the members asserted, as long as the U.S. government was satisfied that a new agreement was in the interests of American national security. Appropriate consultation with Congress would have to occur, of course, but approval could be given by joint resolution of Congress or some other means. If the breakdown of the international control idea and the need for collective security were emphasized forcefully, the administration would even be able to carry its policy to the public and win wide backing. Internationally, the United States might have to take some flak. The French and others would protest exclusion from the nuclear partnership and might even retaliate by making negotiations difficult for the renewal of military arrangements (like the use of bases). But the benefits of nuclear cooperation with Britain and Canada would compensate the United States for its trouble. Nor should a Soviet propaganda barrage charging an Anglo-American–Canadian pact to dominate the world dissuade the administration from carrying out the new policy. The United States had to achieve maximum security/maximum strength and solve the raw material problem once and for all. These two objectives could best be reached by effective collaboration with the British and Canadians.[7]

Achieving maximum security/maximum strength, the committee decided, required a virtual absorption of the British program by the American, similar to what had happened during the war. The United States would permit full cooperation in the weapons field, but the British must agree to a 20-year pact, institute security safeguards and coordination of disclosure of information to other countries (including the Dominions) to prevent dissemination of secret information, and most important of all, locate major production and storage facilities with "due respect for strategic considerations"—that is, either in the United States or Canada. Atomic weapons components might be placed in Britain, but only if war plans required it. The British and Canadians would, in addition, cooperate on defensive measures that might be taken against a potential Soviet attack and especially on providing bases for American bombers armed with atomic weapons. The provision for cooperation on allocation of raw materials was just as sweeping. Although the raw material situation would improve in 1952 due to recycling processes for depleted materials and new sources of uranium in South Africa, the United States would temporarily, in 1950 and 1951, need a larger share of British stocks. Under the principle of most effective use and in possession of the major weapons-producing establishment, the United States could claim up to 90 percent of all raw materials. Britain and Canada could divide the remainder. Anglo-American–Canadian partnership would also improve control of raw materials. British influence with the Belgians and South Africans would assist in the negotiation of new uranium agreements. Those countries that possessed raw materials necessary for nuclear development would have to negotiate for assistance in developing atomic energy and accept terms set out by the United States, Britain, and Canada—as opposed to bargaining with all three and playing off one against the others. A united front would enable the United States to secure its goal of delaying for as long as possible nuclear development and manufacture of atomic weapons in other countries. The Special Committee's March 2, 1949, report became the official policy of the administration.[8]

In April 1949, even as NATO was coming into existence, Lieutenant General Norstad sounded out British Chief of Staff Lord Arthur W. Tedder about the proposal. Reflecting the British chiefs' desire for acquisition by Britain of atomic bombs at the earliest possible moment, Tedder said that if full and effective partnership were established, the British government would probably not insist upon a major production program in the British Isles. From the purely military point of view, the British chiefs could certainly agree to a smaller program as long as a few atomic bombs were kept in Britain for use according to common war plans. Some plutonium production would have to continue for reasons of national prestige and to win public support. But Tedder would attempt to sell the proposal to British officials. Greatly encouraged, the State Department wanted to initiate negotiations as early as summer. Unfortunately, a JCAE investigation of mismanagement by the AEC of the American nuclear program interfered. Kennan explained to Makins that nothing could be done while the JCAE was on the prowl. Makins nodded. The British government too preferred no publicity, he said, for fear the British public might get wind of the more controversial parts of the American plan—the raw materials allocation formula, for example—and react adversely. It did not want to appear to be allowing the United States to dominate.[9]

While prospects for agreement between the administration and the British now appeared promising, the attitude of the JCAE remained questionable. The almost casual manner in which the Special Committee to the NSC glossed over the difficulty of convincing Congress of the advisability of the proposed nuclear partnership indicated clearly misplaced confidence. Based upon past statements, members of the JCAE would favor increased raw material allocation for the United States and location of plants and stockpiles in North America. But they would cite security reasons for opposing exchanges of weapons data or even allowing British scientists to enter the American program. If the British proved intransigent on raw materials, they might threaten economic pressure.

The administration believed, however, that even though cold war tensions had relaxed somewhat in May 1949 with the lifting by the Soviets of the Berlin blockade and the successful creation of the West German state, it had just the ammunition to break down JCAE opposition. In early July the members of the JCAE were shown new estimates predicting a Soviet atomic bomb by mid-1950 or 1951 and were told that other countries, including France, Norway, and British Dominion nations (South Africa, Australia, and New Zealand) too were pushing ahead with development of atomic energy. The British, Acheson said at a meeting on July 6, were the most valuable ally of the United States and could not be coerced into abandoning their program even if Congress used economic pressure. McMahon was not very impressed. The Congress was in a sour mood, he warned, and would give any proposal for cooperation with the British on nuclear matters a rough time. Why not, Acheson replied, have the JCAE approve only the idea of negotiations and leave the matter of final sanction until later? After an agreement with the British was reached, congressional approval could be given by joint resolution of Congress or by executive agreement with JCAE concurrence. McMahon was still skeptical. In response to his question whether the British had any bargaining power—anything the United States truly wanted and needed—Acheson answered vigorously in the affirmative. The British had control of or a great deal of influence with countries that possessed much of the raw material supplies the United States looked to.

McMahon pondered the administration's proposal. Although, he said, the JCAE might consider a plan earmarking bombs for British use, it preferred no American-assisted program in the British Isles. Would the senator and his colleagues, Acheson asked, be willing to meet with the President and his key advisors to discuss the matter? McMahon said yes.[10]

On July 14, 1949, at Blair House in Washington, where the President was staying during the renovation of the White House, the administration made its big push. Present were President Truman, Vice President Alben W. Barkley, new Secretary of Defense Louis Johnson, Secretary of State Acheson, General Eisenhower, Chairman of the AEC Lilienthal, Chairman of the MLC Webster, AEC Commissioner Joseph Volpe, and Gordon Arneson of the State Department. From Congress came Senators Connally, Hickenlooper, McMahon, Vandenberg, and Millard E. Tydings (D., Maryland), Speaker of the House Sam Rayburn, and Representatives Carl T. Durham (D., North Carolina) and W. Sterling Cole (R., New York). Opening the meeting, Truman told the congressmen that the United States would never be able to conclude effective international control of an atomic energy pact with the Soviets. The proper policy for the country, therefore, was to move in the direction of closer cooperation with the British. Lilienthal agreed and said that in order for the United States to keep on schedule with its production of atomic bombs, the cooperation of the British for the control of raw materials was critical. Eisenhower then presented the military/strategic point of view. The fates of the United States and Britain were completely interlinked, he told the the congressmen. He pointed, for example, to the vital importance of British air bases for American strategic war plans. The United States could not fight another war without Britain, he said. Yet the British were so angry and bitter about the state of Anglo-American nuclear relations that he feared they might not cooperate fully in the event of war. Acheson added one other point. The British would have two nuclear reactors operating at full capacity in one year and would produce a bomb in four without American help. Then they might not be so willing to conclude a partnership on terms so favorable to the United States.[11]

In *Present at the Creation* Acheson described Vandenberg's initial response to the administration presentation as his "usual histrionics." With Hickenlooper enthusiastically agreeing, he charged that the American people did not want the United States to give away its atomic know-how to the British. He charged further that the administration was presenting a false impression of the state of Anglo-American relations. The British were far more dependent upon the United States than the reverse, he added, and this time the United States should not bail the British out. Truman, Eisenhower, Acheson, and Barkley, supported by Speaker Rayburn, all tried to convince Vandenberg that assisting the British on atomic energy would redound to the benefit of the United States, but the senator was adamant. He did not want to give the atomic bomb to Britain. The most he would consider was an agreement whereby the United States produced all bombs and earmarked some for British use.[12]

Acheson was disgusted. The British were fully justified in building atomic bombs for their own security, he said, and the United States should not try to prevent them from doing so. Any British government that accepted a proposal like Vandenberg's for the United States to earmark bombs for British use (without giving them actual custody) would be so humiliated that it would fall from power. In order to remove the source of irritation from the overall relationship, the United States had to propose a full partnership or nothing at all. Neither Vandenberg nor McMahon reacted sympathetically. They appreciated the need for talks with the British and Canadians, they said, but beyond that would not commit themselves. Hickenlooper felt the same way. The administration had obviously already made up its collective mind to act contrary to the McMahon Act, and he thought that they were making a serious mistake. The raw material problem was not so bad that the United States had to give away the secret of the atomic bomb. Lilienthal contradicted him. The raw material situation was very bad, he said, and if the United States did not conclude a new agreement to cooperate with the British for the control and allocation of uranium and other materials, the AEC would have to slow bomb production.[13]

Aside from Rayburn and Senator Connally, the administration had no support among the congressmen present at the meeting. Nevertheless, the President and his advisors disregarded the opposition of Vandenberg, McMahon, Hickenlooper, and the others and decided to enter into negotiations with the British with a view toward concluding a new, comprehensive agreement. The members of the JCAE went away seething. In the next few days, Senators William F. Knowland (R., California) and Eugene D. Milliken (D., Colorado) resigned from the committee in protest of the proposed policy, others leaked accounts of the meeting to the press, and still others discussed embarrassing the administration by introducing a congressional resolution to forbid negotiations with the British on nuclear matters without keeping the committee fully informed. McMahon even sent Acheson harsh recommendations for negotiating with the British and Canadians while at the same time lobbying for none. If the administration was determined to open talks with the British over the committee's objections, he wrote the secretary of state, it ought at least to demand the best possible terms.[14]

Out of necessity, the administration arranged another meeting with the JCAE. This time all committee members were present, but not the President and vice president. The administration was on the defensive from the start. When Eisenhower tried to play down the size and importance of the British part of the proposed partnership, the congressmen demanded that the British have no facilities for making atomic bombs located in the British Isles and no atomic bombs. Hickenlooper worried that, bombs in hand, they might attempt to stay neutral in a possible Soviet-American war. But

Cole complained that the British might use the freedom of action possession of the bomb would give to provoke a war with the Soviets. Vandenberg seemed most interested in the value to the United States of maintaining the atomic monopoly, while others wanted to avoid future British competition in the commercial and industrial area. But almost all charged that the administration had no legal right to conclude a new agreement with the British without congressional approval.[15]

Most vocal of all was Senator Knowland, his resignation revoked. He demanded veto power over any new agreement and threatened, if this concession were not granted, to bring up the entire subject on the floor of the Senate. Acheson tried to suggest that the administration had the authority under the McMahon Act to make nuclear arrangements with foreign governments if they were in the best interests of the common defense and security but ran into a hailstorm of criticism. Senator Milliken asserted that Congress, by passing the McMahon Act, had preempted the field of atomic energy and that the administration needed congressional consent even to start negotiations with the British. McMahon said no, that starting negotiations would not violate the McMahon Act but that actually concluding an agreement without congressional approval and exchanging restricted data would. He, Vandenberg, and most of the others demanded that the administration reconsider its entire position. Impressed by the virulence of the criticism and threats hurled by the agitated congressmen, Secretary of Defense Johnson broke ranks with Acheson and said that the Pentagon would reassess its position. The administration's resolve to carry through on its proposed policy of nuclear partnership with the British and Canadians had been badly shaken.[16]

Reluctantly, the President and his advisors abandoned the comprehensive plan. The hostility of the JCAE to nuclear cooperation with the British —compounded by the fact that Congress had yet to ratify the NATO pact and Vandenberg was so opposed to the administration's proposed negotiating plan that he might retaliate by working to delay ratification—compelled them to settle for an extension of the Modus Vivendi to buy time for the formulation of new proposals. Talks would be undertaken to explore the issues in atomic energy with the British and Canadians, but the administration would seek to maintain the status quo and avoid drawing up a new agreement. Delighted, the JCAE agreed to a public statement by the President announcing the opening of exploratory talks on "basic questions underlying any determination of long-range policy" in the field of atomic energy. Still, they insisted that Truman make clear that the talks would not in any way involve agreement or commitment by the United States government prior to further consultation with Congress.[17]

This was hardly a satisfactory conclusion to the policy reassessment begun at the Princeton conference in January 1949. Because the international control idea, due to a vote by the U.N. Atomic Energy Commission to terminate its own deliberations until the Great Powers found a basis for agreement, was now officially dead, and because the military had just proposed a major expansion of the nuclear program through 1956, the United States would need British cooperation more than ever for the control and allocation of raw materials. The administration could not afford to postpone substantive negotiations for too long.[18]

The mood in the State Department in August 1949 turned sour. Overloaded with work on the questions of military aid, NATO, German policy, and devaluation of the pound sterling, Acheson gave way to Under Secretary of State James Webb on nuclear matters. It was Webb, together with Kennan of the PPS, who tried to rally administration officials around a plan to negotiate with the British to extend the Modus Vivendi for one year while simultaneously working out arrangements to preempt that pact with a long-term agreement. Under that latter agreement, the British would give up all pretensions to a leadership role in Western Europe, thus facilitating Western European unity on the basis of Franco-German cooperation, in exchange for cooperation with the United States on atomic energy. Of course, British nuclear production and bomb storage in the British Isles would be severely limited and as much as possible of the British program integrated into the American-Canadian effort. But Kennan believed that the prospects of cooperation with the United States on atomic energy were sufficient incentive for the British to align themselves regionally with North America rather than Western Europe.[19]

Except for a startling international development, Kennan's grand conception would never have had a chance to be implemented, and the administration would have had to settle for limited negotiations to extend the Modus Vivendi. But the Soviets detonated an atomic device in late August 1949 and upset all the old calculations. Negotiations that were to begin September 20, 1949 (the day after the Soviet test was confirmed), took on a new sense of urgency. Although official Washington was still digesting the bad news and congressmen were too shocked to have formulated firm opinions about the event, it was clear that the plan that the JCAE had summarily rejected in July had become suddenly viable.

The CPC met at the State Department on September 20, 1949, and Webb laid out the American objectives for the British. Because of the problem of securing congressional approval of any new agreement, he said, the administration wanted the British to go along with an extension of the Modus Vivendi followed by a long-term agreement. The new partnership would have to include provisions for a continued flow of large quantities of raw materials into the American program, location of most nuclear facilities, raw material stockpiles, and atomic bombs with "due regard for strategic considerations," and adoption of a common policy by the United States, Britain, and Canada toward nonparticipants to the agreement. British Ambassador Franks had reservations. Continuation of cooperation based on the Modus Vivendi, even for a short time, he suggested, might prove difficult because in some of the nine fields the British had not gotten what they wanted. The exchanges were often slow and incomplete. He did, however, look forward to the time when full and effective cooperation could be established and expressed a willingness to discuss British nuclear relations with Commonwealth countries and Western Europe. After C. D. Howe, Canadian member of the CPC, declared that his government supported the American position on all points, the CPC set up three subcommittees to discuss strategic and military affairs, raw material supplies and requirements, and information exchanges.[20]

Differences quickly surfaced. On September 24, 1949, Sir John Cockcroft presented an ambitious British plan agreeing to allocate to the United States enough raw materials for a large expansion of the American program. The British, in return, would be permitted to maintain two atomic piles and a low-separation diffusion plant in the British Isles. They would also enjoy full cooperation without restriction on exchanges of information—including information on the design, production, storage, and delivery of atomic weapons—and participate in combined testing of atomic weapons at American test sites. Because the British program would be kept so small, they would receive from the Americans enriched uranium 235 and other components necessary for making improved atomic weapons. "In accordance with common strategic concepts," weapons would be stored in the United States, Canada, and Britain. Other provisions included establishing common security standards in all three countries, effecting a complete interchange of intelligence information, and promising not to disclose classified data to third countries without prior consultation.[21]

Webb and Kennan became pessimistic about the chances of an agreement. They told the President on September 26, 1949, that the talks had failed because the British wanted much more independence than the JCAE would accept. The President, however, had been invigorated by the crisis atmosphere in Washington and was determined to go ahead with a new long-term agreement if one could be worked out. If he had to, he declared, he would go to the country over the issue. They were more cautious. They advised that the administration consult with the members of the committee first and see if their views, in light of the Soviet atomic test, had softened. They repeated these restraining words on October 1 and 3 after representatives on the subcommittees, now consolidated into a steering committee, had made some progress in raw materials and adjourned to consult with their governments.[22]

With a break in negotiations, the administration briefed the JCAE on October 6 and 13, 1949. In a somber mood even after Congress passed the one-billion-dollar Mutual Defense Assistance Act to give military aid to American allies, and still deeply worried by the news of the Soviet atomic bomb, the members were more inclined than ever to sanction a new agreement for cooperation with the British. McMahon was so discouraged that he saw war between the Soviet Union and United States as inevitable and wanted to blow the Soviets "off the face of the earth, quick, before they do the same to us—and we haven't much time."[23] The mood of the military was equally grim. JCS analysts drew up plans to secure Britain as the primary base for strategic bombing in the event of war. Many top military leaders viewed the next four or five years as the "most critical in the entire history of the country." Some, thinking like McMahon, believed war inevitable.[24]

With negotiations set to resume in late November, the Americans reacted unenthusiastically to the British proposals put forward in September. For two weeks in the first part of the month, Webb, Arneson, and General Nichols toured British nuclear facilities to get a better idea of the progress of the British program. They reported on November 21, 1949, that the first two British piles and certain other associated chemical-processing facilities were so far along that it would be unwise to stop production. The third reactor, the low-separation diffusion plant, was not far along in construction, however, and the British appeared unwilling to cancel it purely for domestic political reasons. They recommended that the American negotiating team insist that the British stop work on that plant and make other cancellations to limit the British program. The American members of the CPC agreed. They would also propose that all nuclear components for British atomic weapons be made in the United States with only a limited number of assembled weapons stored in the British Isles for use in accordance with common war plans. The principle of most efficient use of raw materials and personnel, in addition, would have to be recognized so that the vast bulk of material and all important British scientists would be absorbed into the American program.[25]

When the steering committee met on November 28, 1949, the British had three principal reservations to the American counterproposal. They demanded the right to have a small but complete nuclear program in Britain to take advantage of future commercial and industrial uses of atomic energy and to have the capability of making atomic weapons should the new agreement some day end. They wanted, in addition, the Americans to guarantee a small stockpile of atomic weapons on British soil (about 20) with more stored in Canada and earmarked for British use. They also quarreled with the American proposal for allocating materials. If they were to retain a program in Britain, they would need significantly larger stocks than the Americans were offering.[26]

Attempting to narrow differences, Carroll Wilson of the AEC put forward a compromise proposal on December 2, 1949, based on the principle of increasing the collective strength in the shortest possible time. The British, he said, wanted substantially all the facilities in Britain necessary for the production of atomic weapons. But the United States already possessed the complete information and production capacity to maximize bomb production. The British should, therefore, agree to bring all key scientists to the United States to work in the American program while receiving and facilitating a full exchange of information. British and Canadian design ideas would thus help improve American production facilities. And although the integration of the British program into the American would curtail the independent British weapons program for the next few years, the British would be permitted to develop and manufacture certain weapons components in Britain as long as it was in the interest of the combined effort. The possibility would still exist that the British could complete a full weapons establishment in Britain at some future date.[27]

This proposal did not satisfy the British. Only Sir Henry Tizard, chairman of the main Advisory Council on Scientific Policy, favored acceptance of all weapons production in North America. He did so because he believed that Britain had to rely on the United States for its strategic bombing capability in any future war. The others, however, were not so sure. They dreaded the day when, for the second time, Anglo-American cooperation would break down and they, as in 1945, would be left without functional nuclear plants. Cockcroft and Sir William G. Penney, chief superintendent of armaments research of the Ministry of Supply, told Commissioner Wilson that Britain would eventually want its own weapons establishment. Even should cooperation continue, they needed home development of atomic energy for commercial and industrial purposes. While national pride and public opinion factors were also involved in British reluctance to give in to American desires, Webb and Lilienthal believed that bitterness and mistrust built up since the end of the war impeded rational bargaining. The United States had not dealt properly with the British, Lilienthal thought, and Anglo-American nuclear relations would suffer because of it.[28]

At year's end, the British and Americans had agreed on a broad framework providing for manufacture of most atomic bombs in the United States with "arrangements for a certain number to be allotted to the United Kingdom," but the details were disputed. The British, on December 29, 1949, gave the Americans a draft counterproposal. Limited to three years, the plan permitted the British to build a small, complete program (including later a high-separation diffusion plant to produce enriched uranium 235) and to vary the use of raw materials within their program as they saw fit upon due notice to the CPC. Since atomic weapons production would be fully integrated to produce the maximum number of weapons, and since full cooperation would be established in all aspects of the atomic energy field, the British would have certain constraints on what they could do with their program. But it was clear that they intended to strike out more and more in the direction of developing the commercial and industrial uses of atomic energy. Raw materials, they believed, would be available in sufficient quantities to supply the programs of all three countries.[29]

This was little more than a restatement of the British position of September 1949, and the AEC debated it on January 5, 1950. Lilienthal spoke initially about the way the talks were being handled. It was a mistake, he thought, for negotiations of such importance to be discussed almost entirely in a working-group setting. Far preferable would have been a full discussion between the secretary of state and the foreign ministers of Britain and Canada on the basic questions of Anglo-American–Canadian relations. That way the fundamental nature of the new agreement could have been resolved. After that, working groups could have been given authority to debate specific technical issues. As for the present situation, he was upset that a steering committee meeting had been held on the previous day without consulting him first. Volpe, who along with Wilson had attended, explained what had happened. The British December 29, 1949, proposals had been given by Acheson to Arneson for analysis. At the meeting, Arneson and Adrian Fisher, the State Department's legal advisor, had insisted that further staff work be done before a meeting of all American CPC members was called. Volpe promised in the future to see that Lilienthal received any further calls or memoranda concerning the negotiations immediately.[30]

Procedural questions out of the way, Lilienthal opened the floor to specific objections to the British proposal. Strauss had several. Under the British draft, he charged, the British would be free to "take up any particular development" (a reference to the development of the commercial and industrial uses of atomic energy) they wanted. Theoretically, in addition, they could use atomic weapons delivered to them by the United States outside of common war plans. They could even violate the principle of civilian control of atomic weapons by giving custody to the British military. AEC Commissioner Henry D. Smyth agreed. Under the British proposals, he charged, the British could learn all American nuclear secrets, cancel the agreement at the end of three years, and go ahead with the manufacture of atomic weapons on British soil. Neither he nor Pike nor Strauss was impressed by Volpe's reminder that the British "attached no particular significance" to the three-year time period. Once information was exchanged, they said, it could not be recalled. Gordon E. Dean, newest member of the AEC, expressed another concern. If the United States gave classified information useful for developing power reactors to the British and not to private American companies, it might put American industry at a competitive disadvantage for the future. AEC concerns about the British plan were largely shared by Secretary of Defense Johnson and the JCS. With both sides showing little flexibility, the negotiations stalled.[31]

Interestingly, the British never used a hard line on raw materials to apply pressure. Since the Americans were rapidly expanding their program and would do so again in order to develop the hydrogen bomb, this tactic might have been very effective. But it also might have provoked the JCAE into an economic retaliation that the British would have been unable to resist. British leaders certainly did not want to jeopardize raw material collaboration, the one sure link in the nuclear partnership since 1945. In any event, they made a proposal on December 22, 1949, for an interim raw materials agreement and the Americans accepted. Official approval came on April 25, 1950.[32]

By mid-January 1950, with the administration preoccupied with internal discussions about the advisability of producing a hydrogen bomb (a decision made by Truman on January 31), resolution of the basic argument was not in sight. Fisher and Arneson suddenly came to the conclusion already reached by Lilienthal. Higher policy direction from the secretaries of state and defense and the chairman of the AEC was needed, they realized, before talks with Franks could be held to revive negotiations. The participants on the American side had to be made to understand that although partnership with the British would increase actual atomic explosive power by only 1 percent, it was important to conclude a new agreement to bring nuclear relations into line with the overall status of Anglo-American relations. Some compromise had to be found to reconcile the concerns of both sides.[33]

Determined to manufacture an atomic bomb and maintain a small but intact nuclear program in the British Isles, the British refused to return to the subordinate position of 1945. They would not integrate their scientists and resources into the American program. Insistent upon effective control of any joint program, the Americans refused to help the British unless they did. Whether partnership could eventually have been worked out is doubtful. Each side had at that time given as much as it believed it could to safeguard its national interests. Each was unlikely to concede more. Then, at the end of January 1950, disaster struck. The British arrested Klaus Fuchs, a German-born British scientist and Manhattan Project participant, for passing nuclear secrets to the Soviets. Lilienthal told the JCAE that some of the information was weapons-related. As a consequence, American security had been seriously damaged.[34]

Any possibility of reviving the stalled negotiations had been dashed. Even after Bevin asked the State Department to play down the case, nothing could be done. The JCAE's worst fears had been realized. The members of the committee would now certainly not approve collaboration with the British, and especially not with a "socialist" Labour government badly weakened by losses in parliamentary elections on February 13, 1950. Attlee was left with only a precarious seven-member majority in the House of Commons. Within the administration, too, sentiment for cooperation vanished. Johnson told the JCAE that he believed the United States should go it alone with its program and cut all ties.[35]

Although the United States experienced its own spy scandals in 1950, most notably the Gold and Rosenberg cases, the disaster of the Fuchs case continued to cast a troubled cloud over the administration's yearlong effort to achieve consensus for a new policy for Anglo-American nuclear relations. In retrospect, the administration had had to walk a fine line between resolute JCAE opposition to cooperation and insistent British demands for real partnership. Even after news of the detonation of the Soviet atomic bomb temporarily stilled congressional protests and permitted the administration to open negotiations, and even after the administration softened its position in late 1949 to satisfy some British objections, American policymakers could not find sufficient common ground with the British to forge an agreement. In 1950 they were not inclined to, nor would the JCAE let them, try again.

NOTES

1. Memorandum by Webb, Washington, August 19, 1949, S/AE Files, *Foreign Relations of the United States* (hereafter cited as *FRUS*), 1949, 1:519.

2. Francis Duncan, "Atomic Energy and Anglo-American Relations, 1946-1954," *Orbis* 12 (Fall 1969): 1198; Report by PPS, PPS/48, Washington, February 7, 1949, PPS Files, *FRUS*, 1949, 1:419-28.

3. Ibid.

4. Ibid.

5. David E. Lilienthal, *The Journals of David E. Lilienthal*, vol. 2, *The Atomic Energy Years, 1945-1950* (New York: Harper & Row, 1964), pp. 454-57.

6. Dean Acheson, *Present at the Creation* (New York: W. W. Norton, 1969), pp. 314-15; Memorandum by Souers, Washington, February 10, 1949, S/AE Files, *FRUS*, 1949, 1:429-30.

7. Memorandum by Arneson, Washington, March 1, 1949; Minutes of NSC Special Committee on Atomic Energy Policy, Washington, March 2, 1949; Memorandum by Souers, Washington, March 2, 1949, S/AE Files, *FRUS*, 1949, 1:435-61.

8. Memorandum by Souers, Washington, March 2, 1949, S/AE Files, *FRUS*, 1949, 1:443-61.

9. Memorandum of Conversation by Arneson, Washington, July 25, 1949, S/AE files; Douglas to Acheson, London, July 13, 1949, 811.646/7-1349, *FRUS*, 1949, 1:499-500, 475-76; Acheson, *Present at the Creation*, p. 315.

10. Memorandum of Conversation by Arneson, Washington, July 6, 1949, S/AE Files, *FRUS*, 1949, 1:471-74.

11. Record of Meeting at Blair House, Washington, July 14, 1949, S/AE Files, *FRUS*, 1949, 1:476-81; Lilienthal, *Journals* 2: 543-45, 548; Acheson, *Present at the Creation*, pp. 316-17.

12. Ibid.

13. Ibid.

14. Record of Meeting at Blair House, Washington, July 14, 1949; Memorandum of Telephone Conversation by Acheson, Washington, July 18, 1949; McMahon to Acheson, Washington, July 18, 1949, S/AE Files, *FRUS*, 1949, 1:476-81, 484-89; Acheson, *Present at the Creation*, p. 317; McMahon to Johnson, Washington, July 14, 1949, SCI Files, *FRUS*, 1949, 1:482-84.

15. Record of Meeting of JCAE, Washington, July 20, 1949, S/AE Files, *FRUS*,

1949, 1:490-98; Acheson, *Present at the Creation*, p. 318; Lilienthal, *Journals* 2:548-52.

16. Ibid.

17. Memorandum by Acheson, Washington, July 25, 1949; Record of Meeting of JCAE, Washington, July 27, 1949, S/AE Files, *FRUS*, 1949, 1:498-99, 503-6; *Public Papers of the Presidents: Harry S. Truman, 1949* (Washington, D.C.: U.S. Government Printing Office, 1964), pp. 402-3; Acheson, *Present at the Creation*, pp. 318-19.

18. *FRUS*, 1949, 1:501-3.

19. Memorandum by Arneson, Washington, undated; Memorandum by Webb, Washington, August 19, 1949; Minutes of Meeting of U.S. Members CPC, Washington, September 13, 1949, S/AE Files, *FRUS*, 1:513-14, 519-26; Lilienthal, *Journals* 2:565.

20. Minutes of Meeting of CPC, Washington, September 20, 1949, S/AE Files, *FRUS*, 1949, 1:529-35.

21. Hewlet and Duncan, *Atomic Shield*, p. 306; Margaret Gowing, *Independence and Deterrence: Britain and Atomic Energy, 1945-1952*, vol. 1 (London: Macmillan, 1974), pp. 286-87.

22. Memorandum of Conversation by Webb, Washington, October 1, 1949; Minutes of Meeting of CPC, September 30, 1949; Memorandum of Conversation by Webb, Washington, October 3, 1949, S/AE Files, *FRUS*, 1949, 1:543, 548-54; Lilienthal, *Journals* 2:574-77.

23. Memorandum by Arneson, Washington, October 6, 1949, SCI Files, *FRUS*, 1949, 1:558; Hewlett and Duncan, *Atomic Shield*, p. 307; David E. Lilienthal, *Change, Hope, and the Bomb* (Princeton, N.J.: Princeton University Press, 1963), p. 143.

24. Memorandum by Souers, Washington, October 10, 1949, SCI Files, *FRUS*, 1949, 1:559-64; Walter S. Poole, *The History of the Joint Chiefs of Staff: The Joint Chiefs of Staff and National Policy*, vol. 4, *1950-1952*, (Wilmington, Del.: Michael Glazier, 1980), pp. 161-62; Lilienthal, *Journals* 2:582-83.

25. Hewlett and Duncan, *Atomic Shield*, pp. 307-8; Gowing, *Independence and Deterrence* 1:294-96.

26. Hewlett and Duncan, *Atomic Shield*, pp. 308-10; Gowing, *Independence and Deterrence* 1:296-97.

27. Arneson to Marten, Washington, December 12, 1949, S/AE Files, *FRUS*, 1949, 1:601-3.

28. Gowing, *Independence and Deterrence* 1:230; Hewlett and Duncan, *Atomic Shield*, p. 310; Lilienthal, *Journals* 2:610, 615.

29. Franks to Acheson, Washington, December 29, 1949, S/AE Files, *FRUS*, 1949, 1:620-22.

30. CM 351, January 5, 1950, AEC (DOE, Freedom of Information Act, photocopy).

31. Ibid.

32. Hewlett and Duncan, *Atomic Shield*, p. 311; Minutes of Meeting of U.S. Members CPC, Washington, April 25, 1950, S/AE Files, *FRUS*, 1950, 1:547-58.

33. Memorandum by Fisher and Arneson, Washington, January 18, 1950, S/AE Files, *FRUS*, 1950, 1:499-503.

34. Lilienthal, *Journals* 2:634-35.

35. Memorandum of Conversation by Battle, Washington, February 13, 1950, 761.5211 Fuchs, K.F.J./2-1350, *FRUS*, 1950, 1:527-28; Duncan, "Atomic Energy," pp. 1200-1201; Gowing, *Independence and Deterrence*, vol. 2 (London: Macmillan, 1974), pp. 145-49. About Fuchs and the disappointing end to the 1949 negotiations, Margaret Gowing makes the following points: wartime necessity justified British authorities in clearing Fuchs for top secret work; although circumstantial evidence of a link between Fuchs and left-wing groups (possibly even Communists) was overwhelming, there was no absolute proof; and even had there been no Fuchs case, negotiations would have failed. She asserts that most American leaders "apparently desired that the United Kingdom should do precisely nothing in the atomic field." This is obvious exaggeration. Although rejected, the American proposal had many attractive features, including exchanging all information necessary to manufacture atomic bombs and a small stockpile under British control. As for downplaying the importance of the Fuchs case, the facts do not warrant such a conclusion. Fuchs revealed data not only on the make-up of the plutonium bomb but also about general principles of the hydrogen bomb discussed at Los Alamos, New Mexico, and on planned U.S. and British output of plutonium for the early postwar period.

7
OUT OF THE QUESTION

> I suggested to Mr. Attlee that both in the discussions regarding security measures and in any approaches which the British Government might make to us in Washington on this whole subject the matter should be conducted as far as possible through the regular Embassy staff, pointing out that the presence in Washington of such well-known officials as Sir Roger Makins, with their known connection with this subject (atomic energy), always gave rise to embarrassing speculation in the Press, Mr. Attlee and Mr. Bevin agreed that this was most desirable.
> —Dean Acheson, May 16, 1950[1]

Although in early 1950 the Anglo-American nuclear relationship reached its nadir, the same factors existed that had pushed the British and Americans together in 1949. The Soviets had the atomic bomb and were building a large atomic arsenal. In response to the widespread perception among American leaders that Soviet possession of a nuclear capability magnified the Soviet challenge to the West many times and increased the danger of war, policymakers conducted a complete review of American objectives and programs for national security. In NSC 68 the National Security Council (NSC) depicted American goals and foreign policy as in conflict with Soviet goals and foreign policy. The members wrote that although the United States, if the Soviets ever provoked war, had the present atomic capability (mid-April 1950) to deliver a "serious blow against the war-making capacity of the U.S.S.R.," the Soviets in four years would attain the capability of launching a surprise atomic attack serious enough to damage the vital centers of the United States. Since there was no chance of reaching an effective agreement for the international control of atomic energy, the United States must lead the way to a "more rapid building up of the political, economic, and military strength of the free world." This could be accomplished through programs of active aid but also through the establishment of improved political, economic, and military cooperation with the allies. NSC 68, then, was a general statement of the need for collective security against the Soviet threat. But in one critical area, at least, it called for unilateral American action. The United States should proceed immediately with as great an expansion of its nuclear capability as was possible. No mention was made of improving nuclear cooperation with any other country, including Britain.[2]

Yet a JCS review of long-range raw material requirements for the nuclear program, ordered by President Truman and completed in August 1950, made clear that continued British cooperation for the control and allocation of uranium was an absolute necessity. Their cooperation was especially critical in light of the expansions the United States had undertaken in its nuclear program and would undertake in October 1950 (and again in January 1952 after the Soviets in October 1951 detonated their second atomic device). The JCS reported in August and September 1950 that in order to destroy Soviet nuclear capability in a future war, conduct a strategic air offensive against the Soviet Union, support ground forces fighting in Western Europe, and maintain a general reserve and postwar stockpile, the United States would have to produce twice as many nuclear weapons by 1956 as estimated in 1949. This would mandate acquiring all available uranium ore through 1958. But it was unlikely that the British, with their own nuclear program making slow but steady progress, would agree. The possibility existed, then, that Anglo-American competition over raw materials would damage the American strategic position.[3]

The United States needed cooperation, not competition, with the British in the military field as well. At the beginning of 1950 the Strategic Air Command (SAC) had three bases in Britain but needed seven to accommodate the seven bomber wings to be deployed under wartime plans. In April, therefore, the United States and Britain agreed to improve jointly four more airfields. But it was the Korean War that greatly accelerated the American buildup in Western Europe and created the conditions necessary for the fulfillment of the recommendations of NSC 68. The Truman administration and Congress saw in the North Korean invasion of the South not just a local conflict but a clear harbinger of Communist aggression around the globe. The most obvious and vulnerable target was Western Europe. With the Germans disarmed and only relatively small numbers of American, British, and French troops on occupation duty in Germany, Western Europe lay virtually undefended before the large Soviet armies stationed in Eastern Europe. The only deterrence to attack was the threat of retaliation by American bombers armed with atomic bombs, but the President had yet to authorize transfer of atomic weapons to military custody. Nevertheless, in late June the JCS requested and received permission from the British for the use by SAC of even more British airfields. The larger problem, that of beefing up NATO's conventional strength and preventing a possible drive to the English Channel by the Red Army, was not addressed until mid-1951 when the British and Americans began to deploy the first of several divisions in Germany. Even so, NATO military strength would not be a match for Soviet power until many years after the rearmament of the Germans, begun in 1955.[4]

Despite partnership and progress in NATO, the British and Americans still did not cooperate in 1950 in nuclear matters. The major stumbling block to renewal of negotiations, everyone understood, was improvement in British security standards sufficient to convince the Americans that the British could be trusted to safeguard secrets. The British seemed to be willing to make improvements. On April 17, 1950, the British members of the CPC proposed, in view of the Fuchs case, a conference to examine the comparability of American, British, and Canadian security standards in the nuclear field. Held in June, the conference established that the British needed to make changes, adopt different procedures, and enforce previously written rules and regulations in order to tighten security.[5]

Restoring American confidence in British reliability, the British knew, would require more than promises. It would require actually improving security to American satisfaction and then persuading the Americans over time that the benefits of cooperation and information exchanges outweighed the liabilities. And yet the British were rapidly approaching a time of key decision in their program. By late spring 1950 they were preparing for their first plutonium pile at Windscale to go critical. To proceed with manufacture of an atomic bomb, moreover, British scientists needed certain raw materials from the Americans. In order to obtain those materials, the British government would need export licenses approved by the American government. Concerned, Attlee surprised Acheson in mid-May 1950 by dropping in on a meeting with Bevin, Makins, and Lester Pearson at the foreign secretary's apartment in London.[6]

The problem, he told Acheson, was that politically the United States, Britain, and Canada would be unable to conclude a new nuclear agreement for about a year. But the British had to decide now whether to go on with the program as planned or make alterations demanded by the Americans as a necessary precondition for an Anglo-American nuclear partnership. In the absence of a positive indication that the chances of a new agreement between the United States and Britain in the near future were good, he would have to order the British program to continue full force. But he understood completely the difficulties this might pose for future cooperation. The state of public opinion in Britain was such that he could not, in the absence of an agreement, assure the Americans that he would cancel construction of the third British atomic pile. Did Acheson, he wanted to know, have a solution to the dilemma? Acheson replied that he did not. If the administration decided to renew negotiations during the present congressional session, he said, the news would surely leak to the newspapers and cause problems in the preelection atmosphere. He thought it a good idea for the June security conference to take place first; then the two governments could consider the next step.[7]

Probably expecting the response Acheson gave, Makins remarked that the British government would have to go forward with its program while attempting to avoid creating future difficulties for Anglo-American nuclear relations. The American government could, however, help the British government in the meantime. It could give "sympathetic consideration" to a British request for export licenses for certain materials, the transfer of which would not be in violation of American law but would require a discretionary decision by the U.S. government. He said that an American refusal would cause "misunderstanding and difficulty." Acheson replied that he did not know what the British government had in mind but promised that the administration would give the British request "sympathetic consideration." He went on to warn that any such request for export licenses should be made through the regular British Embassy staff because the presence of Makins or any other British official associated with nuclear matters in Washington would cause embarrassing speculation in the press. In a polite way, he was telling them that the state of Anglo-American nuclear relations was so sensitive that officials of the United States' closest ally had to stay out of the American capital.[8]

In an attempt to avoid making future difficulties for Anglo-American nuclear relations, the British decided in early summer 1950 to drop plans for a third atomic pile, though not the low-separation diffusion plant, which the Americans considered more economical than the others. Maintaining three piles would be too expensive and not needed to develop the bomb. From the American point of view, they realized, three would use up scarce resources. They also may have been attempting to conciliate the Americans to win approval of their request for export licenses, made officially on June 21, 1950.[9]

For once, the timing of the British request was right. Four days later the outbreak of the Korean War plunged Washington into another crisis atmosphere. Cooperation with allies became the order of the day. Gordon E. Dean, new AEC chairman from July 11, 1950, and Senator McMahon's law partner, was therefore inclined to grant the British request. It was a relatively modest order, after all, a request for only 505 tons of slightly enriched uranium 235 and one and one-half tons of Kell-F, a special plastic. But the British case was also aided by the fact that the United States still needed very badly British cooperation on raw materials.[10]

The American need was so acute because on August 8, 1950, the JCS officially doubled strategic requirements for atomic weapons by 1958. Unfortunately, production of Belgian Congo uranium could only be increased marginally to meet American requirements. The result, Dean explained to the American members of the CPC on September 7, was that there would be a raw material shortage through 1951. It would help matters, he suggested, if the United States could win British acquiescence in a greater allocation of raw materials to the American program.[11]

He advised, then, that the United States grant the British request for export licenses for the U-235 and Kell-F. At the same time, they could tell the British that the United States desired to discuss future allocations of raw materials at an early date. He and a majority of his fellow AEC commissioners believed, however, that negotiating on raw materials would once again necessitate discussing the larger problem of overall Anglo-American-Canadian nuclear relations. In order to persuade the British to transfer the plutonium output of their piles to the American program, the United States would probably have to offer a stockpile of atomic weapons for British use. He asked General Omar Bradley, chairman of the JCS, for a military opinion of such an arrangement.[12]

Bradley responded that strictly from a military point of view complete cooperation with the British would be highly desirable. He personally liked the idea of exchanging British plutonium for American atomic weapons but thought that the British would insist on production of at least a token number of bombs by their own efforts. Dean nodded in agreement. The British, he said, had already requested use of the American Pacific testing site at Eniwetok Atoll to detonate their first atomic device. But a continuing British program would be a waste of plutonium. Their best scientists too could make more of a contribution in the American program. Impatient that the American and British programs could be allowed to proceed independently without proper coordination of effort and resources, and practical enough to know that Congress would never consider an amendment to the McMahon Act until after the mid-term election and the start of the new session in January 1951, Dean proposed that the administration attempt to reach a quick consensus for a new negotiating position with the British. They could then open discussions in a month to six weeks with an eye toward concluding an informal agreement. Always in favor of closer nuclear ties with the British, Acheson swiftly agreed. But he suggested that the Department of Defense (the new name of the National Military Establishment after Congress passed the National Security Act of 1949), which had the "greatest interest" in military security, give its recommendations first, followed by the AEC and State Department. This suggestion was adopted.[13]

The State and Defense departments (the latter now headed by George Marshall, who had replaced Johnson as secretary of defense on September 12, 1950, and by Robert Lovett as his under secretary) had no objection to approval of the transfer of slightly enriched U-235 and Kell-F to the British. The transfer went through. Consensus within the administration on a new negotiating position for nuclear discussions with the British, however, was not so easily achieved. Another British spy scandal involving the defection of Bruno Pontecorvo, an Italian-born British scientist, to the Soviets in October 1950 killed any chance for an early revival of talks for improved cooperation. The chill in Anglo-American nuclear relations grew colder.[14]

NOTES

1. Memorandum of Conversation by Acheson, London, May 16, 1950, S/AE Files, *Foreign Relations of the United States* (hereafter cited as *FRUS*), 1950, 1:559-62.

2. Report of NSC by Lay, NSC 68, Washington, April 14, 1950, S/S-NSC Files, lot 63D351, NSC 68 Series, *FRUS*, 1950, 1:234-92.

3. Poole, *The History of the Joint Chiefs of Staff: The Joint Chiefs of Staff and National Policy*, vol. 4, *1950-1952* (Wilmington, Del.: Michael Glazier, 1980), pp. 144-45.

4. Ibid., pp. 168-70.

5. Minutes of Meeting of U.S. Members CPC, Washington, April 25, 1950, S/AE Files, *FRUS*, 1950, 1:547-58; Margaret Gowing, *Independence and Deterrence: Britain and Foreign Policy, 1945-1952*, vol. 1 (London: Macmillan, 1974), p. 300.

6. Memorandum of Conversation by Acheson, London, May 16, 1950, S/AE Files, *FRUS*, 1950, 1:559-62; Andrew J. Pierre, *Nuclear Politics: The British Experience with an Independent Strategic Force, 1938-1970* (London: Oxford University Press, 1972), pp. 122-23; Gowing, *Independence and Deterrence* 1:299-300.

7. Ibid.

8. Ibid.

9. Ibid.

10. Minutes of Meeting of U.S. Members CPC, Washington, September 7, 1950, S/AE Files, *FRUS*, 1950, 1:572-75.

11. Ibid.

12. Ibid.

13. Ibid.

14. Summary Log of Atomic Energy Work in Office Under Secretary of State, May–September 1950, Washington, undated, S/AE Files, *FRUS*, 1950, 1:580-87.

8
RUNNING IN PLACE

> Is the Prime Minister aware of the recent statement by the Leader of the Opposition that this country has not the secret of the atomic bomb? If this is so, is this equal partnership (with the United States)?
> —Emrys Hughes, House of Commons, January 30, 1951[1]

If the British came into 1951 expecting a new round of negotiations, they were to be disappointed. The political atmosphere in Washington was hostile. Alarmed by the dangerous turn the Korean War had taken with the intervention of Communist Chinese troops on the side of the North Koreans, and prodded into action by a nationwide address given by former President Herbert Hoover on December 20, 1950, the United States Congress began an extraordinary debate lasting from January through March 1951 on the wisdom of Truman administration foreign policy, especially the decision to send several divisions of combat troops to Europe. Hoover's speech voiced many of the doubts isolationists felt about collective security. The Korean War was a defeat for the United Nations concept, he charged, the Europeans were so badly divided that the United States should not station troops there to save them, and the British were so untrustworthy that they were "flirting with appeasement of the Communist bloc." Instead of trying to help Europe, therefore, the United States should arm its air and naval forces "to the teeth," exert control over the Atlantic and Pacific oceans, and make impossible invasion of the Western Hemisphere. Safe behind the walls of this "Fortress America," the United States could cut defense costs and balance the budget. Many Republicans and others in Congress sympathetic to anti-interventionist arguments agreed. Although without sufficient votes in the end to prevent the administration from carrying out its plan to build up American defense ties with NATO and increase American troop strength in Europe, they did perpetuate the feeling within the administration that Congress was not yet ready to smile on efforts to improve nuclear ties with the British.[2]

The British had two other problems. Strong doubts about British security—and about British willingness to improve security—persisted in American minds. Equally important, the British government came under crippling attack at home. Blaming the Labourites for the failing economy and diminishing British influence around the world, Winston Churchill applied intense political pressure until he defeated Attlee in the general election in October 1951. Critically weakened, the Labour government failed in all attempts to negotiate Anglo-American nuclear questions.

Churchill fired the opening salvos in a bitterly partisan campaign on January 30, 1951, by scoring the government's atomic energy policies in the House of Commons. Could the Prime Minister, he asked, give assurances that the relationship of equal partnership in nuclear matters (which, he asserted, had been in place when he left office in August 1945) between the United States, Britain, and Canada still existed? It did, the Prime Minister replied, though modified now for certain purposes. Churchill and his followers were skeptical. They challenged the government that the partnership could not be an equal one as long as Britain did not have the secret of the atomic bomb. Churchill complained that the wartime "treaty" of cooperation, a reference to the Quebec Agreement, had been revoked and that therefore there was no further reason for secrecy as to its provisions. The government should make it public. To this demand, Attlee responded that Churchill had his facts wrong. There never was any treaty, just an agreement between the two governments, and that agreement had been changed and altered and new agreements made. The old accord was still being kept secret because the American government wanted it kept secret. But he would ask the Americans if they would be willing to publish.[3]

Anxious to avoid embarrassment, the government did request that the Americans agree to publication of the Quebec Agreement, but the State Department turned thumbs down. Because the JCS were at that time (January 31, 1951) presenting a new proposal to exchange atomic bombs for British plutonium and to effect the exchange without asking for new legislation, the State Department feared arousing Congress over less important issues. The British government would have been well satisfied to let the matter rest, but Churchill turned up the heat once more. He wrote personally to President Truman on February 12, 1951, requesting publication of the Quebec Agreement. He went further than requesting; he threatened. The United States had important SAC bases in East Anglia in Britain, he said, bases from which American bombers would fly in wartime to attack the Soviet Union. But the British government would have to approve atomic bombs for those bases. Such approval would be far easier to give if the Americans agreed to publish the Quebec Agreement. The implication of his statement was that if the Americans balked at publishing the wartime accord, he, when he again became Prime Minister, would give the Americans trouble over use of British bases for bombing missions.[4]

In late March Truman finally got around to turning down Churchill's request. He stated when he did that American air base rights in East Anglia were "mutually satisfactory." Meanwhile, Churchill and his supporters were launching another stern attack in Parliament. They demanded a straightforward answer to the question whether Britain had an equal partnership on nuclear matters with the Americans. They also wanted to know whether Britain had a right to be consulted on the use of the atomic bomb. Britain had earned the right, they asserted, because of its wartime contributions and present position of great risk as the "aircraft carrier of the Western world," and indeed had had the right of consultation during the war. The government, in addition, was not doing enough to chide the Americans for their unfair atomic energy legislation. True, Britain had had damaging spy cases, but the United States had had more. Responding for the government, Minister of State Kenneth Younger revealed that the United States still refused to allow publication of the wartime agreement. He was forced to admit that because of the McMahon Act there existed no formal agreement at present for cooperation with the United States and Canada. Certain areas of cooperation did continue on an ad hoc basis, he hastened to assure, and the British government hoped for more collaboration in the near future.[5]

Meanwhile, the JCS proposal of January 31, 1951, for a new agreement between the United States and Britain received consideration within the administration. Stressing maximum *practicable* (my emphasis) security for classified nuclear information and safe location of weapons production facilities, stockpiles of atomic weapons, and delivery vehicles (bombers), the JCS and Department of Defense (DOD) wanted a new push for Anglo-American nuclear cooperation. Such cooperation would provide maximum exploitation of the best non-Communist uranium sources, increase raw material supplies to the United States, and insure (by an exchange of British plutonium for either American U-235 or finished composite atomic weapons) that raw materials were converted as quickly and efficiently as possible into weapons. From the purely military point of view, it would facilitate the arming of the British with efficient atomic weapons in numbers commensurate with British plutonium production. It would maximize, further, Anglo-American nuclear capability in the event of war by coordinating beforehand British and American plans. It would also maximize the capability of the United States, Britain, and Canada to coordinate active and passive defense measures against a possible Soviet atomic attack. It fit in, lastly, with plans to beef up NATO defenses in Europe.[6]

Solidly in favor of the JCS plan was Dean. As he explained in a May 18, 1951, memorandum, the United States badly needed a long-term agreement to stabilize its raw material outlook for the future. But Dean wanted much more than a raw materials pact. He proposed broad cooperation with the British in military and civilian nuclear areas, acknowledging when he did that Congress's approval of the new arrangement in the form of an amendment to the McMahon Act would be needed.[7]

Dean's plan was in trouble by June. Yet another British spy case placed British security in the worst possible light. The British government announced on June 7, 1951, that Donald C. Maclean, head of the American Department in the British Foreign Office and member of the CPC from January 1947 to August 1948, had disappeared and was suspected (later confirmed) of having defected to the Soviets. Although the information he possessed, the State Department informed Senator McMahon, was far less valuable than that which Fuchs had stolen, the JCAE nevertheless had one more confirmation of British security incompetence.[8]

On the face of things, British security standards in the British nuclear program did appear less stringent than American security standards in the American nuclear program. The British used a personnel screening system called the "nothing known against" system wherein the investigators merely checked if a person had any black mark on his record. In the case of Klaus Fuchs, for example, the British Secret Service suspected that he had had contacts with left-wing, perhaps Communist, groups but did not know for a fact that he maintained an active association with Communists. The Americans, on the other hand, employed a double inquiry or "positive vetting" system wherein investigators scrutinized loyalty and political views. Had the British adopted the positive vetting system after the war, Fuchs's political viewpoint and contacts might have made him, despite his value as a scientist, too great a security risk. Although the differences between American and British approaches were discussed at the security conference in June 1950 and again at a second conference in June 1951, and although the Americans pressured the British to adopt the positive vetting system, the Labour government took no steps to tighten security in this manner before leaving office in October 1951.[9]

The final blow to Dean's plan came in September 1951. The JCS changed their minds about exchanging American atomic weapons for British plutonium. The problem, General Bradley wrote, was that the JCS and DOD had to balance the competing interests of expanded cooperation with the British to acquire new scientific and technical information and gain access to British raw material stockpiles against maintaining the highest level of secrecy to prevent leaks of information to the Soviets. Once the AEC informed them just how much technical weapons data the United States would have to reveal to show the British how to use American atomic weapons, they decided that the danger of leaks of vital weapons information was too high. They were searching, instead, for a way to separate weapons data from scientific and nonweapons technical information to permit exchanges with the British. But until a satisfactory solution was discovered, they favored handling all atomic weapons matters through the DOD to insure maximum security.[10]

In any event, they felt that the United States should transfer no information until the British had progressed in their own program to the point where they were producing enough fissionable material to fabricate a considerable number of atomic weapons, or until there was a better chance that NATO could successfully defend Western Europe. Strengthened NATO forces might improve the security of the British Isles as a strategic location for nuclear facilities, raw material stockpiles, and stockpiles of atomic bombs. The JCS also had another reason to back away from its January 31, 1951, proposal and Dean's more ambitious plan. They were adamantly opposed to an administration-sponsored amendment to the McMahon Act. The members of the JCAE, they felt, were far too critical of proposals for better Anglo-American nuclear ties and far too worried that leaks of secret nuclear information would damage the American military posture. The administration, therefore, should wait for the JCAE to propose new legislation and be content to obtain information from the British and other Western Europeans by means other than a direct exchange. Without JCS support, Dean's proposal for a new agreement to cooperate with the British on nuclear matters faltered.[11]

JCS and DOD opposition also had a negative impact on an official British request, made through military channels and confirmed by Ambassador Franks on August 2, 1951, for use of an American test site for the detonation of the first British atomic device in 1952. Once it became clear that the British were asking for a full-scale joint exercise, Lovett and Deputy to the Secretary of Defense on Atomic Energy Affairs Robert LeBaron refused Acheson's and Dean's urgings that they approve the request. Even if the British withdrew their proposal for free exchange of information between British and American scientists during the test, they said, British security problems and the danger of leaks through the British program required that—in order to gain any American assistance—the British radically cut the number of British technicians involved in the test. In essence, Lovett and LeBaron wanted Attlee and his cabinet to put the testing of the first British atomic device in American hands, with only Dr. Penney and a few other British scientists permitted to participate.[12]

Despite the fact that the counterproposal, approved by the President on September 24, 1951, and tentatively backed by Senator McMahon, would not only have severely limited British participation in their own test but would also have altered the kind of test they wanted, the American estimation of the British position was such that administration officials believed the British would swallow their pride and accept. They were wrong. In late September Penney came to Washington to discuss the counterproposal and found it unacceptable. Attempts to narrow differences satisfied neither side. There the matter rested until after the general election and Churchill's return to power. Ultimately, Churchill insisted on full cooperation and reciprocity in the conduct of the test or nothing at all. The consequence was that the British set off a shallow-water atomic burst without American assistance at the Monte Bello Islands in Australia on October 2, 1952.[13]

Differences of opinion expressed by Dean and the AEC on the one hand and Lovett, LeBaron, Bradley, and the DOD on the other toward how far to go and what steps to take to achieve Anglo-American cooperation on nuclear matters were founded in the first instance on solid and substantial policy concerns. Dean favored moving forward with new legislation because, like Acheson, he wanted to see overall Anglo-American relations put on a better footing. He also, quite naturally, wanted to secure British cooperation for the long-term control and allocation of raw materials. He was therefore willing to run the risk of some security loss in information exchanges with the British in order to guarantee those raw materials. With the backing of all interested parties within the administration, he was confident that he could convince his friend McMahon and the other members of the JCAE to sponsor an amendment to the McMahon Act to remove the legal impediments to cooperation and information exchanges.

The DOD looked at the problem differently. Lovett, LeBaron, and Bradley also worried about the raw material problem but put more emphasis on the necessity of maintaining maximum security for American atomic weapons secrets. Because British security problems might result in leaks to the Soviets, they would oppose any transfer of weapons data to the British. Even should the British bring their security system up to American standards and satisfy them that exchanged data would not fall into the wrong hands, they still opposed seeking new legislation from Congress to permit exchanges. The JCAE, it seemed certain, would raise a disruptive ruckus, turn back all attempts to improve nuclear cooperation, and strain Anglo-American relations at a time when the United States, because of the hot war in Korea and cold war with the Soviets, needed close political, economic, and military cooperation with its most important ally. Until the British actually became an atomic power by their own efforts, the United States should let matters be.

Another, more bureaucratic reason was involved in the differences of opinion between the AEC and the DOD. The DOD desired urgently to assume complete responsibility for the atomic stockpile, while the AEC commissioners passionately opposed military control. The controversy was not new. After international tensions rose sharply in March 1948 over the Communist coup in Czechoslovakia, the JCS had asked for "direct and exclusive control" of the stockpile for strategic planning purposes and to prepare for tactical use. They had repeated this petition to the President in July 1948 when the Soviets imposed the Berlin blockade. At that time, however, the President had issued a public statement that civilian authority would be maintained.[14]

Quite clearly, actual military control of atomic weapons would be required at some point to meet the Soviet threat. That point was finally reached in the midst of the Korean War when on April 6, 1951, Truman decided to approve a JCS request for the transfer of a limited number of completed atomic weapons. He had already, at the start of the war in June 1950, authorized transfer of nonnuclear components of atomic weapons to military control for shipment to American bases in Britain and the Pacific area.[15]

But this victory of the DOD over the AEC did not satisfy the JCS. In his September 7, 1951, memorandum (when he backed away from the January 31, 1951, proposal to exchange American atomic weapons for British plutonium), General Bradley suggested that all atomic weapons matters be handled through military channels to improve security. Subsequently, the growing atomic arsenal, the fact of Soviet atomic capability, and the need to bring readiness to employ atomic weapons to an even higher level made military leaders press their case more and more vigorously in the 1950s.[16]

Under these conditions, tension between the AEC and the DOD was almost inevitable and occurred over matters upon which the two agencies should have been in substantial agreement. One such example was an amendment to the McMahon Act sought by Dean for the purpose of giving the Canadians information on new technology for more efficient production of fissionable material. Because most uranium mined by the Canadians went to the United States, the AEC chairman was easily able to persuade the JCAE and Congress to approve the amendment on October 30, 1951. The only problem was that he neglected to consult extensively with the DOD so that the JCS could conduct a review of the security aspects of the amendment. Lovett, new secretary of defense from September 17, 1951, and Deputy Secretary of Defense William C. Foster angrily registered their objections with Dean in early November.[17]

The struggle between the military and the AEC for control of atomic weapons and the nuclear program had not been finally decided, as Congress had intended, by passage of the Atomic Energy Act of 1946. It continued through the immediate postwar years and had some effect on the conduct of nuclear relations with the British. As nuclear matters grew more complex and the nuclear challenge of the Soviets became more imposing, the struggle between the DOD and the AEC for control of American atomic weapons would be renewed with further consequences for Anglo-American nuclear relations. Together with British security problems and JCAE opposition to cooperation, DOD-AEC conflict had already prevented measures to revive nuclear ties with the British even in areas like joint testing. Joint testing of British atomic devices would at least have fulfilled the reciprocity requirement demanded by the JCAE. Real progress, then, in reviving nuclear relations depended both on active British measures to convince the Americans that they were worthy partners in the atomic energy field and on efforts within the administration to smooth over bureaucratic differences and reforge a consensus in favor of improved cooperation.

NOTES

1. 483 *H.C. Deb.* 5s., pp. 715-16.
2. David W. Reinhard, *The Republican Right since 1945* (Lexington: University Press of Kentucky, 1983), pp. 71-73.
3. 483 *H.C. Deb.* 5s., pp. 715-16.
4. Arneson to LeBaron, Washington, February 9, 1951; Churchill to Truman, February 12, 1951, G/PM Files, lot 68D349, *Foreign Relations of the United States* (hereafter cited as *FRUS*), 1951, 1:690-94.
5. Truman to Churchill, Washington, March 24, 1951, G/PM Files, lot 68D349, *FRUS*, 1951, 1:703-4; 485 *H.D. Deb.* 5s., pp. 2660-65, 2669-71.
6. Memorandum by Lovett, Washington, October 12, 1951; Memorandum by Lay, Washington, May 21, 1951, G/PM Files, lot 68D349, *FRUS*, 1951, 1:776-77, 721-30.
7. Memorandum by Lay, Washington, May 21, 1951; Memorandum by Lay, Washington, July 19, 1951, G/PM Files, lot 68D349, *FRUS*, 1951, 1:721-30, 746-48.
8. McFall to McMahon, Washington, August 13, 1951, S/AE Files, *FRUS*, 1951, 1:752-55.
9. Margaret Gowing, *Independence and Deterrence: Britain and Atomic Energy, 1945-1952* (London: Macmillan, 1974), 1:304-5; 2:139; Memorandum of Conversation by Penfield, London, October 9, 1951, 741.13/10-1651, *FRUS*, 1951, 1:774-75.
10. Informal Statement by DOD, Washington, undated; Memorandum by Lovett, Washington, October 12, 1951, G/PM Files, lot 68D349, *FRUS*, 1951, 1:769-72, 776-77.
11. Ibid.
12. Memorandum of Conversation by Arneson, Washington, August 2, 1951; Minutes of Meeting U.S. Members CPC, Washington, August 24, 1951; Memorandum of Meeting CPC, Washington, August 27, 1951; Draft Memorandum by Arneson, Washington, September 10, 1951, S/AE Files, *FRUS*, 1951, 1:755-69.
13. Memorandum by Arneson, Washington, September 24, 1951, S/AE Files; Memorandum of Conversation by Penfield, London, October 9, 1951, 741.13/10-1651; Franks to Acheson, Washington, December 26, 1951, S/AE Files, *FRUS*, 1951, 1:772-75, 798-99.
14. Hewlett and Duncan, *Atomic Shield*, pp. 99-100, 136-38, 150-72; Larry Dean O'Brien, "National Security and the New Warfare: Defense Policy, War Planning, and Nuclear Weapons, 1945-50" (Ph.D. diss., Ohio State University, 1981), pp. 96-98, 188-96.
15. Hewlett and Duncan, *Atomic Shield*, pp. 521-25, 537-39.
16. Informal Statement by DOD, Washington, undated, G/PM Files, lot 68D349, *FRUS*, 1951, 1:769-72.
17. Foster to Dean, Washington, November 2, 1951, 811.5611/11-251; Dean to Foster, Washington, November 27, 1951, 103-AEC/11-2751; NSC 120, Washington, December 21, 1951, S/S-NSC Files, lot 68D351, NSC 120 Series, *FRUS*, 1951, 1:784-88, 794-98; Hewlett and Duncan, *Atomic Shield*, pp. 480-83; Public Law 235, 82d Cong., 65 Stat. 691.

9
WHO SHALL BE CONSULTED ON THE USE OF ATOMIC BOMBS?

> If it [a decision to use the atomic bomb] has to be made for the welfare of the United States and if the democracies of the world are at stake, I would not hesitate to make it again.
> —Harry S. Truman, April 6, 1949[1]

The other important issue in Anglo-American nuclear relations in 1951 was the question of British right of consultation or veto with regard to possible American use of atomic bombs. In the Modus Vivendi of January 7, 1948, the British had given up all claim to this right, but it sprang to life again because of a statement by President Truman on November 30, 1950. Referring to the Korean War and the measures the United States might take to bring it to a successful conclusion (especially in light of recent Chinese Communist intervention on the side of the North Koreans), the President warned that the administration had under "active consideration" use of the atomic bomb. Although he had not actually authorized use of the bomb, the effect of his statement in Western Europe and Britain was to cause great alarm. Attlee told the House of Commons the next day that the British government would expect to be consulted before the atomic bomb was used by the United States in Korea. "In any case Her Majesty's Government consider that a decision of such grave importance could not be taken on behalf of the United Nations without the fullest prior consultation with those member States who are participating in the international police action."[2]

Truly concerned that the President and his advisors might take some rash action in Korea, Attlee promptly flew off to Washington to discuss the matter with Truman. He brought along Sir William Slim, chief of the Imperial General Staff, Tedder, the chief of staff, and Far Eastern experts from the Foreign Office. Suspicions of Attlee's intentions abounded in Congress. Twenty-four Republican Senators introduced, but failed to pass, a resolution requiring ratification by the Senate of any agreement made by the President and Prime Minister. His reception by Truman and the administration was somewhat friendlier. Still, he made little headway in his talks with administration officials until the last meeting on December 8, 1950. Speaking privately to the President in his office, he succeeded in convincing him to agree to a joint statement conceding Britain the right of consultation on the use of the atomic bomb. The President's advisors were stunned. Lovett whispered to Acheson that the secretary of state had better speak up before the communiqué was drafted and convince the President to reverse himself. Acheson tried. Assembling Truman, Attlee, and Franks away from the others, he reminded the President of his numerous public statements promising to make no commitment that would limit his duty and power under the law to authorize if necessary the use of atomic bombs. A change in that position now would cause an uproar in Congress and the public. His arguments had the intended effect. Everyone reluctantly agreed that the right of consultation on the use of the atomic bomb had to be deleted from the communiqué. In the end, the most Truman could and would promise was to keep the Prime Minister informed at all times of developments that might bring about a change in the world situation.[3]

It is highly unlikely that Truman really intended to give Attlee and the British a right of consultation on the use of the atomic bomb. Attlee's principal motive for rushing to Washington, Franks had informed Acheson prior to the visit, was to secure his domestic political position and reduce public anxiety about recent events. It was probably by emphasizing this side of the question—the political impact—that Attlee convinced Truman. One of two accounts Acheson has given of the conference corroborates this opinion. In any event, Attlee was able to return home and assert that he had received from Truman "assurances which I consider to be perfectly satisfactory" about American caution in the use of atomic bombs in a crisis.[4]

Once the question of consultation on the use of the atomic bomb was broached, it was natural for the British to pursue the matter and seek more definite, if more private, assurances from the Americans. After all, the Americans did have bombers armed with atomic weapons stationed at British bases, and no formal procedure existed for guaranteeing that those bombers would not be used in a way British officials considered injurious to British interests. Attlee and Bevin, in addition, realized that the government was vulnerable to political attack by Winston Churchill and the Conservatives on the whole matter of nuclear relations with the Americans. They did not want to be embarrassed by questions about consultation on the use of the bomb. The Labour government, the Conservatives would charge if the facts became known, was responsible for giving up the right of consultation in the Modus Vivendi, and it would not win them any votes to argue—probably quite correctly—that the Americans would not consult anyway on the use of the atomic bomb.

Anxious then to preempt a Churchillian attack on the issue, Bevin reopened the matter in mid-January 1951. He asserted in a talk with American Ambassador to Britain Lewis W. Douglas that the British had a right of consultation about the use of American planes flying from British bases, especially with respect to planes taking part in an American strategic offensive. The British government, therefore, wanted formal briefings for British military leaders on American strategic air plans. The Americans were reluctant to cooperate. Locked in a "great debate" that would continue through March on American foreign policy and the wisdom of American military commitments to Europe, Congress was in no mood to allow concessions with regard to the atomic bomb. Besides, the British wanted far too much. General Bradley told Lovett, Ambassador-at-Large Philip C. Jessup, and Deputy Under Secretary of State for Political Affairs H. Freeman Matthews on January 15 that he had already talked to Tedder and members of the British Military Mission in Washington and that they had asked for details from the strategic air plans that would violate American security requirements. He had refused to divulge such details. His only concession had been to agree that the United States would communicate the requested information should a war with the Soviets ever occur and the United States need to use British bases. A subsequent meeting was held between the American chiefs of staff and Marshal of the Royal Air Force Sir James Slessor, chief of the British Air Staff. British officials indicated that the two meetings had satisfied Tedder and Slessor that arrangements for consultation between British and American military leaders in the event of a crisis had been made.[5]

The British had good reason to inquire about American plans to use British air bases. According to REAPER, the JCS's "Joint Outline War Plan for a War Beginning on July 1, 1954," strategic bombers based in Britain were absolutely essential for the success of any wartime attack on the Soviets. If war occurred, planes flying from those bases would approach the Soviet Union along the edge of the Mediterranean Sea and deliver 52 atomic bombs in the industrial regions of the Volga and Donets Basin. The Soviets, should the plan ever be carried out, would undoubtedly retaliate against the bases—and Britain.[6]

Despite the plain language of the December 8, 1950, public statement and the January 1951 discussions, the British told the Canadians that they had received from the Americans a firm commitment for consultation on the use of atomic weapons. This was revealed by Franks to Hume Wrong, Canadian ambassador to the United States. Wrong then informed the Americans and added a word of his own. He told Arneson that his government too was concerned about storage of atomic weapons components at the Goose Bay air base in Canada, overflights of Canada by Strategic Air Command planes carrying atomic weapons or parts, and possible atomic bomber strikes flying out of Goose Bay. Canadian officials were particularly worried about this last point, fearful that the Americans would be too quick to act in a crisis and might therefore increase the danger of war. They therefore refused to give prior consent for strike operations and overflights by SAC. The United States worked to set up a prior notification procedure to secure quick approval for strike operations, but negotiations continued through the end of the year without resolution of the basic Canadian concern.[7]

In February 1951 the British pressed the Americans again on the consultation issue. They attempted in a working paper dated February 22, 1951, to determine which Soviet actions or other forms of Communist aggression would trigger war and necessitate the use of atomic weapons by the United States supported by Britain. Their ultimate goal was to conclude a formal agreement in order to define very clearly under what circumstances the United States could use British bases to launch atomic strikes.[8]

The Americans took their time responding. Only after the State Department's Policy Planning Staff and JCS's Joint Strategic Survey Committee debated the issue in the summer did the JCS sit down with State Department officials to talk about how to approach discussions with the British. Present were General Bradley, Army Chief of Staff J. Lawton Collins, Air Force Chief of Staff Hoyt S. Vandenberg, Vice Chief of Naval Operations Admiral Lynde D. McCormick, Secretary of State Acheson, Matthews, Arneson, Deputy Director of the PPS John H. Ferguson, and Secretary of Defense Lovett. Concerned that politico-military discussions would lead to implied agreement or commitment, Bradley wanted to limit Anglo-American discussions to meetings between the British and American chiefs of staff. He suspected that British political leaders were trying to tie the question of the use of the atomic bomb to world developments that might bring on a general war. Should such developments take place, the United States would then be bound to consult on the use of the bomb. He wanted to avoid that situation.[9]

Acheson, while agreeing that this was what the British intended, nevertheless asserted that a genuine connection between general war and the use of the atomic bomb did in fact exist and that the United States should at least discuss the subject in order to secure British cooperation in a future war. Lovett refused to accept his advice. There were two separate questions, he said—conditions precipitating war, and the use of the bomb—and he did not want the two linked. General Collins remarked that this was correct because the United States might at some time want to use the atomic bomb tactically (that is, in some local conflict involving American forces) and that discussions with the British should be limited to what situations would lead to war.[10]

An even tougher, more distrustful line was taken by General Vandenberg. He was suspicious of the British because of the way they had almost tricked Truman into granting the right of consultation in December 1950. He also mistrusted them because of Slessor's and Air Marshal Sir William Elliott's attempts to pin down the American chiefs of staff in the January discussions and because of their February 22, 1951, paper presented to the State Department (not the military). Since he believed that they were after an implied commitment on the part of the United States to consult on the use of the atomic bomb, he insisted that military conversations between the British and American chiefs take place first to find out just what the British were really after. Then, if it was safe, politico-military talks could occur. The State-JSSC paper, therefore, could be discarded for the present.[11]

Acheson tried to find a middle position. The British, he suggested, had a right to know what the JCS and the President were thinking on the questions of what situations would precipitate war and when the United States would use atomic weapons. To them this was a "life and death matter," and they deserved to know if American leaders were "sober and responsible." In the upcoming discussions, the United States should compromise and concede that a general war would mean use of atomic weapons by the United States. Lovett objected. What if the Soviets attacked American forces in Korea, he said, and the allies, Britain included, did not want to go to war? In order to fight the Soviets, the United States would have to use every weapon at its disposal, especially atomic weapons carried by bombers flying out of bases in Britain. Allied neutrality would be disastrous. The United States could not, therefore, commit itself in advance and so tie its hands in some future situation. Collins and Vandenberg concurred. They insisted on military talks before political to discover whether the British would deny use of bases without American commitment to consult. Together with Lovett and Bradley they also opposed, when speaking of the atomic bomb, referring to it only in connection with general war. That would imply that the United States could not use it in other circumstances. In the end, Acheson deferred to their judgment on every point.[12]

The JCS were being extremely cautious. The British had misinterpreted American words before and might, intentionally or not, do so again. It turned out that they were right about British intentions to get a commitment from the Americans concerning consultation on the use of the atomic bomb. On September 11, 1951, Acheson and Jessup met with new British Foreign Secretary Herbert S. Morrison, Elliott, and Franks and discovered that the British desired immediate politico-military conversations between Morrison and Franks on the one hand and Bradley and a State Department representative on the other. Attlee, already under attack for failure to preserve British defense ties with Egypt and because negotiations with Iran concerning continued British control of Iranian oil had collapsed, was again under pressure in the House of Commons to say flatly that the British government had the right of consultation on the use of bombers carrying atomic bombs and flying out of British bases. At the very least, Franks suggested, Bradley and Elliott should begin discussions and have himself and someone from the State Department join in.[13]

Mindful of the wishes of the DOD, Acheson resisted all proposals for politico-military talks. There was not enough time to achieve the desired results, he said, because Morrison would have to return soon to Britain for the election campaign. And even if Morrison's presence was not required for the talks, American law limited the commitments the administration could make. Although, therefore, he could not approve at present politico-military talks, he saw no problem in consulting the British prior to using British air bases—as long as the President had freedom of action on the use of the atomic bomb. He then declined to help the British government frame answers to Conservative thrusts expected in the House of Commons on the right of consultation.[14]

The meeting became strained. Morrison, never an easy man to deal with, gratuitously raised the question of British security standards and the American practice of having all workers sign forms saying they were not Communists. He said he doubted whether implementing this practice in the British program would be "useful." Shifting suddenly to the matter of information exchanges, he told Acheson it would be very helpful if he could receive an understanding (from Acheson) that the United States would seek an amendment to the McMahon Act. Acheson pointed out that the difficult political atmosphere created by the Fuchs and Pontecorvo cases made this impossible. When he refused even to give Morrison a private assurance that the administration would propose an amendment to the McMahon Act when the opportunity arose, the Foreign Secretary went away empty-handed and disgruntled.[15]

Two days later, Franks came back for a meeting with PPS Director Paul H. Nitze, Bradley, and Matthews and softened the British position considerably. There were two general categories of issues in the February 22, 1951, paper, Franks said: military judgments with possible political connotations (including appraisals of the strategic significance of particular areas and principles/qualifications to apply to the manner in which the United States and Britain should handle aggression in particular cases) and problems of consultation. These latter problems were political in essence, having to do with American use of British bases for actual military operations. The Americans stared noncommittally. Franks then tried to justify a British right of being consulted on the use of the atomic bomb in the event of general war by pointing out the importance of British air bases and overseas possessions for the conduct of the war. Again, the Americans sat mutely. Finally, he admitted that the Prime Minister and his cabinet needed real progress on the talks before Morrison's departure from the United States on September 21 in order to answer questions in Parliament about whether the British government retained control over its own bases.[16]

The Americans now understood what Franks was talking about. "Obviously" prior consultation and agreement with the British government would be required, Matthews and Bradley assured, before the United States could use British bases for military operations. But the question of use of bases and British control of those bases was less important than the basic question of Western unity. The Americans preferred to put the discussion in the context of the possibility of general war rather than use of the atomic bomb. However, even though the United States wanted frank discussions of situations that could lead to general war, Nitze remarked, American officials could make no commitment or agreement. Would the United States, Elliott asked, be willing to consult Britain in advance of taking some action? The United States, Nitze repeated, could make no commitment to consult. Frustrated, Elliott gave his opinion that general war, should it come, meant using the atomic bomb. But Bradley quickly brought up the example of a Soviet attack on Yugoslavia to demonstrate that situations calling for use of the atomic bomb could not so easily be defined.[17]

Franks too was frustrated. He (perhaps indiscreetly) said that he was trying to decide what Attlee, or Churchill—should he win the upcoming general election—would want him to press for. The British government, he finally decided, wanted three things. It wanted opportunities for free discussions whenever particular crisis situations arose, opportunities to discuss hypothetical situations that might at some future time arise (for example, a Soviet attack on Yugoslavia), and opportunities to discuss certain more general principles in order to be able to approach borderline cases (where use of the atomic bomb would be a judgment call) to determine how close they were to the Americans in their thinking. The Prime Minister would want, he explained, to communicate with the President during a crisis and have the necessary background information, provided by these discussions, to know how to analyze a given situation. The British government, he stated further, did not want a specific agreement requiring the United States to consult in advance of using atomic bombs in "cases X, Y, and Z," but wanted an expression of general intent to consult in advance of using the bomb, or in other words an informal understanding of intention to consult.[18]

The Americans refused. Nitze declared that the United States would make no commitment limiting American sovereignty in any way either in deciding when a general war situation would occur or on the use of atomic weapons. He would not even commit to talk to the British on the general subject. The best he would do was indicate that at present the United States intended to talk with the British. Franks interrupted. An expression of intent, he tried to suggest, was in a certain sense a commitment. No, Nitze replied firmly. The United States undertook no commitment of any kind for the future. He suggested that they go ahead with talks to bring their viewpoints closer together and set up procedures to facilitate further talks. But there could be no ambiguity this time in what the Americans had said.[19]

Despite Franks's creative attempts to obscure plain meaning in convoluted language, the Americans had stood firm. The British, due to a hopelessly weak bargaining position, could not convince them to reconsider. They had sought the right of consultation and been denied it even concerning American atomic strikes flying from British air fields. They had attempted to bind the Americans to agreed principles and situations in which the atomic bomb could or could not be used and had been rebuffed. They had asked the Americans to give some indication that they would be consulted in a crisis situation and had been told that the United States would make no such commitment whatsoever. The only public statement the Americans would agree to was a simple announcement that the United States and Britain had discussed developments in the world situation and would do so again.[20]

On October 17, 1951, the British finally informed the Americans that if under direct pressure in the election campaign, they would have to respond that in an emergency the United States would not be able to use British bases without British consent. On the question of whether Britain had the right to be consulted as to the use of the atomic bomb, however, they would follow the statement proposed by the Americans that the United States and Britain had discussed developments in the world situation and would do so again. They would avoid, in other words, a direct response.[21]

Advocates of atomic energy cooperation with the British were hopelessly on the defensive in 1951 due to the overriding consideration of security and continued JCAE opposition. As long as the British remained incapable of or unwilling to meet American security demands and as long as American access to raw material supplies, although not guaranteed for the long run as Gordon Dean wanted, remained unimpeded, this situation would not change. The United States would not offer to give Britain a small supply of atomic bombs in exchange for British plutonium, it would not assist the British in detonating an experimental atomic device at an American test site without severe restrictions, and it would not agree to publish the now revoked wartime Quebec Agreement. Nor would the United States make concessions to the British on the question of consultation on use of atomic bombs, even bombs carried by American planes flying out of British bases. Because the DOD and JCS wanted to preserve the President's freedom of action to launch an atomic strike against the Soviet Union, they opposed any intimation that the United States was making a commitment of any kind to the British. Badly weakened politically and under the greatest pressure by Churchill for the lack of cooperation between the United States and Britain in the field of atomic energy (as well as for failure of its domestic and foreign policies), Attlee's Labour government could find no way to persuade or exert leverage on the Americans to reconsider.

NOTES

1. *Public Papers of the Presidents: Harry S. Truman, 1949* (Washington, D.C.: U.S. Government Printing Office, 1964), p. 200.

2. Ibid. (1965), p. 727; *Manchester Guardian*, Dec. 1, 1950, p. 7.

3. Dean Acheson, *Present at the Creation* (New York: W. W. Norton, 1969), pp. 481, 484; Kenneth Harris, *Attlee* (London: Weidenfeld and Nicolson, 1982), pp.

462-65; U.S. Minutes, Truman-Attlee Conversations, Sixth Meeting, The White House, December 8, 1950, Conference Files, lot 59D95, CF 49, *Foreign Relations of the United States* (hereafter cited as *FRUS*), 1950, 3:1787.

4. Memorandum of Conversation, November 30, 1950, *Official Conversations and Meetings of Dean Acheson (1949-1953)*, Presidential Documents Series (Frederick, Md.: University Publications of America, 1980), reel 3, pp. 450-51; Harris, *Attlee*, pp. 464-66.

5. Memorandum of Conversation by Jessup, Washington, January 14, 1951, 790.00/1-1451; Bevin to Acheson, Washington, January 14, 1951, 790.00/1-1451; Memorandum of Conversation by Jessup, Washington, January 15, 1951, 790.00/1-1551; Memorandum of Telephone Conversation by Jessup, Washington, January 26, 1951, 611.41/1-2651; Acheson to Bevin, Washington, January 26, 1951, 611.41/1-2651, *FRUS*, 1951, 1:802-8.

6. Encl. to JCS 2143/6, November 29, 1950, CCS 381 (1-26-50), BP pt. 1, Modern Military Branch, National Archives.

7. Memorandum of Conversation by Arneson, Washington, April 7, 1951, 711.56342/4-751; Acheson to Marshall, Washington, June 14, 1951, 700.5611/6-1451; Memorandum of Conversation by Arneson, Washington, June 14, 1951, PPS Files, lot 64D563; Lovett to Acheson, Washington, November 5, 1951, 742.5/11-551, *FRUS*, 1951, 1:809-11, 843-54, 894-97.

8. Paper by Savage, Washington, April 12, 1951, PPS Files; Memorandum of Conversation by Nitze, Washington, May 4, 1951, 700.5611/5-451; Memorandum by Savage, Washington, May 23, 1951, *FRUS*, 1951, 1:814-21, 826-27, 834-40.

9. Memorandum of Conversation by Ferguson, Washington, August 6, 1951, S/AE Files, *FRUS*, 1951, 1:875-80.

10. Ibid.
11. Ibid.
12. Ibid.

13. Memorandum by Jessup, Washington, September 11, 1951, S/AE Files, *FRUS*, 1951, 1:880-83.

14. Ibid.
15. Ibid.

16. Memorandum by Nitze, Washington, September 13, 1951, S/AE Files, *FRUS*, 1951, 1:883-90.

17. Ibid.
18. Ibid.
19. Ibid.

20. Both Gowing and Harris have given the unfortunate impression that Britain either retained a right of consultation on the use of atomic bombs by American planes flying out of British bases or regained that right in October 1951. See Margaret Gowing, *Independence and Deterrence: Britain and Atomic Energy, 1945-1952*, vol. 1 (London: Macmillan, 1974), p. 318, and Harris, *Attlee*, p. 289.

21. Memorandum of Conversation by Arneson, Washington, October 17, 1951; Memorandum by Arneson, Washington, October 18, 1951, S/AE Files, *FRUS*, 1951, 1:891-94.

10
FULL CONSIDERATION?

> Under arrangements made for the common defense, the United States has the use of certain bases in the United Kingdom. We reaffirm the understanding that the use of these bases in an emergency would be a matter for joint decision by His Majesty's Government and the United States Government in light of the circumstances prevailing at the time.
> —Anglo-American Joint Communiqué, January 9, 1952[1]

On October 25, 1951, the Conservatives won the general election in Britain and Winston Churchill again became Prime Minister. Pleased at the return of the man who had been so great an ally in the fight against Nazi Germany and Imperial Japan, and whose tough anti-Soviet stance paralleled basic American containment policy, administration officials nevertheless had a certain sense of wariness about dealing with Britain's old leader. Because of his tremendous prestige, indomitable stubbornness, and comfortable political position, he might be able to bring pressure to bear on the American government to reestablish at least the level of cooperation that had been maintained during World War II. Yet Churchill was 77 years old upon taking office for the second time, and there were questions as to how vigorous he would be in putting forth Britain's case for better treatment in the field of atomic energy.

On November 9, 1951, the Prime Minister dispelled these doubts. Speaking at the lord mayor's banquet at Guildhall, he declared that it was his intention to return Britain to economic and financial good health. He would, moreover, restore British influence in the world, especially with the Americans. The British government, he asserted, should have "full consideration" from the United States for its point of view on nuclear affairs because Britian had taken and was taking "peculiar risks in providing the principal atomic base for the United States in East Anglia." Just what did the Prime Minister mean by "full consideration"? Was he angling to persuade the United States to give Britain more financial assistance along the lines of the Marshall Plan, expiring on December 31, 1951? Or did he, as members of the State Department believed, want both nuclear information and the right of consultation on all nuclear matters, including American use of the atomic bomb? And there was another question the Americans mulled over after the Guildhall speech. What would Churchill do if they declined to meet his demands? He would not, Churchill told the House of Commons on November 21, tell the Americans to evacuate their bases in Britain. But he would go to Washington just after the beginning of the new year to consult with President Truman and his advisors about atomic energy and other matters important to the two allied nations.[2]

Churchill's desire for a return to the level of cooperation achieved during the war was tempered somewhat by briefings given him by his advisors about the (to British minds) intransigent American attitude in past nuclear talks. Lord Frederick Cherwell, Churchill's German-born but British-raised paymaster general and personal advisor on all scientific matters, suggested that no amendment to the troublesome McMahon Act was possible in 1952, an American election year. The British should content themselves with winning from the Americans a recognition that noncooperation in the field of atomic energy had produced a waste of effort and resources and should be replaced by better relations as soon as possible. This would mean passage of new legislation in the American Congress in 1953. The United States, in addition, should acknowledge that the British nuclear program was a valuable entity and could make a significant contribution to the joint effort. This tack would assure that the United States made no further attempt to subjugate the British program to the American. But there was one area in which substantial progress could be made. The Prime Minister should negotiate with the Americans for the right of consultation before the President took any decision leading to a general war. He should also secure the right of joint Anglo-American decision on atomic attack missions and the right to be briefed on the details of the American strategic air plan.[3]

Since the British nuclear program was at long last about to produce an atomic device, the British believed that they could make a better case to the Americans concerning the value of their knowledge and cooperation. Yet the device would not be assembled and detonated until October 1952. In the meantime, high costs in nonmilitary areas prevented plans for a rapid expansion of Britain's atomic bomb building program and hindered progress toward the development of atomic energy for commercial and industrial purposes. Budget considerations, moreover, caused the new cabinet to put aside Cherwell's plans for a costly reorganization of the nuclear program. Consequently, the British government continued to have difficulty over the next few years assuring the Americans that they were taking steps to improve British security standards to the satisfaction of American experts.[4]

The British arrived in Washington on January 5, 1952, and settled into a series of meetings with their American counterparts lasting through January 10 and again from January 16 through 18. In between, Churchill and Anthony Eden, his foreign secretary, took time off for business in Ottawa, Canada. Ranging over many topics including relations with the Soviets, American and British officials explored their attitudes toward Communist China, the European Defense Community proposal, and growing Arab nationalism in the Middle East (especially Iran and Egypt). The discussions did not always resolve differences but did clarify the positions of both sides. A very friendly atmosphere was created in which Churchill in particular felt free to express his views. This was what the Americans wanted. While they had no intention of making substantial concessions, they were willing to make gestures to win the Prime Minister's support or good will for administration foreign policy. They were largely successful. Even on potentially divisive issues they had their way. When, for example, the Prime Minister made a strong appeal to reverse the NATO decision—concurred in by the Attlee government—to install an American admiral as overall commander of NATO's Atlantic forces, the Americans were able to maneuver Churchill gently away from a confrontation.[5]

The Americans also deflected British thrusts on atomic energy. In direct talks between Truman and Churchill with their key advisors present on January 7 through 10, 1952, the Prime Minister proposed that Cherwell and American officials open negotiations to find a formula under which the British and Americans could carry on effective cooperation in the nuclear field. Since the October 30, 1951, amendment to the McMahon Act did permit some exchange of restricted information under certain circumstances, Acheson and Lovett conceded that this might be possible. But the British would have to put into effect an adequate security system to safeguard American secrets. Churchill responded that he was certain the British could meet American requirements. Promising a full background investigation of all personnel within the British nuclear program, he declared that homosexuals would be excluded and inquiries initiated about persons with relatives living behind the iron curtain or with relatives having Communist sympathies. Even after this assurance, the Americans qualified their promise of improvement by saying the best they could do was work for "maximum cooperation within the limits of the McMahon Act."[6]

That limitation, as Churchill learned when meeting with Senator Brien McMahon, author of the act, would prevent the kind of collaboration for which he had hoped. Although apologetic, saying that had he known about the Quebec Agreement and the extent of Anglo-American wartime cooperation in atomic energy he would never have proposed legislation so restrictive of information exchanges, McMahon explained that undoing the provisions of the act would be difficult. There was still too much opposition in the JCAE and Congress. Within the administration, in addition, sentiment for cooperation was uncertain. The AEC and State Department favored improved contacts. The DOD, particularly Robert LeBaron, did not.[7]

McMahon's assertion about LeBaron was confirmed at meetings on January 10, 1952, in Dean's office involving Dean, AEC Commissioners Henry D. Smith and Thomas E. Murray, LeBaron, and Arneson for the Americans and Cherwell, British Ambassador Roger Makins, and Sir Christopher Steel for the British. Citing the spirit of the Churchill-Truman talks on atomic energy, Cherwell tried to get the Americans to agree to some exchange of classified information. In response, Dean offered to interpret the nine areas of the Modus Vivendi more liberally and to be more sympathetic to other British requests if the British would ask specific questions and meet the requirements of the October 30, 1951, amendment to the McMahon Act. LeBaron, however, was suspicious of Cherwell's intentions. The only important nuclear information the United States possessed, he asserted, related to the design and manufacture of atomic weapons. That information the administration was expressly forbidden from communicating by the McMahon Act. Cherwell countered by observing that the United States possessed important information relating to nuclear reactors and that this data could be exchanged under the October 30, 1951, amendment. LeBaron shook his head. As to that amendment, he observed acidly, the DOD and JCS had not had the opportunity to cooperate with the AEC in its formulation and so would have difficulty approving specific proposals that might be drawn up (by the AEC and the British). The DOD, he explained, had "constitutional responsibilities for the national security" and must be sure that it did not violate those responsibilities by illegally exchanging information with the British.[8]

LeBaron's attitude irritated not only Cherwell but also the AEC commissioners and Arneson. Yet there was little they could do. Dean promised to try to provide the British with some of the information they needed while waiting until 1953 (after the election and with a new administration installed in Washington) to review the situation. If exchanges by that time did not satisfy the British, they would consider again whether to seek new legislation from Congress. What he was in effect telling Cherwell was that the British just would not get restricted information until at least 1953.[9]

Arneson was angry. In a January 15, 1952, memorandum to Acheson, he complained that the assistant secretary of defense's attitude did not match the "spirit and intent of the Truman-Churchill meetings." He speculated that Cherwell would report to Churchill about LeBaron's obstructionism, and Churchill would then prod Truman or Lovett about the DOD's general attitude. It might even be a good idea, he suggested to Acheson, if the secretary of state himself talked to the President or secretary of defense about encouraging DOD officials toward greater flexibility. In any event, he did have some good news to report. In a later meeting on January 10 between Cherwell and Director of the CIA General Walter Bedell Smith, Smith and Cherwell had come to a tentative agreement to use the October 30, 1951, amendment to cooperate on the gathering of scientific nuclear intelligence. Truman himself had raised with Churchill the importance of finding out what the Soviets were up to in atomic energy, and Cherwell and other British officials were pleased with the development.[10]

The Americans also demonstrated a slight degree of flexibility on the question of consultation on the use of the atomic bomb. While the U.S. government would not consult on the use of atomic weapons or before taking actions that might lead to general war, it would consult prior to making use of British bases. Any stronger commitment, the British had to understand, might compromise American freedom of action, especially in the event of an emergency. As a gesture of respect for the Prime Minister, however, Lovett promised Churchill and his advisors a personal briefing on the strategic air plan. This was accomplished at the Pentagon on the morning of January 17, 1952. Later in the year, Lovett authorized joint discussions with the British on strategic and tactical aspects of the air plan, and an important meeting between the JCS and Air Marshal Sir John Slessor took place in July.[11]

Although the joint communiqué of the conference referred only to an American commitment to consult on the use of bases in Britain in an emergency, not on the use of atomic weapons—at best a modest achievement for British diplomacy but more realistically a superficial one—Churchill conveniently decided well after the end of the conference to exaggerate the extent of progress made on nuclear relations. On February 26, 1952, the day after the NATO Council voted in Lisbon to provide 50 divisions for the defense of Western Europe by the end of 1952, he declared in the House of Commons that in Washington the Americans had agreed that they would not use atomic bombs from bases in East Anglia without British consent. This promise, he trumpeted, stated in a "formal and public manner what had already been reached as a verbal understanding between the late Prime Minister [Attlee] and President Truman." And there was more. When he told the Americans that the British were almost ready to test an atomic bomb and that the British had a plant ready for regular production of atomic bombs, a new atmosphere on nuclear matters was created. As proof, he cited McMahon's public statement—referring to the fact that British wartime contributions had been hidden from the Senate during 1946 deliberations on the Atomic Energy Act—in which he said that "now we [the Americans] may consider rethinking the entire situation with all the facts in front of us."[12]

The key to opening the door to American nuclear secrets, Churchill and his advisors seemed to think, was to play up British atomic progress in the press and Parliament, fabricate news about improved Anglo-American cooperation and information exchanges, and in the process entice the Americans into agreeing to information exchanges in order to discover what in fact the British really did know. At the same time, these tactics would make it politically possible at home for the Americans to exchange nuclear information. Accordingly, Churchill made his statement in the House of Commons. Then, British Foreign Office and atomic energy officials suggested that Britain was ahead of the United States in some areas the Americans deemed very important. These included development of smaller atomic weapons for tactical use in support of combat troops and development of power "breeder" reactors that made more fuel than they consumed. Newspaper accounts of supposed British advances did not fool the Americans. When Cherwell sent Sir John Cockcroft, head of the British atomic energy program, to Washington the last two weeks of March 1952 with specific proposals to test the willingness of the Americans to go to the "maximum limit of the McMahon Act," Cockcroft achieved very little. The Americans were willing to offer some cooperation on the gathering of intelligence about Soviet nuclear activities and to revive some of the areas of exchange delineated in the Modus Vivendi but balked at disclosing any information the British really wanted. What they did offer would have amounted, had the British accepted, to an almost one-sided disclosure by the British of their nuclear secrets. Annoyed and indignant, Cockcroft expressed his concern publicly in mid-April that American security restrictions were preventing visits by American scientists to Britain and British scientists to America. Churchill, a month later, announced that American observers would not be invited to witness the British atomic bomb test later in the fall. He would, however, consider "any proposals which the United States government might make for closer collaboration in the future."[13]

The January 1952 Washington conference had shown the British that the Truman administration did not want to cooperate, and indeed was still forestalled by the McMahon Act from cooperating, in the areas of atomic energy the British considered most important. Nor had they afterwards been able to maneuver the Americans into agreeing to greater collaboration. By summer, Churchill had come to understand that progress on an interchange of information could not take place until two events occurred—British demonstration of atomic prowess by successful detonation of an atomic device, and formation by a new President in 1953 of an administration empowered by majority vote of the American electorate to carry out national policy for four full years. He did hope, however, to pursue the question of consultation on use of atomic weapons, seeing in this issue a means whereby Britain could restrain the Americans from any hasty action in Korea, against the Chinese Communists, or even against the Soviet Union. Britain might yet retain a measure of influence with the Americans.

NOTES

1. U.S. State Department, *Bulletin*, 1952, 25:83-84.
2. *London Times*, Nov. 10, 1951, p. 6; Substance of Discussions of State-JCS Meeting, November 21, 1951, PPS Files, *Foreign Relations of the United States* (hereafter cited as *FRUS*), 1951, 1:898-99; 494 *H.C. Deb* 5s., p. 376.
3. Margaret Gowing, *Independence and Deterrence*: vol. 1 (London: Macmillan, 1974), pp. 411-13.
4. Peter Pringle and James Spigelman, *The Nuclear Barons* (New York: Holt, Rinehart, and Winston, 1981), pp. 137-39; Gowing, *Independence and Deterrence*, vol. 2 (London: Macmillan, 1974), p. 56.
5. Dean Acheson, *Present at the Creation* (New York: W. W. Norton, 1969), pp. 594-606.
6. Memorandum for Secretary of State, Secretary of Defense, by Lay, August 28, 1952, Papers of Harry S. Truman, President's Secretary's File, box 201, Harry S. Truman Library; Hewlett and Duncan, *Atomic Shield*, 574-75; Gowing, *Independence and Deterrence* 1:413-14.
7. Gowing, *Independence and Deterrence* 1:414-15; John W. Wheeler-Bennett, *John Anderson, Viscount Waverly* (London: Macmillan, 1962), p. 338.
8. Hewlett and Duncan, *Atomic Shield*, p. 575; Memorandum by Arneson, Washington, January 15, 1952, G/PM Files, lot 68D349, "Truman-Churchill Talks," *FRUS*, 1952-54, 2:846-48.
9. Ibid.
10. Ibid.
11. Gowing, *Independence and Deterrence* 1:413-14; Acheson, *Present at the Creation*, p. 601.
12. 496 *H.C. Deb.* 5s., p. 964; U.S. State Department, *Bulletin*, 1952, 25:83-84.
13. *New York Times*, Feb. 12, 1952, pp. 1, 5; Mar. 3, 1952, p. 24; Apr. 20, 1952, p. 20; May 20, 1952, p. 6; May 28, 1952, p. 5; Gowing, *Independence and Deterrence* 1:415-16; 501 *H.C. Deb.* 5s., p. 31.

11

THE STRUGGLE FOR CONTROL OF ATOMIC ENERGY POLICY

> It is recognized that responsibility for advising the President as to the military desirability of the use of atomic weapons, as is the case with any other weapon in our national armory, rests with the Joint Chiefs of Staff and the Secretary of Defense. Responsibility for advising the President as to the political aspects of the use of atomic weapons rests with the Secretary of State. Military considerations and political considerations are often inextricably interrelated. By law, the power to decide on the use of atomic weapons rests with the President.
> —Special Committee of the NSC on Atomic Energy, October 23, 1952[1]

While Anglo-American atomic energy ties evidenced little improvement in early 1952, Churchill and his advisors believed it only a matter of time until American commitment to the bilateral nuclear relationship caught up to American commitment to overall British and Western European security. That latter commitment was increasing, moreover, and might just be the catalyst needed to rev up the engines of nuclear cooperation. In late February the NATO Council voted to admit Greece and Turkey to formal NATO membership and agreed to provide 50 divisions for the defense of Western Europe by the end of the year. Strong supporters of the decision, American policymakers applauded. They also led the cheers after the representatives of France, West Germany, Italy, the Netherlands, Luxemburg, and Belgium met in Paris on May 27, 1952, to create a European Defense Community (EDC). Designed to establish a single unified command and bind West Germany to the Atlantic defense plan, the EDC concept faced tough sledding in ratifications debates in the signatories' national assemblies, especially the French. But the British and Americans quickly issued a joint statement proclaiming that a threat to the EDC would be regarded as a threat to their own security and gave the concept a need boost. By mid-1952 it did appear that the United States was moving inexorably in the direction of closer ties to Western Europe.

Might not Churchill's hope of Anglo-American nuclear partnership, then, eventually come to pass? The problem was that important obstacles to cooperation still remained. Events within the American nuclear program, in the international sphere, and among the American policymakers all served to complicate greatly formulation of American nuclear policy and once again to shunt Anglo-American nuclear relations off to the side. These events had their origin in the recent past.

In September 1951 McMahon and the other members of the JCAE determined that the United States should maintain and extend its lead in atomic energy over the Soviets and launched a campaign to persuade the administration and Congress to approve a vast expansion of the nuclear program. They insisted that the United States begin to mass-produce atomic weapons, accelerate the project to build the hydrogen bomb, and discover and develop more raw materials to propel the program. The administration took care to listen. By mid-January 1952 the NSC had discussed and approved a five-year, five- to six-billion-dollar program to expand American fissionable material production and increase weapons stockpiling. On January 21 the administration submitted an appropriations request to Congress, then fought off an attempt by the House Appropriations Committee to slash it. The compromise secured much of what McMahon and his colleagues had wanted.[2]

If determination to stay ahead of the Soviets motivated the JCAE to push through expansion of American nuclear capabilities, the perceived growing power of both Soviet and American atomic arsenals persuaded some in the administration and many in the international community that superpower competition in the nuclear sphere was making the world a much more dangerous place to live. With international control of atomic energy foundering in the U.N. over mutual distrust and unworkable plans, the U.N. General Assembly voted over the opposition of the Soviets to dissolve the U.N. Atomic Energy Commission and set up a Disarmament Commission under the authority of the Security Council. Intending to find some way to regulate, limit, and reduce not just atomic but all armaments, disarmament proponents could not get the Americans and Soviets to agree on a plan. The Americans placed great emphasis on developing first an adequate disclosure and verification system. The Soviets opposed permitting on-site inspection of their nuclear and military facilities. They pushed instead for one-third reductions in the armed forces and armaments of the United States, Soviet Union, Britain, France, and Italy. The Americans preferred gradual reductions of both nuclear and conventional weaponry.[3]

While disarmament proposals were worked out within the administration and in consultation with Britain and other allies, a policy debate erupted between the DOD and the AEC concerning custody of atomic weapons and procedure for advising the President on use of those weapons. Like the issues of expanding the nuclear program and negotiating in the U.N. on disarmament, the DOD-AEC quarrel persisted through the first half of 1952 and into the autumn.

Actually, this debate was just another phase in the continuing struggle between the DOD and the civilian agencies of the government over control of the nuclear program and all its aspects, particularly nuclear weapons. It was precipitated by Lovett in November 1951 when he asked the JCS to determine "the exact nature and scope of DOD interest in the use of atomic weapons" and to describe DOD responsibility for determining requirements for atomic weapons, delivery methods, and where and how such weapons would be used. Naturally, the JCS's reply proposed the broadest possible powers for the DOD, asserting that the chiefs of staff could not agree to any other agency "interposing itself between them and the President in submission to him of recommendations for a military course of action, nor could they agree to any such other agency having a voice in determining how, when, and where such military operations are to be conducted."[4]

Other proposals in the JCS reply, including complete military control of the atomic arsenal, had the President responded in the affirmative, would have gutted the AEC's and State Department's authority to advise the President on nuclear matters and to have a significant say in the management of nuclear issues. Prudently, the President on January 29, 1952, referred the JCS/DOD plan to the Special Committee of the NSC for further study. The procedure was for the DOD, AEC, and State Department to submit revised recommendations to James S. Lay, executive secretary of the NSC, for the President's consideration later in the year. While the DOD reiterated the JCS recommendations almost at once, the AEC and State Department dragged their heels. Only in late May did AEC Chairman Dean reply, refuting when he did most JCS points and yielding only to agree to the establishment of a plan to transfer control of atomic weapons to the military in an emergency.[5]

With regard to the questions of who should advise the President on use of atomic weapons and recommendations to the President for exchanges of information with foreign governments, Dean was most emphatic that the JCS was way off base. An NSC study approved April 27, 1951, had already established that the NSC was the principal agency for advising the President on use of atomic weapons. And it was the NSC, not the American members of the CPC as the JCS asserted, that under the October 30, 1951, amendment was directed to recommend exchanges of restricted data with foreign governments. Because of that amendment, moreover, and also because it might be to the advantage of the United States, the AEC wanted to try for a broader exchange of information with foreign governments (the British and Canadian). Yet it understood that the JCS themselves had under consideration legislation to allow information exchanges with NATO allies to facilitate conduct of combined operations. The joint chiefs even contemplated an actual exchange of fissionable material for the very same purpose. The AEC asked to be kept informed.[6]

By mid-June 1952 the dispute had boiled down to four basic issues: the procedure for advising the President on use of atomic weapons and other matters like deployment of atomic weapons, the manner in which atomic weapons production programs should be established, the question whether an amendment to the McMahon Act should be sought to enable the military to transmit information on atomic weapons to foreign governments to facilitate combined military operations and to permit exchanges of fissionable material or weapons material for such operations, and the question whether all or part of the national atomic stockpile should be turned over to complete custody of the military. On June 11 the State Department gave its opinion. The JCS were, as the JCS had asserted, the President's principal military advisors, but the NSC had the responsibility of advising the President with respect to integration of domestic, foreign, and military policies. It was the NSC, therefore, that should render advice on the use of atomic weapons once the JCS had made an initial recommendation that atomic weapons should be used. The JCS statement that other agencies were "interposing" themselves between the JCS and the President on this matter was incorrect. This was the province of the AEC. In fact, the State Department believed that the JCS should not even have a monopoly with regard to advising the President as to the type of weapon (for example, hydrogen as opposed to atomic) and delivery related to target selection. These choices, it was felt, might well have a bearing on the outcome of the conflict and the "possibilities of winning the peace once victory is assured."[7]

Meanwhile, the staff of the Special Committee of the NSC made its own report, paralleling the State Department document but going into greater detail. The procedure would begin with a JCS determination that using atomic weapons in a given situation was "militarily desirable." Then the members of the Special Committee would give their views on political, military, and technical considerations. If time and circumstances permitted, Congress would pass and the President approve a joint resolution declaring war—clear authority for the President to use all means to carry on the conflict. But if the Soviets were launching a surprise attack and time constraints were a factor, the President would have to act under his constitutional powers as commander-in-chief and make such decisions with respect to utilization of atomic weapons as were necessary. He would consult with congressional leaders at the earliest possible moment. In an urgent situation short of surprise attack, the President might have time to consult beforehand with congressional leaders. At a very minimum he would want the advice of the JCS, secretary of defense, secretary of state, and chairman of the AEC. Additional actions to be taken could be decided at a meeting with congressional leaders, again if time and circumstances

The Struggle for Control

allowed. These additional actions might include briefing or consulting other governmental agencies or officials (the full NSC, the cabinet, or the Civil Defense Authority), informing the American people, or communicating with other governments, especially "those whose consent is required before their bases can be used by the United States for atomic strikes."[8]

Taken as a whole, this Special Committee staff study was unclear on the question of consulting foreign governments, in particular the British. The language referring to consent before using foreign bases to launch atomic strikes seems by context and phrasing to be absolutely applicable only when the President and his key advisors had sufficient time to meet first with congressional leaders. In other words, in the event of a surprise attack and if the JCS, supported by the Special Committee, recommended atomic strikes by American bombers using foreign bases, the President might well authorize such strikes without contacting and consulting foreign governmental leaders. He might do this on the basis of an explicit agreement worked out with a foreign government well in advance and designed specifically to provide for such a contingency. Or, in the absence of such authorization, he might imply foreign consent by virtue of the fact that the foreign government in question had permitted establishment of American bomber bases on its soil and subsequently concurred in the arming of those bombers with atomic weapons. Under either reasoning, the President and his advisors would have the freedom of action necessary to respond to a surprise Soviet atomic attack, the freedom of action American policymakers had consistently insisted upon in discussions with the British and other foreign governments. If time and circumstances permitted, the United States would probably consult but did not want to be legally bound to do so.

With respect to the British situation, the joint communiqué of January 9, 1952, was sufficiently vague to support the implied consent interpretation. "Under arrangements made for the common defense," the communiqué read, "the United States has the use of certain bases in the United Kingdom. We reaffirm the understanding that the use of these bases in an emergency would be a matter for joint decision by His Majesty's Government and the United States Government in light of the circumstances prevailing at the time." The British might object, but the United States could make the case that if "the circumstances prevailing at the time" were a surprise Soviet atomic strike threatening American bases in Britain with destruction, and if the attack were so sudden as to leave no opportunity for consultation with British leaders, the President would have full authority to order atomic retaliation from those bases. Fortunately, however, the state of Soviet atomic power in mid-1952 made it very unlikely that the Soviets would consider such a rash action forcing the President to make so fateful a decision. In mid-1952 the number of Soviet atomic bombs was estimated at 50. With bombing capability limited to Western Europe, and with American atomic forces so formidable, the Soviets were hardly in a strong position to provoke war. Yet the balance of forces might look less favorable at the end of the decade. Estimates of the growth of Soviet atomic capability showed the number of Soviet atomic weapons roughly doubling over each of the next three years. Even more dangerous, by the mid- to late 1950s the Soviets might develop delivery systems to threaten the United States itself. By the end of the decade, therefore, having freedom of action on the use of the bomb, freedom from the cumbersome constraint of having to consult with distant allies prior to launching retaliatory nuclear attacks from overseas bases, would take on a critical importance.[9]

The strains between the DOD, the State Department, and the AEC had to be resolved, the President ordered, and a meeting was held on June 17, 1952, with Acheson, Dean, Lay, Arneson, General Bradley, Deputy Secretary of Defense William C. Foster (sitting in for Lovett), and LeBaron in attendance. Despite previous sharp differences, the participants conducted themselves in a spirit of compromise. Almost at once all parties accepted the NSC staff study paper recommendations for the procedure for advising the President on the use of atomic weapons. They agreed that after an initial JCS recommendation, the NSC would help the President decide. Next, they all concurred that new legislation was needed to permit exchange of atomic weapons information with the NATO allies for planning purposes. But the point was made that the JCAE and Congress might well balk at amending the McMahon Act. What was needed, LeBaron suggested, was an interim arrangement prior to passage of another amendment. He asked if it might not be possible for the AEC to make an official determination that the size, weight, shape, yield, and military effects of atomic weapons were no longer "restricted data" within the meaning of the McMahon Act. That might be possible, Dean replied, and such a reinterpretation ought to be investigated, but he warned that the JCAE would have to be informed. LeBaron and Bradley were not deterred, and it was agreed that the AEC and DOD would see what could be done in this area.[10]

The spirit of compromise remained vibrant as the conversation turned to the question of custody of the atomic stockpile. Dean offered to support the deployment of atomic weapons to forward (overseas) bases if the DOD agreed to take responsibility for security, make the necessary arrangements for evacuation, and insure storage so that there would be no physical deterioration of the weapons. He also agreed to support turning over some number of atomic weapons at "fully operational bases" in the United States, but the AEC must continue to have access. Bradley had one reservation. The JCS, he said, felt that the military needed immediate custody of more atomic weapons in order to be ready for emergency use and to improve security in the event of an emergency movement of the weapons from storage facilities to bombers. The stipulation about "fully operational bases" might prevent immediate custody. His argument failed to persuade Dean. After a brief discussion during which LeBaron conceded that the initial estimate of atomic weapons the military should control was too high, it was agreed that the JCS and DOD would study the matter further and find a more realistic number. It was also agreed that the AEC and DOD would work out means for a transfer of a portion of the stockpile to military custody and that the Special Committee would consider their joint recommendation. On the last issue—the question of who should set atomic weapons production rates and goals—Dean suggested that the AEC and JCS were not as far apart as previously thought. "Greater precision of language," he said, was all that was needed to resolve the problem. It was decided that the AEC and JCS would study the situation and present to the Special Committee a joint recommendation.[11]

Final resolution of the disputed issues took place September 10, 1952. The Special Committee adopted and the President approved the compromise proposals worked out between the interested parties. The procedure for determining atomic weapons production would begin with a DOD statement of the numbers, types, and desired military characteristics of atomic weapons it wanted. In light of DOD requirements, the AEC would then propose rates and goals of production for weapons materials and indicate its capabilities to meet DOD requirements. If there were differences between the AEC and DOD proposals, the President would decide. Once the AEC constructed the weapons, in addition, it would conduct tests and evaluations to check quality and performance. The DOD would then have the right to conduct its own tests and evaluations to ascertain whether the weapons met desired military characteristics.[12]

The internal American policy debate of the first half of 1952, combined with work on the nuclear expansion program, discussions about disarmament proposals, events and developments in the Korean War, and other administration business, served to preclude (had the administration entertained the thought of initiating) serious bilateral discussions with the British on nuclear matters or use of atomic weapons. But by summer that debate had largely ended, and the Americans had no excuse for ignoring British calls for talks. British military leaders, in particular, were very interested in examining the implications of atomic weapons capability for the British defense posture and joint Anglo-American strategy. They, and British political leaders, wanted to sit down with their American counterparts before any more time had passed. Despite the nearness of the American election and the certainty that a new President and new administration would take office in January 1953, they wanted no delay in reviving nuclear contacts.

NOTES

1. Memorandum for the President, October 23, 1952, Papers of Harry S. Truman, President's Secretary's File, box 202, Harry S. Truman Library.
2. Memorandum for the President, Washington, January 17, Truman Library, PSF

Subject File, *Foreign Relations of the United States* (hereafter cited as *FRUS*), 1952-54, 2:851-58; Harold P. Green and Alan Rosenthal, *Government of the Atom* (New York: Atherton Press, 1963), pp. 10-11, 237-38; Alfred E. Eckes, Jr., *The United States and the Global Struggle for Minerals* (Austin: University of Texas Press, 1979), pp. 170-73, 179-82. The Korean War served as catalyst for a general reassessment of American raw material needs, including uranium requirements.

3. See *FRUS*, 1952-54, 2:859-63, 980-81, 1043-46.

4. Memorandum by Lovett, Washington, February 6, 1952, G/PM Files, lot 68D349, "Use Policy 1950-55," *FRUS*, 1952-54, 2:863-68; Walter S. Poole, *The History of the Joint Chiefs of Staff: The Joint Chiefs of Staff and National Policy*, vol. 4, *1950-1952* (Wilmington, Del.: Michael Glazier, 1980), pp. 152-54.

5. Ibid., Memorandum by Dean, Washington, May 27, 1952, G/PM Files, lot 68D349, "Use Policy 1950-55," *FRUS*, 1952-54, 2:947-53.

6. Ibid., Note by Secretaries to JCS on Amendment to Atomic Energy Act, June 23, 1952, CCS 471.6 (8-15-45), secs. 28-33, RG 218, Central Decimal File 1951-53, box 168, Modern Military Branch, National Archives.

7. Memorandum by Department of State, Washington, June 11, 1952, G/PM Files, lot 68D349, "Use Policy 1950-55," *FRUS*, 1952-54, 2:969-73.

8. Staff Study Prepared by Representatives of NSC Special Committee on Atomic Energy, Washington, June 11, 1952, G/PM Files, lot 68D349, "Use Policy 1950-55," *FRUS*, 1952-54, 2:973-79; Memorandum for the President by Gleason, October 23, 1952, Papers of Harry S. Truman, President's Secretary's File, box 202, Harry S. Truman Library (parts excised).

9. U.S. State Department, *Bulletin*, 1952, 26:83-84; Annex to Report to NSC by Lay, Washington, August 22, 1952, S/S-NSC Files, lot 63D351, NSC 135 Series, *FRUS*, 1952-54, 2:89-113; Robin Higham and Jacob W. Kipp, eds., *Soviet Aviation and Airpower: An Historical Review* (London, Brassey's, 1977), pp. 198-99; Stephen E. Ambrose, *Eisenhower: The President* (New York: Simon & Schuster, 1984), p. 93. It is unclear whether the Soviets had any atomic bombs deployed operationally in 1952.

10. Memorandum by Acheson, Washington, June 13, 1952, 700.5611/6-1352; Informal Minutes of Meeting of NSC Special Committee on Atomic Energy and Chairman JCS, Washington, June 17, 1952, G/PM Files, lot 68D349, "Use Policy 1950-55," *FRUS*, 1952-54, 2:981, 984-88.

11. Ibid.

12. Memorandum by Lay, Washington, September 10, 1952, G/PM Files, lot 68D349, "Use Policy 1950-55," *FRUS*, 1952-54, 2:1010-13; Poole, *History of the JCS* 4:158-59. Decision about the number of atomic weapons to place in military hands for "operational flexibility and military readiness" was not so easily achieved. In August Lovett persuaded the President to authorize the placement of considerable numbers of nonnuclear components aboard aircraft carriers and at certain overseas bases where they could be secure. In October and November he and the JCS pushed once again for military control of the entire stockpile. They backed off only when Dean persuaded them to wait for Eisenhower to take office in January 1953.

12

ACTIVITY—BUT NO ACTION

> No arrangements have been made for American observors [sic] to witness the test of the United Kingdom atomic weapon. The United States Government is prevented by existing domestic legislation from exchanging reports on atomic weapons with other countries. I should, of course, be willing to consider any proposals which the United States Government might make for closer collaboration in the future.
> —Winston Churchill, May 19, 1952[1]

After the Americans in 1945 and 1946 rejected the idea of a postwar Anglo-American nuclear partnership, British officials fell back on the theory that American policymakers would only grant Britain full equality in the nuclear sphere once the British program produced a workable atomic device. In mid-1952, with preparations for their first atomic test right on schedule for an October detonation, they firmly believed that their opinions should once more count for something in the deliberations of the Americans on nuclear matters. They hoped and expected the Americans would feel the same way.

In order to be able to converse intelligently on the subject, Churchill asked the British chiefs of staff in June 1952 to meet at the Royal Naval College at Greenwich to study global strategy and Britain's role in maintaining the West's atomic deterrent. The British chiefs complied and produced recommendations for the Prime Minister's consideration. Even though, they believed, the United States possessed a large stockpile of atomic weapons and held a sizeable strategic advantage over the Soviets, and even though economic problems made it unlikely that the British government could build many atomic bombs, Britain had to take a share in the West's atomic deterrent. This was necessary for two reasons. An independent British deterrent force would increase British influence on American cold war policy and on planning war strategy. It would also insure that in the event of war with the Soviets the British possessed atomic weapons with which to attack and destroy targets not of direct strategic interest to the United States but of importance to Britain. Specifically, the British could concentrate on producing smaller-yield weapons to use in a tactical role during ground engagements in Western Europe or at sea. The disadvantage of not possessing atomic weapons had been demonstrated only too well at the recent January 1952 meetings in Washington. British atomic power had still only been potential, and the Prime Minister had had a difficult time staking a claim on decision making for strategy in a future war (and as a consequence for the peace terms after such a war). British commanders-in-chief, at the present time, had insufficient information as to how the Americans would use atomic weapons in a future war. They could not, as a consequence, take that all-important factor into account when drawing up war plans. Despite the cost, then, Britain would have to press ahead with a relatively large bomb-building program.[2]

There was a chance, however, the British chiefs believed, that American assistance might yet be forthcoming to reduce the burden. Although arrangements for a supply of American atomic weapons under British control, under discussion in late 1949, had been ruled out by the Fuchs betrayal, it might be possible to revive the idea after the American presidential election in November and after detonation of the first British atomic device. That latter event might just be the lever to move the heavy weight of Anglo-American noncooperation off dead center. In any event, they believed it probable that should war come, the United States would make available to the Royal Air Force a supply of American atomic weapons. It was all the more necessary then for the government to speed construction of atomic-capable V-bombers for strategic air offensive purposes. They recommended, in addition, that the government build more reactors, double the output of plutonium within three years, and accelerate the planned pace of bomb building.[3]

Although the British chiefs were cognizant of the costs of building up Britain's nuclear power, they were even more impressed by the destructiveness of atomic weapons and the potential destructiveness of hydrogen weapons. Slessor and Chief of the Imperial General Staff Sir William Slim, in particular, believed that the advent of the hydrogen bomb would diminish severely the effectiveness of large conventional forces. When Slessor went in July 1952 to the Pentagon and met with the JCS, therefore, he tried to persuade the Americans that a radical change in strategy was necessary. There were two strategic alternatives for the defense of Western Europe, he told the JCS. NATO could build up a force of 98 divisions and 10,000 aircraft—"an economic impossibility, a logistic nightmare and a strategic nonsense"—or the allies could adopt a strategy based primarily upon atomic air power and reduce conventional force levels to cut costs. This, Slessor maintained, was "strategically sound and economically practicable" and afforded "the best hope of preventing war." General Bradley was not convinced that atomic attacks would be decisive. Recalling how the Germans had carried on in the latter years of World War II despite the allies' massive bombing campaign, he suggested that Slessor was not taking proper account of "modern defensive measures." Aside from that, adopting a new strategy was premature. Atomic weapons for purely tactical use would not be available in sufficient numbers until 1955. Unspoken but probably a factor in Bradley's comments was the American desire for the rearmament of Germany and other allied measures to reduce the burden on U.S. forces for the conventional military defense of Western Europe. The upshot of the meetings was that American strategy for deterring Soviet attack, despite the fact that the NATO allies were backing rapidly away from providing the 50 divisions promised at Lisbon, remained the same.[4]

On October 3, 1952, at the Monte Bello Islands in Australia, the British successfully tested their first atomic device. The British Parliament and people were naturally proud, as was the government, but British officials did not pause to pat themselves on the back. They opened another campaign to persuade American policymakers that cooperation in the field of atomic energy was in the best interests of the United States.

Immediately after the detonation of the device, British officials let it be known that they believed their atomic test had demonstrated that they could make a "substantial contribution" to any plan to exchange information. They hinted that their bomb had been different from American models and might offer improvements in design. Since both they and the Soviets now had an atomic capability, moreover, security restrictions on all technical atomic details were less important than in 1946 when Congress had passed the McMahon Act. Certainly nuclear scientists on both sides of the Atlantic believed that this was so and favored pooling information to accelerate research and development efforts. Even the American chairman of the JCS wanted to reveal some information about atomic weapons to the allies, if only to facilitate cooperation on combined operations. Winston Churchill reiterated the British plea for cooperation in the House of Commons on October 23. The British bomb, he said, had been exploded inside a naval vessel in a test to determine the impact of an atomic detonation in a harbor. One of the results of the test, he assured, would be closer ties to the United States in nuclear matters and an interchange of information.[5]

Optimism in the British government about the prospects for Anglo-American nuclear relations became even more marked after the American presidential election on November 5, 1952. Former Supreme Allied Commander Europe Dwight D. Eisenhower won the election by a substantial margin. Knowing that Eisenhower had always believed that the Americans had treated the British very shabbily on nuclear matters after the war and that he had favored and argued for increased cooperation within the administration in 1949, Churchill was publicly ebullient. In response to a question in the House of Commons on November 20, he said that he wanted to exchange information not only about the atomic bomb but about developments in the hydrogen bomb as well once Eisenhower took the oath of office in January 1953.[6]

The Prime Minister's enthusiasm was not just for public consumption. So certain was he that a sea change in Anglo-American nuclear relations was imminent that he refused to support the doubling of plutonium output (to be effected by construction of another atomic pile) proposed by the British chiefs and Lord Cherwell. His understanding had always been, he carefully explained, that the Americans would eventually supply the British with bombs for British use. The change of American administration and the success of the British atomic bomb test should make this kind of collaboration a reality. At any rate, he wanted to postpone the decision to begin a costly expansion of the British nuclear program until he talked to the newly elected President and listened to his views. The Prime Minister's decision to wait sorely disappointed Cherwell. Britain urgently needed a new atomic pile, he argued, not only for military purposes but to produce more fissile material for industrial applications. Even if Eisenhower did decide to give Britain as many as 50 atomic bombs, "new dual-purpose piles" would still be needed to learn how to design and use reactors to make electricity. For only six million more pounds per year for four years, he could launch the full expansion program.[7]

Adamant that negotiations with the Americans had to be tried first, Churchill turned aside Cherwell's arguments and arranged to meet with the President-elect in Washington on January 5, 1953, a year to the day after he had arrived for the meetings with Truman. Britain, he told Eisenhower and the press the day he arrived, could be a "useful partner" for the United States in the field of atomic energy if only given a chance. He did not say, but might well have been thinking, that cooperation between British and American scientists could accelerate the development of the hydrogen bomb. In this he would have been wrong. The United States had already secretly detonated a thermonuclear device on October 31, 1952 (November 1, 1952, Washington time) at the Eniwetok test site in the Pacific. The British and Canadians had been informed a few days before that two explosions were scheduled for early November but had not been informed of the nature of either.[8]

The Americans were seemingly leaving the British further and further behind in the development of atomic energy for military purposes. Because most American policymakers believed that this was so and that the British, even after testing an atomic device, had little new data to offer in an exchange of information, the idea of cooperation was far less enticing than the British had hoped. Then there were the complicating factors of intra-American policy disagreements and persistent American doubts about the adequacy of British security standards. After the negotiations of 1949 and the Fuchs spy scandal of early 1950, the Truman administration had never again put together a consensus on a realistic plan for substantial collaboration with the British on nuclear matters. There had never been an American willingness to consult on the use of atomic weapons. Churchill and a few others might doggedly persist in the idea that the coming of Eisenhower would sweep away all barriers to cooperation, but those who had been involved in negotiations with the Americans on nuclear matters longest had to wonder. Would Eisenhower's broom be strong enough to sweep away opposition from the JCAE? Or would the McMahon Act prove once again mightier than the policymakers?

NOTES

1. 501 *H.C. Deb.* 5s., p. 31.
2. Margaret Gowing, *Independence and Deterrence: Britain and Atomic Energy, 1945-1952*, vol. 1 (London: Macmillan, 1974), pp. 440-43; John Simpson, *The Independent Nuclear State: The United States, Britain, and the Military Atom* (London: Macmillan, 1983), p. 69.
3. Ibid.
4. R. N. Rosencrance, *Defense of the Realm: British Strategy in the Nuclear Epoch* (New York: Columbia University Press, 1968), p. 173; Walter S. Poole, *The History of the Joint Chiefs of Staff: The Joint Chiefs of Staff and National Policy*, vol. 4 (Wilmington, Del.: Michael Glazier, 1980), pp. 309-10.
5. *New York Times*, Oct. 12, 1952, sec. 4, p. 6; 505 *H.C. Deb.* 5s., pp. 1270-71.
6. 507 *H.C. Deb.* 5s., pp. 2042-43; Gowing, *Independence and Deterrence* 1: 448-49.
7. Ibid.
8. *New York Times*, Jan. 6, 1953, p. 1; Memorandum for File, by Arneson, Washington, October 27, 1952, G/PM Files, lot 68D349, "Ivy," *Foreign Relations of the United States*, 1952-54, 2:1036-37.

13
GETTING ORGANIZED

> What they [the British] really want to know is that we are not starting a war.
> —Dwight D. Eisenhower, March 7, 1953[1]

Upon taking office, the new President had very clear in his mind a set of general principles to guide decision making on domestic, foreign, and military policy. His administration must discover a "reasonable and respectable posture of defense," he told the new members of the NSC on February 11, 1953. If this goal could be achieved and maintained over the long haul, the overall budget could be controlled, the economy would continue to grow, and the United States would remain strong enough to combat the growth of Soviet influence around the world. If it could not, the next four years might be difficult ones for the United States both at home and abroad.[2]

Keeping a firm rein on defense spending did not mean that Eisenhower intended to oversee the dismantling of American military might. It did mean that he intended to recast it into a different mold and at the same time redefine American national strategy. Under the leadership of the Truman administration, American and NATO conventional military strength had greatly increased, and the United States had adopted a national strategy of vigorously containing Soviet expansion wherever the Russian Bear prowled. Under the Eisenhower administration, the United States would place more emphasis on building up air and sea power, press the NATO allies to increase conventional strength and permit German rearmament, and rely more heavily on American nuclear superiority to deter Soviet aggression. With 1,600 operational atomic bombs to the Soviets' 50 to 100 in January 1953, the United States was still far ahead in this area. Greater emphasis on atomic weaponry, in addition, would enable the administration to reduce conventional forces and save money. By no means, however, did Eisenhower and Secretary of State John Foster Dulles intend the emphasis on air-atomic and sea power to signal the allies that the United States was backing away from the American commitment to Western European security. American defense ties not only to NATO countries but to Japan, South Korea, Australia, and others were essential to protect the United States' true interests and preserve the peace. Eisenhower was prepared to use nuclear weapons to defend those interests. At the end of March, for example, he told the NSC that he would be willing to employ atomic weapons in Korea if a "substantial victory over the Communist forces" could be achieved and the military stalemate broken. Fortunately, the war in Korea was ultimately resolved by negotiation of an armistice agreement in July 1953, permanently dividing the country along the 38th parallel. But Eisenhower's commitment to resort to nuclear weapons if necessary was clear.[3]

Because the defense policy he was proposing was so different from what had been the norm in the last few years of the Truman administration, Eisenhower understood that a concerted effort would have to be made to win the support of the Republican-controlled Congress. He warned his subordinates to "exercise particular care to make certain of appropriate and timely consultation with Congressional leaders in all matters where this seems necessary or desirable." Already the administration was being challenged by anti-interventionists in the Republican party led by Robert A. Taft, senator from Ohio and the man Eisenhower had bested for the Republican nomination, and John W. Bricker, the junior senator from Ohio and author of the Bricker amendment. The Bricker amendment was designed to limit presidential authority to make treaties with foreign powers that contradicted American law, require specific legislation to ratify all treaties and executive agreements, and possibly even give Congress veto power over presidential authority to send American combat troops into action in the absence of a declaration of war. Isolationist in nature and strongly opposed to foreign aid, the anti-interventionists wanted the United States to develop a Western Hemispheric defense concept. The Eisenhower administration did pursue plans to develop civil and continental defense against Soviet nuclear attack but shrugged off isolationist arguments to draw back from the policy of worldwide alliances. Eisenhower also had to worry about Senator Joseph R. McCarthy (R., Wisconsin) and his publicity-seeking campaign to find Communists in every corridor of power in Washington. Because he thought the junior senator from Wisconsin would eventually overplay his hand and lose influence, and because he too was concerned with security (especially the security of American nuclear secrets, as evidenced by his decision not to grant clemency to the atomic spies Alfred and Ethel Rosenberg), he declined to speak out against McCarthy's excesses. In the end, attempts by the right wing of the Republican party to interfere with Eisenhower administration policy largely failed.[4]

Getting Organized

In no policy-making area would cooperation with Congress be more important than in the field of atomic energy, but relations between the new administration and the JCAE got off to a rocky beginning. Part of the problem involved a bitter battle within the JCAE between senators and members of the House of Representatives over the committee chairmanship. In this nonpartisan struggle, members of the House insisted that the chairmanship, heretofore held exclusively by senators, alternate. Neither side would yield, and the result was stalemate from January through April 1953. Finally, Hickenlooper stepped aside in favor of Representative W. Sterling Cole (R., New York).[5]

The JCAE was also weakened in its dealings with Eisenhower when the FBI discovered that a "vitally important report" prepared by the technical staff of the JCAE had been lost. Upon hearing that the report, consisting of a summary of the development of the hydrogen bomb, had mistakenly been classified secret, not top secret, and sent to a Princeton College professor, Eisenhower was furious. At a meeting of the NSC on February 18, 1953, he said that if the persons responsible for the lost report had been members of the armed forces, they would have been shot. It was small consolation that the JCAE technical staff would (he understood) be abolished after the new chairman was chosen.[6]

Temporarily at least, Eisenhower could use JCAE disorganization to steal a march and reorder the manner in which nuclear matters would be handled within the administration. This he did by appointing former AEC commissioner Lewis L. Strauss as his special assistant for atomic energy affairs, with plans to make Strauss chairman of the AEC on July 1, 1953, when Gordon Dean's term expired. Since the President intended that Strauss remain his special assistant after July 1, members of the JCAE complained that Strauss's dual role would impair relations with the committee. Strauss would attend NSC meetings and international conferences and feel bound to maintain silence about the topics of those conversations. This reticence, in turn, might inhibit his ability to keep the JCAE fully and currently informed about developments within the American nuclear program. The President had made up his mind, however, and the disorganized JCAE could not get him to reverse Strauss's appointment. Nor could they prevent the AEC from drawing up plans for the participation of private industry in the development of "practical nuclear power." Because most Democrats wanted the government to construct and operate power reactors to speed development, the issue continued to be a point of contention between the AEC and the JCAE through both terms of Eisenhower's administration.[7]

With the coming of the Eisenhower administration to power, British officials mapped out potential areas of cooperation with the Americans. Quite naturally, they wanted any information the Americans would be willing to give in the nuclear field, especially if it could be used for the urgent development of nuclear reactors for the production of electric power. But they were also interested in the use of nuclear propulsion. The Americans were working on nuclear propulsion of submarines and other naval vessels, and this might be a possible area of negotiation. Another area in which collaboration would reduce costs was testing. Now that Britain had proven it could detonate an atomic device without American assistance, the question of national pride was no longer so important. Provided arrangements for a reciprocal exchange of information were satisfactory, the British government would be willing to agree to joint tests at American test sites. The outlook for this possibility, however, probably depended upon changes in American law. Until that was accomplished, the British government would have to struggle along on its own or in cooperation with Australia. At any rate, Churchill ordered further steps to allay American concerns about British security. A committee of experts, headed by Lord Waverly (formerly Sir John Anderson), was set up in January 1953 to study plans for the reorganization of the British nuclear program.[8]

Then there was the question of consultation on the use of the bomb. Addressing the Royal Institute of International Affairs in March 1953, Sir John Slessor complained that at the recent ten-day NATO conference in Paris, discussions about strategic air power had been completely avoided by the Americans. American military officers had cited the McMahon Act as a barrier to revealing information about the atomic capabilities of SAC and had referred to the Red-baiting activities of Senator McCarthy as a disincentive to a freer discussion of the issue. As a result, only the United States, Britain, and to a lesser extent Canada knew anything about modern strategic air power. Since the Americans alone had a strategic bomber force of any significance, the British had little influence on American nuclear policy and strategic planning. This situation was intolerable. In order to remain a Great Power, Britain too must have a strategic bomber force no matter what the cost. The United States could no longer be permitted to have a monopoly on this "instrument of such enormous, such decisive influence for peace and war."[9]

On the American side, the importance of consultation had been raised by a State Department Panel of Consultants on Disarmament that had worked through the last year of the Truman administration to recommend an American negotiating position on the arms race and disarmament. The panel, chaired by Robert Oppenheimer and including among its members Vannevar Bush and Allen W. Dulles, issued its report in January 1953. "No small part of the uncertainty which surrounds the field of atomic weapons," they wrote, "derives from a widespread feeling [among the allies] that the United States is clutching the atom to its bosom and may at any moment get angry and hurl it in the general direction of the Kremlin." Greater cooperation, then, with the allies was needed along with attempts at serious bilateral talks with the Soviets to reduce tensions. A first step would be communication of information to the allies to give them a greater understanding of the atomic bomb itself. But the panel did not suggest that the American government "tie its own hands and surrender the right to decide for itself, in an emergency, whether and how it will use its atomic weapons." The new administration felt the same way about it. On March 7, 1953, two days after Joseph V. Stalin died in Moscow, new Secretary of State John Foster Dulles reported to the President about conversations he was having in Washington with Anthony Eden concerning American air bases in Britain, Iran, and elsewhere. Former President Truman, Eden had alleged, had given Churchill a "personal assurance" at the January 1952 meetings that the Prime Minister would be consulted on the use of atomic weapons. Eden and the Prime Minister wanted to insure that Eisenhower would adhere to that agreement. Eisenhower refused to be pinned down. "What they really want to know," he told Dulles, "is that we are not starting a war." As for assurances—well, perhaps Dulles should talk to Bedell Smith (now under secretary of state). Smith, he thought, knew more about the past history of talks on the subject of consultation than did he.[10]

In the early days of the Eisenhower admnistration, the only area of effective Anglo-American nuclear cooperation was in the joint control of raw materials. But as in the past, American officials attempted to limit the British share. Such was the case in April 1953 when British Ambassador Roger Makins sent Dulles a letter requesting a 1953 allocation for the British program of 500 tons of U_3O_8 (uranium ore). Rafford L. Faulkner, assistant director for foreign procurement of the AEC's Division of Raw Materials, wanted the British request reduced by 75 tons to avoid interfering with the American expansion plan.[11]

Any effort to persuade the British to scale back their nuclear program would at this point, however, have been profoundly discouraging to the British, since Churchill had such high hopes for cooperation with the Eisenhower administration. And indeed Eisenhower did desire cooperation, though to what extent was still uncertain. He would listen to the advice of the interested parties within the administration before making his decision. Upon receipt of a policy letter from Dean on March 6, 1953, explaining the AEC's position on the development of practical nuclear power (NSC 145), he decided to have the AEC, State, and Defense Departments put their proposals for major revisions of the McMahon Act before the NSC. This was done on March 11, 1953. Whle the State Department advocated support for the AEC policy of permitting private industry to help in developing nuclear power, Dulles and Arneson also wanted to insert additional language. They wanted authority "to deal with certain foreign governments in this area, not only to assure the continuance of the flow of uranium and other raw materials to the United States from present suppliers, but also to stimulate such a flow from other potential producers." Likewise, the JCS and DOD wanted to tack on language to the AEC's proposal. They wanted legislation to permit the exchange of certain nuclear information with the allies if this was in the interest of national security. Eisenhower thought this and other proposed changes good ideas. He asked the AEC to put together legislation combining the different proposals in "non-technical language" for his consideration.[12]

On June 8, 1953, the President took a public stand on cooperation in the field of atomic energy with the allies. The McMahon Act, he said, had been passed in 1946 when the United States had had a monopoly in the nuclear field and had been designed to preserve that monopoly. Since both the British and the Soviets now had the atomic bomb, the act was outmoded. It had to be revised in a way that permitted exchanges of information with the allies. Although the British were quick to hail Eisenhower's remarks as vindication of their position that excessive American secrecy had led to unnecessary research duplication, a waste of money and materials, and the loss of valuable time in the face of a common threat, new Chairman of the JCAE Cole showed little enthusiasm for the President's pronouncement. The AEC, he said, could release more information to the allies simply by clearing the transfer with the Joint Committee. He urged caution on exchanges of nuclear information, however, and said that there was no need for a change in the law. Acting Senate leader William F. Knowland (R., California) added that there was no chance that new legislation would pass before the end of the current session on July 31, 1953.[13]

The earliest the administration would be able to put its proposals before Congress, then, was January 1954, but that did not stop Dean from arguing in the press for greater cooperation. He even revealed JCS proposals to give the allies data on the size, weight, and shape of American atomic weapons, weapons effects, and other information concerning the use of atomic weapons in joint defense or retaliation operations. But Dean was replaced by Strauss on July 1, 1953, and the administration's atomic energy legislation now passed into the hands of a man who earlier had been a fervent opponent of cooperation with the British and an intense advocate of maximum security for atomic secrets. The British feared he would prove so again. It is interesting to note that Strauss had not sought the chairmanship of the AEC. The President had pressed it upon him because he intended the AEC chairman to be a major policymaker in his administration and wanted a like-minded Republican in the job. After a search for other acceptable candidates failed to produce someone willing to give full devotion to the post, Strauss accepted.[14]

Strauss and Dulles would be the two most important advisors to the President on nuclear matters and would view the idea of collaboration with the British far less enthusiastically than had Dean and Acheson. In fact, they would restrain Eisenhower to a certain extent in his desire to make up to the British for their spare treatment by the Truman administration on nuclear matters. Their sometimes torpid attitude toward improving Anglo-American nuclear relations, however, was partially counterbalanced by the vigor of the new members of the JCS (appointed in May to take office later in the summer of 1953). Chairman Admiral Arthur W. Radford and Chief of Staff of the Air Force Nathan F. Twining, in particular, advocated a far more aggressive American attitude in foreign affairs while the United States maintained its huge strategic advantage over the Soviets. Consequently, they viewed cooperation with allies in a far more favorable light and advocated information exchanges on use of atomic weapons. Despite the different perspectives of his key advisors, the President believed that he had chosen men who would further the basic policies of his administration.[15]

In mid-July 1953 the JCS considered seeking an interim arrangement to permit exchanging information on use of atomic weapons with the allies in the absence of new authorizing legislation. They wanted the AEC to reinterpret the data in question as no longer "restricted data" within the meaning of the McMahon Act and thereby circumvent JCAE opposition. But fearing AEC objections, General Bradley recommended to new Secretary of Defense Charles E. Wilson that he persuade the Special Committee of the NSC to petition the attorney general for a legal ruling that the security provisions of the present Atomic Energy Act did not apply to the DOD in its military application of atomic energy. Granted, a hornet's nest of opposition would arise from the JCAE once the members discovered that Congress was being circumvented, but the administration was currently struggling with plans to use large numbers of atomic weapons for the defense of Western Europe against Soviet attack. The plans would come to naught unless the JCS had authority to familiarize the allies with atomic weapons and their use.[16]

Planning to rely more and more on atomic weapons was being facilitated by the advance of technology. In 1952 stockpiling had begun on small atomic bombs to be carried by fighters, fighter-bombers, light bombers, and general purpose aircraft operating from forward airfields and aircraft carriers. More advances were to come. The military was developing atomic weapons to destroy submarines, subsonic turbojet guided missiles (maximum range 500 miles) to be deployed in two to five years on land, from submarines, and on surface ships, and ground combat assisting weapons—unguided ground-fired rockets and short-range (75-150 miles) guided missiles—to be deployed in 1953-54. These weapons would supplement the main bomber striking force of B-47s (fully operational in 1953) and longer-range B-52s and B-60s (fully operational in 1956). But it was clear that emphasis in the future would be on guided missiles, including those with intercontinental range.[17]

In light of these technological advances, and with an eye toward finding a reasonable and economic defense posture as ordered by the President, the NSC conducted a review of U.S. policy and strategy called Project Solarium. In a memorandum on July 22, 1953, Lay described the three basic alternatives open to the administration. The United States, he wrote, could adopt a strategy of defending only its vital interests in the world, or it could draw a line around NATO and the Western Pacific to repel all aggression that violated those boundaries, or it could attempt to disturb and weaken the Soviet bloc while simultaneously strengthening the free world to "assume the greater risks involved" in such an undertaking. The long-term objective of this latter strategy would be not only to defend American interests but ultimately to free from Soviet control the Eastern European satellites and mainland China. The discussion of the last option included a section on insuring counter-air-atomic strikes in the event of Soviet attack. In order to preserve a retaliatory capability, assembled atomic weapons would have to be given to tactical units on foreign soil. Intergovernmental agreements with NATO allies would probably be necessary.[18]

Although a final decision on basic American national policy and strategy was three months away, the British were anxious to open discussions right away. While announcing in the House of Commons that Britain would test its second atomic device in October 1953 in Australia, Minister of Supply Duncan Sandys declared on July 31 the British government's "extreme readiness to have a frank exchange" of nuclear information with the United States on a completely reciprocal basis. Britain, he added, would take steps to assure the security-conscious Americans that British safeguards would be the same as those in effect in the United States.[19]

On August 8, 1953, the cause of Anglo-American cooperation received an unexpected boost from the Soviets. Premier Georgi M. Malenkov announced that the United States no longer possessed a monopoly on the hydrogen bomb. Prepared to back up words with action, the Soviets did explode a hydrogen bomb on August 12. Since the Soviets had closed the gap between their nuclear program and the American, confirmation of the Soviet test had a significant impact in Washington, though not perhaps as dramatic a one as had occurred after the first Soviet atomic test in the late summer of 1949. Bradley, now retired as chairman of the JCS, called publicly for relaxation of atomic energy regulations to permit cooperation between the United States and the NATO allies. Of far more importance was the reaction of JCAE Chairman Cole. "I presume," he wrote the President on August 21, 1953, "that this latest sign of Soviet atomic progress will be reflected in the plans you and your advisors are formulating for more effective defenses against nuclear attack from land or sea." He also gave his support from further steps to expand the American nuclear program, a policy of releasing information on the effects of atomic weapons to promote greater awareness of the threat, and administration efforts to pursue a prudent international control of atomic energy agreement. But noticeably absent from his list was expanded cooperation on nuclear matters with the allies. The administration would have to do more to convince him.[20]

In its first eight months in office, the Eisenhower administration laid the foundation for improving Anglo-American nuclear cooperation. The bedrock ideas of a sound, growing economy, stable, prudent defense spending, greater reliance on nuclear weapons in the event of war, and greater cooperation with allies dictated early on a thorough reassessment of American national security policy and the state of nuclear relations with the allies. Almost immediately, a consensus began to form among the interested parties that some revision of the McMahon Act to permit exchanges of nuclear information with the allies and on the utilization of atomic weapons was desirable. The only question was, would the administration go as far toward complete collaboration as Churchill wanted? Or would it leave untouched the restrictions against revealing information applicable to the design and manufacture of atomic weapons, the production of fissionable material, and the use of fissionable material for the production of power? To a large extent, the outcome of the national security policy review, the ability of the AEC, State, and Defense Departments to consolidate the consensus, and the opinions of the members of the now reorganized JCAE would influence President Eisenhower's decision.

NOTES

1. Dulles, Telephone Call to Eisenhower, March 7, 1953, *Minutes of Telephone Conversations of John Foster Dulles and Christian Herter, 1953-1961* (Frederick, Md.: University Publications of America, 1980), reel 8, p. 704.

2. Memorandum of Discussion at 131st Meeting of NSC, February 11, 1953, Eisenhower Library, Eisenhower Papers, Whitman File, *Foreign Relations of the United States* (hereafter cited as *FRUS*), 1952-54, 2:236-37; Samuel P. Huntington, *The Common Defense: Strategic Programs in National Politics* (New York: Columbia University Press, 1961), pp. 64-69.

3. Huntington, *Common Defense*, pp. 63-64; Memorandum of Discussion at Special NSC Meeting, March 31, 1953, Eisenhower Library, Eisenhower Papers, Whitman File, *FRUS*, 152-54, 2:264-81; Ambrose, *Eisenhower*, pp. 50, 94. In late January and early February 1953 the Europeans were urging the United States to deploy more American atomic weapons to Europe to allow them to control defense expenditures. The United States had only 16 atomic bombs of 20 kilotons each deployed at this time in Europe.

4. Memorandum by Eisenhower, White House, March 3, 1953, *Minutes and Documents of Cabinet Meetings of President Eisenhower (1953-61)*, Presidential Documents Series (Frederick, Md.: University Publications of America, 1980), p. 214; Memorandum by Nitze and Savage, Washington, May 6, 1953; Report of NSC by Special Evaluation Subcommittee of NSC, Wahsington, May 18, 1953, PPS Files, lot 64D563, "National Security, Civil Defenses," *FRUS*, 1952-54, 2:318-23, 328-49.

5. Harold P. Green and Alan Rosenthal, *Government of the Atom* (New York: Atherton Press, 1963), pp. 12, 55-56.

6. Memorandum of Discussion of 132d Meeting of NSC, February 18, 1953, Eisenhower Library, Eisenhower Papers, Whitman File, *FRUS*, 1952-54, 2:1106-9.

7. Report to NSC by AEC (NSC 145), Washington, March 6, 1953, S/S-NSC Files, lot 63D351, NSC 145, *FRUS*, 1952-54, 2:1121-25.

8. 510 *H.C. Deb.* 5s., pp. 673-76; *New York Times*, June 25, 1953, p. 14; Peter Pringle and James Spigelman, *The Nuclear Barons* (New York: Holt, Rinehart, and Winston, 1981), p. 139.

9. Sir John Slessor, *The Great Deterrent* (New York: Frederick A. Praeger, 1957), pp. 122-26.

10. Report by Panel of Consultants on Disarmament, Washington, January 1953, Disarmament Files, lot 58D133, *FRUS*, 1952-54, 2:1056-91; Dulles, Telephone Call to Eisenhower, March 7, 1953, *Telephone Conversations of Dulles*, reel 8, p. 704; Walter S. Poole, *The History of the Joint Chiefs of Staff: The Joint Chiefs of Staff and National Policy*, vol. 4, *1950-1952* (Wilmington, Del.: Michael Glazier, 1980), p. 159 n. 32. On June 24, 1953, Eisenhower agreed that nuclear components could be sent "to those storages afloat and ashore wherein the decision to so deploy rests solely with the United States."

11. Memorandum for Files by Hamilton, Washington, April. 13, 1953, AE Files, lot 57D688, "CDA-General"; Memorandum by Arneson, Washington, December 3, 1953, PPS Files, lot 64D563, "AE," *FRUS*, 1952-54, 2:1141-44, 1251-55.

12. Minutes of Cabinet Meeting, March 6, 1953, *Cabinet Meetings of Eisenhower*, pp. 211-13; Memorandum by Arneson to Dulles, Washington, March 10, 1953, PPS Files, lot 64D563, "AE-Armaments 1952-53"; Memorandum of Discussion at 136th Meeting of NSC, Wednesday, March 11, 1953, Eisenhower Library, Eisenhower Papers, Whitman Files, *FRUS*, 1952-54, 2:1125-33, 1180.

13. *New York Times*, June 9, 1953, pp. 1, 3.

14. Ibid., June 26, 1953, p. 4; Lewis L. Strauss, *Men and Decisions* (Garden City, N.Y.: Doubleday, 1962), pp. 333-35.

15. Note by the Secretaries to JCS on Military Objectives to be Provided for in Proposed Atomic Energy Legislation (JCS 2172/26), December 14, 1953, CCS 471.6 (8-15-45), sec. 46, RG 218, Central Decimal File 1951-53, box 170, Modern Military Branch, National Archives.

16. Memorandum by Bradley, July 14, 1953, CCS 471.6 (8-15-45), sec. 39, RG 218, Central Decimal File 1951-53, box 169, Modern Military Branch, National Archives.

17. Memorandum by Lay, Washington, November 5, 1952, Truman Library, Truman Papers, PSF-Subject File, *FRUS*, 1952-54, 2:165-81.

18. Memorandum by Lay, Washington, July 22, 1953, S/S-NSC Files, lot 66D148, "Solarium," *FRUS*, 1952-54, 2:399-434.

19. *New York Times*, Aug. 1, 1953, p. 9.

20. Ibid., Aug. 31, 1953, p. 4; Cole to Eisenhower, Washington, August 21, 1953, S/S-NSC Files, lot 66D95, "NSC 151 Memos," *FRUS*, 1952-54, 2:1185-88.

14
FUNDAMENTAL DECISIONS

> In many ways, he's just a little Peter Pan.
> —Dwight D. Eisenhower on
> Winston Churchill, October 23, 1953[1]

In early September 1953, with the news of the Soviet hydrogen bomb fresh in his mind, President Eisenhower contemplated a future of growing American and Soviet nuclear stockpiles, perhaps an increased danger of war, and certainly increased risk to the United States. Programs to defend the country and develop civil defense, he must have reflected, would not be completely effective once the Soviets accelerated nuclear weapons production and devised delivery systems to carry those weapons. They might not work at all if the Soviets perfected the technology for intercontinental ballistic missiles. Nor did the prospects for disarmament look promising. The Soviets had consistently refused to agree to an adequate system of inspection and verification to insure compliance with any proposed agreement. They gave no intimation that they would do so anytime soon. No, this dilemma required a different kind of solution. If only the fissionable material the superpowers used to make weapons could be turned to peaceful uses, the waste of a nuclear arms race might still be avoided. It was an idea that Eisenhower continued to think about until he developed the Atoms for Peace plan in early October.[2]

While the President brooded about great issues, the British opened another front in the campaign to persuade the United States that Britain too was a factor in the nuclear age. In September 1953 they attempted to arouse American curiosity about their new highly advanced Delta-winged jet fighters and bombers, showcased at a defense exhibition at Farnborough. Next, they dropped hints in the press about supposed progress in the development of guided missiles and of "certain mechanisms" associated with atomic bombs. Finally, in late September Churchill dispatched Cockcroft and Sir Christopher Hinton, deputy controller of British atomic energy production, to North America for technical discussions with the United States and Canada. The Prime Minister also arranged simultaneously for the United States to send two B-29 "Flying Laboratories" to help obtain final data on atmospheric conditions so that the British could set and plan the exact time of their upcoming atomic tests at the Woomera rocket range in Australia in October.[3]

Churchill indicated the importance he attached to the talks with the Americans by sending Lord Cherwell to Washington in early October 1953. Unfortunately, the Americans were willing to give away promises but little else. Strauss informed the British that the administration was preparing an amendment to permit private industry to enter the nuclear power field and that included in this legislation was a provision for exchanging information and materials applicable to nuclear power development with foreign governments. Prospects for passage appeared good, since many members of the JCAE approved. But less certain of success was an amendment to permit the JCS to collaborate more fully with the British and other NATO allies in nuclear planning. Congress still vigorously opposed communicating atomic weapons secrets to foreign governments.[4]

During the talks, Cherwell attempted to elicit information about the important field of weapons effects, in particular debris analysis. That data would be invaluable, he explained, to British scientists currently conducting atomic tests. Strauss told him bluntly that the administration could not help. Discussing debris analysis required using American atomic weapons and weapons tests as a "base of reference." That would be a violation of American law. Although he personally favored communicating nonweapons data, including the effects on certain targets of blast, heat, and radiation resulting from atomic explosions, even this kind of exchange would have to be cleared with the JCAE.[5]

Subsequently, JCAE permission for a partial transfer of weapons effects information was secured. During another meeting with Cherwell in early November 1953, Strauss contacted members of the JCAE by telephone and won their agreement to an exchange with the British of nonweapons information. Cole further heartened the British by telling the newspapers that he was now ready to support a greater exchange of information on the atom and atomic weapons with at least "the top people of our allies."[6]

On October 30, 1953, the President approved NSC 162/2 as a new statement of American national policy and strategy. In order to meet the threat posed to the United States by the Soviet Union, and to do so without "seriously weakening the United States economy or undermining our fundamental values and institutions," the United States had to emphasize in its military posture the massive retaliatory capability and deterrent effect of American offensive striking power. In conjunction with the allies, in addition, the United States had to maintain an adequate level of readiness to counter Soviet attacks, hold vital areas, and keep open lines of communication. The American mobilization base had to be preserved and protected.[7]

Reliance on American strategic air power, the document went on, and nuclear weapons generally would continue to require overseas bases. In a war, the United States would "consider nuclear weapons as to be as available for use as other munitions." That meant that the United States needed advance consent, where such consent was required, from foreign governments to launch atomic strikes and otherwise use nuclear weapons from foreign bases. The administration, therefore, should pursue such understandings by diplomatic means and secure prior allied consent for such actions where possible. Cooperation of allies was important in one other respect. Since the United States was shifting to reliance on its nuclear deterrent, the allies would have to assume a greater share of the ground combat burden. Germany and Japan would have to be rearmed, even over the objections of France and others. Overall, the key to the new strategy was providing an adequate defense while maintaining a sound and growing economy over the long haul. Accomplishing this goal would probably require "redeployments" of American combat troops from Western Europe and Korea to the continental United States.[8]

Adoption of NSC 162/2 had important implications for American atomic weapons policy. The intention to rely primarily on strategic air power and tactical atomic weapons to deter aggression, and to use those weapons immediately if the Soviets attacked, made it necessary to transfer custody of more, if not all, atomic weapons to the DOD. The State Department approved such a transfer. But it did not believe that the military should have the right to use nuclear weapons automatically in all situations—especially not in limited or localized wars. It wanted the President to decide on a case-by-case basis when to authorize use, although in certain cases like an atomic Pearl Harbor, automatic use would be appropriate.[9]

The new national security policy also gave greater urgency to administration efforts to collaborate with allies on use of atomic weapons. But Cole and most members of the JCAE were far from convinced that McMahon Act restrictions ought to be relaxed to the extent desired by some within the administration. They still rigidly opposed, for example, giving atomic weapons, or information applicable to the design and manufacture of atomic weapons, to Britain or other allies. Nor did they see any longer a critical need to cooperate with the British on control of raw materials. As revealed in hearings of a Special Senate Subcommittee on Minerals, Materials, and Fuels Economic on November 12, 1953, in Salt Lake City, Utah, the United States was no longer a have-not nation in uranium. Because production from the Colorado River Plateau was increasing and new supplies had been discovered in Wyoming, Idaho, and Nevada, the United States would soon be self-sufficient in that critical mineral.[10]

Now that the administration could no longer use joint control of uranium as an overriding reason for improving nuclear ties with the British, cooperation for the common defense and security became the main theme. At the same time, fears about leaks through the British program to the Soviets began to recede somewhat. But some members raised another concern. They charged that while the United States concentrated on building a larger and more diverse stockpile of bombs, the British would use information exchanges to construct power reactors and gain a competitive advantage. They cited, for example, a breeder reactor currently being built in Britain designed to produce 50,000 kilowatts of electricity a day. Although the AEC was building a breeder reactor with a 60,000 kilowatt capacity, the British were slightly ahead. Democrats on the committee blamed this state of affairs on the administration's plan to encourage the development of nuclear power by private enterprise. If the AEC had been given the proper encouragement and resources, they thought, American development of power reactors would be second to none.[11]

In early November 1953 a December conference in Bermuda between Eisenhower, Churchill, and French Premier Joseph Laniel was arranged to discuss the EDC idea, Germany, Iran, and other topics of interest. It was anticipated that Churchill would want to hold private discussions with Eisenhower about atomic energy and press enthusiastically for greater cooperation. As would the Americans, he and his advisors planned to shift away from the previous emphasis on the mutual advantages of exchanging data to arguments that focused on the danger posed to the collective security of the West by Soviet nuclear development. Since the Soviets had progressed so far, the added security risk created by a complete exchange of atomic energy and weapons data was acceptable. Although they realized that the administration could not pool British and American information and efforts until Congress passed amendments to the McMahon Act, they intended to ask for details on the scope of the legislation Eisenhower would put before Congress and prospects for passage. If the proposals did not provide for significant improvement over the kinds and amount of cooperation agreed to in the Modus Vivendi of January 7, 1948, they would object strenuously.[12]

On November 18, 1953, Strauss forwarded to the President a summary of the proposed major revisions of the McMahon Act. The legislation pertaining to disclosure of nuclear information to selected allied governments was subsequently set forth in detail in NSC 151/1 on December 2, three days before the start of the Bermuda conference. If greater cooperation with the allies on atomic weapons matters was permitted, the document declared, the allies would be able to "participate intelligently" in military planning for their own defense and in combined operations with the United States, would be better able to understand atomic weapons effects and so take precautions to protect government officials and the general populace in the event of nuclear attack, and would be inspired to "act with the United States in crises and thus give the United States greater freedom of action to use atomic weapons as required." But even if the new legislation did not provide for atomic weapons data exchanges, it would still permit the United States to continue cooperation with the British and Canadians on nuclear intelligence, control of uranium, and in the nine fields of the Modus Vivendi.[13]

Believing, however, that the allies immediately required greater knowledge on the use of atomic weapons, the JCS had recently given some data—none considered restricted under the McMahon Act—to allied commanders and certain key staff officers in the Supreme Headquarters, Allied Powers Europe, on a strictly need-to-know basis. They had been told the number of American atomic weapons available for the tactical defense of Western Europe, the fact that they were all of the airburst variety, and that they averaged 20 kilotons of explosive power apiece. Under the proposed legislation, they intended to be more exact about specific kilotonnages, numbers of weapons within the various yield ranges, tactical use, and estimated results. But ominously, a dispute between the AEC and DOD over the meaning of "restricted data" as defined in the McMahon Act threatened to make the proposed legislation almost useless as a vehicle to transmit more information to the allies. As originally drafted, restricted data had been defined as "all data concerning the manufacture or utilization of atomic weapons, the production of fissionable material, or the use of fissionable material in the production of power." Although the DOD believed that the elimination of the words "or utilization of atomic weapons" would give it authority to make the desired exchanges, AEC officials had begun to think otherwise. They worried that data on utilization of atomic weapons would necessarily reveal information about the design and manufacture of atomic weapons. And in light of the past history of internal administration policy debates on nuclear matters, it would be very difficult to keep the AEC-DOD disagreement out of earshot of the members of the JCAE.[14]

NSC 151/1 was discussed in the NSC on December 3, 1953. In that debate Eisenhower overrode reservations by Strauss and the JCS and communicated his determination to promote the fullest possible cooperation and trust with Britain and other allies. Specifically, he rejected Strauss's insistence that the "rules governing the disclosure of information relating to numbers of [nuclear] weapons in the [U.S.] stockpile, past and present" be made more stringent for security reasons. "With some heat," the President stated that he wanted to treat the allies as allies. By this he did not mean that the United States was obligated to "reveal everything we know as to the number of weapons which would be made available for the defense of the allies in a general war, but, since you are asking your allies to take some pretty terrible risks in standing with you, it is certainly incumbent upon you to give them some good idea of the magnitudes which would be available for their defense. In short we should be in a position to reveal to them the nature and character of the military impact that our atomic weapons would have against an enemy attack."[15]

Nor was Eisenhower happy with a JCS suggestion that the NSC adopt a policy of giving information related to the numbers of American nuclear weapons available to Western European defense to NATO commanders rather than to NATO governments. Allied governmental leaders, he said, had to be given "some idea of the sweep of powers in our hands." Only in this way would the administration win their complete support for the new strategic concepts the United States was pushing with respect to increased reliance on nuclear weapons and redeployment of substantial numbers of forces from Europe to the United States. He himself and Dulles had to feel free to disclose nuclear information in high-level conferences with heads of allied states if such disclosure was in their judgment necessary.[16]

In his remarks, the President demonstrated to the members of the NSC his great displeasure with any interpretation of NSC 151/1, that limited cooperation with Britain and other NATO allies beyond those restrictions imposed by the McMahon Act. Nor would he feel obligated to withhold from allied leaders information vital to their defense, whether wording in the document seemed to require it or not. Lamely, Special Assistant to the President for National Security Affairs Robert Cutler attempted to diffuse Eisenhower's anger by suggesting that NSC 151/1 was only meant to be a general guidance. "It was assumed that the President would make such exceptions to this guidance as were in the national interest."[17]

What Eisenhower thought was in the national interest was sharing with the British not only the results of past American research but also atomic weapons, means of delivery, and strategy. But he understood full well that the McMahon Act and JCAE opposition made full and effective cooperation politically impossible. He would have to hide his true feelings at Bermuda and confine words and actions to the limitations set by NSC 151/1, adopted with minor changes as NSC 151/2 on December 4, 1953. He approached the conference apprehensively for one other reason. Churchill was reported to be almost deaf, reduced in stamina to the point where he worked mainly in the mornings, and increasingly unrealistic both about his own age and Britain's status in the world. He still believed his country a Great Power. If the Americans did not agree to significantly improved Anglo-American nuclear relations, Eisenhower worried, the Prime Minister might become difficult. It was very important, then, to project optimism about the possibility of improvement while politely holding the line against commitment.[18]

At a late morning meeting on the first day of the Bermuda conference, December 5, 1953, in Eisenhower's quarters at the Mid-Ocean Club, the President responded to a predictable Churchillian plea for a resumption of full-scale cooperation by quoting chapter and verse of the McMahon Act.

He himself was personally sympathetic to the Prime Minister's position, he assured, but his authority to act was limited by the law. Still, he promised to take steps to get Congress to pass an amendment to the McMahon Act when the next session began in January 1954. As proof of American good will, he cited the recent exchanges arranged by Strauss and Cherwell. Dreading the Prime Minister's reaction, he was pleasantly surprised to find Churchill reasonably vigorous and mentally alert. The older man appeared to realize that Britain was not dealing from a position of strength. Tacitly admitting that the British program had yet to, and would not in the near future, produce a sizeable stockpile of atomic bombs, he offered that in the event of war with the Soviets, the United States would probably want British planes to assist in the retaliatory strikes against the Soviet Union. But currently the new British V-bombers were being designed and built with no proper knowledge of the characteristics of American atomic weapons. The Royal Air Force needed to know at minimum the weight, dimensions, and ballistics of American bombs to build compatible bomb bays and release mechanisms into British planes. Bomb bays and release mechanisms had so far been designed to handle only British-made atomic weapons. Could not the Americans release this information?[19]

Strauss handled the reply. The weight, dimensions, and ballistics of American bombs, he said, were basic weapons data. He was sorry, but that information could not be provided. The Prime Minister experienced a moment of exasperation. Britain, he confessed, could not afford to spend so many millions of pounds to learn what the United States, its closest ally, already knew. This noncommunication between friends made no sense at all because Britain and the United States were faced by a common, very dangerous enemy. Cherwell nodded in agreement. Collaboration was essential to maximize their strength, he said, but the Americans need not tell all they knew. Because British strategists believed one-or two-megaton booster fission bombs were sufficient for almost all targets the British would want to attack, the British government had no intention of developing the hydrogen bomb. The administration need not contemplate revealing information in the thermonuclear area. The Americans would not reconsider. Exchange of basic atomic weapons information was expressly forbidden by the McMahon Act, they reiterated, and there was no possibility Congress would agree to lift the restriction.[20]

The discussion moved on to other nuclear questions, and Churchill tried to salvage what he could. After agreeing with Eisenhower that atomic weapons—in principle only—should be regarded as a proper part of conventional armaments, he inquired about a greater exchange of information concerning intelligence on enemy weapons and capabilities. Already the two allies were exchanging raw intelligence information and some finished intelligence reports on the Soviet nuclear program. Under the October 30, 1951, amendment, in addition, the United States had transmitted information pertaining to certain materials used in intelligence collection.

Why not go the full way? Once again, Strauss had to disappoint him. The United States, he explained, could not exchange information on evaluation methods for intelligence data because evaluation was done in terms of existing American nuclear weapons. Thwarted on all his major objectives, Churchill startled the Americans by producing suddenly the British copy of the 1943 Quebec Agreement. He wanted it published, he declared, along with all related documents. The idea was to reveal to the world and the American Congress the full extent of Anglo-American wartime cooperation in the field of atomic energy and so build public support for a return to collaboration. Eisenhower groped for words. He could only think to suggest that Strauss prepare a white paper on the subject with Cherwell's assistance.[21]

Perhaps it was Bermuda's warm climate or perhaps the stimulating environment of a major international conference, but Churchill refused to give up on making some kind of progress in atomic energy. On the morning of December 7, 1953, he handed Eisenhower a memorandum written by Cherwell expressing the British government's desire to extend interchanges on intelligence regarding Soviet nuclear tests. A little later in the day, he gave the President a second note, this time reminding Eisenhower that Strauss and Cherwell were to compile a white paper of documents to tell the story of Anglo-American relations about the atomic bomb. He and the President would then reconsider whether to publish. He intimated that he expected the President to agree since they both desired a greater interchange of information and believed that secrecy was "evaporating the growth of knowledge between us."[22]

Although Churchill had at the December 5, 1953, meeting agreed to the principle that atomic weapons be considered as a proper part of conventional weapons, he and his advisors (and the French too when the Americans raised the matter with them) stubbornly resisted automatic use of atomic weapons. They disliked the idea even in the event Communist forces struck again in Korea—unless the U.N. allies of the United States agreed in advance. American use of atomic weapons, the Prime Minister emphasized, even in Korea might cause the Soviets to retaliate by "attacking the population centers of the British Isles." Although he and his advisors continued to insist that the United States agree to consult in such crisis situations, the Americans refused to renounce their "right to use atomic weapons if war were forced upon us by the Soviets."[23]

The strong position taken by the Prime Minister, Eisenhower told the NSC on December 10, 1953, was motivated mainly by political considerations. In his last talk with Churchill in Bermuda, he confided, the Prime Minister had said that he was more concerned that the United States not announce its proposed automatic use of atomic weapons in the event of a Soviet attack than opposed to the American intention and planning to actually use them if necessary. Telling the world that the United States and its allies would resort so quicky to atomic weapons, especially in light of

Eisenhower's U.N. speech (given on December 8, 1953) on the peaceful uses of atomic energy, would be a terrible political mistake. Eisenhower thought that he had a temporary solution. The United States would continue to count on use of atomic weapons in the defense of Western Europe but would have the British and American chiefs of staff meet privately to discuss planning. Since Europeans generally thought of the use of atomic weapons as the "gateway to annihilation," not as a "great new source of defensive strength" like the Americans, no further mention would be made of it for the time being to the French and other Western European governments. Nor would the United States mention redeployment of troops from Western Europe and Korea to the continental United States. Statements on that topic might tip the American hand on use of atomic weapons or, conversely, send a false signal that the United States was backing away from its commitment to Western European security. Such statements would certainly complicate negotiations on EDC ratification. Four days later at the NATO conference in Paris, Secretary of State Dulles managed both to send the wrong signal and to complicate the EDC negotiations. Angered by NATO failure to meet agreed military commitments, he warned that unless a European army was approved soon, the United States would undertake "an agonizing reappraisal" of basic American policies.[24]

As he had indicated at his first meeting with the President at Bermuda, the Prime Minister was placing great emphasis on the perception of cooperation. If the Americans would agree to publication of the Quebec Agreement, for example, this would contribute to a better public and political atmosphere in which to press for actual Anglo-American collaboration on atomic energy. Churchill also held out hope that Eisenhower's Atoms for Peace speech to the U.N. General Assembly on December 8, 1953, would stimulate public and congressional acceptance of the idea of cooperation. In that speech Eisenhower proposed disarmament negotiations and that the United States, Soviet Union, and Britain contribute "X" amount of fissionable material to a U.N. organization for peaceful uses.

Hoping to build on the highly favorable international reaction to Eisenhower's speech (and on what little momentum had been carried out of the Bermuda conference), Churchill set to work drafting a speech to the House of Commons on the progress made at the conference. In an advance copy transmitted to Eisenhower for his comments on December 16, 1953, he stated that definite progress had been made and gave the distinct impression that further agreement would follow. Then, despite Eisenhower's concern that the Prime Minister was perhaps revealing too much about Strauss's and Cherwell's chore of drawing up a history of Anglo-American cooperation on atomic energy and his reservations about inaccuracies in minor facts and in timing of events, Churchill gave the speech on December 17.[25]

While all British officials wanted cooperation on nuclear matters, only Churchill wanted to insist on publication of the Quebec Agreement and the subsequent history of postwar nuclear relations. Eden, Cherwell, and

Makins, for example, had indicated privately at the Bermuda conference and afterwards that they took a "dim view of the enterprise" and would rather not have it done. It was "ancient history," they said, and publishing old facts would only recall if not revive British bitterness about Truman administration policy. Nevertheless, Churchill felt so strongly about the matter that the AEC staff began to work leisurely on a first draft. By late January 1954 the draft was complete and given to the State and Defense departments for their review.[26]

The administration moved much more quickly to build public support for changes in the McMahon Act. On December 16, 1953, the day before Churchill read his speech to Parliament, Eisenhower declared at a press conference that he wanted wider authority from Congress to decide what information, materials, and weapons could be exchanged with allies. He wanted, further, to be free to tell the allies how to use atomic weapons and how to protect themselves from atomic attack in the field of battle. He even left ambiguous the question of giving the allies atomic weapons themselves depending on the circumstances—for example, if the allies ratified and successfully implemented the EDC treaty. In an effort to persuade Congress to give him the proposed authority, he met with congressional leaders at the White House on December 18 and 19. Predictably, Senator Hickenlooper declared his adamant opposition to "giving away our atomic secrets to any foreign countries." But the majority believed that the President did have a good case to make for the revision of the McMahon Act. Although the administration was winning its battle to improve nuclear cooperation with Britain and the NATO allies, the extent of its victory was still in doubt.[27]

The Bermuda conference was yet another demonstration for the British of their limited ability to influence American policy. Although the administration naturally had to formulate proposed changes to the McMahon Act with the expectation that the JCAE and Congress would give short shrift to plans for a rapid, leaky disclosure of American nuclear secrets, the real determinants of its negotiating position were the policy conclusions of NSC 162/2 and NSC 151/2. In order to shift to a strategy for the defense of Western Europe based upon the early tactical and strategic use of atomic weapons, the United States needed the cooperation of its allies. In order to cooperate, the allies required information on the utilization of atomic weapons. But Eisenhower and especially Strauss, the President's key advisor in the nuclear discussions, would go no further. Churchill's argument that Soviet (and British) progress in the nuclear field made the basic restrictions of the McMahon Act against exchanging atomic weapons and fissionable material data obsolete impressed the President but did not persuade him to act. Emphasis on security considerations was still very important to American policymakers and to the members of the JCAE. Also important, even vital, was maintenance of the President's freedom of action on use of nuclear weapons. Not only must he remain absolutely

Fundamental Decisions   131

unfettered in order to launch an immediate retaliation against the Soviets in the event of a surprise attack, he must also be free to order American nuclear retaliation should the Soviets confine their attack to Western Europe. Since this policy was consistent with the new strategy detailed in the national security documents, the Americans resisted British attempts to win the right of consultation. If Churchill and his advisors could take some satisfaction in the knowledge that the Americans were at last serious about seeking changes in the McMahon Act, they still had to ask themselves how great an impact those changes would have for Anglo-American nuclear relations.

NOTES

1. Ambrose, *Eisenhower*, p. 146.
2. Lewis L. Strauss, *Men and Decisions* (Garden City, N.Y.: Doubleday, 1962), pp. 356-57; Peter Pringle and James Spigelman, *The Nuclear Barons* (New York: Holt, Rinehart, and Winston, 1981), pp. 121-22.
3. *New York Times*, Sept. 14, 1953, p. 3; Sept. 16, 1953, p. 4; Sept. 25, 1953, p. 3; Sept. 27, 1953, p. 5.
4. Ibid., Oct. 5, 1953, p. 14; Strauss, *Men and Decisions*, pp. 372-73; Arneson to Penfield, Washington, November 9, 1953, S/AE Files (State, Freedom of Information Act, photocopy).
5. Ibid.
6. Ibid.
7. Report to NSC by Lay (NSC 162/2), Washington, October 30, 1953, S/S-NSC Files, lot 63D351, NSC 162, *Foreign Relations of the United States* (hereafter cited as *FRUS*), 1952-54, 2:577-97.
8. Ibid.
9. Memorandum by Smith, Washington, December 3, 1953, PPS Files, lot 64D563, "NSC 153-162 September-December 1953," *FRUS*, 1952-54, 2:607-8; Telephone Conversation between Dulles and Wilson, December 22, 1953, *Minutes of Telephone Conversations of John Foster Dulles and Christian Herter, 1953-1961* (Frederick, Md.: University Publications of America, 1980), reel 1, pp. 766-67.
10. "Stockpile and Accessibility of Strategic and Critical Materials to the U.S. in Time of War," *Hearings by Special Subcommittee on Minerals, Materials, and Fuels Economic of the Committee on Interior and Insular Affairs*, U.S. Senate, 83rd Cong., 1st and 2d sess., 1954; Alfred E. Eckes, Jr., *The United States and the Global Struggle for Minerals* (Austin: University of Texas Press, 1979), pp. 201, 204-12.
11. 520 *H.C. Deb.* 5s., pp. 586-87.
12. Memorandum by Gleason, November 13, 1953 (170th Meeting of NSC on November 12, 1953), Eisenhower Papers as President, Ann Whitman File, Eisenhower Library; Aldrich to Dulles, London, November 27, 1953, 396.1/11-2753:Tele; Memorandum of Conversation by MacArthur, Washington, December 2, 1953, CFM Files, lot M88, box 166, "Big Three Bermuda," *FRUS*, 1952-54, 5:1722, 1725-26; Memorandum by Arneson, Washington, December 3, 1953, PPS Files, lot 64D563, "AE," *FRUS*, 1952-54, 2:1251-55.
13. Note by the Secretaries to JCS on Military Objectives to be Provided for in Proposed Atomic Energy Legislation (JCS 2172/26), December 14, 1953, CCS 471.6

(8-15-45), sec. 46, RG 218, Central Decimal File 1951-53, box 170, Modern Military Branch, National Archives; Report to NSC by Lay (NSC 151/2), Washington, December 4, 1952, S/S-NSC Files, lot 63D351, NSC 151 Series, *FRUS*, 1952-54, 2:1256-85.

14. Report to NSC by Lay (NSC 151/2), Washington, December 4, 1953, S/S-NSC Files, lot 63D351, NSC 151 Series, *FRUS*, 1952-54, 2:1256-85.

15. Memorandum by Gleason on 173d NSC Meeting, December 3, 1953, Washington, December 4, 1953, Eisenhower Papers as President, Ann Whitman File, Eisenhower Library.

16. Ibid.

17. Ibid.

18. Ambrose, *Eisenhower*, pp. 145-46.

19. Eisenhower-Churchill Meeting, Eisenhower's Quarters, Mid-Ocean Club, Bermuda, December 5, 1953, Notes by Strauss, Eisenhower Library, Whitman File, "Bermuda State Department Report," *FRUS*, 1952-54, 5:1767-69; Strauss, *Men and Decisions*, p. 373.

20. Ibid.

21. Ibid., Strauss, *Men and Decisions*, pp. 369-70.

22. Churchill to Eisenhower, Bermuda, December 7, 1953, Eisenhower Library, Eisenhower Papers, Whitman File, *FRUS*, 1952-54, 2:1289.

23. Memorandum by Gleason, December 11, 1953 (174th NSC Meeting on December 10, 1953), Eisenhower Papers as President, Ann Whitman File, Eisenhower Library.

24. Ibid.

25. Churchill to Eisenhower, Bermuda, December 7, 1953, Eisenhower Library, Eisenhower Papers, Whitman File; Churchill to Eisenhower, Washington, December 16, 1953, Presidential Correspondence Files, lot 66D204, "Churchill Correspondence," *FRUS*, 1952-54, 2:1289, 1301-2, 522 *H.C. Deb.* 5s., p. 584.

26. Arneson to Penfield, Washington, January 26, 1954, AE Files, lot 57D688, "Quebec Agreement," *FRUS*, 1952-54, 2:1355-56.

27. *New York Times*, Dec. 17, 1953, pp. 1, 22; Dec. 19, 1953, pp. 1, 9; News Conference of December 16, 1953, *Public Papers of the Presidents: Dwight D. Eisenhower, 1953* (Washington, D.C.: U.S. Government Printing Office, 1960), p. 836.

15

AMENDING THE McMAHON ACT

> I ask that authority be provided to exchange with nations participating in defensive arrangements with the United States such tactical information as is essential to the development of defense plans and to the training of personnel for atomic warfare. Amendments to the definition of "restricted data" recommended later in this message will also contribute to needed administrative flexibility in the exchange of information with such nations concerning the use of atomic weapons.
> —Dwight D. Eisenhower, February 17, 1954[1]

The challenge facing the administration in 1954 was to propose changes to the McMahon Act necessary to improve cooperation with the allies for the defense of Western Europe without going too far and alienating Congress. Many, including Chairman of the JCAE Cole, were convinced that new legislation ought to be passed, but only if restrictions on exchange of the most important nuclear secrets—nuclear weapons information at the very least—were left intact. They also wanted assurances that the British and others would protect American secrets and that the administration had adequate means of verifying that this was being done. If these conditions could be met, the likelihood that Congress would amend the McMahon Act before the end of summer was high.

Only progress in disarmament talks with the Soviets or Soviet agreement to adhere to the President's Atoms for Peace idea (and thereby match the amount of fissionable material the United States intended to contribute to an international pool of material for peaceful uses) could have changed the basic international conditions that necessitated formulation of the new nuclear strategy. American policymakers did not expect either of these contingencies to occur. As long as the Soviets refused to allow adequate inspection and verification of proposed arms reductions, nuclear and conventional, no disarmament agreement was possible. Nor did it seem that the United States and the Soviet Union, even in direct, bilateral talks, could come to agreement on the terms of a disarmament treaty. The Soviets wanted nuclear disarmament only without conventional disarmament and had responded to the President's December 8, 1953, speech to the U.N. with a public call for the banning of the use of atomic weapons. Since NATO did not have the conventional military strength to deter a Soviet attack, the United States could agree to neither of these proposals.[2]

While Secretary of State Dulles met in Berlin from January 25 to February 18, 1954, with the foreign ministers of Britain, France, and the Soviet Union to discuss the problems of Germany and Austria, Eisenhower prepared a special message to Congress on atomic energy. He gave the address on February 17. Using rhetoric Churchill would heartily have endorsed, he declared that because the American atomic monopoly had disappeared in 1949, and in light of the fact that the Soviets were now catching up to the United States in the nuclear arena, the McMahon Act was now obsolete. The Congress should agree to lift restrictions inhibiting exchanges of information pertaining to use of and defense against atomic weapons. This would permit the United States and its allies to develop joint defense plans and arrange for training of allied personnel for nuclear warfare. But the administration did not want a blank check to reveal nuclear weapons data. The President assured Congress that exchanges of restricted data would be regulated according to the importance of the information being transferred, specific uses that could be made of it, the contribution it would make to the common defense, and the ability of the recipient foreign government to provide adequate security standards and practices.[3]

In order to insure that information was protected according to the required security standards, Eisenhower wanted responsibility for safeguarding nuclear information transferred from the AEC to the DOD. The DOD could presumably make security arrangements more easily and effectively with the military establishments of foreign governments than the AEC. In his speech, the President went on to ask for amendments to the McMahon Act to permit cooperation on the exchange of "restricted data" for the industrial applications of atomic energy. He also requested authority to release fissionable material in amounts adequate for industrial and research use. These amendments would permit the United States to carry out the President's Atoms for Peace plan. Not mentioned in the speech was another motivation for information exchanges on the industrial applications of atomic energy, a desire by the DOD to assist the British in the development of nuclear-powered ships, technically within the category "industrial applications of atomic energy." Since British naval power was important in the event of war for the control of the sea lines of communication between the United States and Western Europe, NATO's ability to defend against Soviet submarine attacks could only be enhanced by nuclear-powered British submarines and ships on patrol in the Atlantic Ocean and North Sea.[4]

While the JCAE went to work holding committee hearings on the proposed amendments to the McMahon Act, the British House of Commons debated in March 1954 the defense budget and the advisability of the government's plans to build up the British nuclear deterrent. Although some Labour members of Parliament decried the expense of building bombs and equipping the Royal Air Force with V-bombers to deliver them, the majority clearly wanted to provide full funding for the British nuclear program. There was greater opposition, however, to the proposed strategy for the early use of atomic weapons in the defense of Europe. Several days after Dulles, on March 16, said that the NATO and Rio treaties gave the President the power, without consulting Congress, to order instant retaliation in Europe and the Western Hemisphere if an ally was attacked, the Prime Minister was asked directly whether Eisenhower would consult with Britain before using atomic weapons in the event of all-out war in Europe, or if he would consult should the United States only be attacked and American retaliation originate in part form USAF bases in Britain. Referring to the language of the January 9, 1952, communiqué from his talks with President Truman, Churchill would say no more about the matter.[5]

The Prime Minister and his cabinet might very well have escaped with no more probing questions had not the world's and the British public's fear of nuclear war been brought to the surface by an event in the middle of the Pacific Ocean. American hydrogen bomb tests in the Marshall Islands March 1 and March 26, 1954, resulted in the accidental contamination of a Japanese fishing vessel and its crew. Although the Japanese boat had apparently strayed inside the warning range, the repercussions for the United States were severe. The world, Dulles told Strauss, believed that due to the enormity of thermonuclear explosions, the United States was using vast areas of ocean for its tests. In Britain, many people feared that a few hydrogen bombs might suffice to destroy most of the British Isles. Appeasement talk was in the air. In Parliament too the debate revived. Churchill came under intense pressure to ask the United States and the Soviet Union to postpone further nuclear tests. The members wanted to know, moreover, whether the British government had any intention of developing hydrogen bombs. All this agitation caused the aged Prime Minister great unease. Assuring the members that the Americans were taking extra precautions to prevent a repeat of the accident, he appealed openly for restraint. The American Congress was currently examining Eisenhower's proposals for changes in the McMahon Act, and he feared that too-harsh criticism of American hydrogen bomb tests would damage the favorable atmosphere for passage in Washington.[6]

Because the Labour party would not let up, Churchill was forced to schedule a speech on April 5, 1954, to clear up misconceptions about the hydrogen bomb. Using nontechnical information provided by Eisenhower, he attempted to put to rest the exaggerated fears of the British public. He also tried to revive awareness of the importance to Britain of nuclear ties with the United States. His method was to disclose the provisions of the Quebec Agreement of 1943 without mentioning the Modus Vivendi of 1948 and its provisions canceling the British right of consultation on the use of atomic weapons. Reaction in Washington was swift. Within hours, Senator Hickenlooper revealed that the Quebec Agreement had been nullified in 1948. The next day, April 6, the administration confirmed Hickenlooper's statement.[7]

Nor had Churchill's pronouncements had the desired effect in London. Labour members of Parliament embarrassed the Prime Minister by forcing him to admit that the Americans had permitted no British observers at the recent hydrogen bomb tests. His remark that the Americans had allowed an RAF flight in the vicinity hours after the explosion to collect data seemed small consolation. They also pressured the government to use American air bases in Britain as a diplomatic weapon to force the United States to agree to a joint policy for hydrogen weapons. Attlee's Labour government, they insisted, had successfully kept the spirit of the Quebec Agreement alive by obtaining assurances from Truman that the United States would seek Britain's consent before using nuclear weapons against a third party. The culmination of a very bad few weeks for the Prime Minister came on April 13, 1954. Under questioning, Churchill confessed that present Anglo-American relations regarding the civilian use of atomic energy covered only information exchanges in a limited field. There was no agreement in addition to exchange data on the design or manufacture of atomic weapons.[8]

On May 4, 1954, the Conservative party struck back. A right-wing member of Parliament asked Churchill if it were true that the Attlee government had—as alleged in the just-published book, *The Private Papers of Senator Vandenberg*—given up in the Modus Vivendi of 1948 the British right of veto over American use of atomic weapons in exchange for American financial aid. To Attlee's outrage, Churchill's reply amounted to a smile of satisfaction. When the question was repeated on May 18 in words charging a "surrender" and "sell-out" of Britain's right of veto, Attlee could no longer keep silent. He insisted that there had been no surrender, no sell-out. But as with the Labour attack on Churchill, the damage had already been done.[9]

Although Churchill spent a good deal of time and effort defending the United States in the Parliamentary debates of March, April, and May 1954, he himself had grave concerns about the impact of the hydrogen bomb on the continued security of the British Isles. Acquisition of hydrogen bombs in some numbers by the Soviets, he realized, would mean that the British government would have to reassess its civil defense and city defense programs. Shelters would have to be dug far deeper in the ground than originally conceived, plans would have to be created for a wider dispersal of the population, and antiaircraft artillery and fighter squadrons would have to be strengthened to take a higher toll of an invading bomber force. The American hydrogen bomb test incident, then, presented both a headache and an opportunity. It was a headache because of the political problem it created both within Britain and between the United States and Britain. It was an opportunity because it permitted the British government to open discussions with the Americans on the hydrogen bomb and, once again, on the question of consultation.[10]

On April 12, 1954—just as the administration began contemplating intervention with air power, possibly with atomic bombs, in Vietnam on the side of the beleaguered French—Eden met with Dulles in London to discuss the feasibility of a moratorium on further hydrogen bomb experiments. He did so again on May 2. British scientists, Eden said, had determined that two well-placed observatories, one in Scandinavia and one in Switzerland (or even better, one in Europe and one in North America), could detect explosions equivalent to 50,000 tons of TNT and pinpoint the site of such explosions. It would be a good idea, then, to interrupt the acceleration of the nuclear arms race to propose a moratorium on nuclear tests of such a magnitude. The Soviets would be put on the spot. If they accepted, the American lead in nuclear technology might well be preserved. The only drawback was that Britain too, should the government decide to develop a hydrogen bomb capability, would be disadvantaged. He hoped that under such circumstances the United States would be "as kind to the United Kingdom as possible within United States laws." If the Soviets refused, they would suffer in the eyes of world opinion.[11]

Simultaneously with its efforts to win approval of a moratorium on testing, the British government attempted to reopen the question of consultation. Because of the debate in the House of Commons and the negative American reaction to Churchill's revelation of the terms of the Quebec Agreement, the inescapable impression left with the public was that the British right of consultation no longer existed. This perception particularly annoyed Eden, now asserting himself as Churchill declined. It was his opinion, he told Dulles at the April 1954 meetings of the North Atlantic Council, that the United States was obligated to consult the British government "prior to any decision to use atomic weapons." Now Dulles became annoyed. The British, he believed, were obviously trying to maneuver into the position of having a veto on American use of nuclear weapons. On May 6 he told the NSC that Eden was fully aware of American policy on the subject. His, Dulles's, statement to a restricted group on April 23, 1954, at the NATO meeting had put all the allies on notice regarding that policy and should, he maintained, constitute the necessary "consultation with our allies." He had said that the United States assumed that the Soviets would, in the event of general war, make use of atomic weapons with maximum surprise. In response, and since NATO relied so heavily on atomic weapons for its defense, the United States would employ atomic weapons like conventional armaments to repel the Soviet attack. While the administration intended to consult and cooperate with the allies, the allies had to understand that "under certain contingencies, time would not permit consultation without itself endangering the very security we seek to protect. So far as feasible, we must seek understanding in advance on the measures to be taken under various circumstances. In these ways, our joint capacities will be best calculated to deter aggression against any of us and to protect us in case it should occur."[12]

On May 7, 1954, Dulles said publicly that there was a distinct possibility that the United States might be forced to intervene militarily in Indochina. A French force of several thousand soldiers had just surrendered to the North Vietnamese at Dienbienphu. Concerned that the Americans might strike precipitously in Southeast Asia and eager to discuss the continued debate over the EDC treaty and the question of consultation on use of nuclear weapons, Churchill asked for a conference with Eisenhower. This was arranged for May 20, 1954, but was postponed until June 25 because of a conflict with the Geneva meetings on Vietnam. While Churchill and Eisenhower left discussion of technical matters related to atomic energy to their advisors, they concentrated on fundamental policies. In order to win British support for the EDC, for example, Eisenhower told Churchill that the United States would give Britain atomic bombs in the event of an emergency. The British, he was thinking, had more bombers than bombs. Besides, he did not want to see only American bomber crews suffer casualties. This promise to the Prime Minister could not, of course, go into the public statement of June 28 or the final communiqué of June 29.[13]

Eisenhower's willingness to let the British share the burden of atomic air attacks in the event of war did not mean that he intended to consult before deciding in an emergency to use nuclear weapons. But he and his advisors realized that the question of consultation—not only with the British but with all Western European governments—had a bearing on the stability of the NATO alliance. In NSC 5422/2, a statement of policy adopted by the NSC on August 7, 1954, the administration sought to maintain a balance between consultation and freedom of action. The document read,

> As a broad rule of conduct, the U.S. should pursue its objectives in such ways and by such means, including appropriate pressures, persuasion, and compromise, as will maintain the cohesion of the alliances. The U.S. should, however, act independently of its major allies when the advantage of achieving U.S. objectives by such action clearly outweighs the danger of lasting damage to its alliances. In this connection, consideration should be given to the likelihood that the initiation of action by the U.S. prior to allied acceptance may bring about subsequent allied support. *Allied reluctance to act should not inhibit the U.S. from taking action, including the use of nuclear weapons, to prevent Communist territorial gains when such action is clearly necessary to U.S. security.*[14]

The policy adopted unofficially by the Truman administration, confirmed in the Modus Vivendi of 1948, maintained by American officials after American strategic bombers were introduced into Britain in summer 1948 and armed in 1951 with atomic weapons, and adhered to by President Eisenhower through the first 20 months of his administration had now become official American policy. The United States would not let allied claims to consultation on, let alone veto of, American use of nuclear weapons hinder presidential freedom of action to respond to Soviet conventional or nuclear attack. The most the administration would be willing to do was discuss far in advance possible scenarios that would trigger a decision to use nuclear weapons and plans on how those weapons should be employed. Even then, the United States would make no commitment to alter its strategy. If the British and other NATO governments wanted American assistance in the defense of Western Europe, they would have to accept such assistance on American terms.

The unseemly bickering between Labour and Conservative members of the British Parliament over the consultation question and the British government's attempt to capitalize on the controversy to put pressure on the Eisenhower administration to make concessions did not affect the progress of the proposed amendments to the McMahon Act. Bickering between Strauss and the JCAE almost did. The dispute revolved around Strauss's dictatorial rule and the administration's decision to open negotiations with the Mississippi Valley Generating Company to provide power in an AEC plant in Paducah, Kentucky, in place of power generated by the government-controlled Tennessee Valley Authority (the so-called Dixon-Yates proposal). With AEC Commissioner Thomas E. Murray complaining to the JCAE that Strauss did not permit him and his colleagues access to information, and with Murray siding with Democrats on the committee opposed to the involvement of private industry in the development of nuclear power reactors, tension btween Strauss and his critics grew. Then Strauss alienated the entire JCAE. In response to a JCAE letter of May 20, 1954, he refused to turn over some information on AEC meetings for the past ten months so that the Joint Committee could look into AEC activities. When he refused once again during hearings on the proposed changes to the McMahon Act, the JCAE inserted into the legislation language requiring the AEC to keep the committee "fully and currently informed with respect to all AEC activities."[15]

Strauss's troubles with the committee also complicated the task of pushing the amendments through Congress. But Cole and Hickenlooper in late May 1954 hit on the idea of tying international/security issues to domestic issues like the Dixon-Yates plan so that Republicans who generally opposed the former but favored the latter and Democrats who generally opposed the latter but favored the former would not be able to pick apart the legislation piecemeal. The maneuver was successful. On July 13, 1954, the JCAE recommended to Congress that it pass the amendments to the McMahon Act. The end of the atomic monopoly had created a new international situation, they acknowledged, and the allies needed information on the use of atomic weapons to "dam the tide of Red military power and prevent it from engulfing free Europe." Giving this information to the allies, they were convinced, would be beneficial to U.S. national security.[16]

The full Congress agreed. On August 30, 1954, it passed the Atomic Energy Act of 1954 and the President signed it. Under proper security safeguards, the United States could now give its allies certain formerly restricted data for training in the use of and defense against atomic weapons, and for evaluating the atomic capabilities of a potential aggressor. The act also provided for certain exchanges of nonmilitary nuclear technology, for example to assist the allies to build nuclear reactors for research purposes and to generate power. Exchanges of information, however, would be neither simple nor unfettered. There would be no transmission of data pertaining to the design or manufacture of nuclear weapons. If the United States transmitted data—say, on the external characteristics of atomic weapons and their yields—the recipient government had to guarantee maintenance of mutually agreed security standards and promise not to transmit the information to third parties. If the United States transmitted a certain quantity of fissionable material for peaceful uses, the recipient government had to guarantee that it would not divert that material to military purposes. The procedure for concluding agreements with foreign governments was also drawn out and involved. First, the administration and the recipient government had to negotiate an Agreement for Cooperation. The AEC had then to approve that agreement, including the detailed terms and the various guarantees previously discussed. Next, the President was required to approve execution of the agreement and make a written determination that performance would promote the defense and security of the United States. Finally, the administration had to submit the proposed agreement to the JCAE for a period of 30 days while Congress was in session. Only at the end of the 30 days would the bilateral Agreement of Cooperation have the force of law. But it would be an executive agreement, not a treaty.[17]

What was remarkable (or perhaps unremarkable) about the Atomic Energy Act of 1954 was how precisely it fulfilled the desires of the Eisenhower administration. American policymakers had wanted participation by private enterprise in the development of nuclear power and had secured that objective despite the opposition of congressional Democrats and Strauss's unwillingness to provide the JCAE with all the information about AEC activities it demanded. They had wanted measured cooperation with the allies on the use of and defense against atomic weapons and had won this battle rather handily. The international reaction to the March 1954 hydrogen bomb test accident and British attempts to capitalize on the incident had caused ripples of concern among the administration and Congress but had not halted the steady progress of the amending legislation.

In light of the new American strategy to employ large numbers of atomic weapons in any future war with the Soviets in Europe, the case in favor of the proposed changes had far outweighed the possible loss of security. The members of the JCAE and Congress had not even said no to exchanges of information applicable to the construction of power reactors, an area where the British appeared to be in competition with the United States. But they had retained their power of oversight and had no intention of letting the administration engage in an orgy of uncontrolled cooperation. Information exchanges would be regulated and limited and the Joint Committee kept "fully and currently" informed by the AEC of nuclear matters and decisions. This provision for strict accountability of the AEC to the JCAE would have a significant impact when Strauss and the commissioners made a final determination on whether exchanging data on the external characteristics and yield of atomic weapons would reveal actual atomic weapons information.

NOTES

1. *Public Papers of the Presidents: Dwight D. Eisenhower, 1954* (Washington, D.C.: U.S. Government Printing Office, 1960), pp. 260-69.

2. *New York Times*, Jan. 18, 1954, p. 6; *Foreign Relations of the United States* (hereafter cited as *FRUS*), 1952-54, 2:1324-31. Dulles, in fact, was publicly pushing "massive retaliation" by nuclear means to deter the Soviets and gave a speech on the subject before the Council of Foreign Relations, January 12, 1954.

3. *Public Papers of the Presidents: Eisenhower, 1954*, p. 260; *New York Times*, Feb. 18, 1954, p. 8.

4. Ibid.; Lewis L. Strauss, *Men and Decisions* (Garden City, N.Y.: Doubleday, 1962), p. 373.

5. 524 *H.C. Deb.* 5s., pp. 1362, 1465-69, 1476-90; 525 *H.C. Deb.* 5s., pp. 1050-51.

6. Memorandum of Telephone Conversation between Dulles and Strauss, March 29, 1954, Eisenhower Library, Dulles Papers, "Telephone Conversations," *FRUS*, 1952-54, 2:1379-80; 525 *H.C. Deb.* 5s., pp. 1836-42.

7. 526 *H.C. Deb.* 5s., pp. 36-60, 191, 963-64; *New York Times*, Apr. 5, 1954, p. 10; Apr. 6, 1954, p. 12; Apr. 7, 1954, p. 3; Apr. 9, 1954, p. 4.

8. Ibid.

9. 527 *H.C. Deb.* 5s., pp. 200, 1890-92.

10. 530 *H.D. Deb.* 5s., pp. 34-36.

11. Dulles to State Department, Geneva, May 2, 1954, 396.1-GE/5-254:Tele, *FRUS*, 1952-54, 2:1418-19.

12. Memorandum of Discussion at 195th NSC Meeting, May 6, 1954, Eisenhower Library, Eisenhower Papers, Whitman File, *FRUS*, 1952-54, 2:1423-29; Statement by Dulles to North Atlantic Council Close Ministerial Session, Paris, April 23, 1954, 740.5/4-2454, *FRUS*, 1952-54, 5:509-14.

13. Ambrose, *Eisenhower*, pp. 205-8; 530 *H.C. Deb.* 5s., pp. 34-36; Dulles calls Hagerty, June 22, 1954; Eisenhower calls Dulles, June 28, 1954, *Minutes of Telephone Conversations of John Foster Dulles and Christian Herter, 1953-1961*

(Frederick, Md.: University Publications of America, 1980), reel 8, pp. 941, 936; U.S. State Department, *Bulletin*, 1954, 30:49.

14. My emphasis; Statement of Policy by NSC (NSC 5422/2), Washington, August 7, 1954, S/S-NSC Files, lot 63D351, NSC 5422, *FRUS*, 1952-54, 2:715-31.

15. Harold P. Green and Alan Rosenthal, *Government of the Atom* (New York: Atherton Press, 1963), pp. 14-15, 92.

16. Strauss calls Dulles, May 22, 1954, *Telephone Conversations of Dulles*, reel 2, p. 442; John Simpson, *The Independent Nuclear State: The United States, Britain, and the Military Atom* (London: Macmillan, 1983), p. 113; "Amending the Atomic Energy Act, Statement by Dulles Before JCAE," U.S. State Department, *Bulletin*, 1954, 30:926-28; *New York Times*, June 3, 1954, p. 1; June 4, 1954, p. 19; June 5, 1954, p. 6; July 14, 1954, pp. 1, 10; Memorandum of Discussion of 203d Meeting of NSC, June 23, 1954, Eisenhower Library, Eisenhower Papers, Whitman File, *FRUS*, 1952-54, pp. 1467-72.

17. Public Law 703, 83d Cong., 68 Stat. 919; Statement by President upon Signing Atomic Energy Act of 1954, August 30, 1954, *Public Papers of the Presidents: Eisenhower, 1954*, pp. 776-77.

16
STRIVING TO ACHIEVE A MINOR VICTORY

> It [the Anglo-American Agreement for Cooperation of June 15, 1955] is of vital importance to the maintenance of our common freedom.
> —Dwight D. Eisenhower, June 20, 1955[1]

Having convinced the full Congress to grant limited authority to improve nuclear cooperation with the allies, the administration now had the task of negotiating and concluding a bilateral agreement with the British, then submitting it to the members of the JCAE for their inspection. Therein lay the crux of a difficult problem. If American policymakers interpreted the terms of the 1954 Atomic Energy Act too liberally, they might agree to a broad exchange of information only to have an aroused Joint Committee block the arrangement. If, on the other hand, they interpreted the terms too rigidly, they might please the JCAE but completely alienate the British. The result would be no agreement at all and frustration of administration plans to tighten Anglo-American nuclear ties for the defense of Western Europe. Skillful diplomacy was needed, then, and fortunately, American policymakers had time to prepare their approach. Because the new act stipulated that an Agreement for Cooperation with a foreign government had to be submitted to the JCAE for 30 days while Congress was in session, there was no reason to rush into talks. The 1954 mid-term elections were coming up, and the new Congress would not convene until January 1955.

Anglo-American talks to discuss a new accord on atomic energy finally began in mid-October 1954 with the arrival in Washington of Plowden and Cockcroft. Along with Makins, they met with members of the AEC and DOD for preliminary talks on possible further collaboration on the industrial and military uses of atomic energy. They were quickly given to understand that the terms of the 1954 Atomic Energy Act did not permit the administration to exchange the kind of information the British nuclear program badly needed. This great disappointment caused Churchill and his cabinet to reassess British atomic energy policy. A stark danger existed, they concluded, that Britain—its stockpile of atomic weapons so tiny—would be locked into a position of permanent inferiority by an international movement to place a moratorium or outright ban on nuclear testing and nuclear weapons production. British public opinion, they realized, strongly approved the moratorium idea. They could no longer wait, therefore, for a breakthrough in Anglo-American nuclear relations but had to make an immediate decision to accelerate the British program.[2]

Accordingly, they took a number of actions late in 1954 to create a British stockpile of nuclear weapons of the most modern design. First, they allocated substantially more money for a stepped-up testing program in Australia to develop bombs of greater yield and less weapons weight. Only three atomic tests had so far been conducted. By 1956 the government hoped to be in position to conduct several more. Next, they authorized construction of six additional reactors to expand production of military plutonium and highly enriched uranium. When British scientists knew more about designing and building weapons, the fissionable material would already be on hand to build them. So would the necessary manufacturing facilities. In a few years, the government hoped to turn out "tens of weapons each year."[3]

Most importantly, Churchill and his cabinet made the decision to initiate research and development of the hydrogen bomb. It had become clear in the postwar world that in order to have political influence and be taken seriously by the superpowers, Britain too had to have the same nuclear capabilities as the United States and Soviet Union. Since it was foreseen that there might be problems with conducting thermonuclear testing at the Australian test site, separate facilities would be built on Christmas Island in the Pacific. Finally, the British government would officially adopt nuclear deterrence as the basis of its national defense policy. Once British V-bombers began to come off assembly lines in sufficient quantities and a larger stockpile of atomic bombs was achieved, Britain would have its deterrent force.[4]

Although British officials believed that a hydrogen bomb capability would persuade the Americans to exchange weapons data and take greater account of British opinions, they thought it highly unlikely that Britain's independent nuclear deterrent would cause the Americans to back away from their commitment to NATO and Western European security. American actions swiftly demonstrated that the British were correct. On December 4, 1954, Dulles convinced the NATO Council of Ministers to adopt a declaratory policy of being prepared to use nuclear weapons to defeat any Soviet conventional (and of course nuclear) attack on Western Europe. In fact, the United States was moving rapidly to improve American military readiness to do just that by drawing up plans to deploy additional atomic weapons to overseas bases. The President ordered the State

Department to insure the cooperation of foreign governments. He directed the AEC, in addition, to facilitate dispersal of atomic and hydrogen weapons within the continental United States. The Soviets, it was believed, would have the capability in five years to "strike a crippling blow at the United States." But if expansion of the American nuclear arsenal combined with dispersal continued apace, the United States would still be able to retaliate with at least equal force. Subsequently, 36 percent of American hydrogen bombs and 42 percent of atomic bombs were sent overseas.[5]

Relying on massive retaliation to deter the Soviets might cause political problems within NATO, however, because of allied fears of nuclear war and its consequences for Western Europe. This was recognized by the NSC Planning Board in a mid-December 1954 draft statement of policy intended when finally approved to supersede NSC 162/2. But despite possible strains with the allies, the planners concluded that the United States had no other viable option but to continue to rely heavily on nuclear weapons to deter Soviet aggression. It must also retain the option of using those weapons even in the case of local aggression. Many people in Britain were not enthusiastic about the new NATO policy. Statements by Field Marshal Montgomery and General Alfred M. Gruenther, supreme NATO commander, that atomic weapons would definitely be used if war broke out provoked more questions in the House of Commons about arrangements between Churchill and Eisenhower for consultation. Labour party leaders wanted to know whether the United States had a unilateral right to use atomic weapons without talking to the British government and whether control of atomic weapons, in light of the recent NATO decision, had actually been transferred from political to military authority. Not in good health and unwilling to engage in another debate like the one in the spring, Churchill avoided a meaningful response. He left members of Parliament with severe doubts about the extent of American willingness to give the proper weight to informed British opinion on use of nuclear weapons in a crisis.[6]

At the beginning of 1955 the American strategic advantage over the Soviets reached its highest point prior to the age of intercontinental ballistic missiles. The American nuclear stockpile and operational nuclear weapons dwarfed the Soviet, American superiority in long- and medium-range bombers was well established, and, with the French prepared to accept German rearmament and membership in NATO, the North Atlantic Treaty Organization looked stronger than ever. At home, too, the United States government was secure. Despite Democratic gains in the 1954 mid-term elections, Eisenhower's popularity was very high. Part of this was no doubt due to the fact that the administration had scored notable foreign policy triumphs. But the more telling factor was the balanced budget and growing economy. Eisenhower had restrained defense and other spending as he had promised.

The New Look defense policy and basic national security policy as detailed in NSC 162/2, however, concerned the JCS. They wrote on December 17, 1954, that the administration was emphasizing too much a "preponderant commitment to a policy of reaction." It was imperative, they thought, "that our basic security policy, when revised, reflect throughout the greater urgency of the situation." It must further "define concretely the conditions which it is the aim of our security policy to create, and direct formulation of courses of action designed to achieve the basic objective." What they wanted specifically was for the United States, during the period in which it retained overwhelming nuclear superiority, to try to overthrow Communist domination of mainland China and Eastern Europe. To achieve these goals, the United States would have to build up its conventional forces, as it was doing with its strategic forces, and put maximum pressure on the Soviets.[7]

The timing of the JCS memorandum was no accident. Since September 3, 1954, when the Chinese Communists had shelled Quemoy and Matsu, two offshore islands controlled by the Chinese Nationalists, the administration had been very concerned about possible aggression by the mainlanders against Formosa (Taiwan). Finally, in late January 1955, when it appeared that the Chinese Communists might be contemplating an attack on Formosa, Eisenhower secured a congressional resolution (the Formosa Doctrine) granting him authority in advance to engage in war at his own time and choosing if the Chinese Communists did attack.

If the United States had to fight the Chinese, Eisenhower realized, he would need the cooperation of the allies. He therefore sent Dulles to London in mid-February 1955 to lobby for British support for the defense of Formosa. But on March 10, 1955, contrary to advice the British had given in London, Dulles argued before the NSC that the United States should use atomic weapons if the Chinese Communists attempted to capture Quemoy and Matsu. He then persuaded a reluctant Eisenhower to sanction his March 15 public statement that the United States had to be prepared to use tactical atomic weapons in the event of war in the Formosa Straits. To Anthony Eden, Prime Minister after Churchill's retirement on April 5, 1955, the announced American intention to use atomic weapons unilaterally was a very serious matter. He had always insisted that Britain had the right to be consulted before American resort to nuclear weapons. Such a decision might trigger a Communist atomic counterattack against the British Isles. Although the Chinese did not have a nuclear capability, the Soviets did. And even if the Soviets chose not to go to the aid of their Chinese allies, the Chinese themselves would probably react to American atomic strikes by overrunning British-controlled Hong Kong. At the very least, then, Eden wanted the British point of view on use of nuclear weapons represented in American decision making. Against this tense international backdrop, Strauss and Assistant Secretary of Defense for Research and Development Donald A. Quarles went to London on April 19 to visit British nuclear installations and meet with Eden. The topic of conversation was cooperation, but Eden could well have been thinking that a full exchange of nuclear information would be to no avail if the United States went to war with China. Fortunately, the Formosa crisis eased with an offer by Chinese Premier Chou En-lai to negotiate. The question of consultation would not now become a factor affecting Anglo-American negotiations for a new nuclear accord.[8]

What did become an issue was DOD plans to incorporate in a new agreement a provision to exchange with the British nuclear submarine propulsion information. On April 19, 1955, the day Strauss and Quarles flew to London, the JCAE sent a letter to the AEC requesting information about proposed exchanges with the British and other nations of restricted data pertaining to military-type reactors. Although the committee members were willing to sanction some cooperation in the development of civilian reactors—an essential provision of the President's Atoms for Peace plan—they wanted the American technological lead in the military reactor area preserved. They were very proud that the *Nautilus*, the world's first nuclear submarine, was ready to be handed over to the United States Navy for sea trials on April 22, 1955. In reply to the JCAE's letter, Strauss wrote on May 16 that it was the opinion of the AEC's general counsel that the 1954 Atomic Energy Act did not permit exchanges of restricted data on submarine, aircraft, or military package power reactors.[9]

The JCAE still did not relax. The members had learned of two AEC-DOD communications regarding proposed categories of information to be included in a possible agreement for cooperation with the British and Canadians. They wanted copies of those communications and the AEC general counsel's opinion. Knowing full well that the AEC-DOD communications contained information on DOD wishes to exchange with the British information on nuclear submarine propulsion, Strauss did not want to jeopardize Anglo-American negotiations by letting the JCAE know what was afoot. On June 9, 1955, therefore, he claimed executive privilege for the AEC-DOD communications. He did waive that privilege for the document containing the opinion of the AEC's general counsel.[10]

Fearful that the DOD proposal to exchange nuclear submarine propulsion information, actually already negotiated with the British and Canadians, would blow up in their faces and cause the JCAE to reject the entire agreement for cooperation, Strauss lobbied feverishly within the administration to get the proposal dropped. He was essentially successful. Although an exchange of nuclear package power-plant information was provided for in a separate agreement for cooperation with the Canadians, the exchange of nuclear submarine propulsion information was excised from the Anglo-American Agreement for Cooperation concluded on June 15, 1955, in Washington.[11]

The Anglo-American agreement did, however provide (on paper) for a degree of cooperation not achieved since World War II. There were two parts. The British and Americans would exchange information on the civilian uses of atomic energy and on the military uses. The civilian agreement contained a very important restriction. It stated that the signatories were prohibited from exchanging data of military significance, or data "not relevant to current or planned programs." This meant that the United States would not give the British information on military power reactors (including nuclear submarine reactors) and isotope-separation plants. Data on heavy water and U-235 could be transferred if exclusively for civilian research purposes. All information, in addition, had to be exchanged on the basis of reciprocity. If the British had no information of equal value, the United States would be free to refuse to divulge its secrets. The military agreement was the more important of the two. It stated that since the United States and Britain were participating in "international arrangements for their mutual defense and security and making substantial and material contributions thereto," they would make atomic information available to each other so as to facilitate the development of defense plans, assist in the training of personnel in the employment of and defense against atomic weapons, and cooperate in the evaluation of the capabilities of potential enemies (that is, the Soviet Union) in the employment of atomic weapons. The signatories further agreed to maintain mutually satisfactory security standards and not to communicate exchanged atomic information to any third party. No atomic weapons or special nuclear material could be transferred.[12]

Overall, the terms of the Anglo-American Agreement for Cooperation of June 15, 1955, amounted to a conservative step in the direction of greater cooperation in the field of atomic energy. This moderation was important. It convinced new JCAE Chairman Senator Clinton P. Anderson (D., New Mexico) and his colleagues that, despite their anger at Strauss's decision to withhold the two AEC-DOD communications and despite suspicions that the administration had almost made an agreement to give the British military reactor information, they should approve the arrangement. They did so in hearings in July. But the moderation of the agreement also created problems. Although a better atmosphere between British and American officials resulted, many in Britain felt that the accord did not go far enough. The restrictions against disclosing weapons design and manufacturing information was scored in Parliament, the *London Times*, and the *Manchester Guardian*. The feeling was widespread in Britain that duplication of effort and waste would continue in the British and American programs. The agreement certainly would not help Britain reduce costs.[13]

There was a more fundamental obstacle to using the agreement for greater cooperation, however. The AEC and DOD still disagreed as to the extent of information exchanges possible under the agreement. Not only had Strauss and his colleagues shot down the proposal to exchange nuclear submarine propulsion information, but they were increasingly inclined to refuse to sanction information exchanges on atomic weapons characteristics—size, weight, and yield. Transferring this information, they felt, would reveal information about the design and manufacture of American atomic weapons. If the JCAE learned of this, there would be a backlash from the members. In the end, the AEC blocked exchanges of information the British needed to design delivery systems to carry American atomic weapons. Informed British participation in defense planning, as a result, remained an unfulfilled goal. Despite DOD protests to the President, this state of affairs endured until early 1957. The June 15, 1955, agreement was, therefore, a very unsatisfactory (albeit temporary) conclusion to the high hopes Churchill had had for nuclear cooperation with the Eisenhower administration.[14]

The decision by Churchill and the British government in late 1954 to expand dramatically the British nuclear program had been vindicated by the disappointing terms of the Anglo-American Agreement for Cooperation. If Britain was to build up a relatively large stockpile of bombs, it must for the time being do so on its own without significant American help. But British leaders had not abandoned the hope that patience and persistence would eventually pay off in establishment of full cooperation on atomic energy and weapons. For just this reason, they made the decision to develop the hydrogen bomb. Using the same rationale, they settled for the minor victory provided in the June 15, 1955, accord. Although under that agreement information exchanges, especially on the utilization of atomic weapons, turned out to be severely circumscribed by AEC-DOD disagreement, the British came tantalizingly close to achieving a real breakthrough. The Americans very nearly agreed to transfer nuclear submarine propulsion information. Again, the JCAE was the villain. This time, however, there was a realistic possibility that the administration, particularly the DOD, would rally its forces and increase efforts on behalf of cooperation. Basic American national security policy and the American-inspired strategy of early use of nuclear weapons in defense of NATO were being thwarted by inability to collaborate with Britain in the nuclear sphere. As Soviet nuclear capability grew in the next few years, therefore, the pressure to match the rhetoric of cooperation with actual cooperation would become immense.

NOTES

1. *New York Times*, June 21, 1955, p. 17.
2. Merchant to Smith, Washington, November 1954, S/AE Files (State, Freedom of Information Act, photocopy); Memorandum of Conversation by Raynor, Washington, October 27, 1954, 741.5611/10-2754, *Foreign Relations of the United States* (hereafter cited as *FRUS*), 1952-54, 2:1542; *New York Times*, Oct. 24, 1954, p. 19; John Simpson, *The Independent Nuclear State: The United States, Britain, and the Military Atom* (London: Macmillan, 1983), p. 114.
3. Simpson, *Independent Nuclear State*, pp. 221-22, 244-45.

4. Ibid.; Leon D. Epstein, "Britain and the H-Bomb, 1955-1958," *The Review of Politics* 21 (August 1959): 515-17.

5. Memorandum by Goodpaster, Washington, undated, Papers of Dwight D. Eisenhower as President, Ann Whitman File, Eisenhower Library; Draft Statement of Policy Prepared by NSC Planning Board (NSC 5440), Washington, December 13, 1954, S/S-NSC Files, lot 63D351, NSC 5440, *FRUS*, 1952-54, 2:806-22, 1576-77; Ambrose, *Eisenhower*, pp. 224-25.

6. Ibid.; 535 *H.C. Deb.* 5s., pp. 1973-76.

7. Memorandum by JCS, Washington, December 17, 1954, S/S-NSC Files, lot 63D351, NSC 5440, *FRUS*, 1952-54, 2:828-32.

8. Memorandum by Bryan, Washington, March 10, 1955, S/AE Files (State, FOI, photocopy); *New York Times*, Mar. 5, 1955, pp. 1, 3; Mar. 16, 1955, p. 1; Apr. 20, 1955, p. 2; Apr. 21, 1955; p. 12; Apr. 23, 1955, p. 2.

9. *Hearings before Subcommittee on Agreements for Cooperation, JCAE, Amending the Atomic Energy Act of 1954—Exchange of Military Information and Material with Allies*, 85th Cong., 2d sess., 1958, pp. 516-19, 576-77; Simpson, *Independent Nuclear State*, p. 116; Discussion at 251st NSC Meeting, June 19, 1955, Washington, Papers of Eisenhower as President, Ann Whitman File, Eisenhower Library. Strauss reported to the NSC that the "spate of rumors" in the press about Britain being ahead of the United States in the nuclear power production field was based on false information. After spending a week visiting British nuclear installations, he could report that the U.S. effort was "ten times as great" as the British.

10. Ibid.; Palmer to Merchant, Washington, May 24, 1955, 711.56341/5-2455 (State, FOI, photocopy). Draft agreements for cooperation between the United States and Britain and the United States and Canada were completed by representatives of the AEC, State, and Defense departments by the last week in May, and Wilson recommended that Dulles go ahead and open negotiations with both countries. On May 25, 1955, State and Defense Department officials were scheduled to meet with staff members of the JCAE to review the draft agreements. It is possible that the JCAE first learned of plans to exchange nuclear submarine propulsion data with the British at this meeting.

11. *Hearings before Subcommittee, JCAE*, 1958, pp. 516-19; *Minutes of Telephone Conversations of John Foster Dulles and Christian Herter, 1953-1961* (Frederick, Md.: University Publications of America, 1980), reel 3, p. 850; Simpson, *Independent Nuclear State*, p. 114; *Agreement between Government of United Kingdom of Great Britain and Northern Ireland and Government of United States of America for Co-operation Regarding Atomic Information for Mutual Defense Purposes*, Washington, June 15, 1955, in John Baylis, *Anglo-American Defense Relations, 1939-1980: The Special Relationship* (London: Macmillan, 1981), appendix 8, pp. 159-61.

12. Ibid.

13. *New York Times*, June 16, 1955, p. 15; June 21, 1955, p. 17; June 22, 1955, p. 1; 542 *H.C. Deb.* 5s., pp. 1034-38; *Hearings before Subcommittee, JCAE*, 1958, pp. 18, 23, 175, 289-90.

14. Ibid.

17

COOPERATION ON HOLD

> While Her Majesty's Government will at all times welcome arrangements which contribute to world security, they are not prepared to accept agreements which would put the U.K. in a position of decisive inferiority to other Great Powers, a position which is not justified by the state of our scientific knowledge and resources. Her Majesty's Government are however prepared to discuss methods of regulating and limiting test explosions which take account of their own position as well as that of other powers.
> —Anthony Eden, House of Commons, December 6, 1955[1]

By summer 1955, the New Look policy of keeping a tight rein on overall defense spending and relying on the overwhelming American nuclear advantage to deter Soviet aggression began to draw pointed, sometimes public, criticism in the United States. Military leaders like new Army Chief of Staff Maxwell D. Taylor and new Chief of Naval Operations Arleigh A. Burke observed that as Soviet nuclear forces grew in strength (and possibly approached the power of the American nuclear arsenal), deterrence of Soviet conventional military attack in Europe and elsewhere by preponderance of strategic nuclear forces alone would increasingly lack credibilty.[2]

According to the Killian Report, Taylor and Burke had reason to be concerned. Presented to the NSC on February 14, 1955, by the Technological Capabilities Panel chaired by Dr. James R. Killian, president of the Massachusetts Institute of Technology, the report said that the American nuclear advantage was seriously threatened because of Soviet advances in thermonuclear warhead technology and missile development. Although it was more likely, Killian and his colleagues thought, that the Soviets would develop intermediate range ballistic missiles (IRBMs) much earlier than intercontinental ballistic missiles (ICBMs) due to easier accuracy and range requirements, it was of the utmost importance for the United States to keep pace with Soviet long-range missile capabilities. In seven years, the Soviets would probably be close to deploying ICBMs.[3]

Killian Report predictions soon began to come true. The Soviets constructed a liquid-fueled rocket with a thrust of 250,000 pounds, more than enough thrust to send a missile to any major European capital. In response, President Eisenhower ordered acceleration of the IRBM and ICBM projects. For the present, however, the American nuclear advantage was secure. With 11,000 servicemen stationed at 20 major air bases in the United Kingdom, SAC was at peak strength.[4]

Criticizing excessive reliance on nuclear deterrence did not mean that members of the JCS and others in the DOD wanted to scale back the American nuclear buildup. On the contrary, they wanted more money for conventional military and naval forces in addition to, rather than instead of, full funding for nuclear forces. They supported, moreover, the deployment of American nuclear weapons in Europe in cooperation with the NATO allies. They pressed forward, therefore, with plans to enhance Anglo-American nuclear relations under the June 15, 1955, Agreement for Cooperation.

In July 1955 the DOD and JCS prepared to exchange information with the British on the external characteristics of American nuclear weapons—size, weight, center of gravity, attachment systems, and yield. This information was essential, of course, for the British to be able to design their own delivery systems to be compatible with American nuclear weapons. In order to achieve complete compatibility, however, the British also asked for details of American safety features, vulnerability of weapons to countermeasures, fusing and firing mechanisms, loading checks, and in-flight preparation procedures. The DOD and JCS were willing. Chairman of the AEC Strauss was not. He surprised defense officials by saying that he now adamantly opposed revealing the external characteristics of American nuclear weapons because a transfer of that information would necessarily reveal data concerning the design or fabrication of the nuclear components of the weapons. Under section 144b of the Atomic Energy Act of 1954, the administration was forbidden from revealing nuclear weapons data.[5]

Never an enthusiastic proponent of Anglo-American nuclear cooperation, indeed in the late 1940s a fervent opponent, Strauss had no personal inclination to argue on behalf of information exchanges that risked violating the Atomic Energy Act. More importantly perhaps, he wanted to take no action that aroused JCAE anger and opposition to administration policy on overall atomic energy matters. Key members of the JCAE like Chairman Anderson, he knew, had protested his dual role as chairman of the AEC and special assistant to the President for atomic energy affairs. Anderson had been sharply critical of the way Strauss appeared to wield almost total control of AEC policy-making, in addition, and he and other Democrats had opposed plans pushed through Congress by the administration for development of nuclear power by private industry. It was true, on the other hand, that more and more members of the JCAE viewed increased cooperation on nuclear matters with the British in a favorable light. But all the members were still very jealous of their oversight function and considered administration actions testing the limits of the law a serious challenge to their power. Acutely aware, then, that the eyes of the JCAE were on him and fearful that transfer of data on the external characteristics of American nuclear weapons would reveal weapons design or fabrication secrets, Strauss blocked DOD plans for fulfillment of the military part of the June 15, 1955, Agreement for Cooperation.[6]

Since Eisenhower looked on Strauss as his principal atomic energy advisor, Strauss's objection to the transfer of information froze the plan through the summer. But the chairman of the AEC felt less strongly about a renewed DOD effort to transmit information to the British on nuclear submarine propulsion. If the DOD could find a way to justify the exchange, he would not object.

In fact, DOD officials were already actively looking for legal justification for the exchange. In late May 1955, when they learned that the JCAE would not permit inclusion of a provision for an exchange with the British of information on nuclear submarine and other military power reactors, they took steps to checkmate congressional opposition. Secretary of Defense Wilson wrote Attorney General Herbert Brownell, Jr., asking for a legal opinion as to whether the Atomic Energy Act of 1954 permitted the exchange. Brownell replied on June 13. The act did permit an exchange of information on military nuclear power plants, he wrote, but he reserved judgment on whether information on nuclear submarine propulsion could be revealed.[7]

Neither Brownell nor DOD officials informed members of the JCAE about the attorney general's ruling. They all feared the political consequences if Anderson and his colleagues learned that administration officials were plotting to circumvent JCAE wishes. At the July 6, 1955, executive session of the JCAE Subcommittee on Agreements for Cooperation to confirm the June 15, 1955, agreement, it did come out in passing that the attorney general had determined that exchange of information on military package power reactors would be legal. But AEC officials assured members of the Joint Committee that it was AEC opinion that nuclear submarine propulsion data could not legally be revealed. Since DOD officials did not then attempt to act contrary to this opinion, the JCAE did not rise in protest. Like the AEC-DOD impasse over transfer of information related to the external characteristics of American nuclear weapons, however, the question of transferring nuclear submarine propulsion data remained fundamentally unresolved through summer 1955. The DOD wanted to act on both matters but had insufficient support within the administration to contravene JCAE wishes.[8]

Unaware of the internal American debate, Prime Minister Eden and his advisors looked forward to the first exchanges of information under the June 15, 1955, agreement. The time of that pact and the apparently good prospects for improved cooperation on nuclear matters were important in two respects. The British economic outlook into 1956 was such that in order for Britain to carry through with plans to complete its expensive nuclear expansion and to proceed as rapidly as possible with the buildup of the British atomic (and eventually hydrogen) bomb stockpile, American assistance was essential. Construction of nuclear power plants, further, was expected to provide great commercial benefit in the future. On the strategic front, equipping British bombers with British-made nuclear weapons would create an independent British deterrent to Soviet attack and further permit cutbacks of expensive conventional military forces. While at first Britain would become more dependent on its superpower ally, in the long run the country would become economically and strategically self-sufficient.[9]

No sooner was the ink dry on the June 1955 agreement, however, than a glitch in Eden's plans, wholly unrelated to intra-American difficulties, appeared. The opposition Labour party began to bring political pressure to bear on the government to halt the nuclear arms race. On June 28, 1955, for example, the Prime Minister was asked if in view of the improved prospects for general nuclear disarmament, he would be willing to halt British research and development of the hydrogen bomb. No, Eden responded, he would not. Prospects for disarmament had only improved because the Western Powers had increased efforts to build up military strength. They must continue to do so. A month later, Labour members of Parliament opened a new line of questioning. They inquired whether the government viewed as desirable a suspension of all nuclear testing. Minister of State Anthony Nutting responded that the Prime Minister and his advisors did not favor a halt to nuclear testing for the same reason they would not suspend research and development of hydrogen bombs. His response failed to satisfy. Political pressure in the House of Commons for nuclear disarmament, as a result, continued through the year. Although as a practical matter it amounted for the time being to nothing more than a nuisance, Eden and his advisors realized that public pressure to halt nuclear testing might suddenly swell and compel the British government to scale back the British nuclear program, interfering with plans to build an independent nuclear deterrent force.[10]

The British government needed American cooperation in the atomic energy field, then, as soon as possible to accelerate the British nuclear program. But the Americans took no action to fulfill the military provisions of the June 15, 1955, agreement into the fall. AEC-DOD disagreement, the British eventually discovered, had paralyzed the ability of the U.S. government to comply with the agreement. Finally, in December 1955 the DOD officially requested that the AEC agree to transfer information on the size, weight, and attachment systems of American atomic weapons to the British.

Strauss refused. The AEC still held that such a transfer would reveal design or fabrication data and thus violate American law.[11]

Little more progress was achieved on exchanging nuclear submarine propulsion information. On October 12, 1955, in London, First Sea Lord Admiral Louis S. Mountbatten disclosed to the newspapers that because of American legal prohibitions against cooperation, Britain was starting to design its own nuclear reactors for submarines and other warships. His intention was to induce the Americans to cooperate out of a desire to gain access to British secrets. But Britain had a nuclear submarine reactor program in name only. British officials still counted on assistance from the United States Navy (USN) to save Britain millions of pounds in research and development costs. In acknowledgment of that fact, Mountbatten traveled to the United States in the first week of November to discuss with Chief of Naval Operations Burke the possibility of an exchange of data on nuclear submarine propulsion. The administration tried to cooperate. On November 12, 1955, the *New York Times* reported that the First Sea Lord's visit had caused the attorney general to study (for the second time) whether the Atomic Energy Act of 1954 permitted transmission of information to the British on military nuclear reactors.[12]

The first study by Brownell had taken place, of course, back in June 1955 and had resulted in a ruling that the administration could legally exchange data on military nuclear power reactors. The attorney general had yet, however, to render a definitive opinion on the legality of transmitting data on nuclear propulsion reactors for submarines. With JCS plans to exchange information on the external characteristics of American atomic weapons blocked by Strauss's interpretation of the law, and with the British sure to clamor angrily about American inability and unwillingness to carry through with the June 15, 1955, agreement, the DOD pressed Brownell for a favorable decision on the nuclear submarine propulsion question. Unless the Eisenhower administration began to act on its declared policy of cooperating with the British (and to a lesser extent with other NATO allies) in atomic energy matters, its plans to increase the collective strength of the West vis-à-vis the Soviet Union might never come to fruition.

NOTES

1. 547 *H.C. Deb.* 5s., pp. 195-96.

2. Lawrence J. Korb, *The Joint Chiefs of Staff: The First Twenty-five Years* (Bloomington: Indiana University Press, 1976), pp. 39-40, 57-59, 68-69, 108-9.

3. Michael H. Armacost, *The Politics of Weapons Innovation: The Thor-Jupiter Controversy* (New York: Columbia University Press, 1969), pp. 50-51.

4. Ibid., p. 53; Duncan Campbell, *The Unsinkable Aircraft Carrier: American Military Power in Britain* (London: Michael Joseph, 1984), pp. 48-49.

5. *Hearings before Subcommittee on Agreements for Cooperation, JCAE, Amending the Atomic Energy Act of 1954—Exchange of Military Information and*

Material with Allies, 85th Cong., 2d sess., 1958, pp. 175, 189-90, 269-79, 280-89.

6. Ibid., pp. 70-71, 267-68. Strauss's refusal to sanction communication of data on the external characteristics of American atomic weapons to the British precipitated another AEC-DOD quarrel over responsibility for recommending to the President action on nuclear information exchanges of a military character. DOD officials cited section 142 of the 1954 act providing that the DOD had an "equal voice" with the AEC in declassifying restricted data primarily related to military utilization of atomic weapons and other military application. If the DOD and AEC disagreed, section 142 provided for a decision by the President resolving the dispute.

7. Ibid., pp. 516-19.

8. Ibid.

9. R. N. Rosencrance, ed., *The Dispersion of Nuclear Weapons: Strategy and Politics* (New York: Columbia University Press, 1964), p. 92; Anthony Eden, *Full Circle: The Memoirs of Anthony Eden* (Boston: Houghton Mifflin, 1960), pp. 348-49, 412.

10. 543 *H.D. Deb.* 5s., pp. 200-201; 544 *H.C. Deb.* 5s., pp. 818-20; 547 *H.C. Deb* 5s., pp. 195-96.

11. *Hearings before Subcommittee, JCAE*, 1958, p. 378.

12. John Simpson, *The Independent Nuclear State: The United States, Britain, and the Military Atom* (London: Macmillan, 1983), pp. 116-17; *New York Times*, Oct. 13, 1955, p. 4; Nov. 6, 1955, p. 31; Nov. 9, 1955, p. 9; Nov. 12, 1955, p. 18. Sensitive to congressional opposition to the proposed transfer, Mountbatten denied to the newspapers that he had come to acquire American nuclear submarine information at all.

18

DECEIVING THE JCAE

> [The U.S.-U.K. agreement of June 13, 1956, will permit] a broader exchange of materials in the Atomic Energy programmes of the two countries. It will also provide for the exchange of information concerning military package power reactors and other military reactors for the propulsion of naval vessels, aircraft, and land vehicles.
> —Selwyn Lloyd, House of Commons, June 20, 1956[1]

During the Truman administration, progress in Anglo-American nuclear relations could only occur after interested agencies within the government had hammered out policy differences and presented a united proposal to the President. Even then, the JCAE could thwart negotiations or block administration plans to cooperate with the British. The one man—Truman himself—with the authority to override interagency disputes and overcome congressional resistance never exerted himself to push determinedly and consistently for cooperation.

When Eisenhower took office in January 1953, a sharp change occurred in the role of the President in Anglo-American nuclear affairs. Instead of waiting for advisors to reach consensus on the need for greater Anglo-American cooperation, Eisenhower declared in favor of the general goal of improved nuclear relations and eventual construction of an Anglo-American nuclear partnership. Yet, despite speeches criticizing the McMahon Act's restrictive provisions and despite negotiating the June 15, 1955, agreement, Eisenhower had not provided active and vigorous leadership to resolve AEC-DOD differences. Nor had he directly challenged the influence of JCAE members over American nuclear policy. If Anglo-American nuclear relations were to advance, he would have to do so.

Immediately after the turn of the new year, administration officials tried again to move ahead on the issue of transmitting to Britain information on nuclear submarine propulsion. With Eden coming to Washington at the end of January 1956, swift progress was needed. On January 12 the DOD officially informed the JCAE of the attorney general's opinion of June 13, 1955, that the administration could legally exchange military nuclear reactor information with the British. Next, Secretary of State Dulles phoned Brownell on January 23 to pressure him into rendering a definitive response as to how much nuclear data the administration could legally give Britain. He reminded the attorney general that he had said in June 1955 that he thought he would soon be able to give Dulles a "favorable opinion" on the nuclear submarine propulsion question but had not yet done so. When Brownell promised that he would immediately look into the matter, Dulles informed him that from Eisenhower's point of view, the more the administration could give Eden the better. The next day, Brownell called back to ask Dulles to arrange a meeting with AEC technical experts and State Department representatives. He felt confident, he said, that once he had talked with these officials, he could make his report.[2]

Brownell fulfilled his promise in a letter to Wilson and Strauss on January 26, 1956. But although he gave them the "favorable opinion" of the proposed transfer they desired, he clearly felt uncomfortable in assuming responsibility for such a politically charged decision. In his letter he asserted that the AEC could, under the provisions of the Atomic Energy Act of 1954, enter into an Agreement for Cooperation with the British or Canadians to exchange restricted data pertaining to nuclear submarine propulsion. He advised, however, that doing so unilaterally would be unwise. "In view of the sensitive subject matter here involved and its apparent importance," he wrote, "I believe that, in this instance, the matter should be discussed with Joint Committee before the agreements are entered into. This, presumably, would be undertaken on an informal basis in the interest of ascertaining preliminarily the views of the committee and, at the same time, permitting the committee to become aware of proposed developments in the field of international cooperation which might have significant effects upon the atomic energy program."[3]

Aside from American pride in the accomplishment of launching the first nuclear submarine and taking a clear lead in this important military area, the reason that the subject of nuclear submarine propulsion was so "sensitive," as Brownell put it, was JCAE fears that transmission of American nuclear submarine propulsion information would enable the British to apply the technology not only to construction of nuclear-powered submarines but to civilian commercial activities as well. It so happened that Rear Admiral Hyman G. Rickover, director of the USN's submarine reactor development branch, was also manager of the AEC's Shippingport, Pennsylvania, civil power reactor project. Some members of the JCAE believed that an exchange of nuclear submarine propulsion information, therefore, would include transmission of nuclear power reactor data. Thus, the British would get American military and civilian technological information and, since the British nuclear submarine program did not really exist, would give nothing in return. If that occurred, it would be a clear violation of the civilian part of the June 15, 1955, agreement that stipulated that all exchanges be conducted on the basis of reciprocity.[4]

It was not as if, members of the JCAE complained, the British had nothing in their nuclear program of value to trade. At Calder Hall, for example, they had constructed a gas-cooled, graphite-moderated nuclear power station using technology the United States did not possess. But Eden and his advisors refused to reveal that technology as part of exchanges under the civilian part of the June 1955 agreement because they insisted that Calder Hall was a military production plant and not properly included within any civilian exchange. Highly suspicious of British intentions, however, many members of the JCAE believed that the Calder Hall reactor had important commercial nuclear applications and that the British were unwilling to reveal its secrets for that reason. In any event, they viewed nuclear submarine propulsion information as military in character, not civilian, and were determined to deny it to the British. They certainly would not listen to administration entreaties to consider the transmission of that data unless the British offered to exchange Calder Hall technology.[5]

Well aware of JCAE sentiment on this point, administration officials decided against informing members of the committee about Brownell's January 26, 1956, opinion. They began instead to draft secretly an amendment to the June 1955 agreement to mollify Eden when he arrived in a few days. That action and Brownell's legal opinion did cheer the Prime Minister sufficiently so that he did not criticize the administration too severely for failure to live up to the military part of the June 1955 agreement. On the contrary, on his return to London he told the House of Commons that he had talked with Eisenhower about Anglo-American nuclear relations and was "well satisfied with the way the exchange of information is now working under those Agreements and with the results which they are giving to us." Eden was misleading the Commons, of course, about the true state of Anglo-American nuclear relations—something Attlee and Churchill had done without compunction when they had headed the British government. But in this case there was genuine cause for optimism. In the coming months, the Eisenhower administration would make a good-faith effort to improve cooperation with Britain in the nuclear sphere.[6]

One area in which the British believed that the Americans could render timely assistance was British nuclear testing. On March 20, 1956, accordingly, J. C. A. Roper, first secretary of the British Embassy in Washington, met with Outerbridge Horsey, director of the State Department's Office of British Commonwealth and Northern European Affairs, to inform him of British plans to use Christmas Island in the Pacific Ocean for nuclear tests in 1957. Located approximately 1,000 miles south of Hawaii, Christmas Island was claimed both by Britain and the United States. The British government, Roper told Horsey, needed the cooperation and assistance of the American government to carry off its top secret series of tests. The problem was that the British government had given permission to South Pacific Air Lines (SPAL), an American company, to use an airstrip on the island. Since the actual lease to SPAL had been made by the USAF in 1953, Roper wondered whether the American government might not be able to help concoct a cover story to revoke the lease temporarily without arousing suspicion. The British government also welcomed, he went on to say, the cooperation of the American government in facilitating necessary arrangements for the tests. He wanted to know if Britain could use nearby Malden Island, American territory, as an observer point.[7]

Reflecting the administration's growing determination to cooperate with the British on nuclear matters, Horsey was helpful. The USAF's lease with SPAL, he told Roper, contained cancellation provisions that could be invoked on the ambiguous grounds of "military necessity." His office would contact the Air Force to see if this could be done. He added that any American assistance for the conduct of British nuclear tests would in no way prejudice American claims of sovereignty to Christmas Island. Roper replied that he had no specific instructions on this latter point but assumed that the reservation would be taken care of later. He asked Horsey not to talk to the USAF until he reported their conversation to London.[8]

That the Americans would in no way inhibit, but would work to facilitate, the British hydrogen bomb tests in 1957 was an important signal to the British government that the Eisenhower administration really did intend to work for Anglo-American nuclear cooperation. A more important signal came on April 18, 1956, when, without informing the JCAE, the DOD delivered officially to the AEC the draft amendment to the June 1955 agreement to permit transmission to the British of nuclear submarine propulsion information. Almost immediately and again without JCAE knowledge, the administration opened negotiations with the British to arrange the terms of the transfer.[9]

Although armed with Attorney General Brownell's January 26, 1956, opinion that the administration could legally negotiate to transmit nuclear submarine propulsion information to the British, officials in the AEC, DOD, and State Department did not feel sure enough of their case to reveal at once their plans to amend the June 1955 agreement. Instead, they embarked on a surreptitious course of action. They would complete negotiatins with the British, then submit to the JCAE the amendment, the new agreement, and Brownell's legal justification as a kind of fait accompli. But the plan soon came unraveled.

On May 21, 1956, even as the United States conducted the first airborne detonation of a hydrogen bomb, the JCAE held executive hearings to determine the technological progress made by foreign civilian reactor programs and to take testimony from AEC and State Department representatives concerning the state of Anglo-American and Canadian-American contacts under the civilian part of the June 1955 agreement. Reacting to rumors, Senator Henry M. Jackson (D., Washington) asked Gerald C. Smith, counsellor to the secretary of state for atomic energy affairs, whether consideration was being given by the administration to modifying the exchange agreement with the British to permit transmission of classified nuclear propulsion technology. Smith dissembled. The administration, he said, was "preparing to amend the British agreement to permit transfer of that information." But he did not tell the JCAE that the draft amendment had already been drawn up and was being used as a basis for negotiations with the British.[10]

The members of the JCAE clearly did not believe Smith and the administration. Former Chairman of the Committee W. Sterling Cole subsequently requested a written report from the AEC summarizing the results of meetings between the United States and Britain and the United States and Canada held since summer 1955. Again, administration officials dissembled. In a letter dated June 5, 1956, to Anderson, Strauss revealed that discussions to exchange information with the British and Canadians in a number of specific scientific and technical fields had taken place but made no mention of ongoing negotiations to give the British information on nuclear submarine propulsion. Nor did the letter inform the JCAE that an amendment to the June 1955 Anglo-American agreement had been drafted on April 18, 1956.[11]

Withholding information from the JCAE at this point made little sense. Since the end of the current congressional session was less than two months away, the administration had to consult the JCAE in a matter of days anyway so that the members would have 30 days left during the session to consider the proposed exchange as required by the Atomic Energy Act of 1954. Otherwise, the British would have to wait until Congress reconvened in 1957.

Aware of the urgent need for haste, then, Strauss gave Eisenhower the amendment to the June 1955 agreement on June 7, 1956. He recommended that the President approve it and authorize the AEC and DOD to transmit to the British restricted data on nuclear submarine and other nuclear propulsion reactors. Eisenhower said that he intended to look over the papers and sign them the next day. On June 8, therefore, Strauss went before a hastily convened meeting of the JCAE subcommittee on bilateral agreements to brief the members on the administration's proposal. The JCAE erupted in protest. Cole said that in his opinion the Atomic Energy Act of 1954 did not permit an exchange with the British of nuclear submarine propulsion information and demanded that the administration drop the plan.[12]

Plainly expecting a strongly negative reaction from some JCAE members, administration officials attempted to weather the storm. Unfortunately, Eisenhower was suddenly sent to Walter Reed Hospital in Bethesda, Maryland, later on June 8, 1956, for an emergency operation for ileitis. Not only was he unable to lobby the committee but could not even put his signature on the papers amending the June 1955 agreement. Despite this setback, Strauss and other administration officials persisted. Once the operation took place, they brought the President the necessary documents (along with papers pertaining to 27 other legislative bills) and obtained his signature. That same day, June 13, Strauss, Acting Assistant Secretary of State for European Affairs C. Burke Elbrick, and British Ambassador Makins signed the new Anglo-American agreement.[13]

Aside from the provision for the transmission of information on nuclear submarine propulsion, the agreement called for exchanging information on "other military reactors for the propulsion of aircraft and land vehicles" and for a barter deal on raw materials. The British would send the United States stocks of depleted uranium (uranium containing less than 0.7 percent of fissionable U-235) for reprocessing into usable fuel, and the United States would send Britain equivalent quantities of enriched uranium. British officials in the defense establishment and Foreign Office were extremely pleased. Not only would the agreement on nuclear submarine propulsion information eliminate the need for wasteful research duplication, saving Britain millions of pounds, but it would put into British hands a minimum of two years earlier than expected the weapon viewed by British defense officials as the key to the future of the Royal Navy. Nuclear-powered submarines, possibly equipped with nuclear-tipped missiles, would keep Britain a first-class naval power, they believed, for the next two decades.[14]

On June 15, 1956, Strauss set the stage for another in the long series of battles on atomic energy matters between the executive branch and Congress by putting before the JCAE the new Anglo-American agreement. As in the past, many members of the Joint Committee rose in outraged opposition and attacked the proposal on a number of fronts. The agreement violated American law, Cole reiterated, and should be abrogated. Exchanging nuclear submarine propulsion information would give away not only vital military secrets but result in a one-way transfer of commercial nuclear technology to the British, others complained. This would result in long-term commercial disadvantages for American companies. Then there was the old argument that Britain was an unsafe recipient of American nuclear secrets. On June 25, 1956, AEC Commissioner Thomas E. Murray wrote a letter to Anderson stating that he was withdrawing his approval of the agreement due to new information provided by the FBI that detailed the inadequacies of British security procedures. A long-time critic of Strauss over Strauss's domineering style and support of private-industry development of nuclear power, Murray provided more detail for his charges with a second letter on June 26.[15]

Since the 30-day waiting period would expire on July 15, 1956, Anderson scheduled an executive session hearing of the JCAE subcommittee on bilateral agreements for July 9, 1956. At that hearing, JCAE members reviewed the attorney general's opinion of January 26, 1956. They came away still dubious as to the legality of a transfer of American nuclear submarine propulsion technology. The administration was trying to make the case that although mines, torpedoes, and missiles might be carried on a submarine, a submarine itself was not a weapon. Transferring nuclear submarine propulsion information would not, therefore, violate the prohibition in section 144b of the Atomic Energy Act of 1954 against revealing information concerning the design or fabrication of nuclear components of nuclear weapons. While only Cole thought the new agreement blatantly illegal, most JCAE members believed that the proposed transmission went beyond the limits set by Congress under the 1954 Atomic Energy Act.[16]

During the hearing, Anderson extracted from Strauss a pledge to review reports of British security problems. But he and the other members of the JCAE did not intend to wait for a change of heart on the part of the administration. They were too angry at what they viewed as months of intentional deception, misinformation, and withholding of information and were determined to open a strong campaign to thwart the new agreement. On July 13, 1956, accordingly, Cole introduced a bill in the House of Representatives to amend the atomic energy laws to block any exchange of information concerning nuclear submarines. On July 17, 1956, a day after the 30-day waiting period technically expired, Anderson raised the matter on the floor of the Senate. That same day he and JCAE member Senator Albert Gore (D., Tennessee) publicly criticized the AEC's handling of the entire situation and demanded "proper and adequate" security safeguards before any exchange of vital information with the British. The members of the JCAE were doing their best to make the administration wriggle uncomfortably in the bright light of public scrutiny.[17]

The JCAE blitz had the desired effect. At an executive hearing of the full JCAE on July 23, 1956, Strauss and other administration officials testified and revealed doubts about British security. Although officials differed as to whether the British actually met the security standard required by the June 1955 agreement, an FBI study dated July 23, 1956, acknowledged known security problems in the British program. With this evidence in hand, Anderson and the other members sent a letter to Eisenhower on July 27 asking that implementation of the new agreement be suspended until the JCAE could consider the matter further. Since Congress was adjourning that very day in anticipation of the upcoming election campaign, the members would not be able to meet again until the 85th Congress convened on January 3, 1957.[18]

Unwilling to challenge a united JCAE so close to the presidential election, Eisenhower decided to comply with the JCAE's strongly worded request. His letter to Anderson of August 3, 1956, assured the JCAE chairman that he was referring the matter back to the secretaries of state and defense, the chairman of the AEC, and the attorney general for further study. The administration would keep the JCAE fully informed. In keeping with this new policy of deference to congressional sensitivities, Assistant to the Secretary of Defense for Atomic Energy Affairs General Herbert B. Loper informed Anderson by letter on August 16 that the secretary of defense had directed that no transfer of nuclear submarine propulsion data take place until the President made a specific decision to do so. In another letter on the same day, General Manager of the AEC Kenneth E. Fields assured Anderson that recent arrangements made for Rickover to go to Britain concerned unclassified discussions only and had nothing to do with nuclear submarine information.[19]

To Eden and the British, the unfulfillment of yet another Anglo-American nuclear agreement must have been almost too much to bear. With popular war hero and strong proponent of close Anglo-American ties Dwight D. Eisenhower in the White House, they had every right to expect steady if not rapid progress in the nuclear field. Yet, although Eisenhower had early on set forth a strategic program embodied in the policies issued in NSC 162/2 and 151/2 that mandated improved Anglo-American nuclear ties, and despite the fact that he had argued publicly and forcefully on behalf of greater cooperation with the British and other allies in the nuclear sphere, he had stopped short of directly challenging the obstructionist tendencies of the members of the JCAE. Until he did assume a more vigorous leadership stance, moreover, the roadblocks in the path of Anglo-American nuclear cooperation would remain.[20]

NOTES

1. 554 *H.C. Deb.* 5s., p. 1406.

2. *Hearings before Subcommittee on Agreements for Cooperation, JCAE, Amending the Atomic Energy Act of 1954—Exchange of Military Information and Material with Allies*, 85th Cong., 2d sess., 1958, pp. 516-19; Brownell calls Dulles, January 24, 1956, *Minutes of Telephone Conversations of John Foster Dulles and Christian Herter, 1953-1961* (Frederick, Md.: University Publications of America, 1980), reel 4, p. 582.

3. *Hearings before Subcommittee, JCAE*, 1958, p. 516.

4. John Simpson, *The Independent Nuclear State: The United States, Britain, and the Military Atom* (London: Macmillan, 1983), p. 117.

5. Ibid., p. 118.

6. *Hearings before Subcommittee, JCAE*, 1958, pp. 516-19; *New York Times*, Feb. 2, 1956, p. 4; 548 *H.C. Deb.* 5s., p. 2084.

7. Memorandum of Conversation (Roper and Horsey), March 20, 1956, 741.5611/3-2056 (State, Freedom of Information Act, photocopy).

8. Ibid.

9. *Hearings before Subcommittee, JCAE*, 1958, pp. 516-19; Simpson, *Independent Nuclear State*, p. 117.

10. *Hearings before Subcommittee, JCAE*, 1958, pp. 513-19.
11. Ibid., pp. 516-19.
12. Ibid., pp. 513-19.
13. Ibid.
14. 554 *H.C. Deb.* 5s., p. 1406; *New York Times*, June 15, 1956, p. 1; June 16, 1956, p. 6.
15. *Hearings before Subcommittee, JCAE*, 1958, pp. 516-19, 456.
16. Ibid., pp. 41, 516-19.
17. Ibid., pp. 516-19; *New York Times*, July 18, 1956, p. 18.
18. *Hearings before Subcommittee, JCAE*, 1958, pp. 513-19.
19. Ibid.
20. In *Independent Nuclear State*, p. 119, Simpson gives his opinion that the conflict between the administration and the JCAE over transfer of nuclear submarine propulsion data to the British was the turning point in Anglo-American nuclear relations. He describes Eisenhower, the AEC, the DOD, and the State Department as now determined to proceed with exchanges even in the face of active JCAE opposition. The facts do not support this interpretation, as Eisenhower and the administration backed away from the nuclear submarine deal once JCAE protests erupted.

19
FIRST CATALYST FOR NUCLEAR PARTNERSHIP

> The political and psychological impact on the world of the early development of a reliable IRBM [will] be enormous, while its military value [will], for the time being, be practically equal to that of the ICBM.
> —Dwight D. Eisenhower[1]

By summer 1956 the state of Britain's strategic and foreign policy in the world was both alarming and exciting. It was alarming because the island nation's global position continued to erode in the face of economic difficulty. Economic realities, Foreign Minister Selwyn Lloyd and Chancellor of the Exchequer Harold Macmillan told the Prime Minister, required further cuts in the military establishment. Britain, and more generally NATO, would no longer be able to depend upon conventional forces (if they ever had been able to depend on them) to provide a significant measure of deterrence against possible Soviet aggression in Europe. NATO's principal military protection, they said, would have to arise from nuclear weapons targeted on the Soviet heartland. Outside Europe, too, Britain's position was deteriorating. In Egypt, radical Arab nationalist President Gamal Abdel Nasser was moving closer to a decision to nationalize the Suez Canal. Should he take that action, Britain's sea lines of communication with its Far Eastern territories and Commonwealth allies Australia and New Zealand would be in great danger. In wartime they might ultimately be severed.[2]

But the situation facing British leaders in mid-1956 was not all bleak. Even as the country's economic and diplomatic position faltered, British nuclear strength appeared to be waxing. Already in May 1956 British scientists had conducted the first two atomic tests in two and one-half years. Now they were planning four more for the fall and accelerating preparations for the detonation of Britain's first hydrogen bomb sometime in the first half of 1957. Once that latter event took place, moreover, Britain would be catapulted, British officials believed, to the same nuclear level as the United States and Soviet Union.[3]

In the short term, however, British leaders still depended heavily upon American good will and assistance for British security and progress in the nuclear sphere. They did so because the country's nuclear stockpile totaled only about a dozen weapons. That number was not even enough to arm the 50 or so nuclear-capable Valiant bombers scheduled for delivery by the end of the year. In order to build up a significant nuclear arsenal by the early 1960s, then, British leaders counted on the Eisenhower administration carrying through with plans for an Anglo-American nuclear partnership.[4]

Although the July 13, 1956, agreement to transfer data on nuclear submarine propulsion was quickly blocked by the JCAE, administration officials did continue work to clear the way for British use of Christmas Island in the Pacific for the planned British hydrogen bomb test. A comprehensive American position on the issue emerged in mid-August 1956 with a letter from Dulles to the British ambassador. The letter was the official response to a British Embassy note of June 8, 1956. The U.S. government agreed, Dulles wrote, that the British could conduct their test but that such action would have no prejudice to the American claim to sovereignty over the island or to the British claim. With respect to the "considerable financial loss" claimed by South Pacific Air Lines from being evicted from its airstrip on the island, the British government had already promised to consider any claim on its merits. But since the British test might subsequently prevent development of an air route between Honolulu and the Society Islands, 2,500 miles to the south, or impede development of efficient air routes between the United States and the South Pacific, the U.S. government reserved the right to make claims against the British government for any damage. The U.S. government also wanted the British government to relieve the United States from any liability for canceling the 1953 lease to SPAL. In sum, the U.S. government wanted the British government to be completely responsible for any damage or liability arising out of the British hydrogen bomb test at Christmas Island, including possible adverse effects to American islands, territorial waters, fisheries, air and surface navigation, and especially populated areas.[5]

Since the possiblity of claims other than those put forward by SPAL would arise after the British detonated their hydrogen bomb, the issue of liability for damages would not of course provoke the Americans to withdraw cooperation. In light of the administration's failure, moreover, to carry out the terms of the June 1955 agreement for a transfer of information concerning the external characteristics of American nuclear weapons and to overcome congressional opposition to the July 1956 agreement to transfer data on nuclear submarine propulsion, American officials were all the more eager to help facilitate the British hydrogen bomb test. Once the British pledged to cooperate with the Fish and Wildlife Service investigation of the potential effects of the nuclear test on population centers and fisheries, American good will was assured. British and American officials could take up other issues outstanding between the two allies.[6]

The one issue that was to dominate Anglo-American nuclear relations for the next 18 months arose because of a JCS plan to put into effect the strategy of arming NATO countries, and especially Britain, with American nuclear weapons for wartime use. In a March 22, 1956, memorandum for the chairman of the JCS, the Joint Strategic Survey Committee set forth the latest intelligence estimates concerning Soviet nuclear missile development. It was expected, the JSSC said, that the Soviet Union would have IRBMs with a range of 1,600 to 1,800 nautical miles by 1958 or 1959, about the same time the American IRBM program would bear fruit. The Soviets would have, in addition, the ability to produce and deploy ICBMs by 1960-61. Since NATO's conventional military forces were far outnumbered by Warsaw Pact forces and had little possibility, due to budget restraints and the Eisenhower administration's intention to redeploy American troops from Western Europe to the United States, of catching up, a deployment by the Soviets of IRBMs and ICBMs in great numbers would be gravely alarming. Tactical American nuclear weapons deployed in Europe might be checkmated by longer-range Soviet nuclear forces.[7]

To prevent Soviet nuclear superiority in Europe and forestall the possibility of Soviet nuclear blackmail of the NATO allies, and to give the allies confidence that they could stop a Soviet attack if necessary, the JSSC proposed that the administration give serious consideration to "providing our more stable and reliable allies with nuclear weapons with delivery capabilities up to say a thousand miles." In other words, the United States should build IRBMs and persuade the British and other key NATO allies to accept installation of these missiles on their soil. The JSSC saw one major problem, however, with such deployment. If in a time of tension with the Soviets the United States tried to launch the IRBMs from allied soil for the resolution of issues not considered vital to allied officials, allied governments might protest or even try to prevent the launching for fear of retaliation against the missile bases or other targets on their soil by the Soviets.[8]

As with the presence of American bombers armed with nuclear weapons on British soil, then, the proposal to deploy American IRBMs in Britain and elsewhere would focus on the question of consultation on the use of those nuclear-armed missiles. Unlike the situation that existed with respect to American bombers based in Britain, however, British officials intended to insist on a strong right of consultation if not veto over use of any American IRBMs deployed on British soil. The ideal solution from the British point of view would have been for Britain itself to develop IRBMs, arm them with

British-made nuclear weapons, and deploy them as a deterrent force against Soviet attack. Unfortunately, Britain had neither the economic nor the scientific resources to develop and produce IRBMs in time to match Soviet deployment. Only the well-advanced American program could do that. Still, the British government hoped to be able to deploy American IRBMs and retain control over their use. On May 3, 1956, Minister of Supply Reginald Maudling revealed in the House of Commons how this goal might be accomplished. In response to a question about the possibility of an exchange of information with the United States on guided missiles and then a follow-up question about the utility a transfer of guided missiles would have without transfer and pooling of the nuclear weapons for those missiles, Maudling replied that "it is quite possible to design a warhead in one country and put it on a weapon built in another country." British officials were contemplating, in other words, obtaining American IRBMs and fitting them with British-made nuclear warheads.[9]

Even if British and American policymakers could ultimately agree on political questions involving control of American IRBMs in Britain and on related technical questions, the British public remained to be convinced. Sentiment in Britain continued to run strongly in favor of curbing the nuclear arms race. In some quarters, there was even support for disarming unilaterally to reduce the attractiveness of British targets to Soviet nuclear planners. In preliminary meetings on the IRBM question in summer 1956, therefore, State Department representatives and British officials discussed a campaign to convince the British Parliament and people to accept the missiles. Walworth Barbour of the American Embassy in London wrote B. E. L. Timmons, director of the State Department's Office of European Regional Affairs, that initially at least the British public was sure to believe that deployment of American IRBMs in Britain would make Britain a more attractive target for Soviet nuclear strikes. But the U.S. government could counter that impression with the argument that because of Britain's nuclear infrastructure, because of the British bomber force, and because of American nuclear-armed bombers already stationed in Britain, the Soviets would "have to deal with this island promptly and completely in the event of hostilities" anyway. American IRBMs in Britain not only did not increase the target attractiveness of Britain to Soviet nuclear planners but, on the contrary, added to the "defensive strength" of the United Kingdom and to the "deterrent force" of the West.[10]

From discussions he had held with the British, Barbour went on, he felt certain that British Ministers agreed with his reasoning. The main problem from a public relations/political point of view, he thought, would be to convince a majority in the House of Commons to deploy IRBMs and to do so in time to match Soviet IRBM deployment. There might also be a political problem arising from the December 1954 NATO agreement in principle to deploy American tactical atomic weapons in great numbers for use by NATO military forces in the event of war. Some of the NATO allies might protest that deployment of IRBMs in Britain was taking place outside of NATO channels (and so demonstrate a special arrangement between the United States and Britain). But Barbour did not believe that an initial agreement with the British would materially detract from a subsequent proposal to the other NATO partners through the NATO Council for deployment of American IRBMs in Western Europe.[11]

In a certain sense, Anglo-American discussions to begin working out plans to deploy American IRBMs in Britain were premature. Since the JCAE had prevented the administration from transferring to Britain data on nuclear submarine propulsion, the likelihood of congressional sanction for giving Britain information on, control of, or veto over use of American IRBMs had to be considered problematical at best. Only some dramatic turn of events to produce a shift in congressional thinking about the necessity of cooperating with Britain in the nuclear field—or some event or development to rouse Eisenhower to use his vast prestige as a popular President, sound strategist, and admired war hero to override JCAE obstructionism—would make politically possible an Anglo-American deal on IRBMs.

The real turning point in Anglo-American nuclear relations occurred ironically in late October 1956 with the falling-out of the United States and Britain over the Suez crisis and the subsequent decision by Eisenhower to use improved nuclear ties as a way to compensate the British for their deep political and international embarrassment over Suez. Prime Minister Eden and his advisors had long been concerned by the erosion of British influence around the world in the wake of the post–World War II dissolution of much of the British Empire. They had been particularly concerned that radical Arab nationalism in the former British protectorate state of Egypt would endanger British sea lines of communication through the Suez Canal to the Persian Gulf and the Far East. They had sought, therefore, in cooperation with the United States to bring pressure to bear against President Nasser to induce him to lessen his anti-Western policies and prevent Soviet influence from taking root in Egypt. One such tactic was to withdraw offers of aid for the construction of the hydroelectric power-generating dam at Aswan on the Nile on July 19 and 20, 1956. But Nasser, instead of being intimidated, took the decision on July 26 to nationalize the Suez Canal to generate revenue for construction of the dam.

Alarmed, Britain, France, the United States, and 19 other interested nations met at a hastily called conference in London on August 16, 1956, to try to negotiate a settlement with Nasser. When negotiations broke down in early September, the British and French agreed to apply economic pressure on Egypt to accept international control of the canal. While supporting a plan to have the users of the canal form an association to run it, the United States government declared its opposition to the use of force to resolve the dispute.

The crisis continued through October. Suddenly, on October 29, 1956,

Israeli forces invaded Egyptian Sinai and drove toward the canal. The next day Britain and France rejected an American suggestion, supported by the Soviet Union, for an Israeli-Egyptian cease-fire and issued an ultimatum to both Cairo and Tel Aviv to end the fighting. They must withdraw, moreover, from a ten-mile zone on either side of the canal and permit a Franco-British force to occupy key points in the zone. France and Britain then vetoed U.N. Security Council resolutions on October 31 to refrain from the use of force and opened air and naval bombardments of Cairo and the canal area. Their troops invaded Egypt and seized the canal.

Since it quickly became obvious that Britain, France, and Israel had conspired to instigate the Suez crisis, they were universally condemned by the world community. President Eisenhower and his advisors were particularly outraged because the British and French action had occurred on the eve of the American electon. It had also diverted attention from the brutal Soviet repression of the Hungarian revolution. Lastly, it threatened to damage relations between the United States, the ally of Britain and France, and moderate Arab states like Saudi Arabia. In order to distance the United States from the Franco-British action, therefore, and to avoid damaging American interests in the Middle East, Eisenhower ordered steps to undermine the British pound and French franc. This severe economic pressure, combined with diplomatic condemnation, compelled Britain and France to agree on November 6, 1956, to a cease-fire and eventual evacuation of their forces. By December 22 no British or French military personnel remained on Egyptian soil.

In Britain the failure of Eden's bold gamble to seize the canal, bring down Nasser, and so secure the Suez lifeline to the Persian Gulf and Far East led ultimately on January 9, 1957, to the fall of his government. More generally, it shattered the illusion many British leaders had tried to keep alive of British independence from and equality with the United States. Confronted at last by the cold reality of reduced British power and influence in the world, some British Conservatives directed harsh words at the United States. They blamed the Americans for insuring the failure of the Suez operation. The most extreme among them talked of ordering American military forces, including nuclear-armed SAC bombers, out of their bases in Britain. Eden, however, stated categorically that American bases in Britain would be maintained, even after Britain acquired the hydrogen bomb.[12]

Although Eisenhower and his advisors did not doubt that they had acted properly in opposing the Franco-British invasion of Suez, they also realized the necessity of conciliating the British now that the crisis was over. DOD officials in particular wanted to open negotiations within the context of putting together the 1957 Mutual Aid Program (MAP) package for a transfer to Britain of IRBMs.

But the DOD, as Timmons pointed out to Elbrick on November 21, 1956, before a DOD-State Department meeting on MAP of the same day, had yet to settle on any one IRBM proposal. Earlier in the year the DOD had intended to seek base rights in Britain and elsewhere for American IRBMs similar to existing base rights for American bombers. But the British, as has been mentioned, wanted physical control of the missiles or at least veto power over use. The most recent DOD proposal, therefore, spoke of providing "weapons" to the British—missiles, that is, but not American nuclear warheads. Handing over American nuclear warheads was expressly forbidden by American law, and there was no chance that Congress would remove the ban. But even if Congress could be persuaded to sanction transfer of American IRBMs to the British, American officials would face another problem. The other NATO allies on whose soil the DOD contemplated installing American IRBMs might refuse to accept arrangements providing base rights to the United States for its IRBMs. They might demand the same deal as the one given to the British. The United States might have to yield, then, effective control of IRBMs to several different countries.[13]

Despite these potential sticking points, the prospects for cooperating with Britain and other NATO countries in the nuclear field got a boost at the NATO Council meeting in December 1956 when Britain, France, West Germany, the Netherlands, and Turkey requested that American tactical atomic weapons and short-range nuclear-capable Honest John and Corporal missiles be made available to NATO forces for the defense of Western Europe. More importantly, the British by now were intensely interested in acquiring American IRBMs. During the Suez crisis, the Soviets had threatened to intervene militarily to end the fighting and protect their Egyptian friends. They had even hinted at an action against the British Isles with nuclear weapons. That kind of danger no British government could afford to ignore. So the British (especially Duncan Sandys, new defense minister after January 10, 1957) wanted nuclear-armed missiles to deter a Soviet attack. They were now prepared to open preliminary discussions between the USAF and RAF in preparation for governmental-level negotiations in 1957.[14]

But the feeling of frustrating impotence in the face of American pressure over Suez had made a dramatic impression on British policymakers. No one seriously believed that Britain and the United States might some day become open antagonists, but it was credible that the United States might again abandon Britain on some matter vital to British national interests. Since economic limitations and vulnerabilities precluded a buildup of British conventional military forces, Britain must press on with testing the hydrogen bomb and creation of potent nuclear forces. An independent British nuclear deterrent would provide security against Soviet attack irrespective of what the United States did or did not do. An independent nuclear force might provide, in addition, benefits vis-à-vis the United States. American policymakers would certainly have to give more weight to British opinions on a variety of important bilateral and world issues, British officials believed, once Britain built up an arsenal of atomic and hydrogen bombs. And establishing a degree of equality in Anglo-American nuclear relations might even convince the American Congress to entrust Britain with the most important American nuclear secrets. That was what British officials had said after British development of the atomic bomb, of course. But now, with the Eisenhower administration growing increasingly determined to improve nuclear relations with Britain and other allies, and with American concern about British security standards and practices largely alleviated, a true Anglo-American nuclear partnership might be close at hand.[15]

NOTES

1. Dwight D. Eisenhower, *Mandate for Change, 1953-1956* (Garden City, N.Y.: Doubleday, 1965), p. 457.

2. Anthony Eden, *Full Circle: The Memoirs of Anthony Eden* (Boston: Houghton Mifflin, 1960), p. 417; R. N. Rosencrance, ed., *The Dispersion of Nuclear Weapons: Strategy and Politics* (New York: Columbia University Press, 1964), p. 92.

3. 553 *H.C. Deb.* 5s., pp. 695-96, 1283-86; John Simpson, *The Independent Nuclear State: The United States, Britain, and the Military Atom* (London: Macmillan, 1983), pp. 244-45.

4. Simpson, *Independent Nuclear State*, pp. 247, 254.

5. Dulles to British Ambassador, Washington, August 14, 1956, 741.5611/6-856 (State, Freedom of Information Act, photocopy).

6. Memorandum of Conversation, Washington, December 26, 1956, 741.5611/12-2656 (State, FOI, photocopy).

7. Memorandum for Chairman JCS, Washington, March 22, 1956, CCS 381 (Military Strategy and Posture), RG 218, Chairman's File, Admiral Radford 1953-57, Modern Military Strategy and Posture), RG 218, Chairman's File, Admiral Radford 1953-57, Modern Military Branch, National Archives.

8. Ibid.

9. Michael H. Armacost, *The Politics of Weapons Innovation: The Thor-Jupiter Controversy* (New York: Columbia University Press, 1969), pp. 58-59; 552 *H.C. Deb* 5s., pp. 590-91.

10. Barbour to Timmons, London, September 11, 1956, 711.56341/9-1156 (State, FOI, photocopy).

11. Ibid.

12. 562 *H.C. Deb.* 5s., pp. 1099-1100.

13. Timmons to Elbrick, Washington, November 21, 1956, 711.56341/11-2156 (State, FOI, photocopy).

14. Armacost, *Thor-Jupiter Controversy*, pp. 189-91; 564 *H.C. Deb.* 5s., pp. 1307-15; Simpson, *Independent Nuclear State*, p. 124.

15. R. N. Rosencrance, *Defense of the Realm: British Strategy in the Nuclear Epoch* (New York: Columbia University Press, 1968), pp. 236-46; Leon D. Epstein, "Britain and the H-Bomb, 1955-1958," *The Review of Politics* 21 (August 1959): 515-21, 525-27.

20

EISENHOWER TAKES COMMAND

> I have one further thought regarding the next steps required in the matter of the Intermediate Range Ballistic Missile. As you are aware, the only decision taken on this matter at Bermuda by the President was a decision in principle that arrangements would be worked out to make available some of these missiles to the United Kingdom. It seems to me that the next step is to produce an overall draft agreement which will incorporate the various understandings—political, technical, financial, etc.—which will have to be agreed.
> —John Foster Dulles to Wilson, March 29, 1957[1]

As the year 1957 opened, the fate of Anglo-American nuclear relations rested primarily in the hands of one man—Dwight D. Eisenhower. Unsuccessful in his first term in creating effective cooperation in nuclear matters with the British, he now had the opportunity in the aftermath of the Suez crisis to complete the policy of arming the NATO allies, especially Britain, with American-made nuclear weapons for wartime use. By taking the lead in arguing that strained Anglo-American relations required conciliating the British with an offer of American IRBMs and greater overall nuclear cooperation, Eisenhower had an excellent chance of overcoming waning resistance from the most recalcitrant members of the JCAE. Without a vigorous and personal effort by the President, however, DOD plans to deploy IRBMs in Britain and other allied countries might come to naught.

The fall of the Eden government on January 9, 1957, and accession to power of Harold Macmillan greatly improved the political atmosphere between the United States and Britain. Eden's bitterness toward the Americans, especially Dulles, who had undercut him in the Suez crisis, might have made friendly talks on nuclear matters impossible. Instead, Eisenhower looked forward to renewing his friendship with Macmillan, British liaison officer to Eisenhower in North Africa in 1942. On January 22, 1957, therefore, the President directed the American Embassy in London to invite Macmillan to a conference March 21-24 in Washington or Bermuda. Still recovering from the international repercussions of the Suez debacle, Macmillan and his advisors were delighted to accept. They were particularly pleased that the first conference between Eisenhower and the new Prime Minister could be held on British soil at Bermuda.[2]

The invitation to come for a conference meant that Eisenhower had made a basic decision to push on with improvements in Anglo-American nuclear relations even if members of the JCAE and Congress objected. To that end, the administration invited Sandys to come to Washington on January 29, 1957, for negotiations at the Pentagon. Newspapers in Britain and the Untied States speculated that Sandys would offer British nuclear weapons secrets in exchange for American guided missiles. In fact, what occurred was that DOD officials offered Sandys four squadrons (60 missiles) of American IRBMs to be deployed in Britain under a unique arrangement. As required by American law, the nuclear warheads themselves would remain under American control to be released for loading onto the missiles only in the event of war. But the missile sites would be manned by British personnel as soon as they were trained. A joint Anglo-American decision, then, would be required before any missile could be launched. Although details remained to be worked out, the basic agreement was expected to be announced at the conclusion of the Bermuda conference in March. That, of course, was wonderful news for Sandys to take back to Macmillan. But before he left Washington, he got more. The Americans promised to store and earmark for British use nuclear weapons in the event that an international moratorium agreement interfered with British nuclear testing. Even though those particular weapons would remain entirely in American custody in peacetime, the British were assured that in the event of war they would participate in nuclear strikes against the Soviet Union.[3]

The American rationale for wanting to deploy IRBMs in Britain and in other NATO countries went beyond the reasoning behind deploying purely tactical atomic weapons. While shorter-range missiles like the Honest John and Corporal permitted NATO to overcome Soviet conventional military superiority, IRBMs offered distinct strategic advantages. Based overseas and widely dispersed, they would severely complicate Soviet calculations for a surprise attack. Should such an attack take place, their destruction would warn the United States to launch its SAC bombers from American bases and (later when they were deployed) fire its ICBMs and submarine-based missiles. IRBMs would also compound Soviet defense problems. Their relative proximity to Soviet territory and theoretically increased accuracy would offer greater assurance of target destruction. The Soviets would have to reallocate defense funds away from offensive systems to disperse and harden strategic targets. With respect to the European theater itself, deployment of American IRBMs would provide psychological assurance to the NATO allies that the United States was committed to defend Western Europe with its most advanced technology. Under dual control arrangements, moreover, closer integration of American and allied forces would be achieved. The NATO alliance would be reinvigorated. IRBM deployment, lastly, gave the United States strategic advantages over the Soviets even if the Soviets countered with deployment of their own IRBMs. These Soviet missiles would only be able to hit European targets. American IRBMs would be able to strike targets inside the Soviet Union. Unless the Soviets decided to escalate to an all-out exchange using ICBMs, the American homeland would be untouched. American strategists had good cause, therefore, to be cheered by the tentative agreement to deploy IRBMs in Britain.[4]

The British too had cause for rejoicing. Not only did the prospect of American IRBMs in Britain appear as a breakthrough in Anglo-American nuclear relations, it dovetailed nicely with the white paper Sandys was preparing to bring out in April 1957 on the new British defense strategy.

Actually, this strategy had been evolving since summer 1952, when the British chiefs of staff first postulated that Britain should build an independent nuclear deterrent force. Britain, the white paper said, would henceforth follow a strategy of relying primarily on nuclear weapons for deterring major aggressions and for dealing with those aggressions should they occur. Relying on nuclear weapons, it was explained, would permit the British government to implement a whole range of cost-cutting measures while still remaining a first-rate military power. Programs for new generations of supersonic aircraft would be abandoned, the size of the armed forces would be reduced from 690,000 personnel at present to 375,000 by the end of 1962, that personnel reduction would permit an end to conscription by the end of 1961, and force levels for the British Army of the Rhine and Second Tactical Air Force stationed in Germany would be significantly reduced. Overall, British defense expenditures would decline from 1.7 billion pounds in fiscal year 1957-58 to 1.42 billion by 1962.[5]

While all these reductions in conventional military force levels were occurring, the British military establishment would be building up the British nuclear stockpile to about 250 weapons by 1962. They would also build more bombers. But since subsonic British V-bombers were no match for Soviet IRBMs and ICBMs expected to be deployed by 1960, American IRBMs would provide a temporary deterrent force until Britain could develop the nuclear-armed Blue Streak missile for deployment in an underground silo. Once the Blue Streak was acquired, British strategists believed, they would have an independent nuclear force and a greater measure of political maneuverability should British and American interests diverge. On the other hand, construction of an independent nuclear deterrent based on British-built missiles and thermonuclear warheads might improve Britain's standing with the United States. It might persuade the Americans to liberalize laws preventing close collaboration in the nuclear field. This was important because British officials still coveted access to American nuclear technology with applications for civilian purposes.[6]

But it was precisely this information, along with American nuclear weapons secrets, that members of the JCAE wanted to deny the British. British officials, they continued to complain, showed no willingness to reveal information about the British nuclear power development program, in particular the gas-cooled reactor at Calder Hall. Until they were more forthcoming, Anderson and others insisted, the United States should not discuss exchanging nuclear submarine propulsion information. Eisenhower had other ideas. Although he had agreed under JCAE pressure in August 1956 to postpone implementation of the July 1956 agreement to transfer to Britain nuclear submarine propulsion information, he still had the legal justification in the form of the attorney general's January 1956 opinion to do so. The 30-day waiting period had already expired back in the summer, in addition, and his mood was such after Sandys's successful visit that he was determined to effect the greatest possible cooperation with the British in the nuclear sphere in the shortest possible time. On February 5, 1957, he ordered the AEC, DOD, and State Department to put into effect the July 1956 agreement. The President was out front and leading on Anglo-American nuclear relations.[7]

Assured that Eisenhower now intended to promote improved nuclear ties to the British even in the face of JCAE opposition, administration officials prepared to discuss at Bermuda and afterwards questions related not only to IRBMs and nuclear submarine propulsion information, but other atomic energy issues as well. Because the President had acted so quickly and decisively in the aftermath of Suez, however, American policymakers had insufficient time to develop and coordinate negotiating positions and proposals. This was contrary to the situation that had existed in the past when proposals for the improvement of Anglo-American nuclear relations had bubbled up laboriously and often with great discord through the various interested agencies. Now, the President had made a basic decision to promote Anglo-American nuclear cooperation, leaving his advisors scrambling to work out the details. AEC and DOD officials had to hurry, for example, to draw up a draft statement of the proposed scope of cooperation on nuclear submarine propulsion exchanges and means by which such exchanges would be undertaken. A meeting of British and American technicians was then held on March 15, 1957, with a second planned for mid-April.[8]

As for other issues Macmillan and his advisors might wish to raise for discussion, administration officials could only stake out general positions. On the question of future British support for the American-led International Atomic Energy Authority (IAEA), AEC and State Department representatives expected the British to decline to commit themselves to support it. They lacked funds, were short of nuclear-related materials like uranium, and could spare no scientific manpower. With the British nuclear program expanding so rapidly, in other words, the British would be unable to divert resources to the international effort. Nor would they be eager to discuss at an early date application of IAEA safeguards to restrict or eliminate nuclear testing. The British test program had, after all, only resumed testing in May 1956 after a 30-month inactive period. Until British scientists tested the first British hydrogen bomb, American officials observed, and completed a heavy schedule of testing to perfect nuclear warheads for the British deterrent force, Macmillan and his advisors would probably reject a moratorium. AEC and State Department officials sympathized with British concerns and decided only to ask for full support and cooperation in principle for creation of the IAEA.[9]

American policymakers also wanted to avoid controversy at Bermuda over American support for the European Atomic Community, otherwise known as Euratom. Evolving out of Eisenhower's December 1953 Atoms for Peace speech at the U.N. and the American desire for closer integration of the so-called "Six"—France, West Germany, Italy, and the Benelux countries—Euratom would set up a regional Western European program for the peaceful development of nuclear power. American officials considered it the best instrument to accomplish that goal. The British, on the other hand, preferred a broader effort under the aegis of the older Organization of European Economic Cooperation (OEEC), established in 1948 and including in its membership all countries that had participated in the Marshall Plan. Although British officials would not, it was expected, oppose creation of Euratom, they would want the "main instrument" of Western European nuclear power development to be the OEEC. In that way, they would reap the benefits of Euratom developments, would avoid falling behind other Western European nations in the commercial development of nuclear power, and would maintain a vital link with the continental powers. Since the United States had in the past given some assistance to OEEC nuclear development projects and would do so again in the future, American officials did not plan to reject out of hand British desires in this matter. In fact, they too wanted to see closer relations among OEEC countries and thought that placing Euratom under the aegis of the OEEC would be an acceptable arrangement. But they would make clear to the British that Euratom's integrity had to be maintained and that they would defer to the wishes of the Six.[10]

One reason the British were so concerned at being excluded from Western European nuclear development schemes was that, despite the recent American commitments on IRBMs and exchanging nuclear submarine propulsion information, they were still uncertain about the long-term prospects for cooperation with the United States in the nuclear field. Not only did British scientists need technical assistance from the United States to forward the British nuclear power program, but they needed American cooperation on acquiring raw materials as well. Need for uranium would become acute, for example, once a plan, announced March 5, 1957, to triple production of nuclear power by 1965 geared up.

Anticipating the increased British raw material needs, AEC and State Department officials wrote in a March 18, 1957, briefing paper that the President should expect Macmillan to raise the possibility of Britain purchasing Canadian uranium already under contract or option to the United States. He might, in addition, ask for a greater share of the uranium output from South African mines controlled jointly by the United States and Britain. Fortunately, the United States was in a "favorable position" with respect to uranium supplies because of huge American domestic sources currently under production. Because the AEC had over the years financed Canadian uranium production, the United States also controlled that nation's supply. Since in 1959 three-quarters of the free world's 40,000 tons of uranium production would come from the United States and Canada, the United States government could afford to be generous with the British.[11]

In fact, the AEC had already agreed to permit the United Kingdom Atomic Energy Authority to purchase 5,500 tons of Canadian uranium concentrates that would otherwise have gone to the United States between mid-1958 and March 31, 1962. At Bermuda, the AEC would be able to tell the British that the United States would give "sympathetic consideration" to British requests for additional Canadian uranium. Strauss could also hint that the entire output from the expanded South African program, a total of 3,000 tons of uranium per year after March 31, 1962, would probably go to Britain. Although the AEC did not intend to make a final decision on these matters until a study of American military and civilian requirements for the next ten years was completed in July 1957, American officials could intimate that the British would get most, if not all, of what they needed.[12]

Because of the January 1957 offer of American IRBMs to Britain, the success of the Bermuda conference, March 21-24, 1957, was guaranteed. But the President went well beyond merely formalizing the IRBM commitment and promising cooperation on raw materials. He agreed to expand joint intelligence operations with the British and to initiate joint military planning. He further directed Strauss and the AEC to brief the British on the dimensions and weights of American nuclear weapons so that British bombers and bombing mechanisms could be designed and adjusted to carry American atomic bombs. The British reciprocated by revealing the dimensions and weights of their own atomic weapons. Even though the joint communiqué issued on March 24 spoke only of the agreement to provide "certain guided missiles" to the British, and of the renewal of Anglo-American mutual security ties and friendship, the Bermuda conference amounted to a giant stride in the direction of Anglo-American nuclear partnership. Over the next year, negotiations went forward on deploying IRBMs in Britain, on exchanging nuclear submarine propulsion information for British Calder Hall nuclear reactor information (agreed to by the British but only in principle at Bermuda), and on establishing between the RAF Bomber Command and the SAC direct communication links and liaison for exchanges of ideas on operations planning and targeting.[13]

At Bermuda, DOD and State Department representatives decided that the DOD would draw up a draft overall agreement for the transfer of American IRBMs to Britain. It was essential that this be done promptly and prior to the next meeting with British officials, Dulles wrote in a memorandum to Wilson on March 29, 1957, because the only decision the President had made at Bermuda on IRBMs was a "decision in principle that arrangements would be worked out to make available some of these missiles to the U.K." Eisenhower himself had admitted at lunch on March 22 with Dulles and Elbrick that he had questions about the political, technical, and financial details of the IRBM deal. He wanted a document to review, therefore, to serve as a basis for discussion and negotiation with the British. A "fully cleared U.S. Government position" had to be worked out, Dulles told Wilson, before American officials again sat down with their British counterparts.[14]

Using a March 14, 1957, State-Defense memorandum to the President as a general guide, DOD officials worked quickly. On April 3 Elbrick informed Dulles that Wilson had now approved a DOD draft document recommending the basis on which the proposed IRBM deal should be made. The secretary of defense wanted State Department comments and approval so that he could send a letter to Sandys to arrange to open talks in Washington on April 10.[15]

The DOD draft, Elbrick suggested to Dulles, contained certain political understandings that he thought should be slightly altered. He did not believe Wilson would object. But the key question the secretary of state had to decide was how many IRBMs were to be transferred to the British and the manner in which this was to be done. With respect to the legal justification for the transfer, the administration could give the British the missiles on a loan basis under section 102 of the Mutual Security Act of 1954, as amended, or on a grant basis under the 1954 act with reimbursement to the USAF for the number of squadrons transferred. With respect to numbers, the USAF could provide the British with two squadrons (30 missiles) at a cost of $36.5 million or four squadrons (60 missiles) at a cost of $73 million.[16]

Deputy Secretary of Defense Donald A. Quarles, Elbrick told Dulles, opposed transferring missiles on a loan basis, as did Wilson. One reason was that Macmillan had interpreted the President's commitment to deploy IRBMs in Britain as meaning that the missiles would become British property and be manned by British personnel. He had then returned to London and told the House of Commons the same thing. To avoid embarrassing the Prime Minister and upsetting the IRBM deal, Quarles and Wilson argued, the administration must go along with the grant idea. But the secretary of state had more discretion, Elbrick said, on funding for the IRBM transfer. The old "Plan K" account authorized in 1954 for the modernization of the RAF still had $64.4 million left and could be supplemented by "reclaiming certain Plan K sterling accounts and using them to fund current OSP dollar payments." This manipulation of Plan K funds had a drawback, however.

The British had intended to make use of the money for its original purpose. In any event, funds were still available under fiscal year 1957 Mutual Defense Assistance Program (MDAP) accounts to supplement the Plan K account or to finance the entire IRBM transfer.[17]

A final question for Dulles to consider, Elbrick advised, was whether to put all the IRBMs into British hands or to keep some in American possession. According to the March 14, 1957, State-Defense memorandum, only two squadrons were to be transferred to the British and two controlled by the United States without prejudice to a later decision to turn over the American squadrons. But the DOD, and especially Quarles, who had opposed the idea from the start, now recommended putting all four squadrons into British hands as soon as British crews were trained and the missiles could be installed. Quarles and Wilson contemplated paying for the transfer out of Plan K funds to be supplemented by more dollars converted from pound sterling accounts.[18]

Loaning two or four squadrons of American IRBMs to the British, Elbrick advised Dulles, would have political advantages for the administration in dealing with Congress but would cause "something of an explosion" in Britain. He personally believed that the DOD strongly opposed the loan idea because of Quarles's desire to use up remaining Plan K funds and have the $73 million IRBM costs reimbursed to the USAF. But if Dulles did concur in the DOD's desire to transfer the missiles on a grant basis, the secretary of state still had to decide whether the administration should give the British all four squadrons or keep possession of two. He and Dulles's other State Department advisors, Elbrick said, continued to feel that keeping two in American hands would greatly ease the political problem of winning congressional sanction for the transfer. But they all agreed that the other two squadrons should be transferred on a grant basis using Plan K funds. Trying to loan Britain the IRBMs instead of giving them outright would just be asking for another Anglo-American rift.[19]

Dulles saw the wisdom of the grant proposal and signed off on it. He opposed, however, a no-strings transfer of the IRBMs to Britain. It was understood, of course, that American law required that the actual nuclear warheads be kept in American hands until use. But in order to have a better case to put before Congress, Dulles wanted to find some formula to retain a measure of American control over the missiles. In commenting on the DOD's draft, therefore, he tried to arouse interest in a "recapture clause" to permit the United States to recover the missiles at some future date. He was unsuccessful. DOD and State Department officials meeting in Deputy Under Secretary of State Robert A. Murphy's office on April 15 and 16, 1957, decided that such an explicit recapture clause was politically impossible at that time and would be unacceptable to the British. Even so, since the entire transfer would take place under the Anglo-American Mutual Defense Assistance Agreement of 1954, Dulles could make the case that the general recapture clause for transferred military equipment under that agreement applied. Such an interpretation might prove useful in overcoming congressional resistance to the IRBM transfer.[20]

Dulles was even more seriously concerned about language pertaining to conditions under which the IRBMs would be launched. He wanted a clause inserted in the draft requiring the British to use IRBMs only in accordance with agreed NATO plans. But again State-Defense draftees decided that specific language to this effect would be absolutely unacceptable to the British. According to British plans, American IRBMs were to provide a temporary nuclear deterrent force until British-made nuclear forces, including nuclear-armed Blue Streak missiles, could be built and deployed. The British did not want their hands tied by a clause restricting use to the defense of purely NATO interests. Nor did they want to be compelled to use nuclear-armed missiles against the Soviets—thus risking Soviet retaliation against targets in Britain—if a Soviet first strike hit targets in the United States and not Britain. Looking for a compromise, State Department officials inserted in the draft a general reference to the purposes of the North Atlantic Treaty and the obligations of the parties to the agreement thereto. Lastly, the draftees stipulated that the transfer would be on a grant basis for four squadrons of IRBMs to be put into British hands as soon as was practicable. The deal would be financed by Plan K funds. On April 18, 1957, Wilson sent Sandys a letter containing the agreed American negotiating position.[21]

Although Eisenhower and Macmillan had agreed in principle to deploy American IRBMs in Britain, and despite the sense of urgency and purpose with which American policymakers worked to complete a detailed proposal, missiles would not be transferred to Britain anytime soon. For one thing, the IRBMs would not be ready for deployment until 1959. For another, the British had reservations about the American proposal of April 18, 1957. And even if Anglo-American differences could be resolved, the British government faced ever-increasing political pressure from the British Parliament and public to declare in favor of a moratorium on nuclear testing or even a general nuclear disarmament agreement. If domestic political turmoil surrounding nuclear issues got out of hand, more to the point, it might disrupt progress in Anglo-American nuclear relations, including deployment of the IRBMs. Macmillan and his advisors were determined, therefore, to control the political debate. To do so, they would have to secure transfer of IRBMs on conditions favorable to Britain.

NOTES

1. Dulles to Wilson, Washington, March 29, 1957, 711.56341/3-2957 (State, Freedom of Information Act, photocopy/parts excised).

2. Harold Macmillan, *Riding the Storm, 1956-1959* (New York: Harper & Row, 1971), pp. 240-42.

3. Ibid., pp. 245-46, 260-61; *New York Times*, Jan. 21, 1957, p. 3; Jan. 30, 1957,

p. 7; Dulles calls Radford, June 17, 1957, *Minutes of Telephone Conversations of John Foster Dulles and Christian Herter, 1953-1961* (Frederick, Md.: University Publications of America, 1980), reel 6, pp. 216-17.

4. Michael H. Armacost, *The Politics of Weapons Innovation: Thor-Jupiter Controversy* (New York: Columbia University Press, 1969), pp. 183-85.

5. See chapter 12; R. N. Rosencrance, ed., *The Dispersion of Nuclear Weapons: Strategy and Politics* (New York: Columbia University Press, 1964), pp. 92-95.

6. John Simpson, *Independent Nuclear State: The United States, Britain, and the Military Atom* (London: Macmillan, 1983), p. 254; Armacost, *Thor-Jupiter Controversy*, pp. 192-93; Laurence W. Martin, "The Market for Strategic Ideas in Britain: The 'Sandys Era,' " *American Political Science Review* 56 (March 1962): 23-24.

7. *Hearings before Subcommittee on Agreements for Cooperation, JCAE, Amending the Atomic Energy Act of 1954—Exchange of Military Information and Material with Allies*, 85th Cong., 2d sess., 1958, pp. 513-14; *New York Times*, Feb. 25, 1957, p. 14.

8. BEM D-5/2, Washington, March 13, 1957, 57D688 808 (411.25 U.K.-U.S. Berm. Disc.) (State, FOI, photocopy); *Hearings before Subcommittee JCAE*, 1958, pp. 513-14.

9. BEM-5/2, Washington, March 13, 1957, 57D688 808 (411.25 U.K.-U.S. Berm. Disc.) (State, FOI, photocopy); Simpson, *Independent Nuclear State*, pp. 244-45.

10. Ibid.

11. BEM D-5/4, Washington, March 18, 1957, 57D688 808 (411.25 U.K.-U.S. Berm. Disc.) (State, FOI, photocopy).

12. Ibid. Because the Canadians did not want to enlarge their uranium mining and milling industry unless there was a "reasonably assured market," they were waiting to see whether the Americans would exercise their option on Canadian uranium after March 31, 1962. In the meantime, however, AEC and State Department officials thought that the Canadians would be willing to give the British an assurance that the Canadian expansion would be able to meet British needs if necessary.

13. US DEL Bermuda to USIA, March 24, 1957, 57D688 808 (411.25 U.S.-U.K. Berm. Disc.) (State, FOI, photocopy); *Hearings before Subcommittee, JCAE*, 1958, pp. 175, 189; Simpson, *Independent Nuclear State*, pp. 125-26; *New York Times*, June 2, 1957, pp. 1, 3.

14. Dulles to Wilson, Washington, March 29, 1957, 711.56341/3-2957 (State, FOI, photocopy/parts excised); Timmons to Murphy, Washington, April 9, 1957, 711.56341/4-357 (State, FOI, photocopy/parts excised).

15. Ibid.

16. Timmons to Murphy, Washington, April 9, 1957, 711.56341/4-357 (State, FOI, photocopy/parts excised).

17. Ibid.

18. Ibid.

19. Ibid.

20. Memorandum by Timmons to Murphy, Washington, April. 16, 1957, 711.56341/4-1457 (State, FOI, photocopy/parts excised).

21. Ibid.; Tab II-H (U.K.) Intermediate Range Ballistic Missiles, Washington, May 9, 1957, 711.56341/5-957 (State, FOI, photocopy).

21

POLITICAL COMPLICATIONS

> When announcing last June Her Majesty's Government's intention to hold trials of megaton weapons in 1957, Sir Anthony Eden said that the explosions would take place far from any inhabited island and that the tests would be so arranged as to avoid danger to persons or property. The tests would be high air bursts which would not involve heavy fallout. All safety precautions would be taken in the light of the Government's knowledge and of experience gained from the tests of other countries. Since then, detailed plans for the Operation have been made with this as their basis and these assurances can be categorically reaffirmed. There is no question of Hawaii being in the slightest danger. Firing will not take place under any conditions in which inhabited islands might be affected by radioactive material.
> —J. C. A. Roper, January 24, 1957[1]

The success of the Bermuda conference and rapid progress in opening negotiations on IRBMs and nuclear submarine propulsion information greatly strengthened the Prime Minister's hand when he opened the debate in the House of Commons in late March and early April 1957 on Bermuda and Sandys's white paper on defense. The new British defense strategy, he could point out, instead of being based on largely nonexistent nuclear forces had gained form and substance at Bermuda. The IRBM deal with the Americans would provide a temporary but powerful deterrent to Soviet aggression as early as 1959. But by the early 1960s a British-made nuclear deterrent force would take over. The RAF's strategic bomber force would reach full strength, the British nuclear arsenal would expand from 20 weapons to over 200, and research and development on the Blue Streak long-range missile would be well advanced.[2]

The left wing of the opposition Labour party did not intend to let the Prime Minister trumpet his success without comment. Immediately after Macmillan returned from Bermuda, Arthur Henderson inquired whether the government would end hydrogen bomb tests after the first detonation in May 1957 pending the outcome of disarmament discussions currently taking place in the U.N. The British public, Henderson and others in the Labour party pointed out, was still keenly interested in an international moratorium agreement to end nuclear testing. Macmillan and his advisors were well aware of it, but they had another concern. If they halted testing before safe, reliable nuclear warheads for British bombers and missiles were acquired, the country would be permanently and helplessly dependent upon the United States for developing what was to have been an independent British nuclear force by the 1960s. If the Soviet Union then balked at concluding an end to nuclear testing, further, Britain would fall hopelessly behind in the nuclear sphere. Responding to Henderson's question, then, Minister for Home Affairs and Lord Privy Seal Richard Butler said that the policy of the British government remained not to abandon nuclear testing until a comprehensive disarmament agreement with proper safeguards and effective controls against testing was concluded. In the meantime, the security of the free world depended primarily on nuclear deterrence. In order to maintain nuclear deterrence, testing had to continue. He did not say but certainly knew that most British officials, including Macmillan, hoped that a comprehensive disarmament agreement and test ban would not be concluded until after Britain had finished all testing required to build up the British nuclear deterrent force.[3]

On April 1, 1957, Macmillan addressed the House of Commons and discussed the importance of the Bermuda conference. The talks with Eisenhower, he declared, had rebuilt Anglo-American ties strained after the Suez crisis. They had also resulted in an American promise to give Britain guided intermediate range missiles under a "two-key" arrangement. Britain would have physical control over the missiles, he explained, while the United States kept possession of American nuclear warheads. This arrangement compared favorably to the situation that now existed with respect to American nuclear bombers stationed in Britain. With the bombers, the British government had a right of joint consultation but no hands-on control. With the missiles, Britain could exercise a veto over use. The British government also had the right to make its own warheads to replace American nuclear warheads in the future. In this manner, Britain would ultimately exercise total control over the missiles.[4]

Turning to the question of disarmament and a moratorium on nuclear testing, the Prime Minister took an even tougher stand than had Butler a few days earlier. The hydrogen bomb, he stated flatly, was essential for British deterrence of and defense against aggression. Since without testing,

British military forces would have to forego deployment of hydrogen bombs, it would have to continue. Although the British government might agree to some limitation of testing, there could be no outright moratorium. Nor could there be nuclear disarmament without a disarmament agreement on conventional military weapons. Without a concomitant conventional military disarmament pact, he pointed out, the Soviets would gain a huge advantage over NATO forces in Europe. The security of all the allies would be severely jeopardized. Although Macmillan did not command the universal assent of the House of Commons for his statements, he did win a strong endorsement from Labour party leader Hugh Gaitskell for the IRBM agreement with the United States. At least with respect to forging closer nuclear ties with the Americans, the leading figures in both major political parties stood squarely with the Prime Minister.[5]

Such was not the case with Macmillan's position on nuclear testing. On the eve of the first British hydrogen bomb test in early May 1957, political pressure intensified to cancel future nuclear tests. Meeting in London, the U.N. subcommittee on disarmament attracted widespread interest among the British public. While most Britons wanted the government to carry through with the first test, support for future nuclear detonations was less certain. A sizeable percentage of the British electorate wanted the Prime Minister to declare in favor of a moratorium on testing and negotiate with the Americans to rely on existing American nuclear forces for deterrence.[6]

On May 15, 1957, British scientists successfully detonated a hydrogen bomb near Christmas Island in the Pacific Ocean. Instead of praising this important technological and strategic achievement, opposition politicians and much of the public reacted by calling louder for disarmament. They received encouragement from an unlikely source. Harold E. Stassen, Eisenhower's special assistant on disarmament and American representative at the London disarmament conference, put before the U.N. subcommittee a proposal for an early end to production of fissile material for military purposes. At once, Henderson and other disarmament proponents asked the Prime Minister in the House of Commons on May 16 whether the government would adhere to this American call for disarmament. An angry Macmillan, feeling that the Americans had undercut him just in the moment of Britain's finest nuclear achievement, curtly answered that the British government would continue with its nuclear testing schedule. Even though "the bomb works," he explained to the Commons, there was much more to be done before it could be employed "to the purposes for which it has to be prepared." A few days later he tried to quiet the disarmament uproar and deflect criticism of the government's stand by confiding that the government was now formulating a proposal for complete Anglo-American pooling of all information on nuclear weapons. If the Americans accepted, Britain would be able to reduce radically the number of tests required to build up the British deterrent force. But he would accept nothing less than equal partnership with the United States in the nuclear sphere. Britain would not become an American satellite.[7]

Some British officials suspected that the Stassen proposal to the U.N. disarmament subcommittee was a plot authorized by Eisenhower and the American government to embarrass Britain and prevent accumulation of a larger British stockpile of nuclear weapons. This was untrue. Stassen, it turned out, had acted entirely on his own initiative without the prior knowledge or sanction of the President and his advisors. Since Stassen's relations with other American policymakers were poor—Dulles, for one, sought to undermine his influence with Eisenhower at every occasion—he had not bothered to clear his proposal with Washington. Upon hearing of Stassen's actions, moreover, administration officials hastened to disavow them.[8]

By early June 1957 the pressure on the British government to declare for a moratorium on testing diminished somewhat with the temporary recess of the London disarmament conference. The Soviets had blundered and precipitated the recess by insisting that any disarmament agreement include as a first step a pledge to bar use of nuclear weapons. Badly outnumbered in Europe by Soviet conventional military forces, the United States and Britain could never make such a promise. Yet despite this breathing space from the intense heat of public pressure, Macmillan was still angry. He sent Eisenhower a letter complaining that Stassen's proposal had generated great political difficulty for his government. Referring to the late January 1957 suggestion made by American officials to Sandys that the United States would be willing to work out something "special" in the event a moratorium on testing went into effect before British scientists finished the planned test schedule through 1958, the Prime Minister informed Eisenhower that he wanted to send over a negotiating team right away to discuss the matter.[9]

After reading Macmillan's letter, Dulles called Strauss on June 17, 1957, and asked what he thought. Strauss was pessimistic. What the British wanted, he said, was American nuclear weapons and testing information to make further British tests unnecessary. But as he had recently pointed out to Sir Edwin Plowden, head of the British atomic energy program, if a meeting was held with British officials to discuss that kind of proposal, the news would assuredly leak out. The JCAE would react swiftly and negatively. Since the administration could transfer no nuclear weapons information anyway without legislative action, the British were sure to go home disappointed and disgruntled. It made no sense, then, for the British to come at all. Instead, he would write Dulles a personal note indicating that the administration was studying the idea. Dulles could forward the note to Macmillan.[10]

Dulles agreed. Having the British send a negotiating team would only "stir up the animals." It just was not practical to work something out on a nuclear weapons information exchange. Besides, if they made a special deal with the British at this point, other NATO allies would demand a similar arrangement. The most they could promise, he said, was "some stockpiling of weapons earmarked" for British use. That, of course, was the same promise made to Sandys back in January 1957. He added that he had already spoken to Eisenhower about this and the President had authorized him to write Macmillan and say that Strauss, Quarles, and someone from the State Department, probably Murphy, would be willing to talk with the British. He, however, did not think that the idea of a meeting was wise, especially if it took place in Washington. Strauss said that he would go ahead and write his letter to Dulles. It would be a "stall."[11]

Dulles also called Chairman of the JCS Radford to brief him on Macmillan's letter. At the same time, he inquired about the availability for possible transfer to British control of American nuclear warheads stockpiled in Canada, Britain, and Western Europe. Radford said that the United States had a "large number" stockpiled in Britain but that it was his understanding that Congress would have to change the law before any transfer could be arranged. He thought Dulles should tell the British that "frankly we could not get it [a change in the law] at present time because of their lack of cooperation [in refusing to reveal information about the Calder Hall nuclear reactor] and the Chiefs et al. feel it would hurt us with our other allies." Agreeing that no change in the law was presently possible, Dulles asked for an explanation of what precisely had been said to Sandys in January 1957. What he and the other chiefs had not said, Radford responded, was that they would transfer American nuclear weapons to British control. Instead, they had only mentioned storing weapons in Britain under American control—the current situation—and releasing them for British use when hostilities were imminent. They had told Sandys, he assured Dulles, that they could go no further without congressional sanction. The only peacetime release of nuclear weapons Congress might agree to would be transfer of control of stockpiled weapons to Canada because Canada was part of the Continental defense system. In that request, in his opinion, the administration would be justified.[12]

After Radford went on to reiterate that a special deal with the British providing for a peacetime transfer of American nuclear weapons would raise cries of favoritism from the other NATO allies, Dulles responded that it was his impression that the JCS had under consideration stockpiling of nuclear weapons under NATO control. No, Radford said, the JCS had not been considering that. American military officers in Europe, including Supreme Allied Commander General Lauris Norstad, had sent back messages that NATO-controlled stockpiles of tactical nuclear weapons would facilitate plans to use the weapons in the event of a Warsaw Pact attack on Western Europe. But he and the other members of the JCS did not believe that was the way to go. Both the JCS and most of the Europeans themselves, he pointed out, preferred bilateral agreements for installation or stockpiling of nuclear weapons under American control.[13]

Ultimately, Dulles came to an understanding with the British. He committed the administration to consider giving them American nuclear weapons and fissionable material if an international agreement to cease testing of nuclear weapons interfered with essential British nuclear tests. When in July 1957 the news of this "special deal" with the British leaked out to the press, Dulles put out a "red herring" and misled the newspapers into believing that the administration was only considering some ambiguous arrangement for NATO as a whole. In any event, although Dulles and the administration agreed to consider transferring American nuclear weapons to British control, they made no promise to do so. Transfer of American nuclear weapons to foreign, even allied, control in peacetime, they understood, required congressional sanction in the form of a change in American law. On the whole, the administration had recovered quite nicely from Stassen's unauthorized actions at the London disarmament conference and the deleterious impact his proposal had had on the political position of Macmillan and the British government.[14]

Meanwhile, negotiations went forward on the proposals to exchange nuclear reactor information with the British and to deploy IRBMs in Britain. The second Anglo-American meeting on military nuclear reactors, April 15-17, 1957, resulted in formal agreement to limit an initial transfer of information to nuclear submarine propulsion data. Although important members of the JCAE like Senator Anderson still opposed the exchange, DOD officials and Chairman of the AEC Strauss felt emboldened to proceed. A submarine, they continued to insist, was not in itself a weapon but a vessel that could be used for military purposes. Nuclear submarine propulsion information could be considered nonmilitary in nature, then, and not subject to the most severe restrictions against transfer imposed by the Atomic Energy Act of 1954. The attorney general of the United States, in his January 1956 opinion, concurred. With President Eisenhower strongly behind the plan, administration officials paid less attention to JCAE protests.[15]

But the members of the JCAE no longer presented a united front in opposition to dramatic advances in Anglo-American nuclear relations. Indeed, the new chairman of the committee, Representative Carl T. Durham (D., North Carolina), was inclined to agree with the President's assertion that closer nuclear cooperation with NATO and especially with Britain was necessary for the collective defense against possible Soviet aggression. He and other like-minded members of the committee understood, in addition, that atomic energy laws, many still surviving from the original McMahon Act of 1946, were outmoded and did not take into account the acquisition by the Soviet Union and Britain of nuclear forces and nuclear technical knowledge. The premise of the McMahon Act that secrecy for American nuclear weapons information overrode all other considerations no longer held true. Even old-time hardliners like Senators Hickenlooper and Knowland realized that administration moves in the direction of greater cooperation with the allies were necessary. Slowly, if at times grudgingly, they adjusted their thinking. In June 1957, for example, Hickenlooper played an important role in Senate ratification of the treaty establishing the International Atomic Energy Agency. Dulles phoned him personally to thank him and to brief him on the London disarmament talks.[16]

By spring 1957, then, even those JCAE members who opposed administration efforts to forge a nuclear partnership with Britain did so on grounds other than an intractable belief that the United States should protect its nuclear secrets at all costs. They wanted assurances, of course, that the British would adequately protect whatever information, fissile materials, or missiles the administration eventually put into British hands. But they felt even more strongly that British officials should reciprocate by handing over all important British nuclear secrets—including those necessary for the commercial application of atomic energy. That is why British unwillingness to reveal information about the gas-cooled nuclear reactor at Calder Hall aroused so much anger and suspicion. To the JCAE it appeared that the British were trying to acquire American nuclear power secrets without reciprocating and so win a tremendous competitive advantage for the future.[17]

By far the most bitter opposition to administration maneuverings came from former Chairman of the JCAE Anderson. He charged that administration officials, especially Strauss, had systematically withheld information from the committee and intentionally deceived committee members about the state of Anglo-American nuclear relations. Strauss, Anderson said in a conversation with former SACEUR General Alfred M. Gruenther on May 11, 1957, was "totally uncommunicative and largely mistrusted in the Senate." The recent decision by the President not to renominate Thomas E. Murray as a member of the AEC was another point of friction, moreover, because Murray had been the only member of the AEC from whom he could get any information at all. He was "very bitter" against Strauss, he emphasized, and might withhold his support for the IAEA treaty (subsequently ratified by the Senate) as a result. No doubt Anderson's personal animosity toward Strauss increased his hostility toward the proposed transmission of nuclear submarine propulsion information to the British.[18]

In a letter dated May 9, 1957, Strauss informed Durham that the administration was going forward with the nuclear submarine propulsion data transfer. Little more than two weeks later, on May 27, Rear Admiral Rickover led a team of American naval experts to Britain for the first transmission of information. Rickover stayed through May 30, but other naval personnel continued to meet with British experts through the first week in June. By taking the first step, the Americans hoped to persuade the British to fulfill the agreement in principle made by Plowden at Bermuda to discuss Calder Hall technology and other British developments in the commercial nuclear power field. For over a year they had refused to do so for fear that the AEC, in accord with its policy under the Eisenhower administration, would then turn over without cost all commercially valuable information in its possession to private American companies. British government policy, by contrast, was to demand royalties. Although British officials understood that an arrangement to have American companies pay royalties of some kind to the British government could not be worked out, and since British companies were and would be competing with American companies for the international market for nuclear power reactors, they wanted the AEC to agree to confine dissemination of information acquired from Britain to AEC contractors working on an AEC plant similar to Calder Hall. They also wanted reciprocal data on the AEC plant at Shippingport, Pennsylvania.[19]

Once Rickover and his mission completed the first transmission of nuclear submarine propulsion information and invited British nuclear and naval experts to come to the United States for further talks June 10-25, 1957, the British eased terms on revealing information about Calder Hall. But in an attempt to limit criticism that the government was willing to trade vital British commercial secrets for military information, they held back information about Calder Hall's magnox fuel cans and about nuclear reactors being built by private British firms. Still, the AEC had the right to disseminate to American companies the information it did receive.[20]

Details of the proposed deployment of American IRBMs in Britain, the centerpiece of improved Anglo-American nuclear relations, were not so quickly resolved. Negotiations began to drag out, in fact, and ultimately consumed most of the time and effort of British and American atomic energy officials into early 1958. By summer 1957 Anglo-American discussions narrowed to five basic issues—custody of missiles deployed in Britain, division of costs, conditions under which the IRBMs would be used, selection of targets to be attacked, and terms under which the British might replace the missiles or warheads with British built missiles or warheads.[21]

As to the issue of custody of the IRBMs, only Dulles and his State Department advisors had wanted the United States to retain control of two of the four squadrons to be deployed in Britain, and it had been Dulles's idea to try to insert a provision or understanding in any IRBM agreement that the missiles, once outmoded or no longer needed, be returned to the United States. The British, on the other hand, consistently insisted on four squadrons to be placed in British hands. Only the nuclear warheads would remain in American custody until time of use. Since DOD officials had no objection to British control of all four squadrons, and since the Prime

Minister had already stated publicly that all four would come under British control, American negotiators early on conceded the basic point. But the issue was in danger of being revived because the administration was having trouble coming up with funds for the deployment of four squadrons. The United States might only be able to give Britain two squadrons on a grant basis.[22]

The problem of cost arose in part because the projected $73 million pricetag had more than doubled to $149 million due to the added expense of "peculiar ground support equipment" and spare parts. This had upset administration plans. Whereas before officials had contemplated taking the money from leftover Plan K funds amounting to about $99 million, the increased costs of the IRBMs might now make it impossible to pay for deployment even with already authorized and appropriated Mutual Defense Assistance Program funds. The administration might have to seek additional funds from Congress under the fiscal year 1959 Mutual Security Appropriations bill. This would create the possibility of JCAE intervention and a political ruckus in Congress. Nor was it clear that the British, despite cancellation of development of supersonic fighter planes, would let pass without objection diversion of Plan K funds from their original purpose. That money, British officials argued, could help defray the cost of constructing numerous nuclear-capable V-bombers, or it could be applied to fund Britain's share of the IRBM deployment—$57 million more than the initial estimate of $28 million. But perhaps worst of all, if the administration could not come up with its share of the deployment costs, or if a fight with Congress developed placing funding in doubt, the British might take it as a sign that the United States was yet again reneging on an already-concluded commitment to the British in the nuclear field. The political repercussions would be enormous.[23]

Two other issues with political overtones were the related questions of conditions of use and selection of targets. But the American negotiating position was dictated largely by strategic considerations. According to USAF doctrine, American IRBMs required centralized command and control under American jurisdiction. This was necessary because in the event of war quick decisions would have to be made to attack and destroy Soviet targets such as missile sites and air bases from which retaliation could be expected. But without a high degree of coordination between all American strategic forces—bombers, ICBMs, and IRBMs—some Soviet nuclear forces might escape destruction and strike back.[24]

Optimally, then, American negotiators wanted to secure British agreement to use IRBMs in Britain in accordance with American strategic plans and against targets selected by American strategic planners. At the very least, they hoped to constrain the British to use the missiles only in accordance with the NATO Principle that an attack on one was an attack on all. Such a stipulation would compel the British, American strategists believed, to agree to launch the missiles in the event the Soviets attacked the United States without simultaneously attacking Britain.[25]

The British, however, did not want to launch IRBMs against the Soviet Union unless British soil itself was attacked. They feared, quite naturally, that if they did launch, the Soviets would instantly retaliate with nuclear weapons against British targets. A relatively small country in terms of area and much closer to the Soviet Union than was the United States, Britain was vulnerable to great destruction by Soviet medium-range bombers and IRBMs. British negotiators resisted, therefore, American attempts to require automatic launch of American IRBMs in Britain in the event of a Soviet attack on the United States. They also insisted on a degree of independence with respect to targeting. One reason that British strategists had always wanted an independent nuclear force was to have the freedom of action to attack targets more threatening to Britain. These might include Soviet submarine pens, IRBM sites, and bomber bases. But they definitely believed that the American priority target list differed sufficiently from their own to make British control of IRBM target selection highly desirable.[26]

Related to the questions of use and of custody of the missiles was the British intention to replace American nuclear warheads at some future date with British-made warheads for installation on the IRBMs, and whether Britain could replace the IRBMs altogether with a British-made missile like the planned Blue Streak. The Americans, of course, could not stop the British from developing and deploying a British-made missile with a British-made nuclear warhead. But such a project would be expensive and difficult to finance considering British economic limitations. Well within the realm of fiscal plausibility, however, was replacing American warheads with British-made ones. If that were to occur, the "two-key" joint decision for the launch of the IRBMs would no longer exist and the United States would lose all control over British use of the missiles. To avoid this situation, some American officials wanted to retain the right to block replacement of American nuclear warheads with British warheads and perhaps to "recapture" the missiles, as Dulles desired, should the British attempt to proceed without American sanction. DOD officials, in addition, had in mind a plan to station even more American IRBMs in Britain, although these would remain under exclusive American control.[27]

On June 21, 1957, Sandys officially replied to Wilson's April 18 proposal and listed eleven specific points of disagreement related to these five issues. Except on one point, Dulles considered them "basically policy questions" requiring State Department involvement. He accordingly told the American Embassy in London to decline a British request to have a USAF team in Britain June 27 and 28 for technical discussions with the RAF to negotiate Sandys's objections. The Air Force team should limit its discussions, Dulles said, to selection and preparation of missile sites, site security measures, and measures to be taken to establish appropriate safety conditions and training of British military personnel in operation of the IRBMs and related duties.[28]

In analyzing Sandys's reply, American officials did not at first focus on politically and strategically important points concerning control of the missiles and conditions for their use. Instead, Quarles and DOD officials "urgently" studied the question of how, through adjustments in costs and timing of deployment and turnover to the British, the 60-missile, four-squadron plan could be financed. As mentioned earlier, Plan K funds fell about $50 million short of total costs to the United States. It now appeared that the administration would be unable to make up the difference from other currently available sources. Reacting to this news Walworth Barbour at the American Embassy in London reported to Dulles in early August 1957 that he feared that the lack of funds might require scaling back the IRBM plan from four squadrons to a lesser number. Should this occur, the British might reject the deal entirely and retaliate by canceling "certain rights [American base rights in Britain] important to U.S. military security."[29]

In British minds, Barbour explained, the "basic proposition" of deployment of 60 American IRBMs in Britain had already been agreed at Bermuda in March 1957. Any deviation from that commitment by American officials for whatever reason might have disastrous consequences for Anglo-American relations. He offered a possible solution to the problem of funding. Administration officials could go ahead and sign the final IRBM deal and begin deployment using available Plan K funds. Then the administration could request money to complete deployment from Congress under Defense or Mutual Security appropriations for 1959. In this manner, the U.S. government could begin to carry out its commitment to the British. Then, even if Congress ultimately denied the administration additional funding, American officials could at least tell the British that in 1957 and 1958 they had had no reason to doubt that congressional approval would be forthcoming.[30]

On August 15, 1957, a joint Anglo-American study group issued a report on IRBM costs. Quarles, indisputably the most important DOD official familiar with Anglo-American nuclear relations now that Wilson was retiring from his position as secretary of defense and being replaced by Neil H. McElroy, informed the State Department that nothing in the report precluded continued planning for the deployment of four IRBM squadrons in Britain. The DOD, he went on to say, was combining the USAF's Thor and U.S. Army's Jupiter IRBM projects in the interest of economy of resources. They were also making some changes in the scheduling of this combined development program. If the State Department would cooperate in delaying negotiations of detailed agreements with the British and putting off preparation of base sites, the entire delivery and deployment schedule could be pushed back. Costs would thus be stretched out, easing the funding problem.[31]

Dulles agreed to help. On August 27, 1957, he directed officials at the

London Embassy to stall but to assure Sir Richard Powell, permanent British under secretary of defense, that there was "no fundamental change in our thinking." Still, there was little possibility that discussions could be resumed before the end of September 1957. In London, Barbour did inform the British of the delay but not that there had been "no fundamental change" in American thinking on the IRBM deal. Such an assurance, he advised Dulles, would only raise the very doubts it was their intention to avoid.[32]

Annoyed by the delay, the British would not wait until the end of September 1957. On the 17th, British Ambassador to the United States Harold A. Caccia went to Quarles's office in the Pentagon to find out why the Americans had not yet responded to Sandys's eleven points. To buy time, Quarles commented verbally on each of the points and promised that a detailed, written response would soon be delivered. Even so, administration officials delayed another three weeks before approving a draft reply. That response was sent October 12 and closely followed Quarles's remarks to Caccia. The administration promised, for example, that the estimated $33 million cost of each IRBM squadron would now exclude training costs. The DOD would meet those costs out of non–Plan K sources.[33]

On one point, however, the October 12, 1957, letter differed from Quarles's comments of September 17. In response to a request from the USAF, the note omitted his statement that the United States had no present plans for the establishment in Britain of American-controlled IRBM squadrons in addition to the squadrons to be turned over to the British. In light of the disturbing intelligence reports of late September and early October 1957 that the Soviets were about to (indeed did on October 4) launch into orbit around the earth a small satellite, the USAF wanted to keep its options open. If the Soviets, it was believed, had the technological know-how to put a satellite into orbit, no doubt they would soon be able to construct and deploy numerous ICBMs against targets on the continental United States. If the American ICBM program was not sufficiently advanced to match Soviet deployment, moreover, the United States would desperately require allied, especially British, cooperation to deploy additional IRBMs under American control within striking distance of the Soviet Union.[34]

By fall 1957 Anglo-American IRBM negotiations had bogged down. The original impetus provided by the Bermuda conference had long since dissipated in a morass of details and disagreements. Part of the reason for this troubling development was the complicated technological nature of the agreement under negotiation and its political, strategic, and financial consequences. Part was the fact that British and American policymakers still viewed IRBM deployment from a national rather than an allied perspective. The British wanted IRBMs as a first step on the ladder to an independent nuclear deterrent force. The Americans wanted IRBMs in Britain as an adjunct to American strategic forces. Urgently needed was a reminder that the overarching reason for pursuing Anglo-American nuclear cooperation was to increase the collective strength vis-à-vis the Soviets. As in the past, the Soviets themselves would provide that reminder, this time in the form of a 184-pound satellite flying around the earth at 18,000 miles per hour.

NOTES

1. Roper to Irwin, Washington, January 24, 1957, 741.5611/1-2457 (State, Freedom of Information Act, photocopy).

2. John Simpson, *The Independent Nuclear State: The United States, Britain, and the Military Atom* (London: Macmillan, 1983), pp. 247, 254. The range of the Blue Streak was projected to be 2,500 miles as compared to 1,600 for Thor and Jupiter.

3. 567 *H.C. Deb.* 5s., pp. 968-69.

4. 568 *H.C. Deb.* 5s., pp. 37-58.

5. Ibid., pp. 37-58, 63-65, 71-72. Gaitskell also wanted the government to carry through with the first hydrogen bomb test and to build an independent hydrogen bomb capability but wanted in addition limits on nuclear testing at a later date.

6. *New York Times*, May 9, 1957, p. 9.

7. Simpson, *Independent Nuclear State*, pp. 127-28; 570 *H.C. Deb.* 5s., pp. 567-69, 575-76, 1035-39; *New York Times*, May 22, 1957, p. 15.

8. Simpson, *Independent Nuclear State*, pp. 127-28; Michael H. Armacost, *The Politics of Weapons Innovation: The Thor-Jupiter Controversy* (New York: Columbia University Press, 1969), p. 209.

9. Dulles calls Strauss, June 17, 1957, *Minutes of Telephone Conversations of John Foster Dulles and Christian Herter, 1953-1961* (Frederick, Md.: University Publications of America, 1980), reel 6, p. 220.

10. Ibid.

11. Ibid.

12. Dulles calls Radford, June 17, 1957, *Telephone Conversations of Dulles*, reel 6, pp. 216-17.

13. Ibid. Dulles added that he wanted to talk to Norstad. He hastened to assure Radford that he did not think there should be a stockpile of nuclear weapons under Norstad's control as SACEUR but that there should be a stockpile "under U.S. control which could make it available to our allies or SACEUR in the event of war." Radford replied that that situation already existed where allied governments had agreed. Some nuclear weapons had been stockpiled in Italy, for example, but the French had balked. Dulles said that although eager for control of nuclear weapons, the French were afraid of the consequences.

14. Dulles calls Eisenhower, July 17, 1957, *Telephone Conversations of Dulles*, reel 9, p. 1090.

15. *Hearings before Subcommittee on Agreements for Cooperation, JCAE, Amending the Atomic Energy Act of 1954—Exchange of Military Information and Material with Allies*, 85th Cong., 2d sess., 1958, pp. 41, 513-14.

16. Dulles calls Hickenlooper, June 19, 1957, *Telephone Conversations of Dulles*, reel 67, p. 198.

17. *New York Times*, Feb. 28, 1957, p. 14; 569 *H.C. Deb.* 5s., pp. 33-53. The

British understood the potential for rivalry with the United States in the commercial application of nuclear power, but they were counting on nuclear power in the long run to reduce the negative British balance of payments caused partially by the cost of imported oil.

18. Memorandum of Telephone Conversation, Dulles and Gruenther, May 11, 1957, *Telephone Conversations of Dulles*, reel 6, pp. 364-65. So enduring was Anderson's bitterness toward Strauss that in 1959 he was instrumental in blocking Strauss's confirmation 49-46 by the Senate as secretary of commerce.

19. *Hearings before Subcommittee, JCAE*, 1958, pp. 513-14; *New York Times*, June 2, 1957, pp. 1, 3.

20. Ibid., *New York Times*, June 6, 1957, p. 19; June 7, 1957, p. 7; Simpson, *Independent Nuclear State*, p. 127.

21. Tab II-H (U.K.) Intermediate Range Ballistic Missiles, Washington, May 9, 1957, 711.56341/5-957 (State, FOI, photocopy).

22. Memorandum by Herter, Washington, August 15, 1957, 711.56341/8-957 (State, FOI, photocopy/parts excised).

23. Ibid.; Barbour to Dulles, Washington, August 9, 1957, 711.56341/8-857 (State, FOI, photocopy).

24. U.S. Congress, House, *Committee on Armed Services, Hearings, Investigation of National Defense Missiles*, 85th Cong., 2d sess., 1957, pp. 4761-63.

25. Memorandum, Timmons to Murphy, Washington, April 16, 1957, 711.56341/4-1657 (State, FOI, photocopy/parts excised); Dulles calls Murphy, February 4, 1958, *Telephone Conversations of Dulles*, reel 7, pp. 404-5.

26. Ibid.

27. Ibid.; Elbrick to Murphy, Washington, October 9, 1957, 711.56341/10-957 (State FOI, photocopy).

28. Dulles to U.S. Embassy London, Washington, June 25, 1957, 711.56341/6-3557 (State, FOI, photocopy).

29. Barbour to Dulles, London, August 9, 1957, 711.56341/8-957 (State, FOI, photocopy); Memorandum by Herter, Washington, August 15, 1957, 711.56341/8-957 (State, FOI, photocopy/parts excised).

30. Barbour to Dulles, London, August 9, 1957, 711.56341/8-957 (State, FOI, photocopy). By 1959 some of the IRBMs would have been deployed, tangible evidence of American commitment to British security and intention to continue to improve Anglo-American nuclear ties even if Congress balked at funding more missiles.

31. Dulles to U.S. Embassy London, Washington, August 27, 1957, 711.56341/8-957(State, FOI, photocopy/parts excised).

32. Barbour to Dulles, London, August 28, 1957, 711.56341/8-857 (State, FOI, photocopy).

33. Elbrick to Murphy, Washington, October 9, 1957, 711.56341/10-957 (State, FOI, photocopy).

34. Ibid.

22

SECOND CATALYST FOR NUCLEAR PARTNERSHIP

> Naturally, the United States is bound for years to come to enjoy a vast superiority over the other countries of the free world and to be relatively safer, but the resources of applied science and technology have somewhat changed the situaton and, to be frank, the American people are no longer confident that even their great country can do everything itself without allies to secure its own survival and still less to secure the survival of the ideals for which they stand. This new move, this new situation in the United States, will be of far-reaching importance to us all.
> —Harold Macmillan, House of Commons
> November 5, 1957 (after Sputnik)[1]

On August 21, 1957, the Eisenhower administraton tried to take the offensive in the propaganda war over nuclear disarmament. The President announced that the United States would suspend all nuclear weapons tests for two years if the Soviets agreed to halt production of fissionable material for weapons purposes and to join in the establishment of a reliable inspection system. The Soviets responded swiftly—and negatively. On August 23 they resumed nuclear weapons testing. On August 26 they announced that they had successfully tested an intercontinental ballistic missile. Although the ICBM claim went unconfirmed, the United States answered the Soviet challenge by announcing on September 15, 1957, that American nuclear testing would resume in the Pacific in April 1958. A few days later the AEC set off the first recorded underground nuclear explosion. The nuclear arms race was heating up.

The United States, the world believed at the beginning of October 1957, still led in that race. But the successful Soviet launching of the man-made satellite *Sputnik I* into orbit around the earth on October 4, 1957, shocked the scientific community and radically changed the perception of Soviet technological capabilities. Suddenly, the Soviets apeared to be the ones with the superior technology. Incredibly, they appeared to be on the verge of racing past the United States in the nuclear arms competition.

The immediate concern of American policymakers was not that the Soviets *had* gone ahead but that they might do so by early deployment of numerous ICBMs. Secretary of State Dulles called his brother Allen W. Dulles, director of the CIA, on October 8, 1957, to discuss that very subject. He had felt for some time, Allen said to John, that the Soviets were shifting their research and development efforts away from heavy bombers to missiles. That, he believed, was "dangerous" for them in that they might not be able to make the technological leap successfully. The secretary of state nodded. Chairman of the JCS Nathan F. Twining had said the same thing at dinner the night before, he said. Twining's opinion was that it would be quite a long time before the Soviets would have operational ICBMs. But although the consensus of knowledgeable American leaders, including the Dulles brothers, was that the real importance of Sputnik was its propaganda value, they wanted to respond as quickly as possible to dispel the destructive perception of Soviet technological superiority. John Foster Dulles called Twining, therefore, to find out if the head of the American Vanguard satellite program was in Washington. He wanted to talk to him to discover whether an American satellite would soon be launched into orbit.[2]

In Britain Macmillan, Sandys, and other British leaders suffered little loss of morale over Sputnik. On the contrary, they viewed it and its tremendous international impact as an opportunity to convince the Americans to break down all barriers to Anglo-American nuclear cooperation. On October 10, 1957, at the Conservative party conference, Sandys said that American officials would get a ready response if they now brought forward a proposal for greater Anglo-American exchanges of information. Such an agreement, he stressed, would eliminate wasteful duplication in the British and American programs. It would permit faster development of nuclear forces like ICBMs to match Soviet advances. Within the Eisenhower administration, too, American officials recognized that progress in Anglo-American nuclear relations—perhaps even a repeal of all legal restrictions against cooperation—might now be possible. After Sandys's comments of October 10, Strauss contacted Macmillan and suggested that the Prime Minister come to Washington in two weeks for a conference with Eisenhower. After British Foreign Secretary Lloyd received a similar message from Dulles a few days later, Macmillan agreed. The British were now convinced that the Americans were serious about repealing the remaining McMahon Act restrictions against nuclear cooperation and about building a genuine collective defense against the Soviet threat.[3]

This was, in fact, what the Americans had in mind. Dulles told Ambassador Extraordinary and Plenipotentiary to Canada Livingston T. Merchant on October 17, 1957, that Eisenhower was ready to go "pretty far" with the British, and the President expected Macmillan to respond favorably if they offered him anything tangible. They might even use the conference "to work out some closer understanding and arrangements between the two of us and perhaps which might be projected into NATO and SEATO etc. for closer cooperation in the military field, atomic energy, nuclear weapons, economic cooperation, etc." But administration officials were not yet ready to inform the JCAE of their intentions in this respect. Dulles told Senators Knowland and Lyndon B. Johnson (D., Texas), Senate majority leader, that the purpose of the conference was merely to discuss liberalization of present American laws so as to permit a "greater unity of action and greater pooling of assets and divisions of responsibility." The administration certainly had no intention of trying to work out any "exclusive U.S.-U.K. relationship" or "actually to turn over nuclear weapons" to the British or any other foreign country. That latter disavowal was true. Dulles told the President about his conversation with Knowland and indicated that in fact he did not think it necessary to offer American nuclear weapons to the British. But his statements to congressional leaders hardly gave an accurate picture of administration intentions. They were therefore misleading.[4]

Arriving in Washington on October 23, 1957, Macmillan immediately sensed that American confidence and "cocksuredness" had been shaken by Sputnik. But there was nothing wrong with American get-up-and-go. That same day Eisenhower agreed in principle to improve dramatically Anglo-American nuclear cooperation. The next morning the President and his advisors proposed etablishment of two committees to work out details. The first would be headed by Sir Richard Powell and would deal with Anglo-American collaboration on nuclear weapons systems, including IRBMs. A second committee would be chaired jointly by Plowden and Strauss to discuss overall nuclear collaboration and exchanges of nuclear information. Macmillan was amazed, moreover, when Dulles appeared at lunch with a "Declaration of Common Purpose" to be issued at the end of the conference and to call openly for amending the Atomic Energy Act of 1954 to permit "close and fruitful collaboration" with the British and other allied governments. The Americans, Macmillan suddenly realized, could move very swiftly indeed when they made up their minds to do so. Eisenhower made the day's events even sweeter by publicly describing the McMahon Act as a "deplorable incident in American history" of which he personally felt ashamed.[5]

The initial meetings of the two committees went smoothly and resulted that afternoon in agreement to hold further meetings at the end of November or in early December 1957. Of more immediate importance, Strauss, Quarles, and Gerald C. Smith, counsellor to the secretary of state for atomic energy matters, met with Plowden and Powell to draw up a draft statement setting forth general points of agreement. Strauss and Quarles,

Smith told Dulles by phone that evening, had confided afterward that they thought the document "excellent." But then Strauss, Smith learned later from General Loper, had gone to the White House to tell Eisenhower that "all important principles of modern weapons would be in the area which is completely excluded" from exchanges with the British. What that meant, Strauss had told Smith, was that the United States would give Britain everything the Russians knew about nuclear weapons matters and nothing more. No exclusively American nuclear weapons secrets would be revealed. In his opinion, Smith said, such an interpretation of the draft document would be a "bitter pill" for the British and would only amount to a "pretense of cooperation." Strauss seemed to Smith to be counting on the President to explain the document to the British, however, and had breezed over the danger of a negative reaction from Macmillan and his advisors when Smith had raised the point. If carried out in good faith, Smith concluded, the document could still be a first-rate basis for further negotiations.[6]

Dulles subsequently talked to Eisenhower and found the President inclined to downplay the matter. It was a misunderstanding, the President said, and applied only to two or three little things that were unimportant. Dulles thought otherwise. Strauss's reservations against giving the British American nuclear weapons secrets "could go to the heart of the whole program," he thought. Unfortunately, Eisenhower had an "inadequate appreciation" of the situation. The morning of October 25, 1957, therefore, he called Quarles and asked him to go with Loper to talk to the President. Although Quarles too believed at first that the problem was insignificant, Dulles insisted that there was nothing worse than an appearance of agreement with the British only to have that agreement "blow over" later. Reluctantly, Quarles said that he would talk to Eisenhower but wanted Dulles and Strauss there too. Dulles agreed and called Strauss to arrange the meeting for the early afternoon. He wanted, he told the chairman of the AEC, a "clarification in our minds, the President's mind, and maybe Macmillan's as to the scope of the reservations regarding weapons information exchanging."[7]

There may, as Dulles suggested, have been confusion among the Americans as to the scope of nuclear weapons information cooperation. But there was none in the minds of Macmillan and the British. They wanted design and fabrication information for both atomic and hydrogen weapons. This was important for two reasons. First, it would permit British scientists to perfect nuclear warhead designs especially for hydrogen bombs without additional testing. The British government would thus save millions of pounds in expenses and avoid political difficulty over the moratorium on testing question. Second, obtaining American nuclear warhead information would make easier design of British warheads to fit American delivery systems like IRBMs. It would also permit Britain to purchase nonnuclear parts for nuclear weapons at a lesser cost than could be obtained by British production. The Americans, it was well understood, enjoyed economies of scale in their production of nuclear weapons parts.[8]

At the very least, however, British officials wanted to know the weight, dimensions, and yield of American hydrogen weapons along with safety features, vulnerability of weapons, fusing and firing features, loading checks, and in-flight procedures. This kind of information would enable the British to design delivery systems (perhaps the Blue Streak long-range missile) compatible with American warheads. It would also reveal indirectly some information on the design and fabrication of the hydrogen bomb. If the United States in addition agreed to supply Britain with information about the moment of inertia of the warhead of the bomb, its center of gravity, and possibly even design information on the atomic device inside the hydrogen warhead, British scientists might be able to deduce substantial information about the design and fabrication of American hydrogen weapons. Specifically, they could guess both the amounts and arrangements of the nuclear material inside the warhead and the details of the electronic and mechanical equipment that caused detonation.[9]

The DOD favored giving the British information on the design and fabrication of American atomic weapons. Quarles and other defense officials also supported giving the British at least sufficient information on the external characteristics, yields, and delivery systems for hydrogen weapons. That data was essential if the British were to make their hydrogen weapons or delivery systems compatible with American ones. Strauss opposed communicating this latter data, however. He feared that the JCAE would seize upon an administration plan to reveal the most important American nuclear weapons secrets—hydrogen bomb secrets—and refuse to make any liberalization of legal restrictions against cooperation and exchange of information. Although in the October 25, 1957, meeting and later he could not forestall the President from agreeing to give Britain substantial information on American atomic weapons design and fabrication, he did persuade Eisenhower not to push too hard with Congress to reveal hydrogen weapons information. Rather, administration officials would draw up amendments to the 1954 Atomic Energy Act that could be interpreted as giving considerable leeway in revealing nuclear weapons secrets to the British. Then Strauss, Quarles, and Loper would testify before the JCAE and probe carefully to determine just what kind of information exchanges the Joint Committee and Congress would sanction. The administration would insist on nothing that a majority of the JCAE opposed.[10]

In early November Macmillan told the House of Commons that the Washington conference was a great triumph. In the Declaration of Common Purpose, he said, President Eisenhower had accepted the "doctrine of interdependence."[11] In fact, Eisenhower had done nothing of the kind. Certainly in agreeing to push for changes in the law to permit dramatic improvement in Anglo-American nuclear relations he was acknowledging that nuclear cooperation with Britain (and other allies) was necessary to increase the collective strength of the West vis-à-vis the Soviets. But he was in no substantial way acting to impede the independence of the American nuclear program and the ability of the United States to respond forcefully and quickly to Soviet aggression. Negotiations over the next two months would reveal, for example, that the proposed "exchange" of nuclear data, parts, and materials would essentially be a one-way transaction—from the United States to Britain. The United States would receive little from the British beyond information about nuclear weapons designs the United States already possessed, some valuable data on nuclear reactor types the United States did not have, and the right to buy from Britain plutonium produced as a by-product of use in nuclear reactors of American U-235. Nor was Eisenhower, despite the intention to put IRBMs in Britain under a two-key arrangement, compromising American freedom of action on the use of nuclear weapons. He had made no commitment to give Britain a veto over use of nuclear weapons by American bombers flying from British bases. Contrary to creating a situation of "interdependence" in the nuclear sphere, the outcome of the Washington conference of late October 1957 was to increase British dependence upon the United States without markedly increasing British influence with the Americans.

In the aftermath of the Washington conference, Eisenhower and his advisors attempted to quiet public fears that Soviet scientific achievements threatened U.S. national security. On October 28, 1957, Secretary of Defense McElroy announced that he was reversing the order that would have reduced military research, development, testing, and evaluation of new weapons. On November 7, four days after the Soviets launched into orbit a live dog aboard *Sputnik II*, Eisenhower addressed the nation on radio and television to announce the appointment of James R. Killian, Jr., president of the Massachusetts Institute of Technology, to fill the newly created position of special assistant to the President for science and technology. A week later he gave another nationwide speech proclaiming his intention to seek from Congress large increases in future defense spending to meet the Soviet challenge. On November 19 McElroy announced that the administration was speeding up IRBM production for more rapid deployment in Western Europe in 1959.

At the same time, AEC, DOD, and State Department officials proceeded with studies in preparation for further talks on nuclear and military cooperation with Plowden and Powell set for November 23-24, 1957. These discussions would precede more technical talks December 3-5, with December 20 set as a deadline for Anglo-American agreement on areas of cooperation. When Plowden and Powell arrived, progress was achieved on the British request for American assistance to assure Britain of future supplies of uranium after March 31, 1962. American estimates now indicated that the United States would be able to divert uranium from

Canadian or American sources and still have enough U-235 to supply American needs in the future. American officials wanted the British, however, to sell back to the United States plutonium produced as a by-product of use in nuclear reactors of enriched uranium. The British appeared favorable to this suggestion.[12]

In discussions with Strauss, Murphy, and Philip J. Farley, special assistant to the secretary of state for atomic energy affairs, Plowden and Powell also raised the possibility of British use of American nuclear test facilities—Eniwetok in the Pacific, for example. While the Americans did believe that they had the international legal authority under the U.N. Trusteeship Agreement (by which the United States administered Eniwetok and other Pacific atolls and islands) to grant the British request, "serious difficulties" might arise from political considerations. Chief among these, Farley thought, was the danger that limiting access to American test facilities on Eniwetok "might afford plausible grounds for charges of discrimination by other U.N. members who might wish to test nuclear weapons." He was referring to the French. In light of these considerations, American officials carefully avoided making any commitment to the British on use of American nuclear test sites.[13]

At the end of November 1957 the question of consultation on American use of nuclear weapons again became entangled in the British debate over improving cooperation with the United States. Specifically, public and parliamentary protests arose over SAC operation "Reflex Alert" exercises originating out of British bases. Beginning in October, nuclear-armed American B-47 bombers flew continuous patrols with the intention of turning immediately to attack targets in the Soviet Union if the war alert sounded. The purpose of the operation, of course, was to insure that some American bombers would escape from a Soviet first-strike missile attack. But opposition Labour party politicians angrily charged in the House of Commons that USAF operations keeping some B-47s continuously on patrol insured that Britain would not have a right of consultation on their use. Denis W. Healey, for example, cited a public statement made by Dulles on November 19, 1957, that there was "no question of a veto on the use of [American] nuclear weapons being exercised by other countries. No government could legally cast a veto against a decision of another government taken for its own defense."[14]

On November 28, 1957, Prime Minister Macmillan stumbled badly in his response to the Labour party's attack. Citing an agreement made in 1948 (perhaps the Modus Vivendi of January 7, 1948), he said that then Prime Minister Clement Attlee had obtained a right of "joint decision" on American use of atomic bombs carried by American bombers flying from British bases. Winston Churchill, he added, had later confirmed this arrangement. Two weeks later he referred to an Anglo-American understanding of October 1951 making use of British bases in an emergency a matter for joint decision in light of circumstances prevailing at the time and said that this agreement had been the one confirmed by Churchill in Washington in January 1952.[15]

In point of fact, the January 7, 1948, Modus Vivendi had canceled the British wartime right of veto over American use of the bomb. In October 1951, further, the Americans had completely rebuffed British assertions of a right of consultation. Although Churchill had persuaded President Truman and his advisors in January 1952 to include in a joint communiqué that the use of British bases in an emergency would be a matter of joint decision in light of circumstances prevailing at the time, the Americans never meant to commit to anything approaching a right of joint decision. Rather, as Dulles assured Knowland on December 11, 1957, an asserted right of joint decision or veto would not apply "where we have base rights or bases." That meant that by permitting the United States to maintain and operate bases on their territory for nuclear-armed bombers, the British were sanctioning use of those bases by the United States to launch nuclear strikes against the Soviet Union in the event of war. If the circumstances permitted, the United States would certainly consult but would not be bound by British advice and wishes.[16]

In Washington, British Ambassador Caccia and First Secretary of the Embassy Roper tried to insure that Anglo-American negotiations set for December 3-5, 1957, did not contribute to the British government's difficulties. They suggested to Admiral Paul F. Foster, assistant general manager of the AEC for international activities, and General Alfred D. Starbird, AEC director for military applications, that meetings of the two technical committees set up in October at the Washington conference should not include "policy people." Policy had already been set, they said, by the Eisenhower-Macmillan talks of October 23-25, which had in turn been confirmed by Plowden, Powell, and their American counterparts on November 23. They would only send technical and military experts, therefore. The Americans were baffled. Technical questions, Starbird pointed out, often got mixed up with policy questions, and so the United States would include policy people in its delegation. He agreed, nevertheless, to Roper's request that most meetings be held in utmost secrecy in the Pentagon and that American military officials be prepared to meet privately with members of the British Embassy military mission. Discussions would take place in the areas of nuclear materials, antisubmarine detection and defense, nuclear warheads (bombs and missiles), aircraft and aero engines, delivery systems, military propulsion and power reactors, defense against ballistic missiles, and possibly chemical and radiological warfare, infrared research, and thermionic valve research.[17]

Before the December 20, 1957, joint report could be issued, two other important areas of Anglo-American disagreement needed attention. Transmission of nuclear submarine propulsion information to the British and negotiations on the IRBM deal had bogged down. Cooperation between Rickover and the USN on the one hand and the Royal Navy on the other had run into rough seas over the past few months due to friction between British and American personnel and because of internal American developments. The Royal Navy, for one thing, was asking to station many permanent liaison officers inside the AEC and the USN's nuclear program. This caused Rickover to complain that the sheer size of the British presence and time consumed in answering questions would delay critically important work. After Sputnik, moreover, Rickover's worries were heightened by concern that the Air Force, competing with the Navy for defense dollars to build nuclear weapons systems to counter the projected danger from Soviet ICBMs, might win over the President and Congress to a program of IRBM and ICBM development in combination with purchase of more strategic bombers. Navy plans to build long-range missile-launching Polaris submarines might be delayed or cut back. Rickover and his team bridled, therefore, at any obstacle that prevented them from preparing the first Polaris for sea trials by late 1959 or early 1960 to match Thor IRBM deployments in Britain.[18]

By December 1957 relations between the prickly Rickover and the insistent British were severely strained. British naval officers complained that they were not getting adequate information. Part of the problem was the tiny scale of the British nuclear submarine development project. The British were only spending about $7 million a year on their program. At that rate, even if the Americans patiently and thoroughly answered all British questions, it would take many years to produce a successful nuclear submarine reactor. Finally, Rickover proposed a solution. The British should contract to buy a nuclear submarine reactor from Westinghouse, the major American contractor. By acquiring their own model, the British would reach their goal of developing the capacity to build nuclear submarines in the shortest time. They would save money in the long run. Rickover and his people could then proceed with their work without interference. The British liked the proposal at once and tentatively accepted it. Administration officials, as a consequence, inserted a provision for such a purchase in legislation they were preparing to put before Congress in 1958.[19]

Even as negotiations with the British began to bear fruit, prospects for changing the Atomic Energy Act of 1954 to remove most restrictions on information exchanges with allies improved dramatically. Not only did Eisenhower and his advisors pick up the endorsement of Durham and a majority of the JCAE for the basic idea of revising the atomic energy laws, but they won support from outside the committee. On December 3, 1957, for example, the President met with leaders of the House and Senate. Since the world situation was changing so rapidly, he said, the administration needed more discretion to cooperate with all the NATO allies, not just Britain. While some congressional leaders like Chairman of the Senate

Armed Services Committee and member of the JCAE Richard B. Russell (D., Georgia) reserved judgment until they heard the details of the administration's proposed amendments to the Atomic Energy Act, few rose in outright opposition. Those who did, like Anderson, failed to rally sufficient support. The best the senator from New Mexico could do was send Eisenhower a letter cosigned by Durham demanding "proper safeguards" before American IRBMs were given to the allies or nuclear information was exchanged. But Durham quietly told Strauss that the letter did not represent his point of view. Anderson, he intimated, was also misrepresenting the opinions of other JCAE members, some of whom were as strongly in favor of administration proposals as was he.[20]

Ironically, although the administration succeeded in rallying support for greater nuclear cooperation with allies based on increasing the collective strength vis-à-vis the Soviets, administration belief in the strategic necessity of placing American IRBMs in Western Europe faltered. Intelligence estimates originating both in the CIA and the Defense Department predicted that the Soviets would have operational ICBMs in two years. They would have a considerable number in three to five. The significance of early Soviet deployment of ICBMs was that it made American nuclear forces everywhere vulnerable to destruction. This would be especially true for IRBMs stationed in Britain and other NATO countries. Thor missiles intended for installation in Britain and Thor and Jupiter IRBMs being readied for Italy and Turkey would neither be deployed in hardened silos nor have a mobile capacity. Missiles on British soil, in addition, would be difficult to fire preemptively due to the two-key firing system. By the time they were deployed, then, American IRBMs might be outgunned by Soviet ICBMs of longer range and greater striking power.[21]

By November and December 1957 Dulles and Quarles largely discounted the strategic importance of the missiles. They would still be deployed, to be sure, to fulfill the deal with the British and to provide further evidence of the American commitment to NATO and the defense of Western Europe. But chances were that they would soon be replaced by better missiles (or removed altogether). Highlighted by a successful test on December 17, 1957, of an Atlas ICBM, the American long-range missile program was making rapid progress. Not only Atlas but Titan ICBMs and Polaris submarine-launched ballistic missiles would soon be available. When in early 1958 development of solid-fueled Minuteman ICBMs looked promising, liquid-fueled intermediate range Thor and Jupiter missiles seemed outmoded even before installation. Nevertheless, for political reasons the United States secured NATO approval for establishment of IRBM bases under American control at the NATO meeting in Paris on December 19, 1957.[22]

At the same time, British and American negotiators resolved differences on the terms of the proposed deployment of IRBMs in Britain. They also concluded agreements on nuclear weapons information, nuclear warhead production, and raw materials. In late December 1957 the British informally accepted an American proposal on the issue of conditions of use of the IRBMs by agreeing that decisions would be made in light of the undertakings in article 5 of the North Atlantic Treaty. Since that article defined an attack on one as an attack on all, the United States seemed to get an assurance that the British would agree to launch the IRBMs in the event the Soviets attacked targets in the United States but not Britain. But the language was ambiguous enough that the British could claim they were not automatically bound to launch the IRBMs and so risk a Soviet counterstrike at targets in Britain.[23]

Less ambiguity, but more uncertainty about congressional approval, marked the agreement on nuclear weapons information. British and American officials decided that only nuclear warhead design data for nuclear weapons essentially similar to those types produced by the other party could be exchanged. In practice, this would mean that the British would only get information on those types of nuclear weapons they had under active development. They would also have the right to purchase from the United States nonnuclear components for those weapons. To save money, in fact, Britain might be supplied with complete sets of nonnuclear components for certain standard fission (atomic) weapons. They could monitor American development of strategic delivery systems, moreover, and purchase or license-produce either the complete systems or some of their components. Since American nuclear forces were far larger than the British and the United States enjoyed economies of scale in production of delivery systems, it would be to Britain's advantage—both from a financial and technological point of view—to purchase American delivery systems and adapt British nuclear warheads to fit. This they would have to do because under American law the administration could not in peacetime transfer completed nuclear weapons to foreign governments. That provision of the Atomic Energy Act of 1954, at least, Congress would not touch.[24]

Nor was it certain that congressmen would agree to so broad an exchange of nuclear weapons information, nonnuclear parts of nuclear weapons, and delivery systems. Strauss was concerned that wording of the legislation might be too permissive and result in reinvigorated opposition from the JCAE. The problem with the draft amendments, he pointed out to Quarles on December 12, 1957, was that they could be interpreted as authorizing the administration to give too much information on American nuclear weapons not only to Britain but to a "fourth power" (France) as well. In order to be sure that Congress passed the bulk of their proposals, he advised, they had better tighten up the language. JCAE hearings were little more than six weeks away.[25]

More pleasing to members of the JCAE would be the agreements for the coordination of nuclear warhead production and exchange of raw materials. They would tend to increase British dependence on the United States.

Motivated as always by a desire to keep defense expenditures as low as possible, the British had promised not to develop nuclear artillery shells or nuclear warheads for American supplied short-range artillery rockets. Neither would they produce in Britain all their requirements for nuclear bombs and depth charges. Instead, the United States would supply Britain with these nuclear armaments in the event of war under "standard NATO arrangements." That meant that Britain would draw its weapons from the general NATO stockpile the United States was committed to build up. As a quid pro quo, the British—aside from gaining wartime access to a whole array of American nuclear weapons—would receive information to modify British delivery systems to carry American-made warheads and weapons.[26]

Coordinating nuclear warhead production and relying on the United States to supply a large part of British needs in the event of war permitted the British leeway to conclude the materials deal with the Americans. In exchange for enriched U-235 and the vital material tritium, Britain would send to the United States plutonium produced as a by-product of use of U-235 in nuclear reactors. While American U-235 would be used in nuclear reactors and to make bombs, tritium was needed in the cores of British nuclear weapons, both atomic and hydrogen. British plutonium, on the other hand, would enable the United States to fulfill a variety of needs. It could be used to make atomic bombs, both for the United States and to build up NATO's stockpile of tactical nuclear weapons, and to supply Western European states with nuclear material under the Euratom agreement for nonmilitary research. Internationally, the exchange of nuclear materials had an additional advantage. It permitted the United States and Britain to pool resources so that should an agreement with the Soviets be concluded to halt production of fissile material for military purposes, the collective Anglo-American stockpile would be sufficient for both the British and American nuclear programs. The collective strength to deter the Soviets by nuclear means would be maintained well into the future.[27]

Frightened by the Soviet Sputnik successes, the Eisenhower administration accomplished more in Anglo-American nuclear relations in two months than American officials had in twelve previous years. Yet one last obstacle to an effective Anglo-American partnership in the military nuclear sphere remained. Congress had to be convinced to change the law and agree to administration proposals. Unlike past attempts to improve Anglo-American nuclear relations, however, administration officials could expect substantial support on Capitol Hill. Chairman of the JCAE Durham and other key players were very sympathetic to proposals to amend the Atomic Energy Act of 1954 to remove most restrictions against nuclear cooperation with the British. They would also agree to a significant degree of improvement in nuclear relations with other NATO countries. After five years of trying, President Eisenhower and his advisors were very close to forging an Anglo-American nuclear partnership.

NOTES

1. 577 *H.C. Deb.* 5s., p. 37.
2. Dulles calls Allen W. Dulles, October 8, 1957, and Dulles calls Twining, October 8, 1957, *Minutes of Telephone Conversations of John Foster Dulles and Christian Herter, 1953-1961* (Frederick, Md.: University Publications of America, 1980), reel 6, pp. 752-53.
3. Harold Macmillan, *Riding the Storm, 1956-1959* (New York: Harper & Row, 1971), pp. 315-16; *New York Times*, Oct. 11, 1957, p. 10.
4. Dulles calls Merchant, October 17, 1957; Memorandum for Macomber, October 23, 1957; Dulles calls Johnson, October 23, 1957; Memorandum by Peacock, October 23, 1957, *Telephone Conversations of Dulles*, reel 6, pp. 722, 681-83, 685; Dulles calls Eisenhower, October 23, 1957, Dwight D. Eisenhower Papers as President, Ann Whitman File, Eisenhower Library.
5. Macmillan, *Riding the Storm*, pp. 320-23; *New York Times*, Oct. 26, 1957, pp. 1, 4.
6. Smith calls Dulles, October 24, 1957, *Telephone Conversations of Dulles*, reel 6, p. 680.
7. Dulles calls Quarles, October 25, 1957 (10:13 A.M.); Dulles calls Strauss, October 25, 1957 (10:20 A.M.), *Telephone Conversations of Dulles*, reel 6, pp. 674-75.
8. *Hearings before Subcommittee on Agreements for Cooperation, JCAE, Amending the Atomic Energy Act of 1954—Exchange of Military Information and Material with Allies*, 85th Cong., 2d sess., 1958, pp. 174-76, 189-91.
9. Ibid., pp. 189-91, 146-49.
10. Ibid., pp. 174-75. A careful reading of the transcript reveals that administration officials constantly tested the limits to which they could go in forwarding Anglo-American nuclear ties without alienating a majority of the JCAE.
11. 577 *H.C. Deb.* 5s., p. 37.
12. Farley to Dulles, Washington, November 14, 1957, 57D688 808 (411.26 U.S.-U.K. Tech. Disc.), (State, Freedom of Information Act, photocopy); Memorandum of Conversation, Murphy, Caccia, Farley, Washington, December 2, 1957, 711.5612 (State, FOI, photocopy/parts excised); Dulles calls Quarles, November 4, 1957; Dulles calls Strauss, November 18, 1957, *Telephone Conversations of Dulles*, reel 7, pp. 223, 160.
13. Farley to Becker, Washington, November 16, 1957, and Memorandum for Foster and Loper, November 29, 1957, S/AE Files, U.K. Use of U.S. Test Facilities (State, FOI, photocopy).
14. Duncan Campbell, *The Unsinkable Aircraft Carrier: American Military Power in Britain* (London, Michael Joseph, 1984), pp. 55-57; 578 *H.C. Deb.* 5s., pp. 1152-54;. 579 *H.C. Deb.* 5s., pp. 212-17, 371-73.
15. 578 *H.C. Deb.* 5s., pp. 1274-79; 579 *H.C. Deb.* 5s., pp. 1430-31.
16. See chapters 4 and 9; Knowland calls Dulles, December 11, 1957, *Telephone Conversations of Dulles*, reel 7, p. 29.
17. Memorandum for Files (U.S.-U.K. Atomic Energy Talks), Washington, December 2, 1957, 57D688 808 (411.26 U.S.-U.K. Tech Disc.) (State, FOI, photocopy); Memorandum of Conversation, Murphy, Caccia, Farley, Washington, December 2, 1957, 711.5612 (State, FOI, photocopy/parts excised). The Canadians participated

in the technical discussions on antisubmarine detection and defense, aircraft and aero engines, military propulsion and power reactors, and defense against ballistic missiles.

18. Richard G. Hewlett and Francis Duncan, *Nuclear Navy, 1946-1962* (Chicago: University of Chicago Press, 1974), pp. 313-14, 371; *Hearings before Subcommittee, JCAE*, 1958, p. 164. The first Polaris submarine, the *George Washington*, started sea trials on November 15, 1960.

19. *Hearings before Subcommittee, JCAE*, 1958, pp. 162-73.

20. Ibid., pp. 5-6; *New York Times*, Dec. 4, 1957, p. 3; Strauss calls Dulles, December 10, 1957, *Telephone Conversations of Dulles*, reel 7, p. 34.

21. Allen W. Dulles calls John Foster Dulles, October 22 and 23, 1957, *Telephone Conversations of Dulles*, reel 6, pp. 689, 695; Michael H. Armacost, *The Politics of Weapons Innovation: The Thor-Jupiter Controversy* (New York: Columbia University Press, 1969), pp. 204-6.

22. Dulles calls Quarles, November 4, 1957, *Telephone Conversations of Dulles*, reel 7, p. 223; Armacost, *Thor-Jupiter Controversy*, pp. 213-15. Ultimately, the United States only deployed a total of seven squadrons of Thor and Jupiter IRBMs in NATO countries. In October 1959 the Eisenhower administration announced that no more liquid-fueled missiles would be based in Western Europe.

23. Elbrick to Dulles, Washington, December 27, 1957, 711.56341/12-2757 (State, FOI, photocopy/parts excised).

24. *Hearings before Subcommittee, JCAE*, 1958, pp. 5-6; John Simpson, *The Independent Nuclear State: The United States, Britain, and the Military Atom* (London: Macmillan, 1983), p. 133.

25. *Hearings before Subcommittee, JCAE*, 1958, p. 350.

26. Ibid., pp. 5-6; Simpson, *Independent Nuclear State*, pp. 132-33.

27. *Hearings before Subcommittee, JCAE*, 1958, pp. 5-6; Simpson, *Independent Nuclear State*, p. 132.

23

CLEARING THE FINAL HURDLE

> We don't expect to shoot them [IRBMs] off quicky and the chances are they will be replaced but if it is workable at all there could be value if we could spare them to have one or two [squadrons] over there [in Britain].
> —John Foster Dulles, November 4, 1957[1]

In January 1958 the Eisenhower administration prepared to bring before Congress legislation to remove most barriers to Anglo-American nuclear cooperation. The likelihood of success was extremely high. Across the Atlantic, British officials applauded. But even as the moment for which they had waited so long approached, they found themselves harried and harassed on the questions of a moratorium on nuclear testing and consultation on use of nuclear weapons by American bombers flying out of British bases. While renewal and expansion of efforts in the U.N. to get the disarmament ball rolling again only caused Prime Minister Macmillan and his advisors to desire more a nuclear partnership with a dominant United States, Labour party criticism that the government had no way of enforcing the alleged right of joint decision on American use of nuclear weapons made government spokesmen more inclined to emphasize British nuclear independence. The two positions were basically incompatible.

Insistence that Britain retained a right of joint decision on American use of nuclear weapons, further, raised the possibility of a backlash from the American Congress. While most members of the JCAE were willing to consider administration proposals for closer Anglo-American nuclear cooperation as long as the United States emerged the clearly established senior partner, they were not willing to hand over American nuclear secrets without strings. Nor would they permit in any way infringement of American freedom of action to use nuclear weapons to respond to Soviet aggression. Political turmoil over nuclear questions, then, tended to complicate the task of the Eisenhower administration in convincing Congress to amend the Atomic Energy Act of 1954.

On January 11, 1958, two days after the State of the Union Address, Eisenhower called Dulles to discuss upcoming SAC exercises involving British bases. He wondered, he said, whether he should not order a postponement until Macmillan returned from a six-week tour of Commonwealth nations in the Far East. If the USAF went ahead with its plans while Macmillan was away, the British government might be left open to charges that British officials had no control over the actions of nuclear-armed American bombers flying out of British bases. He left Dulles with the impression that he would ask the DOD to postpone the exercises until Macmillan returned and could be personally consulted.[2]

At Dulles's urging, the President soon changed his mind about postponement. On January 22, 1958, he called American Ambassador to London John H. Whitney and instructed him to inform Acting Prime Minister Butler that the United States desired to carry out SAC exercises February 12-18 and March 10-16, 1958. But Whitney should make clear to Butler, he ordered, that the U.S. government wanted complete understanding and agreement on the matter. The British government should know that Eisenhower and his advisors were well aware that exercises at this time might cause political problems for the British government. Accordingly, the U.S. government wished the responsible British ministers to be fully informed and to give their consent. After contacting Macmillan and Lloyd, British Foreign Office officials replied that the British government was well satisfied that the February exercises should take place as scheduled. But they added that the March exercises might have to be canceled if the February exercises resulted in embarrassment that might make postponement of the March exercises desirable. American officials found this response reasonable.[3]

A few days later, on January 27, 1958, Strauss sent a letter to JCAE Chairman Durham detailing the administration's proposed amendments to the Atomic Energy Act of 1954. The changes were intended to permit implementation of recently concluded agreements with Britain, Canada, Australia, and NATO. But the amendments provided for much greater authority to cooperate with allies in the nuclear sphere than was necessary to authorize those specific agreements. As originally worded, the proposed amendments could have been used to justify virtually any exchange of nuclear information or cooperation. One key to this latitude of interpretation was the meaning of the words "atomic weapon." According to the definition in the Atomic Energy Act of 1954, "atomic weapon" meant "any device utilizing atomic energy, exclusive of the means of transporting or propelling the device (where such means is a separable and divisible part of the device), the principal purpose of which is for use as, or for development of, a weapon, a weapon prototype, or a weapon test device." To make matters even clearer, "atomic energy" was defined as "all forms of energy released in the course of nuclear fission or nuclear transformation." Thus, "atomic weapon" as used in both the Atomic Energy Act of 1954 and amendments proposed by the administration in 1958 meant both fission bombs and hydrogen or fusion weapons.[4]

Keeping that explanation in mind, the proposed amendments to the 1954 Atomic Energy Act were comprehensive. First, the President and his advisors wanted authority to communicate to allies information on the external characteristics of "atomic weapons," even if in the process some design information was revealed. This transmission was necessary, Strauss explained in his letter, to permit essential training and planning by the allies and to make their delivery systems compatible with American "atomic weapons." The administration planned to go even further with the British. In amendments to secton 144 of the 1954 Atomic Energy Act, the President wanted authority to communicate "atomic weapons" information to improve an ally's design, development, or production capacity for "atomic weapons." It was not the intent of new section 144c, Strauss wrote, to permit the entry of additional nations into the "atomic weapons" field but to allow exchanges of restricted data if an ally had made substantial progress in the development of nuclear weapons. The words "substantial progress in the development of nuclear weapons," however, were not in the amendments as drafted, but only in Strauss's letter of explanation.[5]

Aside from greater authority to communicate nuclear information to the British and other allies, the administration sought changes in the law to permit transfer of nuclear equipment and materials. Under new section 91c, the President would have the authority to give, sell, or loan to allies nonnuclear parts of "atomic weapons" to improve an ally's state of training or operational readiness, utilization facilities for military applications (that is, military nuclear reactors), and nuclear materials like U-235 for those military utilization facilities or "atomic weapons." Although the amendments were not designed to promote the entry of new nations into the nuclear weapons field, Strauss explained to the committee, the wording of the legislation permitted the President to give nonnuclear parts of "atomic weapons" and nuclear materials to allies as long as that transfer "will promote and will not constitute an unreasonable risk to the common defense and security." This was hardly an exclusive restriction. Lastly, the administration asked for authority to make long-term contractual commitments to purchase special nuclear materials, particularly plutonium, from foreign governments.[6]

On January 29-31, 1958, the JCAE Subcommittee on Agreements for Cooperation chaired by Senator John O. Pastore (D., Rhode Island) met in executive session to hold hearings on the proposed changes to the atomic energy laws. The members took testimony from Strauss, Murphy, and

Quarles. All three emphasized the necessity of increasing cooperation with allies in the nuclear sphere to improve collective security against the growing Soviet threat. Murphy and Quarles stressed in particular that nuclear cooperation with allies was essential to head off independent nuclear weapons development by these countries and to keep the allies firmly in the American camp.[7]

But Strauss ran into sharp criticism from members of the committee who charged that the proposed amendments, far from persuading allies not to develop nuclear weapons, would in fact promote proliferation of nuclear arms. Senator Anderson pointed out, for example, that the test for whether the administration could give "atomic weapons" design and fabrication information to foreign governments was ambiguous. The problem was, he explained, that the requirement that an ally first have a "nuclear weapons capability" was not written into the legislation. Nor was it clear that language like "nuclear weapons capability" or "substantial progress in the development of nuclear weapon," should it be written into the bill, would provide adequate safeguards against injudicious revelation of American nuclear secrets. Strauss tried to clear up the ambiguity. He said that "nuclear weapons capability" meant that a nation had "demonstrated that it can manufacture and has tested a nuclear weapon and has access to material for the manufacture of nuclear weapons." Since the bill only provided for improving an ally's "atomic weapons" design, development, and production capability, the "nuclear weapons capability" test was implied. Senator Albert Gore (D., Tennessee) was not convinced. He said that the legislation was "troublesome" on this point and would have to be looked at carefully.[8]

Another objection came from Representative Chet Holifield (D., California). Holifield questioned Strauss closely about the possibility of the administration using the proposed amendments to transfer nonnuclear parts and special nuclear material for hydrogen bombs. The chairman of the AEC admitted that there was no specific provision preventing such a transfer but that the administration had no intention of doing so. He went on to add that under section 91c it was not intended to promote the entry of additional nations into the nuclear weapons field "nor to promote the buildup of larger atomic stockpiles in the hands of other nations. It is intended, however, that when an ally [Britain] is proceeding with the buildup of a nuclear stockpile, and where it is expending valuable resources which could be used better otherwise for our common defense, the United States might foreclose such waste efforts by furnishing materials under suitable arrangements." In other words, what he was trying to explain was that for the present the intention of the administration was to provide nonnuclear parts and nuclear materials only to Britain. Since the British were proceeding with a buildup of their nuclear stockpile anyway, the United States might as well help them do so in the most efficient manner. Not only would the British save money, but more nuclear materials would be available for the buildup of the American nuclear stockpile.[9]

Holifield frowned. It seemed to him, he said, that by giving an ally nonnuclear parts and special nuclear material in combination with "atomic weapons" design information, the administration would in effect be giving away a completed nuclear weapon. (This was later described by Anderson as a "do-it-yourself kit" for nuclear weapons.) He feared, moreover, that the language of the proposed amendments might even be used in the future to permit the administration to transfer in peacetime actual atomic and hydrogen bombs to the allies. He suggested at the very least that the Joint Committee consider inserting in the legislation some mechanism for the House, as well as the Senate, to review future bilateral agreements containing such proposals.[10]

If Holifield's objections went to the substance of the proposed amendments, some of Anderson's criticisms did not. The first day of the hearings (and several times thereafter), he condemned the administration for its machinations in summer 1956 and spring 1957 on nuclear submarine propulsion information. He was deeply indignant, he said, that the administration, and Strauss in particular, had gone behind the backs of the members of the JCAE to conclude an arrangement opposed by himself and a majority of the committee. He warned Strauss that past administration policy on nuclear submarine propulsion information would have an adverse effect on the final form of the proposed legislation.[11]

Despite this threat, Anderson did not have the votes to block significant change in the law. Whatever revisions were made by the JCAE in the proposed amendments would result from genuinely held reservations that the administration was going too far too fast in agreeing to give the British and other allies nuclear information, parts, and materials without proper compensation and safeguards against escalation or proliferation of the nuclear arms race.

On January 31, 1958, Holifield, Anderson, and Representative Melvin Price (D., Illinois) again zeroed in on the extent to which the proposed amendments would allow the administration to give "do-it-yourself kits" to allies. Starting off, Anderson asked Quarles if the new legislation permitted a transfer of nonnuclear parts of hydrogen bombs. Quarles gave an indirect response. The plan, he said, was "to use that authority where there is a clear justification for it, to make available parts that might be essential to or integral with their delivery systems in a way that would make it desirable for us to give." Alarm bells went off in the heads of the members of the committee. They quickly asked General Loper to detail the specific nonnuclear parts the administration wanted to tranfer to the allies. Loper did so. His still-classified response caused Anderson to press further. From Loper's explanation, he said, he assumed that the probability was that no thermonuclear weapons or parts would be transferred. Was that correct?

Quarles handled the response. "There is no thermonuclear design," he said, "that we now either have or contemplate that would be of a character that you could transfer under this plan."[12]

The members of the Joint Committee were far from satisfied with this response. Holifield insisted that what the administration had in mind was a "do-it-yourself kit" for nuclear weapons (atomic and hydrogen). He charged further that transferring only nonnuclear parts of "atomic weapons" would permit the British to design their "atomic weapons" to fit. It would be, Anderson agreed, like putting bullets (British nuclear cores) into a gun (American nonnuclear bomb parts). Quarles sought to downplay the importance of the transfer. If an ally had the ability to make nuclear cores, he suggested, receiving nonnuclear components from the United States would only be a minor aspect of the problem. Anderson and Pastore strongly disagreed. They protested that without American help the British would certainly have a hard time making firing mechanisms and other nonnuclear parts of American nuclear weapons. The "do-it-yourself kit," Pastore added, really made it easy for them. It was clear that under the proposed amendments as written, the only limitation on transfers of nuclear weapons information, nonnuclear parts of nuclear weapons, and special nuclear materials for building nuclear weapons was the self-imposed restraint and judgment of DOD officials.[13]

Quarles, of course, did not think that a bad thing. He promised the members of the committee that DOD officials would exercise good judgment in the information, parts, and materials they sent the British and other allies. They would certainly consult with AEC experts and members of the JCAE before doing so. But few members were persuaded that self-imposed restrictions or even active supervision by the JCAE would suffice to restrain transmission of "do-it-yourself kits" to the British and other allies in the absence of express prohibitions written into the law.[14]

On February 5, 1958, Loper tried to persuade the JCAE that section 144b as drafted by the administration provided adequate protection against unnecessary revelation of nuclear weapons information to allies other than Britain. The DOD, he assured, would only provide information on the dimensions, weights, and yields of American "atomic weapons" when an ally supplied the delivery vehicle for American warheads. Granted, an ally could deduce from the information given the "arrangement and composition of the interior," but revealing some design and fabrication data was justified by the necessity of achieving compatibility between allied weapons systems and American warheads. Even so, unless an ally had already attained a "weapon design proficiency equivalent to that demonstrated in the particular United States weapon under consideration, information of the type I have indicated would be important, under the law, and therefore nontransmissible under the act." Holifield's frown deepened. He gave his opinion again that more restrictive language was needed to insure that nuclear weapons information could only be given to those nations with a "weapons capability." He continued to insist, further, that the amendments as written permitted the administration to give allies "do-it-yourself kits" for nuclear weapons. Finally, under intense questioning, Loper admitted that this was so. "Technically," he confessed, "through the application of all sections of the authority, all pieces of the authority granted by this law, one could furnish all parts separately as well as design information to a nation which would permit him to assemble them or manufacture a nuclear weapon." Nuclear weapons design information plus nonnuclear components of nuclear weapons plus nuclear materials, Holifield had established, equaled a completed nuclear weapon.[15]

Interestingly, no member of the JCAE protested or made any negative reference to the administration plan to put IRBMs in Britain under the two-key arrangement. Perhaps they were dissuaded from raising the issue by the fact that the President had made a public commitment to the British on missiles at Bermuda. Or perhaps they were just too distracted by other issues raised by the proposed amendments to bother about the missiles. But IRBM deployment in Britain did not become a significant problem in the JCAE hearings.

It still was, however, in negotiations with the British. By early February 1958 Dulles was very worried that the IRBM deal was falling apart and that the administration would become a "laughing stock" before the world because an agreement in principle to deploy the missiles had been made almost a year before. The crux of the problem was that the British now appeared to be backing away from the language that the "decisoin on use would be taken in accordance with the North Atlantic Treaty principle of an attack on one is an attack on all."[16]

On the morning of February 4, 1958, Dulles called Murphy to talk about the hang-up in the IRBM deal and to discuss what to say to Caccia at the meeting arranged by Quarles for that afternoon. They had to be ready for all contingencies, he said. But if no agreement was possible, if the British rejected the American condition that a decision on use be taken in accordance with the NATO principle that an attack on one was an attack on all, there was a possibility that the French would step in and offer the British a deal to develop an Anglo-French IRBM. That would be a disaster. Upon reflection, however, he had to admit that that was a very remote possibility and so perhaps not worth losing sleep over. Murphy agreed. Their problem was not a French overture to the British but a British rejection of any IRBM deal. One difficulty was that British officials now feared that the IRBMs they were getting were no longer worth anything. Citing Soviet ICBM advances, they said they would be outgunned from the start. But they also complained that the timing was not right. The uproar in Britain over American nuclear-armed bomber exercises and the politically sensitive question of right of consultation had caused them great distress.[17]

Dulles understood the British predicament. Yet in talking with Lloyd, he said, he had not gotten the impression that the British foreign secretary himself wanted to reject the American language on decision for use. Still, if the British government ultimately failed to accept this condition, he thought that the President and his advisors should take a "second look" at the decision to deploy the missiles. He felt strongly on this point, he told Murphy, because without language tying a decision on use to the NATO principle that an attack on one was an attack on all (thus in theory requiring the British to agree to launch the IRBMs in the event the Soviets struck only at American targets and not at British and Western European ones), they would have no way of justifying the deal before Congress. Certain senators would charge that the administration was handing over American IRBMs and giving the British veto power over their use. They would not be able to refute that argument. Murphy entirely agreed.[18]

Aside from not wanting to concede language compelling a launch of IRBMs in the event the United States and not Britain was attacked by the Soviet Union, the British had another reason for resisting the American condition on decision for use. They wanted to keep the IRBMs, or at least some of them, free from NATO military control. As long as they argued that the IRBM arrangement with the Americans was separate from the NATO agreement of December 1957 to deploy IRBMs in other NATO countries, they could reserve the right to target at least some of their IRBMs at the Soviet targets they considered most threatening to Britain. Agreeing to tie use of IRBMs to the NATO principle that an attack on one was an attack on all, however, seemed to contradict that distinction.[19]

Finally, in mid-February 1958, the British did virtually concede the point. While stipulating that the deployment of IRBMs in Britain was being made in consonance with the North Atlantic Treaty, the Anglo-American Mutual Defense Assistance Agreement of January 27, 1950, as supplemented, and related agreements, decision on use was to be a "matter for joint decision by the two Governments." Any such joint decision was to be made "in light of circumstances at the time and having regard to the undertaking the two Governments have assumed in article 5 of the North Atlantic Treaty." Even with this language, however, the British felt sufficiently comfortable in arguing before the NATO Council on February 20, 1958, that IRBMs based in Britain would function similarly to the way American bombers based in Britain did. Some IRBMs, like American bombers, would be subject to complete target coordination with SACEUR. But some would be targeted by Anglo-American agreement, just as some American bombers in Britain came wholly under SAC control without NATO involvement.[20]

Officially concluded on February 22, 1958, the Anglo-American IRBM agreement also stipulated that the United States would supply Britain with four squadrons of IRBMs and their related and specialized equipment and would make available training assistance to facilitate deployment. The

United States would provide, in addition, nuclear warheads for the missiles. But all warheads would remain in "full U.S. ownership, custody, and control in accordance with U.S. law." Pursuant to the United States Mutual Security Assistance Act of 1954 as amended and related agreements, ownership of the missiles and other equipment would pass to the United Kingdom as soon as the British were in position to man and operate them. The British also had the right, by special arrangement with the United States, to test-fire missiles on the Woomera Range in Australia (providing the Australians agreed, of course), although training and test-firing would normally take place on American instrumented ranges. The only major expense incurred by the British would result from preparation of missile sites and supporting facilities. Finally, the entire arrangement was subject to revision by agreement of the two parties, would remain in force for not less than five years, and could be terminated thereafter by either government on six months notice.[21]

Settling the IRBM question was a big relief to administration officials, since negotiations had been "unbelievably prolonged" and had resulted in a backload of work on other issues. The only remaining obstacles to implementation were persistent funding questions and the upcoming debate on defense estimates in the House of Commons. As for funding, the administration had not yet decided whether to seek "infrastructure financing" from NATO sources on the basis that IRBMs installed in Britain would be part of NATO's overall forces. In any event, American officials would not object if representatives of the other NATO governments pressed such a proposal—thus, in NATO minds, establishing that IRBMs in Britain were under NATO, not Anglo-American, command. But the British, whether partial funding came from NATO sources or not, would resist that interpretation.[22]

With a large majority in the House of Commons, Macmillan and the Conservatives were thereby assured of winning the final vote on the IRBM deal. But political pressure applied by opposition leaders on the consultation issue worried the Prime Minister. He suspected that he would be closely questioned as to when American IRBMs would actually be deployed in Britain and if British personnel would take immediate possession. If deployment came before British personnel were fully trained, the British government might again be vulnerable to charges it had no control over American nuclear forces stationed in Britain. A little delay in deployment, then, might not be a bad idea.[23]

On February 26, 1958, the day the debate began in the House of Commons, an alleged misstatement by an American Air Force officer in Britain put the government on the defensive. A certain Colonel Zinc of the USAF claimed that he was about to take over "operational command" of the missiles and missile bases in Britain. Although the United States government repudiated his statement (and although his claim was obviously untrue, since IRBMs would not be deployed in Britain until 1959), the question of consultation had been brought once again to the fore. Stubbornly, Macmillan decided to permit the second SAC exercise on March 10 to proceed anyway, demanding only from American Ambassador Whitney that there be absolutely no publicity of the operation. Leaks from Washington sources, Whitney admitted, had betrayed them in the past. The U.S. government would do its best this time to see that knowledgeable officials kept classified information classified.[24]

In the House of Commons, Labour party leaders did not need to learn about the second SAC exercise to find political bombs to drop on the government. "Nuclear armed bomber patrols" flying over Britain since late October 1957 posed a grave threat to British territory and British interests, they charged. What if an accident occurred during these patrols? What if a bomb were dropped? What would be the danger to the British people? And there was a greater problem, they complained, of which American bomber patrols were just symptomatic. With the American nuclear and military presence so great and growing in Britain, the United Kingdom was slipping into too overwhelming a dependence on the United States. One way of alleviating this concern, some suggested, was to have the United States transfer custody of some of its nuclear warheads and bombs to British control. That way, they explained, British leaders—not American generals—would determine British actions and Britain's fate in the event of war. On March 11, 1958, opposition charges that nuclear-armed American bomber patrols posed a danger to the public gained credence. Even as SAC planes began exercises in Britain, an American bomber flying near Florence, South Carolina, accidentally dropped an atomic bomb resulting in a nonnuclear explosion and injury to six persons.[25]

Resuming on February 27, 1958, with testimony by Strauss, General Alfred D. Starbird, AEC director for military applications, Loper, Rickover, and AEC Commissioner Harold S. Vance, JCAE hearings on the proposed amendments to the 1954 Atomic Energy Act ignored the political problems of the British government. Instead, members of the Joint Committee inquired about the extent to which the British or other foreign governments had already requested restricted nuclear data. They also asked about nuclear submarine propulsion exchanges with the British and about details of the proposed exchange of American U-235 for British plutonium.[26]

In response to a letter from subcommittee Chairman Pastore dated February 13, 1958, Strauss told the committee members on February 27 that from summer 1955 to fall 1957 the DOD had supported a British request for "certain thermonuclear weapons information for compatibility purposes." This information, "even though concerning only external characteristics, yields, and delivery systems, was judged by the Commission 'important information concerning the design or fabrication of the nuclear components of atomic weapons.' " More recently, the DOD had made a second request for a "joint determination" with the AEC (as provided for in the 1954

Clearing the Final Hurdle 223

Atomic Energy Act) to give the British some thermonuclear data "as soon as practical, and as soon as the law was modified." Desiring to know just what the DOD wanted to give the British, members of the JCAE questioned General Loper. Loper explained that the British wanted "atomic weapons" (atomic and hydrogen weapons) information for compatibility purposes, weapons effect data, and information on the characteristics of American nuclear weapons (atomic and hydrogen) in the research and development field. He explained that since design of delivery systems took much longer than design of nuclear warheads, the British wanted to know broadly what the United States was accomplishing in the way of weapons design to enable them to adjust accordingly the design of their delivery systems. For example, they would want to know now all about the dimensions, weights, and yields of weapons scheduled for production in 1960, along with safety features, vulnerability of weapons, fusing and firing features, loading checks, and in-flight procedures. They would want, in addition, information on the moment of inertia of the warhead of the bomb, center of gravity, and possibly design of the atomic devices inside American thermonuclear weapons. But even if the DOD provided all this information, Loper said, the British would not be given in any detail "the internal design of the weapon; that is what the amounts and arrangements of the nuclear material are and the details of your electronic and mechanical equipment."[27]

Since testimony by Quarles on January 31, 1958, had already established that revealing information on the "external characteristics" of nuclear weapons would reveal quite a bit of design and fabrication data, it is doubtful that the members of the JCAE believed Loper's final assertion that fulfilling the British request would not reveal substantial information on the "internal design" of American hydrogen weapons. Holifield and Anderson certainly did not. In any event, they had other issues to examine.

They were particularly interested to hear Rickover's plan to permit the British to buy a nuclear submarine reactor directly from Westinghouse and details of the uranium for plutonium deal. On the first matter, Pastore and Representatives James E. Van Zandt (R., Pennsylvania) and Craig Hosmer (R., California) asked Rickover to describe the events leading up to his December 1957 proposal. He complied. Candidly, he told of his irritation at having his people tied up too long in bothering with the British. He complained that leading British engineers and scientists who had come over to learn how to build a nuclear submarine had just wanted to use American information and technology for commercial purposes in their own industry. Pastore tried to change the subject to ask whether the United States was well ahead of the Soviets in nuclear submarine technology and whether giving Britain more information would lead to leaks to the Soviets. But Rickover only wanted to talk about his problems. The real issue, he said, was not security but interference with his ability to deliver on time nuclear-powered submarines and ships. Van Zandt then asked whether the British had any real nuclear submarine information to exchange. No, Rickover replied, they did not. But they could offer information on their gas-cooled, graphite-moderated reactor at Calder Hall.[28]

With regard to the nuclear materials deal, covered under section 55 of the act, JCAE members did not like the terms. Under the agreement, the United States would loan Britain $200 million through 1963 to buy U-235 and would be repaid after 1964 by shipments of British plutonium produced as a by-product of using the U-235. The great inequity was that the United States would be required to pay a price of $30 a gram for plutonium when it only cost the British $12 a gram to produce it. In effect, the United States would be subsidizing the British nuclear program to the detriment of private American industry. The British would be required to pay nothing. Members of the JCAE were particularly irked by this deal because as early as July 29, 1955, they had sent a letter to Eisenhower pointing out that "existing and presently planned facilities for producing special nuclear material will, in all probability, be inadequate to meet future requirements for nuclear weapons." Over the next two and one-half years, in addition, they had reiterated in letters to Eisenhower and most recently to new Secretary of Defense McElroy that they believed that the United States had a desperate need for stockpiles of additional nuclear material including plutonium, all to no avail. Then to have the administration come before them to plead the necessity of acquiring British plutonium at a price two and one-half times that at which it could be obtained domestically greatly angered them. When Loper realized that JCAE opposition to this provision was nearly unanimous, he stated categorically what Quarles had suggested earlier. The administration would be willing to change the terms of the uranium for plutonium deal to win JCAE approval.[29]

The hearings recessed between March 5 and March 26, 1958. When they reconvened, the administration announced that the controversial provision on the nuclear materials exchange had been excised from the legislation. There was also a change in the wording of section 144 for the communication of information to foreign governments. A revision had been made so that only those nations which had made "substantial progress" in the nuclear weapons field could receive "atomic weapons" information. Even so, Anderson complained to the newspapers that the proposed amendments would still result in a proliferation of the arms race. By acquiring American nuclear secrets, he said, other nations in addition to the United States, Britain, and the Soviet Union would learn how to build nuclear weapons. He then surprised Strauss in an open hearing on March 27, 1958, by quoting from the AEC chairman's December 12, 1957, letter to Quarles in which Strauss had expressed the very same concern about proliferation. Vance and Quarles tried to respond. There would be no "do-it-yourself kit" for any nation other than Britain, they assured the members of the committee, because no other allied power had made substantial progress in the nuclear field. Only nonnuclear weapons components would be offered to France and other fourth powers. Quarles then explained in detail DOD rationale for cooperating more fully with allies in the nuclear sphere. To meet the Soviet challenge, he asserted, the United States required the full assistance of its free world allies in the scientific and technological fields, in industrial areas, and in organization, training, and equipping of their military forces. Cooperation also had to be extended to the nuclear arena. But since the Soviets had already mastered every important area of nuclear weapons technology known to American scientists or would soon do so through their own efforts, the United States could reveal its nuclear secrets to the allies without concern that leaks would greatly advance the Soviet program.[30]

With respect to the United Kingdom, the administration proposed even closer cooperation because the British had already achieved "marked success" in the thermonuclear field at great cost and without American assistance. Anglo-American nuclear relations had moved into a "third phase," Quarles said, in which maximum cooperation was needed in all areas, particularly nuclear weapons. Only by opening the vault to American nuclear secrets, moreover, could the United States find out how far the British had gone, gain from whatever expertise they had achieved, and collaborate to watch over Soviet nuclear developments.[31]

Despite administration assurances that greater cooperation with France and other NATO allies would not assist those countries to acquire independent nuclear arsenals, many members of the JCAE, especially Democrats, were troubled about this possibility. After hearings on March 28, 1958, therefore, they requested that Secretary of State Dulles testify when the committee met again after Easter to explain whether the administration's proposals would "prejudice," as Senator Pastore put it, the diplomatic position of the United States in future disarmament talks. Dulles did not want to wait that long to give his opinion. Fearing a buildup of sentiment against the proposed legislation, he called a press conference for April 1, 1958. The United States, he told reporters, would not assist any nation to acquire nuclear weapons that did not already have them. But the notion that the United States could prevent allies from eventually acquiring nuclear weapons if they chose to develop them by withholding all American nuclear secrets was just illusory. In the case of Britain, of course, that key ally already possessed nuclear weapons. So the important theme in Anglo-American nuclear relations would now be to cooperate, avoid duplication of effort, and increase the collective strength.[32]

Dulles's sense of urgency to fight for creation of the Anglo-American nuclear partnership was shared by the British, but for a different reason. On March 31, 1958, the Soviets surprised the world by announcing that they were unilaterally ending nuclear testing. They would maintain the ban indefinitely while reserving the right to resume if the United States and Britain did not end their testing. At once, Labour party leaders in Britain called on Macmillan to agree to the moratorium. This was a golden opportunity, they said, to halt the nuclear arms race. Macmillan and his advisors could not agree. They would wait until they saw whether the Eisenhower administration pushed through Congress proposed changes to the Atomic Energy Act of 1954. If those changes permitted transfer of nuclear information—especially hydrogen bomb design data reliable and resistant to technical countermeasures—they would be able to cancel British hydrogen bomb tests scheduled for August and September. If they did not, the British government would be unable to conclude a moratorium agreement until fall.[33]

Macmillan and the British were greatly cheered by Dulles's testimony before the JCAE on April 17, 1958. In addition to reiterating that collective security against the Soviet threat required close nuclear cooperation with the allies, especially Britain, he sought to dispel congressional fears that cooperation would get in the way of disarmament efforts. Contrary to inhibiting those efforts, he said, nuclear cooperation between the allies and the United States would actually facilitate disarmament negotiations. The allies, he explained, would never agree to a nuclear disarmament agreement unless they were certain that they could gain access to American-made nuclear weapons in an emergency and receive American-nuclear information to assist peaceful development of nuclear power. Without American nuclear cooperation, on the other hand, they would embark upon programs to build nuclear weapons for their own security. The result would be more nuclear-armed states, not fewer. Nor did Congress have to worry that the administration intended to give away American nuclear secrets. Since only the British possessed a nuclear weapons capability, only the British would receive American nuclear weapons secrets. No actual American nuclear warheads or bombs would be given over to the allies, even Britain, unless and until war was at hand.[34]

Dulles's skillful explanation of the administration's case banished the danger that the proposed amendments to the Atomic Energy Act of 1954 would be defeated in their entirety. But JCAE members still had reservations about giving the British so many American nuclear secrets all at once. They were impressed, for example, with the arguments of former AEC Commissioner Thomas E. Murray, now a consultant for the Joint Committee. Testifying after Dulles on April 17, 1958, Murray said that he opposed the proposed amendments because they authorized the administration to communicate the full range of American nuclear weapons information to the British (and potentially to others). Those amendments made no distinction, moreover, between information on weapons of "undiscriminating mass annihilation" useful in a strategy of absolute deterrence and massive retaliation and information on weapons for "discriminating military use." These latter weapons would be valuable for tactical situations and to fight limited nuclear engagements. The failure of the administration to distinguish between the two categories of weapons, he went on to explain, demonstrated that British and American officials had made no agreement on "nuclear missions." It was his belief that the United States should reserve for itself the more strategic role of deterring a massive Soviet nuclear attack while giving to the allies the wherewithal to combat lower levels of Soviet aggression. Instead of giving Britain (and possibly other allies) information on the full range of American nuclear weapons, then, he favored providing them with actual nuclear weapons up to a yield of two kilotons. But he advised no communication of technological data relating to thermonuclear weapons in the megaton range. Taking Murray's objections to heart, members of the JCAE began discussing changes in the bill to tighten restrictions against revealing hydrogen weapons information and to insure that only Britain qualified for American nuclear weapons secrets.[35]

Meanwhile, pressure on the British government to declare in favor of a moratorium on nuclear testing continued, making Macmillan and his advisors anxious. They must soon decide, they realized, whether to go ahead with hydrogen bomb tests in late summer 1958 or cancel them. Their decision rested largely on whether the final legislation passed by Congress permitted the administration to reveal sufficient data about hydrogen weapons to obviate the necessity of the tests. But even if permissive language slipped through, members of the Joint Committee could forestall the administration from giving the British what they wanted and needed under a new bilateral agreement. Whatever occurred, however, the long wait for the creation of an Anglo-American nuclear partnership was about to end.

NOTES

1. Dulles calls Quarles, November 4, 1957, *Minutes of Telephone Conversations of John Foster Dulles and Christian Herter, 1953-1961* (Frederick, Md.: University Publications of America, 1980), reel 7, p. 223.

2. Eisenhower calls Dulles, January 11, 1958, *Telephone Conversations of Dulles*, reel 10, p. 340; Harold Macmillan, *Riding the Storm, 1956-1959* (New York: Harper & Row, 1971), pp. 462-63. On January 4, 1958, a Conservative party political broadcast asserted that the British government had an absolute veto on U.S. use of nuclear weapons by U.S. bombers in Britain.

3. Memorandum by Dulles, Washington, February 5, 1958, 711.56341/2-558 (State, Freedom of Information Act, photocopy); Dulles to Quarles, Washington, February 5, 1958, 711.56341/2-558 (State, FOI, photocopy/parts excised).

4. Public Law 703, 83rd Cong., 68 Stat. 919 (p. 923); *Hearings before Subcommittee on Agreements for Cooperation, JCAE, Amending the Atomic Energy Act of 1954—Exchange of Military Information and Material with Allies*, 85th Cong., 2d sess., 1958, pp. 2-6, 66-68, 87-88.

5. *Hearings before Subcommittee, JCAE*, 1958, pp. 3-4, 8-11.

6. Ibid., pp. 4-6, 8-11.

7. Ibid., pp. 2-6, 18, 23, 93-94, 96, 105.

8. Ibid., pp. 25-26.

9. Ibid., pp. 33-34, 36-37.

10. Ibid., pp. 61-62, 66-68.
11. Ibid., pp. 41, 70-71.
12. Ibid., p. 102.
13. Ibid., pp. 103-4.
14. Ibid.
15. Ibid., pp. 144-49, 152-54, 191-94.
16. Quarles calls Dulles, February 3, 1958; Dulles calls Murphy, February 4, 1958, *Telephone Conversations of Dulles*, reel 7, pp. 417, 404-5.
17. Ibid.; Whitney to Dulles, London, February 18, 1958, 711.56341/2-1858 (State, FOI, photocopy). One of the key concerns of the British was that the IRBMs be deployed in advance of Soviet deployment of IRBMs and especially ICBMs. See *New York Times*, Feb. 27, 1958, p. 8, and Feb. 28, 1958, p. 2, for reports on Labour party attacks on Thor missiles as being worthless.
18. Dulles calls Murphy, February 4, 1958, *Telephone Conversations of Dulles*, reel 7, pp. 404-5.
19. U.S. Embassy Paris to Dulles, February 20, 1958, 711.56341/2-2058 (State, FOI, photocopy).
20. Ibid.; Dulles to U.S. Embassy Paris, Washington, February 17, 1958, 711.56341/2-1758 (State, FOI, photocopy). In the NATO Council meeting of February 20, 1958, it was the Norwegian representatives in particular who pressed the British on the question of IRBMs being deployed in Britain coming under NATO command.
21. Ibid.; Herter to Caccia (text of February 22, 1958, IRBM agreement), Washington, February 22, 1958, 711.56341/2-2258 (State, FOI, photocopy).
22. Martin to Timmons, London, February 26, 1958, 711.56341/2-2658 (State, FOI, photocopy).
23. Ibid.
24. Macmillan, *Riding the Storm*, pp. 474-75; Whitney to Dulles, London, March 1, 1958, 711.56341/3-158 (State, FOI, photocopy). The author has been unable to confirm the Colonel Zinc incident in a second reliable source.
25. 584 *H.C. Deb.* 5s., pp. 33-194; *New York Times*, Mar. 12, 1958, p. 1.
26. *Hearings before Subcommittee, JCAE*, 1958, pp. 162-275.
27. Ibid., pp. 160, 174-76, 189-191.
28. Ibid., pp. 162-73.
29. Ibid., pp. 111-12, 203, 205-24.
30. Ibid., pp. 298, 311, 350; *New York Times*, Mar. 28, 1958, p. 8.
31. *Hearings before Subcommittee, JCAE*, 1958, p. 311.
32. *New York Times*, Mar. 29, 1958, pp. 2, 4, 6; Dulles calls Strauss, March 31, 1958, *Telephone Conversations of Dulles*, reel 7, p. 236.
33. Macmillan, *Riding the Storm*, pp. 484-85, 487; 586 *H.C. Deb.* 5s., pp. 27-32; John Simpson, *The Independent Nuclear State: The United States, Britain, and the Military Atom* (London: Macmillan, 1983), pp. 244-45.
34. *Hearings before Subcommittee, JCAE*, 1958, pp. 447-49, 456.
35. Ibid., pp. 476-81, 520-21.

24

PARTNERSHIP AT LAST

> The President may authorize the Atomic Energy Commission or Department of Defense to transfer by sale, lease, or loan non-nuclear parts of atomic weapons to nations (having made substantial progress in the nuclear weapons field) provided that such transfer will *not* contribute significantly to that nation's atomic weapon design, development, or fabrication capability, for the purpose of improving that nation's state of training and operational readiness.
> —amended section 91, 1958 amendments to the Atomic Energy Act of 1954[1]

The official American response to the March 21, 1958, Soviet appeal to halt nuclear testing was to call for technical talks on methods necessary to verify that neither side could cheat. In fact, however, many Eisenhower administration officials viewed the moratorium idea and nuclear disarmament generally as impractical and dangerous for the preservation of American national security and the defense of Western Europe. Because an agreement to stop nuclear testing or begin dismantling the nuclear arsenal might erode the huge nuclear advantage the United States still held over the Soviets and eliminate the ability of NATO to counter Soviet conventional military superiority in Europe, nuclear disarmament talks had to be approached with extreme caution. Besides, American policymakers just did not trust the Soviets. They suspected that the Soviets would cheat on any agreement and believed that the Soviet moratorium proposal was intended more for propaganda purposes than as a serious basis for negotiation. They noted, for example, that the Soviets had already completed an important series of nuclear tests in late February 1958 with the detonation of two devices at their arctic test range.

Not impressed with the unilateral Soviet moratorium announcement, then, made formally by Premier Nikita S. Khrushchev on April 4, 1958, President Eisenhower declined to interrupt the American nuclear program. On April 28, the AEC resumed testing at Eniwetok in the Pacific. The administration also took steps to build a defensive system against Soviet bomber attack by announcing on May 19 an agreement with Canada for the establishment of a North American Air Defense Command. Lastly, administration officials continued to push for passage of the amendments to the Atomic Energy Act of 1954 to enable the United States to open wide the doors of nuclear cooperation with the allies, especially Britain.

To this end, DOD officials sent a letter dated May 14, 1958, to the JCAE responding to the objections raised by Murray on April 17. The proposed restriction against communicating information on high-yield nuclear warheads would be a serious mistake, they said, because it would prevent deployment in Britain of IRBMs and other "atomic capable delivery systems which employ high-yield warheads" in the future. Nor did they have much use for Murray's suggestion that the United States give actual low-yield nuclear warheads to the allies. The strategy of the United States was to deter by threat of massive retaliation Soviet attack on NATO countries, not to plan and prepare to fight limited nuclear wars in Western Europe. They pointed out, finally, that turning over custody of American nuclear warheads to foreign governments would be a radical departure from previously accepted policy. The DOD did not think Congress should make that change in the law.[2]

Although administration officials continued to fight against major revisions in the proposed amendments, they did try to cooperate to make the language of the bill more precise. On May 21, 1958, for example, Dulles talked to Strauss about how to reassure the JCAE that American nuclear weapons secrets would not go to fourth powers. Why not have the new legislation provide, he suggested, that American nuclear weapons information only be exchanged with those countries that already possessed a nuclear weapons capacity when the act went into force? The revised language could also state that exchanges with countries that subsequently achieved a nuclear weapons capability would have to be incorporated in a treaty and approved by Congress. In that manner, the new legislation would "take care of the British and would not obviously discriminate against the French." Strauss thought the idea promising and said he would call Senator Pastore to pass it on. Dulles added that he would send Farley to explain the proposal to other members of the JCAE.[3]

The administration also had to explain to the JCAE its proposal for congressional review of a new bilateral agreement with the British. While some senators wanted any new agreement written down in a formal treaty and subject to express ratification by a two-thirds vote of the Senate, administration officials favored automatic approval of a bilateral agreement unless

Congress passed a majority concurrent resolution within 30 days. By the end of May 1958 the JCAE adopted this solution but with a 60-day period for any bilateral agreement signed after January 1, 1959. Until then, the 30-day limit would apply.[4]

Although the staff of the JCAE would not have the proposed amendments ready to go before the full Congress until June 10, 1958, the British wanted to know as soon as possible just what the administration would be able to give them on hydrogen bomb data. On May 30, 1958, therefore, Macmillan sent Eisenhower a letter asking that negotiations begin at once for an exchange of nuclear weapons information. Responsive, Eisenhower called Under Secretary of State Christian A. Herter to see about setting up a meeting with the British. Herter replied that he had already talked to Strauss and that the timetable for negotiations could be sped up "very materially." They would have a draft reply to give to Macmillan that very day stating that the United States would be in position to have preliminary discussions with Plowden when he arrived in Washington on Wednesday, June 4, 1958. Shortly thereafter, they could receive a team of British experts for technical discussions. That was fine, the President said, but they had better plan to get everything done by June 15 rather than July 1 because otherwise they might not be able to lay the new agreement before Congress for 30 days before the congressional recess in August.[5]

Later that afternoon Deputy Special Assistant to the Secretary of State for Disarmament and Atomic Energy Richard C. Breithut met with John Roper of the British Embassy and outlined the substance of Eisenhower's reply to Macmillan. Plowden and the British team of experts could come for talks, Breithut said. But the President pointed out in his letter that it was difficult to know whether the expert discussions could make sufficient progress so that the agreement could be ready for initialing during Macmillan's visit to Washington, now set for June 8-11, 1958. Nor did they know whether the full Congress would make changes in the JCAE report. Breithut assured Roper, however, that the President promised in his letter to do everything in his power to facilitate the negotiations. He only asked that the British understand the importance of giving "no publicity to the fact that even preliminary talks were underway" while Congress had yet to pass on the proposed amendments. After listening to the President's message to Macmillan, Roper told Breithut that the British government fully appreciated the need for secrecy. Unfortunately, there was one problem. British nuclear scientist Sir William Penney would head the group of technical experts coming to Washington. His presence might give rise to speculation. However, they could always explain Penney's presence by noting that there were "many things he could usefully discuss with the appropriate U.S. officials." It was not a very good cover story, but it was the best they could do.[6]

Spurred on by the President, administration officials worked feverishly in the next few days to prepare a negotiating position before Plowden's arrival on June 4, 1958. Strauss personally gave his attention to ironing out what he termed "minor differences of opinion" with the DOD prior to an AEC-DOD staff meeting of June 2. Although officials quickly achieved consensus, developments in Congress cast doubt on whether the President would get all the changes he wanted. Still concerned about escalating the nuclear arms race, the JCAE made known to the administration that they would at that time oppose any attempt to give hydrogen bomb design information to the British, even if the law as adopted technically permitted it. They would only sanction atomic (fission) weapons information exchanges. Senator Anderson intended to attack the bill itself, in addition, by offering in the Senate an amendment to the JCAE report tightening language on "do-it-yourself kits" for allies. If passed, his amendment would legally block transfer of "atomic weapons" information and nonnuclear parts of nuclear weapons to those countries that had not made substantial progress in the nuclear weapons field.[7]

In light of these developments, the British found their early June 1958 discussions with the Americans less fruitful than they had hoped. Eisenhower and his advisors were able to talk about atomic (fission) weapons information and nonnuclear components for these weapons but not about hydrogen weapons information or components. Although at the end of Macmillan's visit British and American officials let out information about the proposed purchase by the British of an American nuclear submarine reactor and its fuel and generally put the best fact on the meetings, the possibility that Congress would approve hydrogen bomb information exchanges disappeared. The administration acknowledged as much when Quarles told a closed-door session of the JCAE on June 14, 1958, that the administration had no plans to give information on the manufacture of hydrogen bombs to anybody, the British included. Strauss added that the United States government would never reveal all its nuclear secrets to another country.[8]

On June 19, 1958, the House of Representatives approved amendments to the Atomic Energy Act of 1954 that limited exchanges of nuclear weapons data to nations that had made substantial progress in the nuclear weapons field. To other allies, the administration was authorized to give details on the external characteristics and effects of American "atomic weapons" as well as nonnuclear components for "atomic weapons." The House reaffirmed that all nuclear components for American weapons had to remain in American custody and could only be turned over to allies in the event of war. The bill also contained a provision permitting the sale to the British of nuclear submarine reactor designs and fuel for those reactors and other types of military nuclear power plants. In the Senate, however, as expected, Anderson's amendment passed, eliminating the provision permitting transfer of nonnuclear components for "atomic weapons" to allies other than those having made substantial progress in the nuclear field. Only Britain would be permitted to obtain nonnuclear bomb parts.[9]

Within the now-concrete guidelines set by Congress in the new legislation, administration officials wrestled in late June 1958 with final details of the new Anglo-American bilateral agreement. One last point of contention remained to be worked out. Having lost for the time being the possibility of receiving American hydrogen bomb information (and thus being compelled to go ahead with British hydrogen bomb tests in late summer despite expected negative political fall-out), the British dug in their heels on an AEC proposal to link the nuclear submarine reactor transfer to transfer of Calder Hall reactor information to the United States.[10] The problem was that the government had taken criticism in the past over undermining Britain's future commercial nuclear position in order to acquire American military nuclear secrets. Now, at the very moment an Anglo-American nuclear partnership was being forged, Macmillan and his advisors did not want to see the triumph spoiled by another political battle on the question. Besides, British officials believed that exchange of nuclear submarine propulsion information and other American nuclear secrets should be made on the basis of strengthening the collective security against the Soviet threat, not as a quid pro quo for commercial nuclear information. Such a linkage made it seem as though the British government was being forced to mortgage the country's future against the strategic imperative of the present. It would be a blow to national pride, British officials asserted, and they refused to permit it.[11]

The reason Strauss and the AEC wanted to link nuclear submarine data with British commercial nuclear information was to remove any danger that the JCAE and Congress would balk at approving that provision of the new Anglo-American bilateral agreement. Strauss thought it a small price to pay for easing opposition from JCAE members like Senator Henry Dworshak (R., Idaho) who were still concerned that revealing informaton about submarines and other military nuclear reactors would permit the state-subsidized British nuclear industry to gain a competitive advantage over private American companies. Efforts to unite administration officials behind the linkage failed, however, because of stiff opposition from the DOD. Quarles, Loper told Strauss on June 26, 1958, had instructed him that listing a "civilian consideration"—transfer by Britain of Calder Hall nuclear reactor information—in what he regarded as a "military agreement"—the provision of the bilateral agreement permitting Britain to purchase a nuclear submarine reactor and its fuel—was a mistake. As long as the British objected, Quarles just would not budge.[12]

On June 27, 1958, Dulles, on Strauss's urging, tried to persuade the British to relent. His half-hearted attempt only caused Macmillan himself to instruct British Embassy officials in Washington to refuse. The secretary of state then told Strauss that in view of the fact that the DOD had lined up with the British on this point, perhaps the AEC should withdraw the language linking the nuclear submarine reactor deal to Calder Hall information. But Strauss would not give up. Meeting with British officials, he argued that the language he proposed was necessary to head off JCAE criticism. The British remained adamant. They would not permit the linkage. At last, on June 30, 1958—Strauss's last day as chairman of the AEC—he withdrew the offending sentence from the draft agreement. The British, he told Dulles, had in his opinion made a big mistake.[13]

On June 30, 1958, the amendments to the Atomic Energy Act of 1954 passed Congress. The President was authorized under section 6 (amended section 144c) of the act to give restricted data on "atomic weapons" to an ally (Britain) that had made substantial progress in the nuclear field in order to improve that nation's "atomic weapon" design, development, or fabrication capability. He could only do so if communicating that information would, in his judgment, promote and not constitute an unreasonable risk to the common defense and security. Under section 1 (amended section 91c), in addition, he was authorized to transfer by sale, lease, or loan nonnuclear parts of "atomic weapons" to an ally (Britain) that had made substantial progress in the nuclear field to improve that nation's state of training and operational readiness. But curiously, he could only sell, lease, or loan nonnuclear parts of "atomic weapons provided that such transfer will *not* [my emphasis] contribute significantly to that nation's atomic weapon design, development, or fabrication capability."[14]

There are three possible explanations for the apparent conflict between the language of section 6 (amended section 144c) on "atomic weapns" data and section 1 (amended section 91c) on nonnuclear components of "atomic weapons." In order to understand those explanations, however, it is first important to examine the thinking of key members of the JCAE and Congress.

By summer 1958 most congressional leaders were convinced that greater cooperation with Britain in the nuclear sphere was essential to improve the collective strength against the Soviets. This certainly was the motivating factor in Durham's support for the changes in the atomic energy laws. But many on the Joint Committee wanted to avoid taking any action that would dramatically escalate the nuclear arms race. Pastore, Holifield, and others demonstrated this concern by questioning administration officials repeatedly in JCAE hearings about the possibility under the proposed amendments of giving fourth powers, in particular France, American nuclear weapons information and nonnuclear components of nuclear weapons. Ultimately, of course, Senator Anderson's amendment struck down the provision permitting the administration to give nonnuclear components to allies that had not made substantial progress in the nuclear field. Given this explanation of congressional goals in revising the proposed changes to the Atomic Energy Act of 1954, and understanding that deep down many members of Congress instinctively hesitated to give away too many American secrets, interpretation of the conflicting articles of the 1958 amendments can be attempted.

The first possibility is that in drafting conflicting passages in articles 1 and 6 congressional leaders were trying to reconcile the goal of cooperating with Britian in the nuclear sphere to improve the collective strength vis-à-vis the Soviets with the goal of restraining the nuclear arms race. Thus, they would be willing to give the British information on nuclear weapons similar to the types they already possessed, but they would not sanction transfer of nonnuclear components for types of weapons the British did not possess. While the British would acquire a larger stockpile more rapidly and more efficiently—thereby increasing the collective strength—they would not acquire any new nuclear capability. This would theoretically put a brake on escalation of the nuclear arms race.

Of course, assisting the British to build any type of nuclear weapon faster and more efficiently would escalate the nuclear arms race in that it would provide greater incentive to the Soviets to build up their supply of nuclear bombs and warheads. But the language of the amendments to the Atomic Energy Act of 1954, under the above interpretation, did not permit the administration to improve dramatically the technological level of British nuclear weapons capability. In that sense, Anglo-American cooperation would result only in a quantitative, not a qualitative, escalation of the nuclear arms race. It would also, by the way, insure that the American qualitative lead would not be eroded by leaks through the British program to the Soviets.[15]

The second possible interpretation of articles 1 and 6 (amended sections 91c and 144c) is that Congress was not concerned with restraining transmission to the British of "atomic weapons" information and nonnuclear components of "atomic weapons" at all. Instead, congressional leaders were searching for a formula to prevent transfer of American nuclear weapons information to fourth powers, in particular France. It will be recalled that on May 21, 1958, Dulles had a conversation with Strauss in which the secretary of state discussed allaying congressional fears that a fourth power could obtain American information and use it to achieve an atomic capability. He had suggested that they revise the legislation to provide that American nuclear weapons information be exchanged only with those countries that already possessed a substantial nuclear weapons capability when the act went into force. That way, France and other nations subsequently detonating a nuclear weapon would not have qualified for transmission of American nuclear weapons information.[16]

That suggestion was not adopted by the JCAE and Congress. But it is possible that congressional leaders intended the wording in article 1 (new section 91c) to be a barrier to American assistance to the French and other allies if and when they achieved substantial progress in the nuclear field.

This interpretation is partially supported by a statement made by Senator Pastore to the Senate on June 30, 1958. Pastore explained that House-Senate conferees working on final wording of article 1 had realized that transfer of some nonnuclear components of "atomic weapons" necessarily revealed restricted weapons data. Transferring other nonnuclear components, however, like bomb attachments did not. He then seemed to suggest—although the wording is far from clear—that the language of article 1 would prevent the administration from giving nonnuclear components of "atomic weapons" involving restricted weapons data to fourth powers (France in particular).[17]

Pastore's explanation was confusing because article 1 only provided for transfer of nonnuclear components of "atomic weapons" to allies who had made substantial progress in the nuclear field. That meant that France and other fourth powers would not qualify for transfer of nonnuclear components of "atomic weapons" even if such transfer did not involve restricted data. Possibly Pastore was saying that the language of article 1 would apply to France and other allies once they achieved substantial progress in the nuclear weapons field and qualified under the law for transfer of nonnuclear components of American "atomic weapons." But if this is the case, the wording of article 6 would still have allowed the administration, as this writer sees it, to give the French information on American "atomic weapons" similar to those the French possessed.

There is one other interpretation of the conflicting language of articles 1 and 6 in the 1958 amendments to the 1954 Atomic Energy Act. It could be that House and Senate conferees, in trying to satisfy the concerns of all, just did a poor job of drafting the legislation. Given congressional statements, public and private, about the administration's amendments to the law, it is possible that the conferees intended both to restrict British access to some American "atomic weapons" information and to block transmission of all American "atomic weapons" data to France and other fourth powers. Certainly the transcript of the JCAE hearings on the proposed legislation strongly supports this more comprehensive view.

Whatever the true intent of Congress, President Eisenhower accepted the wording of the act as presented. He signed it into law on July 2, 1958. The next day, Dulles and British Minister in Washington Samuel Hood signed a new bilateral agreement for "cooperation on the uses of atomic energy for mutual defense purposes." Under article 2 of the agreement, the British and Americans promised to cooperate and exchange information for the "development of defense plans, the training of personnel in the employment of and defense against atomic weapons and other military application of atomic energy, the evaluation of the capabilities of potential enemies in the employment of atomic weapons and other military application of atomic energy, the development of delivery systems compatible with the atomic weapons which they carry, and research, development, and design of mili-

Partnership at Last 237

tary reactors to the extent and by such means as may be agreed." They would, in addition, exchange information concerning "atomic weapons" when, after consultation with the recipient party, the communicating party determined that communication of that information was necessary to improve the recipient's "atomic weapon" design, development, and fabrication capability. That meant that the United States would supply Britain with information about American "atomic weapons" that were essentially similar to British "atomic weapons" but not about other types of American "atomic weapons." It was understood that American officials would at this time supply no information about hydrogen weapons.[18]

The second major article, article 3, provided for the transfer by the United States to Britain of a "submarine nuclear propulsion plant and materials." Subject to terms and conditions acceptable to the United States government, a private American company would be permitted to sell to the British government a complete nuclear submarine reactor and spare parts. That company would also be permitted to sell to the British replacement cores or fuel elements for ten years thereafter. For its part, the United States government would communicate to the British government classified information relating to safety features and information for the design, manufacture, and operation of the reactor. It would, in addition, transfer by sale quantities of U-235 for use in the reactor over a ten-year period and reprocess the used uranium at British request. Enriched uranium recovered in reprocessing could be purchased, however, by the United States, as could other special nuclear material recovered in reprocessing. To satisfy JCAE concerns, AEC officials would set the price the British would pay for the U-235 and the price the United States would pay for reprocessed uranium and special nuclear material at the price it charged for domestic distribution of those materials at the time of the sale. In this way, the United States would not be subsidizing the British nuclear program, as members of the JCAE had complained would occur under the original administration proposal.[19]

Other provisions of the agreement stated that neither party would transfer to the other actual nuclear warheads or bombs, that unless otherwise agreed for civilian uses, all exchanged information, equipment, and materials would be used exclusively for the preparation or implementation of defense plans in the mutual interests of the two countries, and that full security for the same would be maintained. The pact would remain in force until terminated by agreement of the parties, except that if not so terminated, article 2 could be terminated by joint agreement or unilaterally by either party on one year's notice to take effect at the end of a term of ten years, or thereafter on one year's notice to take effect at the end of any succeeding term of five years.[20]

But missing from the agreement were provisions to give Britain two of the three parts of the so-called "do-it-yourself kit" for "atomic weapons." Although the British would get information on American "atomic weapons" (understood in this case to mean fission, not fusion or hydrogen weapons), nothing in the bilateral agreement obligated the administration to transfer nonnuclear components or special nuclear material for use in "atomic weapons." U-235 sold to the British under article 3 of the agreement, it must be remembered, was to be used as fuel for nuclear submarine reactors. For the time being, the British would have to make their own nonnuclear components and utilize enriched uranium and other nuclear materials from their own plants to make nuclear weapons.[21]

Despite the absence of provisions for transfer of nonnuclear components and special nuclear materials for nuclear weapons, members of Parliament generally applauded the agreement as a great accomplishment. But opposition leaders could not resist admonishing the Prime Minister to take care lest the Americans not reciprocate when the government handed over British atomic secrets. There was mild criticism that the new agreement did not provide for an actual exchange of nuclear weapons, as that, it was suggested, would further avoid wasteful duplication of effort. But Macmillan reminded the Commons that American law still forbade such a transfer.[22]

In the United States, the Anglo-American bilateral agreement was defended by administration officials including new Chairman of the AEC John A. McCone. It sailed through JCAE hearings. Once the full Congress approved it on July 30, 1958, the Anglo-American nuclear partnership was fact. Not content to rest on past laurels, however, McCone announced that the United States and Britain had agreed to work for even greater cooperation. If the JCAE permitted, he was signaling, the administration would rewrite the July 3, 1958, bilateral agreement to give the British even more nuclear secrets.[23]

The nuclear partnership created by the Anglo-American agreement of July 3, 1958 was based on the mutual interest and great need of the United States and Britain to increase the collective strength vis-à-vis the Soviet Union. Since that interest and need continued to grow in subsequent years, British and American policymakers worked to broaden cooperation in the nuclear field. Ten months later, on May 7, 1959, for example, amendments to the 1958 bilateral agreement gave Britain nonnuclear components and special nuclear materials for use in "atomic weapons."[24]

But the Anglo-American nuclear alliance, though partnership it was, was hardly a relationship based on equality. Far weaker economically and militarily, the British could not afford to produce numerous nuclear weapons systems like the Americans or nuclear material (U-235 and tritium) sufficient to create large and diverse nuclear forces. In the 1960s and after, therefore, British leaders resigned themselves to a strategy of buying American weapons systems, the Polaris sea-launched ballistic missile and currently the Trident II missile, and adapting British warheads to fit. They also acquired much of their stock of nuclear material from the United States. Rather than a relationship built on interdependence, then, as Macmillan had proclaimed in November 1957, the Anglo-American nuclear alliance was one in which the United States was the senior party and the British very dependent upon the Americans.[25]

It has remained that way to the present time. Although there have been disagreements along the way, the partnership has endured. No longer an irritating anomaly in the overall Anglo-American relationship as it was before 1957-58, the nuclear alliance has become a critical element in the defense plans of both Britain and the United States and an unmistakable indication of the importance of the United Kingdom to U.S. national security.

NOTES

1. Public Law 479, 85th Cong., 68 Stat. 276.

2. *Hearings before Subcommittee on Agreements for Cooperation, JCAE, Amending the Atomic Energy Act of 1954—Exchange of Military Information and Material with Allies*, 85th Cong., 2d sess., 1958, pp. 522, 524, 527.

3. Strauss calls Dulles, May 21, 1958, *Minutes of Telephone Conversations of John Foster Dulles and Christian Herter, 1953-1961* (Frederick, Md.: University Publications of American, 1980), reel 7, p. 522.

4. Ibid.; *New York Times*, May 25, 1958, p. 21; May 28, 1958, p. 13; May 29, 1958, p. 9.

5. Harold Macmillan, *Riding the Storm, 1956-1959* (New York: Harper & Row, 1971), pp. 489-90; Memorandum of Conversation by Herter, Washington, May 30, 1958, S/AE File Copy (State, Freedom of Information Act, photocopy).

6. Memorandum of Conversation, Roper and Breithut, Washington, May 30, 1958, 711.56341/5-3058 (State, FOI, photocopy).

7. Memorandum by Farley, Washington, May 31, 1958, S/AE Files (234.4308) (State, FOI, photocopy); Memorandum by Farley, Washington, June 18, 1958, S/AE File Copy (State, FOI, photocopy).

8. *New York Times*, June 9, 1958, p. 8; June 12, 1958, p. 11; June 15, 1958, p. 17. In both Macmillan, *Riding the Storm*, p. 494, and John Simpson, *The Independent Nuclear State: The United States, Britain, and the Military Atom* (London: Macmillan, 1983), p. 139, there is an assertion that Macmillan and Eisenhower signed an agreement concerning joint control or decision on use by the United States of nuclear bombs or warheads in Britain. It is further claimed that the agreement for joint decision on American use of nuclear bombers flying out of British bases replaced the "loose arrangement made by Attlee and confirmed by Churchill." Quite frankly, this writer believes that no such agreement was concluded. It is my opinion that Macmillan was attempting to create in his memoirs the British right of consultation on American use of nuclear bombs carried by U.S. bombers flying from British bases he could never win during his time in power.

9. *New York Times*, June 20, 1958, p. 1; June 24, 1958, p. 1; June 27, 1958, p. 3.

10. *Hearings before Subcommittee, JCAE*, 1958, pp. 501-3. Information on this last dispute was pieced together from sometimes ambiguous evidence and wording in

the following citations (11, 12, and 13) but is strongly supported by testimony by Rickover before the JCAE in executive session on May 28, 1958, and by comments therein by Pastore, Van Zandt, and Dworshak.

11. Strauss calls Dulles, June 26, 1958, *Telephone Conversations of Dulles*, reel 7, p. 942.

12. Ibid.; *Hearings before Subcommittee, JCAE*, 1958, pp. 501-3.

13. Strauss calls Dulles, June 26, 1958; Strauss calls Dulles, June 27, 1958; Dulles calls Strauss and Memo to Dulles about Strauss's call, June 30, 1958, *Telephone Converations of Dulles*, reel 7, pp. 942, 932, 916.

14. Public Law 479, 85th Cong., 68 Stat. 276.

15. *Hearings before Subcommittee, JCAE*, 1958, pp. 2-6, 36-37, 96-105. This first interpretation is supported by Strauss's explanation of the proposed amendments to the JCAE, especially with respect to helping a nation only to do better what it would do anyway. It also fits nicely with testimony given by Quarles before the subcommittee on January 31, 1958.

16. Strauss calls Dulles, May 21, 1958, *Telephone Conversations of Dulles*, reel 7, p. 522.

17. U.S. Congress, Senate, *Pastore Addressing Senate on House-Senate Conference Report on H.R. 12716*, 85th Cong., 2d sess., June 30, 1958, *Congressional Record* 104:12586-87.

18. *Agreement between Government of United Kingdom of Great Britain and Northern Ireland and Government of United States of America for Co-operation on Uses of Atomic Energy for Mutual Defense Purposes*, Washington, July 3, 1958, U.S. Department of State, *United States Treaties and Other International Agreements* 9:1028.

19. Ibid.

20. Ibid.

21. Ibid. It might have been possible for the British to divert U-235 to fabricate nuclear weapons without American knowledge.

22. 591 *H.C. Deb.* 5s., pp. 198-207, 1009-10.

23. *New York Times*, Aug. 1, 1958, p. 40; Aug. 30, 1958, p. 30.

24. *Amendment to 1958 Atomic Energy Agreement*, Washington, May 7, 1959, U.S. Department of State, *USTIA* 10:1274. It is unclear if by this agreement the United States could now give the British data and nonnuclear components for atomic weapons not similar to those types they already possessed, or even hydrogen bomb information.

25. In *Nuclear Politics*, pp. 142-44, Andrew J. Pierre writes that the most important factor causing resumption of substantial Anglo-American nuclear cooperation was the success of the British program itself. The Americans, he says, were amazed by the extent of British knowledge and expertise after the May 1957 Christmas Island detonation of a hydrogen bomb, were less concerned about leaks to the Soviets because of the extent of Soviet nuclear progress and the fact that British security had improved, and wanted the very valuable data Britain now had to exchange. Pierre also mentions as lesser factors the American desire to balance expanding Soviet military strength with a stable NATO deterrent composed of IRBMs in Britain and tactical nuclear weapons for NATO forces on the continent, and the presence in the White House of the pro-British Eisenhower. He further describes the post-1958 Anglo-American nuclear relationship as one of "interdependence."

Pierre is undoubtedly correct that advances made in the British program contributed to the American decision in favor of substantial nuclear cooperation, but he is wrong that it was the major factor. The major factor was American realization that the growth of Soviet nuclear power and Soviet development of the ICBM—dramatized by the Sputnik launch of October 1957—mandated greater nuclear cooperation with Britain and the NATO allies generally. (See Macmillan, *Riding the Storm*, p. 323. Macmillan's account of the American reaction to Sputnik leaves little doubt that the Soviet threat propelled the administration once and for all to decide upon nuclear cooperation with the British.)

Although it is true that Eisenhower offered Britain greater cooperation in the nuclear area as a way of repairing damage done to Anglo-American relations by the Suez crisis, he was motivated to do so largely because of his realistic assessment of the strategic balance. Nebulous Anglophilic sentiment probably played a very minor role in his thinking. Nor is Pierre's characterization of the post-1958 Anglo-American nuclear relationship as one of interdependence accurate. By no stretch of the imagination, in fact, could the post-1958 nuclear relationship be termed one of interdependence. The U.S. nuclear program was massive, self-sufficient, and infinitely more varied than the British. The American nuclear deterrent dwarfed not only the British but the Soviet as well until the mid-1960s. The British nuclear program, on the other hand, became dependent upon the United States for critical nuclear materials, especially tritium. It ultimately created nuclear forces insufficient to deter Soviet attack by themselves but valuable when linked to the much more powerful American nuclear forces. In *Independent Nuclear State*, British author John Simpson admits as much. Overall British nuclear policy after 1958, he concedes, rested on British ability to "situate Britain's nuclear forces within the context of an alliance policy of maximising the 'common defense'" (pp. 226-27, 238-39; see Simpson's work in its entirety for extensive, though primarily undocumented, details of the Anglo-American nuclear partnership, 1958-81).

Without the connection to the American nuclear forces, in other words, British nuclear forces made little sense. With the connection, they added another element of uncertainty to Soviet calculations. In 1958, Prime Minister Macmillan and other British officials might have preferred to describe the new partnership as one of interdependence, but British dependence would have been more accurate. British authors may believe, in addition, that they are interpreting the past history and present reality of Anglo-American nuclear relations accurately, but their exaggerated assessments of Britain's importance to the United States in the nuclear sphere amount to startlingly foolish self-delusion.

25

CONCLUSION

From the end of World War II to the June 15, 1955, Agreement for Cooperation, Anglo-American nuclear relations were not good. Compared to the level of cooperation that existed in other areas of the bilateral relationship, they were poor. But that is not to say that American policy in this area failed. On the contrary, it was extremely successful in fulfilling American goals.

In the period from August 1945 to August 1949, the United States government set forth and attempted to secure a number of objectives. Chief among these was preservation of the American atomic monopoly to enable the United States to build up a sizeable stockpile of atomic weapons. In order to accomplish that objective, the administration and JCAE emphasized maximum security for American atomic secrets and acquisition of free world raw materials critical for the construction of atomic weapons. Another objective was to free the President from all encumbrance on the use of atomic weapons to respond to Soviet aggression. Although it was not thought that in the immediate postwar period the President would have to resort to atomic weapons, the international situation might require it once the Soviets tested an atomic bomb. When the Soviets did, freedom of action on the use of atomic weapons would be vital to American security.

In light of the above objectives, American policy toward Britain was quite logical. The Congress passed and the administration approved the McMahon Act of 1946 placing severe restrictions on cooperation with foreign governments in the development of atomic energy. This was the best way, American leaders believed, to insure maximum security for American nuclear secrets. Although in 1946 both the Soviets and the British possessed the theoretical knowledge to build an atomic bomb, it would be many years, Americans hoped, before the Soviets detonated a bomb. And even when they did, they would have to spend large sums of money, accumulate large amounts of raw materials, and construct an extensive nuclear infrastructure to build up a stockpile of atomic weapons to rival that of the Americans.

As long as the administration took no action that might assist Soviet development, then, the United States could look forward to holding a decisive strategic advantage over the Soviets for years to come. That advantage would pay huge political and economic dividends in the chaotic postwar world and might help win a war should the Soviets and Americans get into a fight. Neither the administration nor Congress was willing to jeopardize American nuclear superiority by giving away American nuclear secrets to what was considered a leaky British ship of state. Nor would they countenance continuation of the wartime British right of veto over American use of the atomic bomb. That right was a dead letter even before the Modus Vivendi of January 7, 1948, officially terminated it. Only joint control of raw materials remained an active and important area of Anglo-American cooperation and only because it coincided with the American objective of building up as rapidly as possible the American nuclear arsenal and gaining an unassailable lead over the Soviets.

Shortly before the Soviets detonated an atomic bomb in August 1949, a shift in American objectives, and therefore policy, occurred. Although maximum security and American freedom of action on the use of the atomic bomb retained vital significance, American officials began to consider seriously whether cooperation with the British might accelerate the growth of their joint atomic strength vis-à-vis the Soviets and preserve for a longer time the strategic advantage. A problem here was that the Fuchs case of early 1950 highlighted the negative aspects of cooperation—the possibility of catastrophic loss of security due to leaks through the British program to the Soviets—and so the door of opportunity blown open by the sudden blast of a Soviet atomic bomb snapped shut again. The possibility of cooperation disappeared for another three years.

What finally forced the door open once more was the Eisenhower administration's New Look defense policy and emphasis on nuclear weapons to deter Soviet aggression and defend Western Europe. In order to implement that strategy, the United States needed to secure the cooperation not only of Britain but other NATO countries as well. Unfortunately, the new objective of nuclear cooperation clashed with the old objectives—maintaining the highest possible level of security for American nuclear secrets and preserving American freedom of action on the use of nuclear weapons. Because members of the JCAE continued to cling to the maximum security axiom and believed, in addition, that the British wanted to appropriate American nuclear secrets to gain a competitive advantage in the industrial and commercial field, they quarreled with administration (especially DOD) plans to press for greater collaboration on the military uses of atomic energy. Because the U.S. government continued to insist that the President retain freedom of action on the use of nuclear weapons to deal with possible

Soviet aggression, the administration clashed with the British. In the latter battle, the United States would never yield. In the former, the JCAE would do so only grudgingly. At the time of the June 15, 1955, agreement, however, the JCAE still had sufficient influence to prevent significant Anglo-American nuclear cooperation. Once the growth of Soviet nuclear power and Soviet development of the intercontinental ballistic missile took place, the objective of cooperating with the allies in the nuclear sphere would outweigh maximum security considerations.

In sum, the formulation of American nuclear policy toward the British up to 1955 had more to do with the struggle for a strategic advantage over the Soviets and restrictions imposed on administration actions by the JCAE than with British development of atomic energy. But the British might have been able to exert influence on American policy had they demonstrated to the U.S. government that they could contribute to the fulfillment of American nuclear goals.

The major factor inhibiting British ability to reason along these lines was the notion, firmly entrenched in most British minds, that Britain was still a Great Power. Even though in the immediate postwar years British finances were exhausted, British military power depleted, and British political influence diminished, British leaders continued to think of their nation as one of the world's "Big Three." And even though Britain lacked the technical knowledge, scientific and technical personnel, and financial resources to come close to matching the size of the American nuclear program, British leaders believed that they should be taken into an equal and full partnership with the United States in the nuclear sphere. They believed that the Americans owed them this because of their immense contributions to the defeat of the dictators in World War II. The Americans believed, however, that the British were asking for American nuclear secrets while offering precious little in return. Not only would the United States, because of Marshall Plan and other aid, be subsidizing the British program, but the British would be unable to use all the information given them. Instead, the British atomic energy program would be a conduit for the transfer of American nuclear secrets to the Soviets.[1]

Another reason cooperation with the British looked so unattractive to many American officials was that the British simply did not appear to be trying to make cooperation attractive. The British nuclear program moved so slowly that it took seven years just to produce an atomic bomb for testing. The British had no stockpile to speak of until 1954. Worst of all, they refused to see how important security considerations loomed in American calculations. Their failure to make improvements suggested that they wanted American officials to trust them blithely with the most critical of all American secrets—and this in the face of numerous proven leaks of major proportions to the Soviet Union.

British inability to take due consideration of the inequality of the American and British positions carried over to revival of the question of consultation, raised anew in the 1950s. Although British leaders could make an arguable case for consideration of their views with respect to use of American bombers armed with atomic weapons and flying from British bases, broader assertions that Britain had a right of consultation on any American use of nuclear weapons, particularly in an emergency, served only to irritate American officials and complicate the overall nuclear relationship. While British concern that American use of nuclear weapons might precipitate an all-out Soviet-American exchange and result in the destruction of Western Europe was understandable and legitimate, it was all too often played out in public for domestic political advantage. Insistence on the broader right of consultation, moreover, was evidence that the British had not yet shaken free of the fiction of Great Power status.

By the mid-1950s reality began to set in. British officials made a greater, more sagacious attempt to increase the attractiveness of their cooperation to the Americans. Slowly but steadily, they took steps to improve British security. Although much still needed to be done in the 1956-58 period, they at least recognized the importance of this factor in American, especially congressional, deliberations. In late 1954 they also set in motion an accelerated program to build atomic weapons and develop the hydrogen bomb. The importance of this development was that it gave them much more information of value to exchange. Lastly, they did in 1955 what they might have done in 1949—accept a slice of cooperation rather than demand an entire loaf in expectation of receiving further slices later. Even after JCAE opposition excised from the June 15, 1955, Agreement for Cooperation the arrangement to transfer nuclear submarine propulsion data, and even after AEC-DOD disagreement cheated them of early information exchanges on characteristics of American atomic weapons, they took what the Americans gave.

In the period from June 1955 to July 1958, several important and concurrent developments took place that ultimately resulted in the forging of the Anglo-American nuclear alliance. With the growth of Soviet nuclear power, the argument that the United States required the cooperation of its NATO allies to maximize the collective strength became unassailable. President Eisenhower and his advisors increased their efforts to persuade the Western Europeans to accept deployment of American IRBMs and tactical nuclear weapons on their soil. They also demonstrated increasing boldness in expanding nuclear cooperation with the British in contravention of JCAE wishes.

But the members of the Joint Committee themselves acknowledged the unremitting logic of the need for greater cooperation with the allies. They protested less and less, as a consequence, that giving American nuclear secrets to the British and others would result in disastrous leaks to the Soviets. The Soviets, they understood further, already possessed much of that knowledge. Rather, their opposition to information exchanges and other cooperation in the nuclear field rested on the fear that giving nuclear data to the British would enable the British state-subsidized commercial nuclear program to gain a competitive advantage over private American companies. It also grew from a still potent proprietary instinct to keep the most important American nuclear weapons secrets exclusively in American hands. Lastly, it arose from a deeply held desire to avoid taking actions that would result in dramatic escalation of the nuclear arms race. Congressional leaders certainly did not want the Eisenhower administration to begin disseminating information to the NATO allies and risk acquisition by several of those nations of nuclear weapons. The world was dangerous enough as it was with just the United States, Britain, and the Soviet Union as nuclear powers.

There was also opposition in the JCAE based on more political and personal grounds. As administration officials contemplated greater cooperation with the British and sought ways in which to push to the limit of the Atomic Energy Act of 1954 (if not circumvent its restrictions), they withheld information from members of the committee. Such was the case in spring 1956 when Strauss failed to inform then JCAE Chairman Anderson that the administration intended to hand over to the British nuclear submarine propulsion information. Although the JCAE was able to block the exchange temporarily, Democrats already unhappy with administration policies for private industry development of nuclear power carried away very bitter feelings toward Strauss and the administration. In 1958, Anderson fought a furious rearguard action to thwart parts of the administration plan to greatly improve nuclear cooperation with the British and other allies.

As for the British, they remained as eager as always to cooperate with the United States in the nuclear sphere, more so after political pressure built in Britain to agree to a moratorium on nuclear testing. Both the Eden and Macmillan governments opposed the moratorium idea because the British nuclear program trailed well behind superpower nuclear development. Even after the first British hydrogen bomb test of May 1957, Macmillan and his advisors refused to sign on to nuclear disarmament efforts. Like the Americans, they believed that powerful nuclear forces were essential to counter overwhelming Soviet conventional military superiority in Europe and to deter Soviet aggression generally. Creation of a compact but technologically advanced British nuclear force, moreover, was seen as a key to unlocking the door to American nuclear secrets. In fact, British progress in the nuclear field did enable Macmillan and his advisors to convince the Americans that British nuclear cooperation would be of value to the United States and that an Anglo-American nuclear alliance would contribute materially to the protection of U.S. national security and the defense of Western Europe.

Finally, two important international events—the Suez crisis of October–November 1956 and the Soviet Sputnik successes of October–November 1957—served as catalysts to persuade President Eisenhower to assume a vigorous leadership role in forwarding the cause of Anglo-American nuclear cooperation. After the Suez crisis strained Anglo-American relations and brought down the Eden government, Eisenhower made the decision to conclude the deal to put IRBMs into Britain. He also decided to transmit nuclear submarine propulsion data to the British and to agree to other areas of cooperation in the nuclear sphere regardless of JCAE opinion. It was helpful, naturally, but not crucial that the new Prime Minister of Britain was his old wartime friend Macmillan. After Sputnik Eisenhower went further. He sought from Congress amendments to the Atomic Energy Act of 1954 to eliminate restrictions against nuclear cooperation with the British and permit him to create a stable, long-term Anglo-American nuclear alliance. Because Durham, the new JCAE chairman, and most members of the Joint Committee were now convinced that U.S. national security and the defense of Western Europe required close cooperation with Britain in the nuclear field, they gave the President most of what he wanted.

With the signing of the July 3, 1958, agreement, the nuclear alliance came into being. Thereafter, Anglo-American nuclear relations amounted to a strong partnership in which the United States clearly dominated, but to which Britain—as long as the British government maintained a sufficient effort—made a very valuable contribution and derived significant, indeed irreplaceable, benefit. The long wait for the nuclear alliance from the end of World War II to 1958 had been worth it.[2]

The 1958 amendments to the Atomic Energy Act of 1954 undoubtedly gave the U.S. government the legal authority to exchange with allies who had made substantial progress in the nuclear weapons field information on both atomic (fission) and hydrogen (fusion or thermonuclear) weapons. Although the JCAE made certain that the administration did not agree to any exchange of hydrogen weapons data under the Anglo-American bilateral agreement of July 3, 1958, it is unclear whether the May 7, 1959, agreement for transfer of nonnuclear components and special nuclear materials for "atomic weapons" permitted an exchange of hydrogen weapons data. It must be assumed, however, that soon thereafter the British and Americans made arrangements that did permit such an exchange.

I make this assertion for two reasons. First, in the 1960s the British were at last permitted to detonate nuclear weapons at American test ranges. At present, moreover, the British test all their nuclear weapons, hydrogen devices included, in Nevada. While it is possible that in return for access to American test facilities the British were required to reveal unilaterally data on British hydrogen weapons, it is more likely that British scientists were greatly assisted by their American counterparts in detonating British hydrogen devices and that information was thereby exchanged.

Conclusion

Another reason to suspect that the British and Americans have exchanged hydrogen weapons data is the fact that in the 1960s the British purchased from the United States Polaris submarine-launched ballistic missiles designed to carry thermonuclear warheads. In order to design warheads to fit the American missiles, British scientists would probably have had to have received information about thermonuclear warheads the Americans intended to mount on the missiles. And even if the Americans held back this information, British scientists could certainly have deduced some data about American thermonuclear warheads once they reeceived the Polaris missiles.

At the present time (January 1987), the Conservative government of Margaret Thatcher has contracted with the United States to purchase Trident II missiles for British submarines. These missiles, too, take thermonuclear warheads, as many as ten for each. It is logical to assume, therefore, that the British and American governments will again be exchanging hydrogen weapons data after 1988-89 when the Trident IIs become available. Whether this exchange will involve relatively complete information about hydrogen weapons designs or whether it will be so circumscribed as to provide only enough data to make possible British deployment of Trident IIs is unknown. It will be the task of some future historian to find out.

Neil Kinnock, leader of the British Labour party, has said that if returned as Prime Mnister after the next general election, he will disarm Britain's nuclear forces unilaterally. He also vows to remove American cruise missiles and other nuclear-tipped weapons from British soil while still permitting nuclear-powered ships carrying nuclear weapons to enter British ports.

Were such a policy implemented by a future British government, the impact on Britain's relations with the United States and other allies would be severe. Whether the viability of NATO itself would be undermined remains an open question. But it seems clear that whatever influence Britain now possesses in regard to U.S. nuclear policy, American use of nuclear weapons, and the U.S. negotiating position in nuclear arms reduction talks with the Soviets would be effectively destroyed. Britain would go from being a second-level player in the international arena, and the nuclear sphere in particular, to being an insignificant entity.

NOTES

1. Oliver S. Franks, *Britain and the Tide of World Affairs* (London: Oxford University Press, 1955), pp. 7-12, 25, 27-28. Although in this work former British Ambassador to the United States Franks recognized the difficulty for Britons, especially those born near the turn of the century and witnesses to Britain's past power, to adjust to the new postwar realities, he himself still clung to the idea that Britain was a Great Power. In his mind, dependence upon the United States, or "interdependence" as he chose to refer to it, did not mean that Britain was no longer a Great Power.

2. Ibid., pp. 34-35. Franks remarked that one reason for Anglo-American misunderstandings was the failure of both sides to communicate the assumptions of a

proposal. He also gave his opinion that American officials' estimation of the British went up when they (the British) delivered on their promises and did well. See John Simpson, *The Independent Nuclear State: The United States, Britain, and the Military Atom* (London: Macmillan, 1983), pp. 219-20, for a concise summary of the major trends in Anglo-American nuclear relations, 1958-81.

BIBLIOGRAPHY

PRIMARY SOURCES
Unpublished Documents

Department of Energy, Washington, D.C. (documents obtained under Freedom of Information Act)
    Atomic Energy Commission Files, AEC Meetings 184, 351.
Department of State, Washington, D.C. (documents obtained under Freedom of Information Act)
    Files:
    741.5611
    FW741.5621
    57D688 808 (411.25 U.S.-U.K. Berm. Disc., 411.26 U.S.-U.K. Tech. Disc.)
    711.56341
    711.5612
    S/AE Files
Eisenhower Library, Abilene, Kansas:
    Papers of Dwight D. Eisenhower as President, Ann Whitman File.
National Archives, Washington, D.C.:
    RG 59, General Records of Department of State.
    RG 218, U.S. Joint Chiefs of Staff.
Truman Library, Independence, Missouri:
    Papers of Harry S. Truman, President's Secretary's File.

Microfilm Documents

Hearings before Subcommittee on Agreements for Cooperation, JCAE, Amending the Atomic Energy Act of 1954—Exchange of Military Information and Material with Allies. 85th Cong., 2d sess., 1958.
Hearings by Special Subcommittee on Minerals, Materials, and Fuels Economic of the Committee on Interior and Insular Affairs. U.S. Senate, 83rd Cong., 1st and 2d sess., 1954.

Joint Atomic Energy Hearings. 80th Cong., 1st sess., 1947.
Joint Atomic Energy Hearings, 84th Cong., 1st sess., 1955.
Minutes and Documents of Cabinet Meetings of President Eisenhower (1953-61). Presidential Documents Series. Frederick, Md.: University Publications of America, 1980.
Minutes of Telephone Conversations of John Foster Dulles and Christian Herter (1953-61). Frederick, Md.: University Publications of America, 1980.
Official Conversations and Meetings of Dean Acheson (1949-1953). Presidential Documents Series. Washington, D.C.: University Publications of America, 1980.

Published Documents

Public Law 585, 79th Cong., 60 Statute 755-775.
Public Law 235, 82d Cong., 65 Statute 692.
Public Law 703, 83d Cong., 68 Statute 919.
Public Law 479, 85th Cong., 68 Statute 276.
Public Papers of the Presidents: Dwight D. Eisenhower, 1953-55. Washington, D.C.: U.S. Government Printing Office, 1959-60.
Public Papers of the Presidents: Harry S. Truman, 1945-52. Washington, D.C.: U.S. Government Printing Office, 1961-65.
U.K. Parliament. *H.C. Debates*, 5th ser., vols. 416, 483, 494, 496, 501, 505, 507, 510, 520, 522, 524-27, 530, 535, 542-44, 547-48, 553-54, 562, 564, 567-70, 577-79, 584, 586, 591.
U.S. v. Belmont, 301 U.S. 324 (1937).
U.S. Congress. House. *Committee on Armed Services, Hearings, Investigation of National Defense Missiles*. 85th Cong., 2d sess., 1957.
U.S. Congress. Senate. *Pastore Addressing Senate on House-Senate Conference Report on H.R. 12716*, 85th Cong., 2d sess., June 30, 1958. *Congressional Record* 104: 12586-87.
U.S. State Department. *Bulletin*. Vols. 26, 30.
U.S. State Department. *Foreign Relations of the United States.*
    1944, Conference at Quebec, vol. 2
    1945, vol. 2
    1946, vol. 1
    1947, vol. 1
    1948, vol. 1
    1949, vol. 1
    1950, vols. 1, 3
    1951, vol. 1
    1952-54, vols. 2, 5
U.S. State Department. *United States Treaties and Other International Agreements*. Vols. 5, 9, 10.

Books

Acheson, Dean. *Present at the Creation*. New York: W. W. Norton, 1969.
_____. *Sketches from Life of Men I Have Known*. New York: Harper & Brothers, 1959.

Attlee, Clement R. *As It Happened.* New York: Viking Press, 1954.
Bohlen, Charles E. *Witness to History, 1929-1969.* New York: W. W. Norton, 1973.
Brown, Anthony Cave, ed. *Dropshot: The United States Plan for War with the Soviet Union in 1957.* New York: Dial Press/James Wade, 1978.
Bush, Vannevar. *Pieces of the Action.* New York: William Morrow, 1970.
Connally, Tom. *My Name Is Tom Connally.* New York: Thomas Y. Crowell, 1954.
Eden, Anthony. *Full Circle: The Memoirs of Anthony Eden.* Boston: Houghton Mifflin, 1960.
Eisenhower, Dwight D. *Mandate for Change, 1953-1956.* Garden City, N.Y.: Doubleday, 1965.
Franks, Oliver S. *Britain and the Tide of World Affairs.* London: Oxford University Press, 1955.
Gavin, Lieut. General James M. *War and Peace in the Space Age.* New York: Harper & Brothers, 1958.
Groves, Leslie R. *Now It Can Be Told.* New York: Harper & Row, 1962.
Killian, James R., Jr. *Sputnik, Scientists, and Eisenhower: A Memoir of the First Special Assistant to the President for Science and Technology.* Cambridge, Mass.: MIT Press, 1977.
Lilienthal, David E. *Change, Hope, and the Bomb.* Princeton, N.J.: Princeton University Press, 1963.
_____. *The Journals of David E. Lilienthal.* Vol. 2, *The Atomic Energy Years, 1945-1950.* New York: Harper & Row, 1964.
Macmillan, Harold. *Riding the Storm, 1956-1959.* New York: Harper & Row, 1971.
Millis, Walter. *The Forrestal Diaries.* New York: Viking Press, 1951.
Strauss, Lewis L. *Men and Decisions.* Garden City, N.Y.: Doubleday, 1962.
Truman, Harry S. *Memoirs.* Vol. 2, *Years of Trial and Hope.* Garden City, N.Y.: Doubleday, 1956.
Twining, General Nathan F. *Neither Liberty nor Safety: A Hard Look at U.S. Military Policy and Strategy.* New York: Holt, Rinehart, and Winston, 1966.
Vandenberg, Arthur H., Jr. *The Private Papers of Senator Vandenberg.* Boston: Houghton Mifflin, 1952.

SECONDARY SOURCES

Articles and Dissertations

Cable, James. "Interdependence: A Drug of Addiction?" *International Affairs* 59 (Summer 1983): 365-79.
Crandall, William F. "A Party Divided against Itself: Anticommunism and the Transformation of the Republican Right, 1945-1956." Ph.D. diss., Ohio State University, 1983.
Dawson, Raymond, and Richard Rosencrance. "Theory and Reality in the Anglo-American Alliance." *World Politics* 19 (October 1966): 21-51.
Duncan, Francis. "Atomic Energy and Anglo-American Relations, 1946-1954." *Orbis* 12 (Fall 1969): 1188-1207.
Epstein, Leon D. "Britain and the H-Bomb, 1955-1958." *The Review of Politics* 21 (August 1959): 511-29.
Goldberg, Alfred. "The Atomic Origins of the British Nuclear Deterrent." *International Affairs* 40 (July 1964): 409-29.

Gormly, James L. "The Washington Declaration and the 'Poor Relation': Anglo-American Atomic Diplomacy, 1945-46." *Diplomatic History* 8 (Spring 1984): 125-43.
Knight, Wayne. "Laborite Britain: America's 'Sure Friend?' The Anglo-Soviet Treaty Issue, 1947." *Diplomatic History* 7 (Fall 1983): 267-82.
Martin, Laurence W. "The Market for Strategic Ideas in Britain: The 'Sandys Era.' " *American Political Science Review* 56 (March 1962): 23-41.
Millett, Stephen A. "The Capabilities of the American Nuclear Deterrent, 1945-50." *Aerospace Historian* 27 (March 1980): 27-32.
Munro, John A., and Alex I. Inglas. "The Atomic Conference of 1945 and the Pearson Memoirs." *International Journal* 29 (Winter 1973-74): 90-109.
O'Brien, Larry Dean. "National Security and the New Warfare: Defense Policy, War Planning, and Nuclear Weapons, 1945-50." Ph.D. diss., Ohio State University, 1981.
Rosenberg, D. A. "The United States Nuclear Stockpile, 1945-50." *Bulletin of Atomic Scientists* (May 1982): 67-68.
Slessor, Sir John. "British Defense Policy." *Foreign Affairs* 35 (July 1957): 551-63.
Tananbaum, Duane A. "The Bricker Amendment Controversy: Its Origins and Eisenhower's Role." *Diplomatic History* 9 (Winter 1985): 73-93.
Wiebes, Cees, and Bert Zeeman. "The Pentagon Negotiations, March 1948: The Launching of the North Atlantic Treaty." *International Affairs* 59 (Summer 1983): 351-63.

Books

Ambrose, Stephen E. *Eisenhower: The President.* Vol. 2. New York: Simon & Schuster, 1984.
Anderson, Terry H. *The United States, Great Britain, and the Cold War, 1944-1947.* Columbia: University of Missouri Press, 1981.
Armacost, Michael H. *The Politics of Weapons Innovation: The Thor-Jupiter Controversy.* New York: Columbia University Press, 1969.
Bartlett, C. J. *The Long Retreat: A Short History of British Defence Policy, 1945-70.* London: Macmillan, 1972.
Baylis, John. *Anglo-American Defense Relations, 1939-1980: The Special Relationship.* London: Macmillan, 1981.
Campbell, Duncan. *The Unsinkable Aircraft Carrier: American Military Power in Britain.* London: Michael Joseph, 1984.
Condit, Kenneth W. *The History of the Joint Chiefs of Staff: The Joint Chiefs of Staff and National Policy.* Vol. 2, *1947-1949.* Wilmington, Del.: Michael Glazier, 1979.
Cook, Blanche Wiesen. *The Declassified Eisenhower: A Divided Legacy.* Garden City, N.Y.: Doubleday, 1981.
Doenecke, Justus D. *Not to the Swift: The Old Isolationists in the Cold War Era.* London: Associated University Presses, 1979.
Donoughue, Bernard, and G. W. Jones. *Herbert Morrison: Portrait of a Politician.* London: Weidenfeld and Nicolson, 1973.
Eckes, Alfred E., Jr. *The U.S. and the Global Struggle for Minerals.* Austin: University of Texas Press, 1979.

Gelber, Lionel. *America in Britain's Place*. New York: Frederick A. Praeger, 1981.
Gowing, Margaret. *Independence and Deterrence: Britain and Atomic Energy, 1945-1952*. Vol. 1, *Policy Making; Vol. 2, Policy Execution*. London: Macmillan, 1974.
Green, Harold P., and Alan Rosenthal. *Government of the Atom*. New York: Atherton Press, 1963.
Guhin, Michael A. *John Foster Dulles: A Statesman and His Times*. New York: Columbia University Press, 1972.
Harris, Kenneth. *Attlee*. London: Weidenfeld and Nicolson, 1982.
Hathaway, Robert M. *Ambiguous Partnership: Britain and America, 1944-47*. New York: Columbia University Press, 1981.
Herken, Gregg. *The Winning Weapon: The Atomic Bomb in the Cold War, 1945-1950*. New York: Alfred A. Knopf, 1980.
Hewlett, Richard G., and Oscar E. Anderson, Jr. *The New World: A History of the United States Atomic Energy Commission*. Vol. 1, *1939-46*. USAEC, 1972.
Hewlett, Richard G., and Francis Duncan. *Atomic Shield 1947-52*. Vol. 2, *A History of the United States Atomic Energy Commission*. University Park: Pennsylvania State University Press, 1969.
_____. *Nuclear Navy 1946-1962*. Chicago: University of Chicago Press, 1974.
Higham, Robin, and Jacob W. Kipp, eds. *Soviet Aviation and Air Power: An Historical Review*. London: Brassey's, 1977.
Huntington, Samuel P. *The Common Defense: Strategic Programs in National Politics*. New York: Columbia University Press, 1961.
Kinnard, Douglas. *The Secretary of Defense*. Lexington: University of Kentucky Press, 1980.
Korb, Lawrence J. *The Joint Chiefs of Staff: The First Twenty-five Years*. Bloomington: Indiana University Press, 1976.
McLellan, David S. *Dean Acheson: The State Department Years*. New York: Dodd, Mead, & Company, 1976.
Nicholas, Herbert. *Britain and the United States of America*. Baltimore: Johns Hopkins Press, 1963.
Northedge, F. S. *Descent from Power: British Foreign Policy, 1945-1973*. London: George Allen and Unwin, 1974.
Pierre, Andrew J. *Nuclear Politics: The British Experience with an Independent Strategic Force, 1939-1970*. London: Oxford University Press, 1972.
Poole, Walter S. *The History of the Joint Chiefs of Staff: The Joint Chiefs of Staff and National Policy*. Vol. 4, *1950-1952*. Wilmington, Del.: Michael Glazier, 1980.
Pringle, Peter, and James Spigelman. *The Nuclear Barons*. New York: Holt, Rinehart, and Winston, 1981.
Reinhard, David W. *The Republican Right since 1945*. Lexington: University Press of Kentucky, 1983.
Rosencrance, R. N. *Defense of the Realm: British Strategy in the Nuclear Epoch*. New York: Columbia University Press, 1968.
_____, ed. *The Dispersion of Nuclear Weapons: Strategy and Politics*. New York: Columbia University Press, 1964.
Schnabel, James F. *The History of the Joint Chiefs of Staff: The Joint Chiefs of*

Staff and National Policy, Vol. 1, *1945-1947*. Wilmington, Del.: Michael Glazier, 1979.

Seldon, Anthony. *Churchill's Indian Summer: The Conservative Government, 1951-55*. London: Hodder and Stoughton, 1981.

Sherwin, Martin J. *A World Destroyed: The Atomic Bomb and the Grand Alliance*. New York: Alfred A. Knopf, 1975.

Simpson, John. *The Independent Nuclear State: The United States, Britain, and the Military Atom*. London: Macmillan, 1983.

Slessor, Sir John. *The Great Deterrent*. New York: Frederick A. Praeger, 1957.

Wheeler-Bennett, John W. *John Anderson, Viscount Waverly*. London: Macmillan, 1962.

Williams, Francis. *A Prime Minister Remembers*. London: William Heinemann, 1961.

Newspapers

London Times
Manchester Guardian
New York Times

INDEX

Acheson, Dean: and the 1949 Anglo-American meetings, 56, 60, 61; and the 1952 Anglo-American meetings, 91; and administration-congressional relations, 29, 53, 55; and allocation of raw materials, 20, 21, 22, 67–68; appointment of, 47; and the Blair House meeting with congress, 53–54; and British atomic testing, 75; and consulting issues, 80, 82–84; and control issues, 8, 102; and the CPC report (February 1946), 19; and information exchange issues, 23, 27, 50, 53–54, 91, 92–93; Lovett replaces, 30; and the NSC Special Committee report, 50; policies toward cooperation of, 29, 52, 69, 76; *Present at the Creation* author, 53–54; and the Princeton conference recommendations, 50

AEC (Atomic Energy Commission): 1948 report by, 41; and the 1949 Anglo-American meetings, 60; and the 1952 Anglo–American meetings, 92; and the 1955 Anglo-American Agreement of Cooperation, 147, 148–49; and the 1957 Anglo–American Bermuda conference, 178–83; and the 1958 Anglo-American conference, 231–34; and the 1958 (July) Anglo–American bilateral agreement, 248; and allocation of raw materials issues, 29, 30–31, 49–50, 69; and control issues, 77, 98–103; creation of, 26; and the Cyril Smith affair, 42–44; DOD/War Department relations with, 26, 76–77, 152–55, 158–64; and information exchange issues, 3, 34, 39–45, 49–50, 117, 125, 147, 152–55, 192, 233; JCAE relations with, 52, 77, 113, 141, 152–53, 158–64; and McMahon Act revisions, 115–16; mismanagement of nuclear program by, 52; policies toward cooperation of, 41–42, 76, 92; and the Princeton conference recommendations, 49–50; and private industry, 113; and research and development in U.S., 31, 199, 230; review of atomic program in Britain by, 39–40; and security issues, 134; and transfer issues, 233. *See also name of specific individual*

Agreement and Declaration of Trust (1944), 5, 7, 9

Aid. *See name of specific act or plan, e.g.* Marshall Plan

Alexander, Albert V., 43

Allocation of raw materials: and the 1945

Anglo-American conference, 12–13; and the 1947 Anglo-American conference, 32–35; and the 1949 Anglo-American meetings, 56–61; and the 1956 Anglo-American agreement, 162; and the 1957 Anglo-American conferences, 204–5, 209–10; and the 1958 (July) Anglo-American bilateral agreement, 237; and American defense policies, 20, 21–22, 28, 29, 48–49, 68–69; and the Blair House meeting (July 1949), 53, 54; and British defense policies, 3, 7, 20, 21–22, 67–68, 179–80; and British influence with supplying nations, 52–53, 55–56, 60–61, 68–69; congressional views about, 29–30, 123–24, 237, 243–44; and consultation issues, 86; and the Eisenhower administration, 115; and the Princeton conference, 48–49; and the Quebec Agreement, 20; and the Truman administration, 243–44; and the V-J Day trust supplies, 20, 21. *See also name of specific agency/department, individual*

American bases in Britain: and the 1952 Anglo-American meetings, 93; and the 1957 Anglo-American Bermuda conference, 186; and the Blair House meeting, 53; and Churchill's pressure to publish the Quebec Agreement, 72–73; and consultation issues, 80–86, 90, 93, 101, 115, 135, 136, 169–74, 204, 213, 246–47; and control issues, 101; military strength of, 152; and the NSC report (March 1949), 51; and SAC exercises, 205, 214, 222; and the strategic importance of Britain, 38, 66–67; and the Suez crisis, 172. *See also* IRBMs

Anderson, Clinton P.: and the 1955, 1956 Anglo-American Agreement for Cooperation, 148, 162–63; and the Atomic Energy Act (1954) amendments, 208, 216, 217–18, 223, 224; attitude toward cooperation of, 148, 162–63, 247; and the deception of JCAE, 191; and information exchange issues, 190, 232; Strauss criticism by, 152–53; and transfer issues, 232–33, 234

Anderson, John (Sir), 11–13, 114

Anglo-American Agreement of Cooperation (June 1955, 1956), 146–49, 161–64, 246

Anglo-American bilateral agreement (July 1958), 4, 236–39, 248

Anglo-American bilateral agreement (May 1959), 248–49

Anglo-American IRBM agreement (February 1958), 220–21

Anglo-American meetings: in 1945 (November), 9–14, 20, 29; in 1947 (December), 32–35; in 1949 (September-December), 56–61; in 1953 (November) in Bermuda, 124, 126–30; in 1953 (October-December), 121–31; in 1954 (October-December), 143–45; in 1957 (April), 190, 191–92; in 1957 (March) in Bermuda, 175–76, 178–83, 185–86, 195–97, 219; in 1957 (October-December), 200–210; in 1958 (June), 231–34

Anti-interventionists in congress, 71–72, 112

Arms race, 8, 154, 186, 213, 225, 234–36, 247, 249. *See also* Disarmament; Moratorium on atomic/nuclear testing

Arneson, R. Gordon: and the 1945 Anglo-American conference, 9–10, 12; and the 1949 Anglo-American meetings, 61; and the 1952 Anglo-American meetings, 92; and allocation of raw materials issues, 44; and the Blair House meeting, 53; and consultation issues, 81–82; and control issues, 102; and information exchange issues, 43–44, 50; and the McMahon Act revisions, 115; and the NSC Special Committee report, 50; and the Princeton conference, 48; tour of British facilities by, 58

Atlas missiles, 208

Atomic, definition of, 214–15

Atomic bombs: British development/production of, 39–44, 48, 51, 54–55, 69, 90, 93, 106, 127, 138, 243, 245; and

Hiroshima, 7–8; Soviet development/ production of, 47, 56, 62, 65, 66, 243, 244. *See also* Testing, atomic/nuclear

Atomic Energy Act (1946). *See* McMahon Act (1946); McMahon Act amendments

Atomic Energy Act (1954), 4, 140, 147, 152, 153–55, 161, 163, 190, 247. *See also* Atomic Energy Act (1954) amendments

Atomic Energy Act (1954) amendments: and the 1957 Anglo–American conferences, 201; and the 1958 Anglo-American bilateral agreement, 236–39; and the 1958 Anglo-American conference, 231–34; and the arms race, 234–36; British reaction to, 225–27; and British stockpiles, 216–17; and congress, 207–8, 210, 213–19, 222–27, 230–36; and the definition of atomic, 214–15; and deterrence, 230; and the Eisenhower administration, 203, 207, 208, 213–19, 222–27, 230, 248; Eisenhower signs the, 236; and hydrogen weapons, 223; and information exchange issues, 214–19, 222–27, 230–36, 248; and IRBMs, 220–22, 230; and manufacturing issues, 216; passage of, 4, 234; and reactors, 232–33; and transfer issues, 215, 216–18, 232–36

Atomic testing. *See* Testing, atomic/nuclear

Atoms for Peace Plan (Eisenhower, December 1953), 121, 128–29, 133–34, 147, 179

Attlee, Clement: and the 1945 Anglo-American conference, 9–11, 13, 20; and allocation of raw materials issues, 22, 67–68; and British atomic testing, 75; and British research and development, 18–19, 22; and consultation issues, 79–80, 83, 205; and control issues, 7–8, 13, 20–21, 22; defeat of, 72; and deterrence, 18–19; and information exchange issues, 9, 10–11, 22; and the McMahon Act, 19; misleads Commons about cooperation relations, 159; and the Modus Vivendi agreement, 136; and parliamentary elections, 61; and uses of atomic/nuclear energy, 7–8, 19

Ballistic missiles. See ICBMs; IRBMs
Barbour, Walworth, 170–71, 195, 196
Barkley, Alben W., 53
Baruch, Bernard, 30
Belgian Congo, 22, 29, 33, 34, 44, 51, 68
Berlin blockade, 37–38, 42, 52, 76
Bermuda conference (March 1957), 175–76, 178–83, 185–86, 195–97, 219
Bermuda conference (November 1953), 124, 126–30
Bevin, Ernest, 34, 37, 61, 67–68, 80–81
Bikini Atoll, 17, 22
Blair House meeting (July 1949), 53–54
Blue Streak, 194, 203
Bradley, Omar, 69, 74, 76, 77, 81–85, 102, 107, 117, 118
Breithut, Richard C., 231
Bricker, John W., 112
Britain: American tours of nuclear facilities in, 39–40, 58, 146–47; Anglo-American Agreement of Cooperation (June 1955, 1956) reaction in, 148–49, 153–54, 159–60, 164; Anglo-American bilateral agreement (July 1958) reaction in, 238; Atomic Energy Act (1954) amendments reaction in, 225–27; Bermuda conference (March 1957) reaction in, 185–88; Bermuda conference (November 1953) reaction in, 128–30; defense policies of, 38, 48, 51–52, 105–6, 135, 144, 167, 173–74, 177–80, 185–86; dependence on U.S. of, 5–6, 144, 154, 222, 238–39, 245–46, 248; economic situation in, 1, 38, 167, 221, 245; and economic threats by U.S., 31–32, 34, 52, 53, 60–61, 172; expansion of atomic program in, 108, 135, 144, 149, 154, 173–74, 177–80; foreign policy of, 171–74; as a great power, 89, 245, 249; internal politics in, 79–81, 128–30, 154, 170, 183, 185–86, 221–22, 246, 249; IRBM agreement (February 1958) reaction in,

221–22; nationalization of industry in, 22; objectives of, 85; policies toward Anglo-American cooperation of, 7–8, 18–19, 67–68, 103, 107, 108, 177–80; public opinion in, 9, 135, 214, 222; and Soviet relations, 10, 37; Sputnik reaction of, 200; strategic importance of, 58, 66–67, 81–83, 105–6, 170, 239, 247; strength of, 167–68, 177, 185; and the Suez crisis, 171–74; Washington conference (October-December 1957) reaction in, 203. *See also specific conference, name, and topic*

Brownell, Herbert, Jr., 153, 155, 158, 190

Brussels Treaty, 37

Burke, Arleigh A., 151, 155

Burns, James H., 26

Bush, Vannevar, 5, 9–12, 20, 21, 22, 31, 32, 41, 42, 114–15

Butler, George H., 48

Butler, Richard, 186, 214

Byrnes, James F., 8–13, 17, 18, 20–21

Caccia, Harold A., 196, 206, 219–20

Calder Hall, England, 159, 178, 180, 189, 191, 192, 224, 233–34

Canada: and the 1946 CPC report, 18; and the 1949 Anglo–American meetings, 56; and the 1949 NSC report, 50, 51; and the construction/operation of atomic energy plants, 18–19, 147; and consultation issues, 81–82; information base of, 114; and information exchange issues, 77, 147, 161; JSSC view of, 9; and the Kennan proposal, 30; manufacture of atomic weapons in, 42–43; and the North American Air Defense Command, 230; and the Princeton conference, 48, 49; stockpiles in, 19, 31–32, 40, 51, 58, 81–82, 189; uranium in, 77, 180, 204–5; U.S. influence on, 18, 20

Carpenter, Donald C., 40, 42–43, 47

CDT (Combined Development Trust), 5, 11–13, 29, 32, 34. *See also* Allocation of raw materials

Chadwick, James (Sir), 19, 20

Chalk River, Canada, 19

Cherwell, Frederick (Lord), 90, 91–94, 108, 122, 127–30

China, 146–47

Christmas Island, 144, 159–60, 168, 187

Churchill, Winston: and the 1952 Anglo-American meetings, 91–94; and the 1953 Anglo-American Bermuda conference, 124, 126–30; and the 1954 Eisenhower conference, 138; and British atomic testing, 75–76; and British security issues, 3, 114; and consultation issues, 80–81, 90, 94, 135–39, 145, 205, 206; defense policy of, 105–6; and Eisenhower's election, 107–8; election of, 3, 72, 89; and the Hyde Park Memorandum, 5, 6, 11; and hydrogen bombs issues, 136–37; and information exchange issues, 5–6, 107–8, 135–39; and internal politics, 137, 185–86; misleads Commons about cooperation relations, 159; pressure on Labour government by, 86; and the Quebec Agreement, 72–73; and the uses of atomic/nuclear energy, 5

Civilian/commercial uses of atomic/nuclear energy, 5, 10, 12, 134, 148, 223, 233, 237, 244–45, 247

Cockcroft, John (Sir), 19, 57, 59, 94, 122, 143

Cole, W. Sterling, 53, 54–55, 113, 116, 118, 123, 133, 139–40, 161

Collins, J. Lawton, 82, 82–83

Conant, James B., 5, 48

Congress: and the 1945 Anglo-American conference, 13–14; and the 1957 Anglo-American Bermuda conference, 182; and the 1957 Anglo-American meetings, 203; and the 1958 (July) Anglo-American bilateral agreement, 238; and the 1958 (June) Anglo-American conference, 231–33; Acheson briefing about Anglo-American atomic cooperation to, 29; and the allocation of raw materials, 29–30, 123–24; anti–interventionists in, 71–72, 112; and consultation issues, 32, 213–14, 244; and

Index 261

control issues, 23; DOD/JCS relations with, 72, 117, 244; and information exchange issues, 2, 13–14, 19, 122, 209, 213–14, 244; and IRBM issues, 171, 173, 195, 219, 220, 230–31; and McMahon Act amendments, 102; and manufacturing issues, 123; and the NSC report (March 1949), 50, 52; opposition to private industry by, 139, 140, 152–53; and planning issues, 122; policies toward cooperation of, 37, 52, 69, 80, 81, 173, 210, 213–14, 234–35; policies toward NATO of, 71–72; and research and development in U.S., 122; State Department relations with, 72; unilateralists in, 23. *See also* Atomic Energy Act (1954); Atomic Energy Act (1954); Congress-Eisenhower administration relations; Congress-Truman administration relations; Hydrogen bombs, American; JCAE; McMahon Act (1946); McMahon Act amendments; Security, British

Congress-Eisenhower administration relations, 112, 113, 116, 135, 158–64, 201. *See also* JCAE; *name of specific agency/department*

Congress-Truman administration relations, 19, 47, 48–49, 53–55, 57–58, 62. *See also* JCAE; *name of specific agency/department*

Connally, Tom, 13, 29, 53, 54

Conservatives (British), 80–81, 84, 89, 136, 172, 200, 249

Construction/operation of atomic plants: and the 1945 Memorandum of Intention, 20–21; and the 1947 Anglo–American conference, 33–35; and the 1949 Anglo-American meetings, 56–61; British pressures about, 5–6, 20–21, 27–28, 31, 33–35, 48–49, 51–52, 56–61, 93, 144, 154; in Canada, 18–19, 147; and the JCAE, 52; and the JCS, 48–49; and the Kennan proposal, 31; and the NSC report (1949), 51; and the Princeton conference, 48–49; and the Quebec Agreement, 5, 20, 21; Truman's position on, 20–21; and U.N. article 102, 20

Consultation issues: and the 1945 Anglo-American meetings, 12; and the 1952 Anglo-American meetings, 93; and the 1953 Anglo-American Bermuda conference, 128, 130–31; and the 1955 Anglo-American Agreement of Cooperation, 146–47; and the 1957 Anglo-American conferences, 204, 205–6; and allocation of raw materials issues, 86; and American bases in Britain, 73, 80–86, 90, 93, 101, 135, 169–74, 204, 213, 246–47; and the American military community, 81, 82–84, 86; and Anglo-American military cooperation, 130–31; and British internal politics, 79–81, 135–36, 221–22, 246; British pressures about, 73, 79–86; and British security standards, 84, 86; and Canada, 81–82; and congress, 32, 53–55, 135, 213–14; and information exchange issues, 84; and IRBM issues, 169–70, 219; and the Modus Vivendi (January 1948), 34–35, 136, 139, 205, 206, 244; and NATO, 137–39, 144–45; and the NSC 5422/2 (August 1954) report, 138–39; and the NSC Special Committee report (June 1952), 101; and the Princeton conference recommendations, 48; and the Quebec Agreement, 136; and the State Department, 82–84; and the Truman administration, 53–55, 244; and uses of nuclear weapons/energy, 244–47

Control issues: and the 1945 Anglo-American conference, 9–13; and the 1949 Anglo-American meetings, 60; and the 1957 Anglo-American Bermuda conference, 178–83; and American defense policies, 8–10, 74–77, 101, 244; and the Blair House meeting, 53–54; British views about, 10–11; and congress, 23, 53–54; and the CPC report (1946), 17–18, 19–20; and DOD, 123; and IRBMs, 170, 173; and the Kennan proposal, 30; and the McMahon Act (1946), 22–23, 77; and

nuclear testing, 103; and the Soviet Union, 27, 28; struggle about, 97–103; Truman's views about, 8–9, 19, 22; and the U.N., 10, 27, 28, 30, 55–56. *See also* IRBMs; *name of specific agency/department or individual*
Conventional forces/weapons, 106–7, 111–12, 146, 169, 177, 187, 188, 247
CPC (Combined Policy Committee), 5, 7, 12–13, 17–23, 29, 32–35, 39–40, 49, 56–58, 99. *See also* CDT (Combined Development Trust)
Cutler, Robert, 126
Czechoslovakia, 37, 38, 76

Dean, Gordon E., 60, 68, 69, 73–77, 99, 102, 113, 115, 116
Debris analysis, 122
"Declaration of Common Purpose" (Washington conference, October-December 1957), 201, 203
Defense policies, American: and the 1947 Anglo-American conference, 32–35; and the allocation of raw materials, 20, 21–22, 28, 29, 48–49, 68–69; and the Anglo-American Agreement of Cooperation (June 1955), 146–49; and Anglo–American military cooperation, 123–26, 130; and China, 146–47; and control issues, 244; in Eastern Europe, 25, 37–38; of Eisenhower, 3–4, 28–29, 53, 111–12, 117–19, 130, 146, 151, 244–45; and the JCS, 146; and the McMahon Act amendments, 134–35; and the National Security Council, 117–18, 122–23; and NATO, 144–45, 246; and the NSC report (March 1949), 50–51; and the Princeton conference, 48–49; and transfer issues, 230; of the Truman administration, 71–72. *See also* Atomic bombs; EDC; Hydrogen bombs; NATO; Sputnik
Defense policies, British, 32–35, 38, 48, 51–52, 105–7, 144, 167, 185–86, 247. *See also* Atomic bombs; EDC; Hydrogen bombs; NATO; Sputnik
Defense, U.S. Department of. *See* DOD

Democratic party, 113, 124, 145, 152–53, 225, 247
Deterrence: and American defense policies, 66, 111, 122–23, 145, 151, 227; and the Atomic Energy Act (1954) amendments, 230; and British defense policies, 38, 105–6, 135, 144, 167, 169–74, 179, 247; and Eisenhower defense policies, 244–45; and IRBM deployment, 169–70, 173, 185, 196–97; and nuclear testing, 186–87
Development. *See* Research and development
Disarmament: British reaction to, 154, 183, 186–88, 249; and Eisenhower administration policies, 114–15, 121, 129, 199, 230; Kinnock's policy toward, 249; and nuclear testing, 186–88, 226; and the State Department Panel of Consultants on Disarmament, 114–15; U.N. discussions about, 98, 186–88, 213
Dixon-Yates plan, 139–40
DOD (U.S. Department of Defense): and the 1955 Anglo-American Agreement of Cooperation, 148–49; and the 1957 Anglo–American Bermuda conference, 178–83; and the 1957 Anglo–American conferences, 203, 204; and the 1958 (June) Anglo–American conference, 231–34; AEC relations with, 76–77, 152–55, 158–64; and the Atomic Energy Act (1954) amendments, 230; and British security problems, 76; congressional relations with, 158–64, 244; and control issues, 77, 98–103, 123; and information exchange issues, 74–75, 125, 147, 152–55, 190, 203, 218, 244; and IRBMs, 192–95; policies toward cooperation of, 73, 76, 92, 172–73, 225; and security issues, 134; and transfer issues, 218, 222–23. *See also* Military cooperation, Anglo-American; *name of specific secretary of defense*
Do-it-yourself kits, 217–18, 219, 224, 232, 237–38
Douglas, Lewis W., 81
Dulles, Allen W., 114–15, 200

Index 263

Dulles, John Foster: and the 1955 Anglo-American Agreement of Cooperation, 146; and the 1957 Anglo-American Bermuda conference, 181; and the 1957 Anglo-American conferences, 200–210; and the 1958 (July) Anglo-American bilateral agreement, 236; and the 1958 (June) Anglo-American conference, 232–33; and allocation of raw materials issues, 115; and the Atomic Energy Act (1954) amendments, 225, 226, 230; attitude toward cooperation of, 116–17, 188–90, 225, 226; and British atomic testing, 168; congressional relationships of, 191; and consultation issues, 115, 137–38, 205, 206; and defense issues, 112, 129, 225; as Eisenhower's adviser, 116; and hydrogen bombs issues, 137; and information exchange issues, 126, 158, 188–90, 201–2, 225, 235; and IRBMs, 181, 194–95, 208, 219–20; and McMahon Act revisions, 115; and nuclear testing, 190; and SAC exercises in Britain, 214; and Soviet ICBMs, 200; Stassen's relationship with, 188
Durham, Carl T., 53, 190–91, 207–8, 210, 234, 248
Dworshak, Henry, 233

EAC (Euratom), 179
Eastern Europe, 25, 37–38
Economic coercion threats toward Britain by U.S., 31–32, 34, 52, 53, 60–61, 172
Economic situation in Britain, 1, 38, 167, 221, 245
EDC (European Defense Community), 97–98, 129, 130, 138
Eden, Anthony: and the 1952 Anglo-American meetings, 91–94; and the 1953 Anglo-American Bermuda conference, 129–30; and the 1955 Anglo-American Agreement of Cooperation, 146–47; and consultation issues, 115, 137–38, 146; fall of, 172, 175; foreign policy of, 171–74; and hydrogen bombs issues, 137; and information exchange issues, 153–54; misleads Commons about cooperation relations, 159
Egypt, 171–74
Eisenhower administration: and the allocation of raw materials, 115; and the Atomic Energy Act (1954), 140, 247; and the Atomic Energy Act (1954) amendments, 203, 207, 208, 213–19, 222–27, 230, 248; deception of JCAE by, 157–64, 191, 217, 246, 247; and disarmament issues, 199, 230; and the McMahon Act amendments, 130; and the nuclear testing moratorium, 229–30; policies toward cooperation of, 118–19, 159, 160, 174, 200–201, 225, 238, 246–47; and Soviet-American relations, 133–34, 210. *See also* Congress-Eisenhower administration relations; Eisenhower, Dwight D.; *name of specific agency–department, or individual*
Eisenhower, Dwight D.: and the 1953 Anglo-American Bermuda conference, 124, 126–30; and the 1954 Churchill conference, 138; and the 1957 Anglo-American Bermuda conference, 175–83; and allocation of raw materials issues, 134; and the Atomic Energy Act (1954) amendments, 236; and the Blair House meeting with congress, 53; British views of, 3–4; and consultation issues, 115; defense policies of, 3–4, 28–29, 53, 111–12, 117–19, 130, 146, 151, 244–45; elected president, 3–4, 107–8; and information exchange issues, 23, 50, 125–26, 130, 134, 248; and IRBMs, 248; and the McMahon Act, 3, 126, 130, 134, 157, 201; Macmillan letters to, 188–89, 231; and the NSC Special Committee report, 50; policies toward cooperation of, 28–29, 54, 107–8, 115, 116, 125–27, 164, 175–83, 203–4, 247–48; speech to congress about atomic energy (February 1954) by, 134–35. *See also* Atoms for Peace Plan; Congress-Eisenhower administration relations; Eisenhower administration

Elbrick, C. Burke, 162, 172–73, 181
Elections: American, 3–4, 23, 44, 90, 92, 106, 107–8, 163–64, 172; British, 61, 72, 85, 86, 89
Elliott, William (Sir), 82–83, 85
Eniwetok Atoll, 69, 108, 205, 230
Euratom (EAC), 179
European Defense Community (EDC), 97–98, 129, 130, 138
European Recovery Program. *See* Marshall Plan

Farley, Philip J., 205, 230
Farnborough, England, 121
Faulkner, Rafford L., 115
Ferguson, John S., 82
Fields, Kenneth E., 164
Fisher, Adrian, 60, 61
Fisk, James B., 42
Foreign policy, American, 65–66
Formosa crisis, 146–47
Formosa Doctrine (January 1955), 146
Forrestal, James F., 9, 31–32, 40–43, 47, 50
Foster, Paul F., 206
Foster, William C., 77, 102
France, 50, 219, 224–25, 230, 234, 235, 236. *See also* Suez crisis
Franks, Oliver, 44, 56–57, 61, 75, 80, 81, 83, 84–85
Fuchs, Klaus, 28, 61, 74, 84, 106, 244

Gaitskell, Hugh, 187
Germany, 25, 29, 52, 66, 97, 107, 111. *See also* Berlin blockade
Gold spy case, 61
Goose Bay, Canada, 81–82
Gore, Albert, 163, 216
Gowing, Margaret, 23
Greece, 28–29, 97
Groves, Leslie R., 8–9, 11, 12–13, 18, 20–22
Gruenther, Alfred M., 145, 191
Gullion, Edmund A., 31

HALFMOON plan, 37–38
Halifax, Edward (Lord), 11–13, 17–21, 27

Harriman, Averell W., 19
Harwell, England, 39, 42
Healey, Denis W., 205
Henderson, Arthur, 186, 187
Henderson, John H., 43
Herter, Christian A., 231
Hickenlooper, Bourke B.: and the 1947 Anglo-American conference, 34; attitude toward cooperation of, 31–32, 191; and the Blair House meeting, 53, 54; complaints about interagency relations by, 26; and consultation issues, 136; and information exchange issues, 42, 44, 53, 54, 130; isolationist position of, 23; and the Kennan proposal, 30; and the McMahon Act amendments, 139–40; resigns as chairman of JCAE, 113; and stockpiles issues, 34
Hinton, Christopher (Sir), 122
Holifield, Chet, 216, 217, 218–19, 223, 234
Hood, Samuel, 236
Hoover, Herbert, 71
Horsey, Outerbridge, 159–60
Hosmer, Craig, 223
Howe, D. C., 57
Hyde Park Memorandum (1944), 5, 9, 11, 21, 29
Hydrogen bombs/weapons: and the 1958 Anglo-American bilateral agreement, 237; and the 1958 Anglo-American conference, 232; American development of, 60–61, 98, 108, 135–37, 160–61, 233; and Anglo-American military cooperation, 106–7; and the Atomic Energy Act (1954) amendments, 223; information leak about, 113; international reaction to development of, 140; Soviet development of, 3, 118, 121. *See also* Hydrogen bombs/weapons, British
Hydrogen bombs/weapons, British: and British policies of cooperation, 3, 149, 246; cost of developing, 202–3; and deterrence, 247; and disarmament, 154, 186–88, 247, 249; and information exchange issues, 108, 127, 202–3, 226, 231–33, 248–49; initiation of de-

velopment of, 144, 149, 246; and public opinion in Britain, 135–36, 187–88, 227; testing of, 167–68, 179, 186–88, 202–3, 226, 227, 233, 248

ICBMs (Intercontinental ballistic missiles), 151–52, 169, 200, 207, 219
Industrial uses. *See* Civilian/commercial uses of atomic/nuclear weapons
Information exchange: and the 1945 Anglo-American conference, 10–13; and the 1947 Anglo-American conference, 32–35; and the 1949 Anglo-American meetings, 56–61; and the 1952 Anglo-American meetings, 91–94; and the 1955, 1956 Anglo–American Agreement of Cooperation, 147–49, 151–55, 158–64; and the 1957 Anglo-American conferences, 201–3, 206–7, 209–10; and the 1958 Anglo-American bilateral agreement, 237; and the 1958 (June) Anglo-American conference, 232–34; and American elections, 107–8; and the American military community, 74–75; and the Blair House meeting (July 1949), 54; and British detonation of atomic bomb, 107; British pressures for, 20–23, 31, 39, 136; and British security problems, 108–9, 118; and Canada, 161; and congress–Eisenhower administration relations, 158–64; congressional policies about, 2, 13–14, 19, 158–64; and consultation issues, 84; and IRBMs, 170, 171, 208; and manufacturing issues, 3–4, 232; and the National Military Establishment, 39–40, 44; and the NSC report (March 1949), 50–51; and the Princeton conference recommendations, 48–49; and the Quebec Agreement, 6, 29; and the U.N., 10. *See also* Atomic Energy Act (1954); Atomic Energy Act (1954) amendments; Hydrogen bombs/weapons; McMahon Act (1946); McMahon Act amendments; Reactors; Research and development; Security, British; Submarine, nuclear propulsion; *name of specific agency/department or person*
Information leaks. *See* Security
Inspection and verification system, 12, 121, 133–34, 199, 230
Intelligence exchange, 93, 94, 127–28, 180
Interagency relations, American, 48, 157. *See also name of specific agency*
Intercontinental ballistic missiles. *See* ICBMs
Intermediate range ballistic missiles. *See* IRBMs
International Atomic Energy Authority/Agency (IAEA), 178–79, 191
IRBM agreement (February 1958), 220–22
IRBMs (Intermediate range ballistic missiles): and the 1957 Anglo-American Bermuda conference, 175–83, 186; and the 1957 Anglo-American conferences, 201–2, 207, 208–9; American production of, 152, 169, 204; and bilateral agreements, 220–22, 230–31; British development of, 169–70,d 173–74, 202–3; and British public opinion, 170, 187; and congress, 171, 173, 219, 220, 230–31; and consultation issues, 169–70, 219; and control issues, 170, 173; deployment in Britain of, 169–71, 190–97, 204, 208, 219–22, 230; and deterrence, 169–70, 173, 185; Eisenhower's policies toward, 152, 248; and information exchange issues, 170, 171, 208; and the JSSC report (1956), 169–70; and the Killian report, 151–52; and NATO, 152, 169, 170–71, 173, 208, 246; Soviet, 151–52, 169, 208; and the strategic importance of Britain, 170; and transfer issues, 170, 172–73
Isolationists, American, 71, 112
Israel, 171–72

Jackson, Henry M., 161
Japan, 7–8
JCAE (Joint Congressional Committee on Atomic Energy): and the 1947 Anglo-American conference, 33–34; and the

1957 Anglo-American Bermuda conference, 219; and the 1957 Anglo-American conferences, 201; and the 1958 (July) Anglo-American bilateral agreement, 238; and Acheson briefing about wartime cooperation, 29; AEC relations with, 41, 52, 77, 113, 141, 152–53, 158–64; and allocation of raw materials, 29, 33–34, 52, 237, 243–44; amd the 1955, 1956 Anglo-American Agreement of Cooperation, 147, 148–49, 161–64, 246; and the Atomic Energy Act (1954) amendments, 207–8, 214–19, 222–27, 230–36; and the Blair House meeting (July 1949), 53–54; British development of atomic bombs, 54–55; and British security issues, 74–77, 86, 243, 244; British security problems, 61, 74, 226; and British testing program, 188–90; chairmanship fight in, 113; construction/operation of atomic plants, 52; control of atomic weapons, 77; creation/function of, 2, 26; deception by Eisenhower administration of, 157–64, 191, 217, 246, 247; DOD relations with, 158–64; economic threats to Britain by, 31–32, 52, 53, 60–61; and Eisenhower administration relations, 52–55, 152–53, 247; and the expansion of the nuclear program, 98; favorable policies toward cooperation by, 57–58, 190–91, 248; fears of Soviet Union of, 4, 52, 56, 57–58, 98, 118; and information leaks, 113; and IRBM negotiations/agreements, 171, 193, 219, 230–31; and the Kennan proposal, 30; as a major factor in preventing cooperation with British, 2, 52–55, 62, 92, 126, 171, 178, 188–91, 243–45, 246–47; and the NSC report (March 1949), 52; State Department relations with, 158–64; and submarine nuclear propulsion issues, 171, 178, 246, 247; and transfer issues, 246; Truman administration meetings with, 53–55; and uses of nuclear weapons, 243–45. *See also* McMahon Act (1946); McMahon Act amendments; *name of specific individual and topic*

JCS (Joint Chiefs of Staff): and the 1949 Anglo-American meetings, 60; and the 1952 Anglo-American meetings, 92, 93; and allocation of raw materials review by (August–September 1950), 66; arming of NATO nations plan developed by, 169–73; and atomic testing, 17; and congress, 72, 117; and the construction/operation of atomic energy plants, 27–28, 48–49; and control issues, 98–103, 99–100; and defense policies, 58, 146–47; and information exchange issues, 44, 93, 116–17, 125–26, 152–54, 155; and the "Joint Outline War Plan for a War Beginning on July 1, 1954", 81; and the McMahon Act revisions, 115–16; policies toward cooperation of, 60, 73, 74, 116–17, 125–26; proposal for cooperation (January 1951), 73, 74. *See also* DOD; Military community, American; *name of specific person*

Jessup, Philip C., 81, 83
Johnson, Louis A., 47, 53, 55, 60, 61, 69
Johnson, Lyndon B., 201
Joint Chiefs of Staff. *See* JCS
Joint Congressional Committee on Atomic Energy. *See* JCAE
"Joint Outline War Plan for a War Beginning on July 1, 1954," (JCS), 81
JSSC (Joint Strategic Survey Committee), 9, 27–28, 82–83, 169
Jupiter missiles, 195, 208

Kennan, George F., 32–34, 48, 50, 52, 56
Kennan (George F.) proposal (August 1947), 30–32
Killian, James R., Jr., 151–52, 204
Killian (James R.) report (February 1955), 151–52
King, Mackenzie, 9, 11, 20
Kinnock, Neil, 249
Knowland, William F., 54, 55, 116, 191, 201, 206

Index

Korea, 2, 66, 68, 71, 76, 79, 94, 112, 128
Kruschchev, Nikita S., 230

Labour party: and the arms race, 154, 186, 213, 225; and consultation issues, 80–81, 145, 205, 213; and control issues, 222; pressures on Churchill by, 135–36, 154; weakness of, 3, 61, 72, 86. *See also* Attlee, Clement
Laniel, Joseph, 124, 126–30
Lay, James S., 99, 102, 117–18
Leahy, William D., 11–13
LeBaron, Robert, 75, 76, 92–93, 102–3
Lilienthal, David E.: and the allocation of raw materials, 26–27, 49–50, 54; appointed chairman of AEC, 26; attitude toward cooperation of, 31, 32, 49–50, 59; and the Blair House meeting, 53; congressional relations of, 29; and the Fuchs case, 61; and the hydrogen bomb issues, 61; and information exchange issues, 34, 39–42, 49–50, 50; and the NSC Special Committee report, 50; objectives of, 49–50
Lloyd, Selwyn, 167, 200, 214, 220
Loper, Herbert B., 164, 202, 203, 217–19, 222, 223, 224, 233
Lovett, Robert A.: and the 1947 Anglo-American conference, 32–33; and the 1952 Anglo-American meetings, 93; appointed undersecretary of defense, 26, 69; attitude toward cooperation of, 26, 31–32, 76; and British security issues, 76; and British use of American sites for testing, 75; congressional relations of, 31–32; and consultation issues, 80, 82–83; and control issues, 98–103; and information exchange issues, 40–42, 44, 81, 91, 93; replaces Acheson, 30; resignation of, 47; the the McMahon Act amendments, 77

McCarthy, Joseph R., 112, 114
McCone, John A., 238
McCormick, Lynde D., 82
McElroy, Neil H., 195, 204, 224
Maclean, Donald C., 28, 74

McMahon Act (1946): and allocation of raw materials issues, 54; as a barrier to cooperation, 26–27, 73; and congressional-Truman administration relations, 54, 55; and control issues, 22–23, 77; and creation of AEC, JCAE, and MLC, 26; Eisenhower's policies toward, 3, 157, 201; and information exchange issues, 22–23, 27, 29, 30, 39, 54, 114, 116, 123, 191; and the NSC report (March 1949), 50; passage of, 2, 22–23, 243; Truman's views of, 22–23. *See also* McMahon Act amendments
McMahon Act amendments: and the 1952 Anglo-American meetings, 91–92; and the 1953 Anglo-American Bermuda conference, 124; and the AEC, 115–16; and American defense issues, 134–35; congressional policies about, 69, 74, 75, 102; Dean's attitude toward, 76; and the DOD, 75, 115–16; Eisenhower's policies toward, 126–27, 130, 134–35; and elections in U.S., 90; and information exchange issues, 77, 84, 91–92, 99–100, 124–25, 133, 139–40; need for, 119; passage of, 133–41; proposed, 3, 115–16; and research and development, 122; and security standards, 134; and the State Department, 115–16
McMahon, Brien: attitude toward cooperation of, 52–54, 91–92, 93; and the Blair House meeting, 53, 54; and British atomic testing, 75; and control issues, 13; and information exchange issues, 22–23, 27, 29, 30, 39, 44, 54; and Soviet atomic testing, 58
Macmillan, Harold: and the 1957 Anglo-American Bermuda conference, 175–76, 178–83, 186–88; and the 1957 Anglo–American conferences, 200–210; and the 1958 (July) Anglo–American bilateral agreement, 238; and the 1958 (June) Anglo-American conference, 231–34; attitude toward cooperation of, 247; and British dependence on U.S., 239; and the British economic situa-

tion, 167; and consultation issues, 205–6; and hydrogen bomb negotiations, 231; letters to Eisenhower from, 23, 188–89; and nuclear testing, 186, 225–27; and SAC exercises in Britain, 214, 222; and Sputnik, 200; and the Stassen proposal, 188–89

Makins, Roger: and the 1945 Anglo-American conference, 12; and the 1952 Anglo-American meetings, 92; and the 1953 Anglo-American Bermuda conference, 129–30; and the 1954 Anglo-American conferences, 143–45; and the 1956 Anglo–American agreement, 162; and the allocation of raw materials, 20–22, 115; as a CPC member, 18, 20–22; and meetings with Truman administration officials, 26–27, 52, 67–68

Malenkov, Georgi M., 118

Manhattan Project, 29, 34

Manufacture/production issues: and the 1945 Anglo-American conference, 10–13; and the 1949 Anglo-American meetings, 56–61; and the 1952 Anglo-American meetings, 92; and the 1957 Anglo-American conference, 209–10; and the Atomic Energy Act (1954), 140; and the Atomic Energy Act (1954) amendments, 216; and British IRBMs, 169–70, 173–74, 202–3; British views about, 10, 19, 39–40, 42–44, 56–61, 67, 108, 144; Bush's views about, 10; in Canada, 42–43; and congress, 123; and control issues, 103; and information exchange issues, 3–4, 232

Marks, Herbert S., 32

Marshall, George C., 26, 30, 31, 47, 69

Marshall Islands, 135–37

Marshall Plan, 1, 25, 32, 37, 48, 179, 245

Matthews, H. Freeman, 26, 81, 82, 84–85

Maudling, Reginald, 170

Memorandum of Intention (November 1945), 12–13, 20–21

Merchant, Livingston T., 200–201

Military community (American): and the 1949 Anglo-American meetings, 60; and American bases in Britain, 66–67; and consultation issues, 81, 82–84, 86; and control issues, 9; fear of Soviets by, 58, 66; and information exchange issues, 74–75; and the Kennan proposal, 31; policies toward cooperation of, 17, 41–42, 66–67, 69, 72, 73–78; and the Princeton conference, 49; and stockpiling issues, 26, 27–28, 74–75; and the strategic importance of Britain, 66–67. *See also* DOD; JCS (Joint Chiefs of Staff); *name of specific person*

Military cooperation, Anglo-American: and the 1949 Anglo–American meetings, 56–61; and the 1957 Anglo-American Bermuda conference, 180; and the 1957 Anglo-American conferences, 201, 204–5, 206–7; and the 1958 (July) Anglo–American bilateral agreement, 236–39; and American defense policies, 123–26, 130; American military proposals for, 72, 73–78; and the Berlin blockade, 37–38, 42; and consultation issues, 130–31; and the Cyril Smith affair, 42–44; in Eastern Europe, 25, 37–38; in Germany, 25; and hydrogen weapons, 106–7; need for, 38–39, 44; and NSC 151/1-2 (December 1953), 124–26, 130; and NSC 162/2 (October 1953), 122–23. *See also* American bases in Britain

Military Liaison Committee, 26, 42, 47

Milliken, Eugene D., 54, 55

Minuteman missiles, 208

Mississippi Valley Generating Company, 139–40

MLC. *See* Military Liaison Committee

Modus Vivendi (January 1948): and the 1949 Anglo-American meetings, 56–57; and the 1953 Anglo-American Bermuda conference, 124; and the allocation of raw materials, 34; British reaction to, 34; and consultation issues, 34–35, 79, 80–81, 136, 139, 205, 206, 244; and control issues, 34; extension

Index 269

of, 55, 56–57; and information exchange issues, 34, 38, 39, 40, 42, 43, 92, 94; passage of, 244; signing of, 34; Webster's views about, 47
Monte Bello Islands (Australia), 76, 107
Montgomery, Bernard Law, 25, 145
Moore, Henry (Sir), 39, 42, 43
Moratorium on atomic/nuclear testing, 137, 144, 186–88, 190, 199, 213, 225–27, 229–30, 247
Morrison, Herbert S., 83, 84
Mountbatten, Louis S., 155
Murphy, Robert A., 182, 205, 215–16, 219–20, 220
Murray, Thomas E., 92, 139, 162, 189, 191, 226–27, 230
Mutual Defense Assistance Act (1949), 57
Mutual Defense Assistance Agreement (January 1950), 193, 220
Mutual Defense Assistance Program (1957), 172, 182
Mutual Security Appropriations bill (1959), 193
Mutual Security Assistance Agreement/ Act (1954), 181–83, 221

Nasser, Gamal Abdel, 167, 171–73
National Military Establishment, 31, 39–40, 44, 49. *See also* DOD (Department of Defense)
National Security Act (1949), 69
National Security Council: and the 1953 Anglo-American Bermuda conference, 124–25; and control issues, 99, 100; and defense policies, 117–18, 145; and expansion of the nuclear program, 98; and NSC 151/1-2 (December 1953), 124–26, 130; and NSC 162/2 (October 1953), 122–23, 145, 146; and NSC 5422/2 (August 1954), 138–39; and NSC 68 (April 1950), 65–66; Special Committee report (March 1949), 50–52; Special Committee to study control issues, 99, 100–101, 102, 103, 117
NATO (North Atlantic Treaty Organization): American joining of, 1–2; American policy toward, 118, 139, 144–45, 246; and congress, 55, 71–72; and consultation issues, 114, 137–39, 145; creation of, 37, 48; and the defense policies of Eisenhower, 244; and the defense of Western Europe, 93, 107; and deployment of American nuclear weapons in Europe, 152, 173, 177–78, 183, 193–94, 208; and deployment of IRBMs, 152, 169, 170–71, 173, 208, 219, 220, 246; and the EDC negotiations, 129; and information exchange issues, 126; JCS plan for arming, 169–73; leadership/membership of, 91, 97; and the Princeton conference recommendations, 49; stockpiles, 189–90, 210; strength of, 66–67, 73, 75, 106–7, 111, 134–35, 145
Nautilus (nuclear submarine), 147
Nevada, 248
New Look Defense policy. *See* Defense policy: of Eisenhower; National Security Council: NSC 162/2
Nichols, Kenneth, 48, 50, 58
Nitze, Paul H., 84–85
Norstad, Lauris, 48, 51–52, 189
North American Air Defense Command, 230
North Atlantic Treaty, 209
North Atlantic Treaty Organization. *See* NATO
NSC. *See* National Security Council
Nuclear submarines. *See* Submarine, nuclear propulsion
Nutting, Anthony, 154

OEEC (Organization of European Economic Cooperation), 179
Oppenheimer, Robert, 48, 114–15

Parsons, William S., 26
Pastore, John O., 215, 218, 222, 223, 225, 230, 234, 236
Patterson, Robert P., 8–12, 22
Pearson, Lester B., 11–13, 18, 67–68
Penney, William G. (Sir), 59, 75, 231
Pike, Sumner T., 42, 50, 60
Plan K funds, 181–82, 183, 193, 195
Planning issues, 122, 129

Plowden, Edwin (Sir), 143, 188–90, 192, 201–2, 204–5, 206, 231
Plutonium. *See* Allocation of raw materials
Polaris missiles, 207, 208, 238, 249
Policy Planning Staff. *See* Kennan (George F.) proposal (August 1947)
Pontecorvo, Bruno, 69–70, 84
Portal, Charles (Lord), 39
Positive vetting system, 74
Powell, Richard (Sir), 195–96, 201–2, 204–5, 206
President, role of, 157. *See also name of specific president*
Price, Melvin, 217
Princeton conference (January 1949), 47–50
Private industry, American, 113, 115, 122, 139, 140, 152–53,192, 224, 237, 247. *See also* Civilian/commercial uses of atomic/nuclear energy
Production. *See* Manufacture/production issues
Project Solarium, 117–18

Quarles, Donald A.: and the 1957 Anglo-American conference, 201–2, 203; and the Atomic Energy Act (1954) amendments, 217–18; attitude toward cooperation of, 146–47, 215–16; and information exchange issues, 203, 209, 223–25, 232; and IRBM issues, 208, 219–20; tour of British facilities by, 146–47; and transfer issues, 181–82, 195, 196, 233
Quebec Agreement (1943), 5–6, 9–12, 19–21, 29, 32, 72–73, 86, 128–30, 136

Radford, Arthur W., 117, 189–90
Rayburn, Sam, 53, 54
Reactors: and the 1957 Anglo-American Bermuda conference, 180; and the 1957 Anglo-American meetings, 190, 191–92; and the 1958 (July) Anglo-American bilateral agreement, 236–37; and the allocation of raw materials, 204–5; American development of, 113; at Calder Hall, 180, 189, 191, 192, 224, 233–34; and the Atomic Energy Act (1954) amendments, 232–33; British buying American, 224, 237; British development of, 53, 94, 106, 113–14, 124, 144, 155, 207; and information exchange issues, 160–62, 180, 190, 204, 207, 232, 236–37, 60, 92, 113–14, 124, 141, 147, 148, 153, 158
REAPER (JCS "Joint Outline War Plan for a War Beginning on July 1, 1954''), 81
REDOX (uranium recovery process), 48–49
"Reflex Alert" (SAC exercises), 205
Republican party, 23, 71–72, 112
Research and development: and information exchange issues, 107, 116; and the Kennan proposal, 31; and McMahon Act amendments, 122; and OEEC, 179; and the Princeton conference recommendations, 48–49; and the Quebec Agreement, 5–6; Soviet, 30, 52, 57–62, 65, 121, 225, 243–44, 245. *See also* Atomic bombs; CDT (Combined Development Trust); Hydrogen bombs; Research and development, American; Research and development, British; Submarine, nuclear propulsion; Testing, atomic/nuclear
Research and development, American: and the 1957 Anglo-American conferences, 209; and Army-Navy competition, 207; and the Blair House meeting (July 1949), 53; expansion of, 204; and policies about cooperation, 108–9; and stockpiles, 117
Research and development, British: and the 1956 Anglo-American agreement, 162; and the 1957 Anglo-American conferences, 210; and the allocation of raw materials, 57–61, 179; beginnings of, 9; and cooperation with European allies, 179; cost of, 155, 162, 179; expansion of, 57–61, 67–70, 246; and information exchange issues, 48–49, 121–22, 127, 134, 94, 155, 162, 207, 223; and IRBMs, 170; slowness of,

245; and stockpiles, 48–49, 67–68; and transfer issues, 67–70. *See also* Atomic bombs: British; Britain: dependence on U.S. of; Hydrogen bombs: British; Testing, atomic/nuclear: British
Rickover, Hyman G., 158, 164, 191–92, 206–7, 222, 223–24
Rio Pact, 48
Roosevelt, Franklin D., 5, 11, 21, 29, 50
Roper, John C. A., 159–60, 206, 231
Rosenberg, Alfred and Ethel, 61, 112
Rowan, Leslie, 11–13
Royalties, 192
Russell, Richard B., 207–8

SAC (Strategic Air Command) exercises in Britain, 205, 214, 222
Sandys, Duncan, 118, 173, 176, 177, 178, 183, 188, 189, 194–95, 200
Security, American, 61–62, 74, 94, 112, 134
Security, British: and the 1955, 1956 Anglo-American Agreement of Cooperation, 148, 162–63; congressional fears of, 2–3, 74–77, 86, 226, 243, 244; DOD concerns about, 76; and the Fuchs case, 28, 61, 74, 84, 106, 244; improvements in, 67, 90–91, 114, 118, 246; and the McMahon Act amendments, 84; as a major factor in preventing cooperation, 27–28, 40, 41, 49, 72, 86, 90–91, 108–9, 114, 245; and the "nothing known against" system, 74; and the Pontecorvo case, 69–70, 84; receding of American concern about, 49, 124, 141, 223, 225
Shippingport, Pennsylvania, 192
Slessor, John (Sir), 82–83, 93, 106, 114
Slim, William (Sir), 79–80, 106
Smith, Cyril, 42–44
Smith, Gerald C., 161, 201–2
Smith, Henry D., 92
Smith, Walter Bedell, 93, 115
Smyth, Henry D., 60
Souers, Sidney, 50
South Africa, 33, 51, 180
Soviet-American relations, 8, 9, 133–34
Soviet-British relations, 10, 37
Soviet Union: atomic bomb development/production in, 47, 56, 57, 62, 65, 66, 243, 244; atomic strength of, 101–2; and the Berlin blockade, 37–38, 42; Bush's attitude toward, 10; and control issues, 27, 28; effects on Anglo-American cooperation of, 3, 10–12, 50–51, 56, 62; and the hydrogen bomb, 3, 118, 121; and ICBMs/IRBMs, 151–52, 169, 200, 208, 219; and nuclear testing, 57, 118, 199, 225, 229–30; research and development in, 30, 52, 57–62, 65, 121, 225, 243–44, 245; strength of, 28, 111, 145, 151–52, 169. *See also* Defense policies, American; Defense policies, British; Defense policies; Military cooperation, Anglo–American; Sputnik
Special Senate Committee on Atomic Energy, 13
Sputnik, 4, 196–97, 199–200, 201, 204, 210, 247–48
Spy scandals. *See name of specific scandal*
Stalin, Joseph, 115
Starbird, Alfred D., 206, 222
Stassen, Harold E., 187–88, 190
State Department, U.S.: and the 1945 Anglo-American conference, 9, 10; and the 1957 Anglo-American Bermuda conference, 178–83; and the allocation of raw materials, 30; congressional relations with, 72, 158–64; and consultation issues, 82–84; and control issues, 98–103; and IRBMs issues, 192, 195–96; and the Kennan proposal (August 1947), 30–32; and the McMahon Act revisions, 115–16; Panel of Consultants on Disarmament, 114–15; policies toward cooperation of, 32, 41–42, 92; War Department relations with, 26. *See also name of specific individual*
Steel, Christopher (Sir), 92
Stimson, Henry, 8, 9
Stockpiles: American, 26–28, 98, 100, 102–3, 117, 124, 144–45, 216–17, 224, 243; of American weapons in

Britain, 51, 69, 189–90; in Canada, 19, 31–32, 40, 51, 58, 81–82, 189; control of, 76–77; and the Modus Vivendi agreement, 33–34; NATO, 189–90, 210. *See also* Allocation of raw materials; Stockpiles, British

Stockpiles, British: and the 1953 Anglo-American Bermuda conference, 127; and the 1958 Anglo-American bilateral agreement, 235; American reluctance to build, 27, 30, 33–34, 48, 58, 216–17; in Canada, 19, 58; cost of, 68, 216–17; expansion of, 3, 38, 67, 149, 216–17, 235; inferiority to U.S. of, 74–75, 127, 144, 168, 177, 245; and the Stassen proposal, 188; at end of World War II, 7. *See also* Atomic bombs: British

Strategic Air Command (SAC). *See* American bases in Britain; SAC exercises in Britain

Strauss, Lewis L.: and the 1949 Anglo-American meetings, 60; and the 1953 Anglo-American Bermuda conference, 127, 128; and the 1955 Anglo-American Agreement of Cooperation, 146–47; and the 1957 Anglo-American conferences, 200–210, 201–2; and the 1958 (June) Anglo-American conference, 231–34; and American defense policy, 130; and the Atomic Energy Act (1954) amendments, 214–19, 222–27; attitude toward cooperation of, 116–17, 125–26, 152, 188–90, 200, 247; and British manufacture of atomic bombs, 40; and British research and development, 39; and British use of American test sites, 205; as chairman of AEC, 116; congressional relations of, 191; as Eisenhower's adviser, 114, 116; and hydrogen weapons negotiations, 231; and information exchange issues, 39, 41, 42, 44–45, 60, 116, 125–26, 127, 128, 152–55, 158, 188–91, 203, 209, 232, 233, 235; and the McMahon Act amendments, 122, 139–41; and the Princeton conference recommendations, 50

Submarine, Nautilus, 147

Submarine, nuclear propulsion: as an area for Anglo-American negotiations, 114; British development of, 155; and the deception of JCAE, 3–4, 158–64, 247; and information exchange issues, 3–4, 148, 153, 155, 178, 180, 190–92, 206–7, 217, 222, 233, 246–48; JCAE concerns about information exchange about, 3–4, 158–64, 171, 178, 246, 247; and NATO defense policies, 134–35; and transfer issues, 237. *See also* Reactors

Suez crisis, 4, 171–74, 247–48

Taft, Robert A., 112
Taylor, Maxwell D., 151
Tedder, Arthur W. (Lord), 51–52, 79–80, 81
Tennessee Valley Authority, 139–40
Testing, atomic/nuclear: American, 17, 22, 103, 108, 135–37, 199, 229–30; and control issues, 103; and deterrence/disarmament, 178–79, 186–88; and the IRBM agreement (February 1958), 221; joint, 77, 114; moratorium on, 4, 137, 144, 154, 186–88, 190, 199, 213, 225–27, 229–30, 247; Soviet, 57, 118, 199, 225, 229–30
Testing, atomic/nuclear, British: American visitors barred from, 94; at Christmas Island, 144, 159–60, 168–69, 187; at Monte Bello Islands, 75–76, 107; at the Woomera rocket range, 122, 221; and British policies toward cooperation, 105, 106, 107, 144; and deterrence, 178–79, 186–88; and information exchange issues, 107, 118, 122; use of American sites for, 57, 69, 75–76, 86, 159–60, 168–69, 205, 248
Thatcher, Margaret, 249
Thor missiles, 195, 207, 208
Timmons, B. E. L., 170–73
Titan missiles, 208
Tizard, Henry (Sir), 59
Transfer issues: and the 1958 (July) Anglo-American bilateral agreement, 237–38; and the 1958 (June) Anglo-Ameri-

can conference, 232–33; and the 1959 (May) Anglo-American bilateral agreement, 248–49; and the AEC, 233; American defense policies, 230; and the Atomic Energy Act (1954) amendments, 215, 216–18, 232–36; and British internal politics, 233–34; and the DOD, 218, 222–23; and export licenses, 68; and IRBMs, 170, 172–73, 220–21. *See also* Bermuda conference (March 1957); Submarine, nuclear propulsion

Trident missiles, 238, 249

Tritium. *See* Allocation of raw materials

Truman administration: and the 1952 Anglo-American conference, 91–94; and the allocation of raw materials, 243–44; anglophiles in, 33, 47; and the Blair House meeting (July 1949), 53–54; and British security, 244; and consultation issues, 244; defense policy of, 71–72; and information exchange issues, 243–44; interagency relations in, 26, 157; policies toward cooperation of, 2, 14, 45, 94, 109, 243–44, 244; and the Princeton conference, 48–49; and use of nuclear weapons, 243–44. *See also* Congress-Truman administration relations; Truman, Harry S.

Truman Doctrine (March 1947), 1, 25

Truman, Harry S.: and 1945 Anglo-American conference, 11–12, 20, 29; Attlee telegrams to, 7–8, 20; and the Blair House meeting, 53; and British atomic testing, 75; and Churchill's pressure to publish Quebec Agreement, 72–73; and the construction/operation of atomic plants, 20–21; and consultation issues, 80; and control issues, 8–9, 19, 22, 77; and foreign aid, 28–29; and the hydrogen bomb, 60–61; and information exchange issues, 50; and intelligence issues, 93; and the McMahon Act, 22–23; policies toward British of, 11; speech about atomic energy policy of, 8–9; and use of atomic bomb in Korean War, 79. *See also* Congress-Truman administration relations; Truman administration

Turkey, 28–29, 97

Twining, Nathan F., 117, 200

Tydings, Millard E., 53

U-235. *See* Allocation of raw materials

Underground nuclear explosion, 199

Unilateralists, congressional, 23

United States: atomic/nuclear strength of, 111–12, 145; uranium in, 123–24, 204–5. *See also specific agency/department, conference, name, or topic*

U.N. (United Nations): article 102 of, 17, 19–20; and British use of American test sites, 205; and consultation issue, 79; and control issues, 10, 27, 28, 30, 55–56, 98; creation of, 10; disarmament discussions in, 98, 186–88, 213; and information exchange issues, 10; and the Korean War, 71. *See also* Atoms for Peace plan (Eisenhower)

U.N. (United Nations) Atomic Energy Commission, 19–20, 30, 55–56, 98

Uranium. *See* Allocation of raw materials; Belgian Congo; Canada; South Africa; United States

Uses of atomic/nuclear energy. *See specific topic*

Vance, Harold S., 222

Vandenberg, Arthur: and the 1947 Anglo-American conference, 34; attitude toward cooperation of, 31–32; and congressional-Truman administration relations, 53, 55; feelings toward Roosevelt of, 15n19; and information exchange issues, 13, 42, 53–54, 55; Lovett's friendship with, 26; and the Marshall Plan, 32; *Private Papers of Senator Vandenberg* author, 136; and stockpiles issues, 34; unilateralist position of, 23

Vandenberg, Hoyt S., 82–83

Vandenberg Resolution (June 1948), 37

Vanguard satellite, 200

Van Zandt, James E., 223–24

Verification system. *See* Inspection and verification system
Vietnam, 137, 138
V-J Day trust supplies, 20, 21
Volpe, Joseph, 48, 50, 53, 60

War Department, U.S., 9–10, 26. *See also* DOD
Washington conferences. *See* Anglo-American meetings
Waymack, W. W., 41
Webb, James E., 47, 56, 58, 59
Webster, William, 40, 47, 48, 50, 53
Weil, George L., 39, 41
Wende, Charles W. J., 39, 41
West Germany, 52, 97

Westinghouse Corporation, 207, 224
Whitney, John H., 214, 222
Wilson, Carroll L., 29, 48, 50, 58–59, 60
Wilson, Charles E., 117, 153, 158, 181, 194–95
Wilson, Henry (Sir), 12, 27
Windscale, England, 67
Woodward, F. N., 42–43
Woomera Range (Australia), 122, 221
Wrong, Hume, 81

Younger, Kenneth, 73
Yugoslavia, 85

Zinn, Walter H., 39, 41

About the Author

TIMOTHY J. BOTTI holds a Ph.D. in American Foreign Policy History from Ohio State University, and is a historian and former Lecturer/Teaching Assistant at Ohio State University.

LIBRARY OF DAVIDSON COLLEGE

Books on regular loan may be checked out for **two weeks.** Books must be presented at the Circulation Desk in order to be renewed.

A fine is charged after date due.

Special books are subject to special regulations at the discretion of the library staff.